ANDERSON'S
Law School Publications

ADMINISTRATIVE LAW ANTHOLOGY
by Thomas O. Sargentich

ADMINISTRATIVE LAW: CASES AND MATERIALS
by Daniel J. Gifford

ADMIRALTY LAW ANTHOLOGY
by Robert M. Jarvis

APPELLATE ADVOCACY: PRINCIPLES AND PRACTICE (Second Edition)
Cases and Materials
by Ursula Bentele and Eve Cary

A CAPITAL PUNISHMENT ANTHOLOGY
by Victor L. Streib

CASES AND PROBLEMS IN CRIMINAL LAW (Second Edition)
by Myron Moskovitz

THE CITATION WORKBOOK
by Maria L. Ciampi, Rivka Widerman and Vicki Lutz

COMMERCIAL TRANSACTIONS: PROBLEMS AND MATERIALS
Vol. 1: Secured Transactions Under the UCC
Vol. 2: Sales Under the UCC and the CISG
Vol. 3: Negotiable Instruments Under the UCC and the CIBN
by Louis F. Del Duca, Egon Guttman and Alphonse M. Squillante

A CONSTITUTIONAL LAW ANTHOLOGY
by Michael J. Glennon

CONSTITUTIONAL TORTS
by Sheldon H. Nahmod, Michael L. Wells, and Thomas A. Eaton

CONTRACTS
Contemporary Cases, Comments, and Problems
by Michael L. Closen, Richard M. Perlmutter and Jeffrey D. Wittenberg

A CONTRACTS ANTHOLOGY
by Peter Linzer

CORPORATE AND WHITE COLLAR CRIME: AN ANTHOLOGY
by Leonard Orland

A CRIMINAL LAW ANTHOLOGY
by Arnold H. Loewy

CRIMINAL LAW: CASES AND MATERIALS
by Arnold H. Loewy

CRIMINAL PROCEDURE: TRIAL AND SENTENCING
by Arthur B. LaFrance and Arnold H. Loewy

ECONOMIC REGULATION
Cases and Materials
by Richard J. Pierce, Jr.

ELEMENTS OF LAW
by Eva H. Hanks, Michael E. Herz and Steven S. Nemerson

ENDING IT: DISPUTE RESOLUTION IN AMERICA
Descriptions, Examples, Cases and Questions
by Susan M. Leeson and Bryan M. Johnston

ENVIRONMENTAL LAW (Second Edition)
Vol. 1: Environmental Decisionmaking: NEPA and the Endangered Species Act
Vol. 2: Water Pollution; Vol. 3: Air Pollution; Vol. 4: Hazardous Wastes
by Jackson B. Battle, Mark Squillace, Maxine I. Lipeles and Robert L. Fischman

ENVIRONMENTAL PROTECTION AND JUSTICE
Readings and Commentary on Environmental Law and Practice
by Kenneth A. Manaster

Continued

FEDERAL INCOME TAXATION OF PARTNERSHIPS AND OTHER PASS-THRU ENTITIES
by Howard E. Abrams

FEDERAL RULES OF EVIDENCE (Second Edition)
Rules, Legislative History, Commentary and Authority
by Glen Weissenberger

FIRST AMENDMENT ANTHOLOGY
by Donald E. Lively, Dorothy E. Roberts and Russell L. Weaver

INTERNATIONAL HUMAN RIGHTS: LAW, POLICY AND PROCESS
Problems and Materials
by Frank Newman and David Weissbrodt

INTERNATIONAL LAW ANTHOLOGY
by Anthony D'Amato

INTERNATIONAL LAW COURSEBOOK
by Anthony D'Amato

INTRODUCTION TO THE STUDY OF LAW: CASES AND MATERIALS
by John Makdisi

JUDICIAL EXTERNSHIPS: THE CLINIC INSIDE THE COURTHOUSE
by Rebecca A. Cochran

JUSTICE AND THE LEGAL SYSTEM
A Coursebook
by Anthony D'Amato and Arthur J. Jacobson

THE LAW OF DISABILITY DISCRIMINATION
by Ruth Colker

THE LAW OF MODERN PAYMENT SYSTEMS AND NOTES
by Fred H. Miller and Alvin C. Harrell

LAWYERS AND FUNDAMENTAL MORAL RESPONSIBILITY
by Daniel R. Coquillette

PATIENTS, PSYCHIATRISTS AND LAWYERS
Law and the Mental Health System
by Raymond L. Spring, Roy B. Lacoursiere, M.D., and Glen Weissenberger

PROBLEMS AND SIMULATIONS IN EVIDENCE (Second Edition)
by Thomas F. Guernsey

A PRODUCTS LIABILITY ANTHOLOGY
by Anita Bernstein

PROFESSIONAL RESPONSIBILITY ANTHOLOGY
by Thomas B. Metzloff

A PROPERTY ANTHOLOGY
by Richard H. Chused

THE REGULATION OF BANKING
Cases and Materials on Depository Institutions and Their Regulators
by Michael P. Malloy

A SECTION 1983 CIVIL RIGHTS ANTHOLOGY
by Sheldon H. Nahmod

SPORTS LAW: CASES AND MATERIALS (Second Edition)
by Raymond L. Yasser, James R. McCurdy and C. Peter Goplerud

A TORTS ANTHOLOGY
by Lawrence C. Levine, Julie A. Davies and Edward J. Kionka

TRIAL PRACTICE
Text by Lawrence A. Dubin and Thomas F. Guernsey
Problems and Case Files with *Video* Presentation
by Edward R. Stein and Lawrence A. Dubin

APPELLATE ADVOCACY

PRINCIPLES AND PRACTICE

Cases and Materials

Second Edition

by

URSULA BENTELE

Professor of Law
Director, Criminal Appeals Clinic
Brooklyn Law School

EVE CARY

Associate Professor of Legal Writing
Brooklyn Law School

ANDERSON PUBLISHING CO.
CINCINNATI

ISBN 0-87084-045-2

To our families:
Buzz, Susanna and Daniel;
Richard, Peter and Anne.

Contents

Chapter 3: Scope of Review and the Preservation Requirement

Chapter 4: Standards of Review

Chapter 5: The Harmless Error Doctrine

Chapter 6: The Role of Appellate Counsel

Chapter 7: The Appellate Brief

Chapter 8: Oral Argument

Preface

We had several goals in writing this book. First, by helping law students to understand the basic principles behind appellate litigation, the book should enhance their study of law in general. Since law school texts in the United States consist primarily of appellate opinions, it is not surprising that law study will be more comprehensible if the student has some understanding of how appellate courts work, and what appellate attorneys must do to have those courts consider the issues that may benefit their clients.

Second, the book provides a set of materials to help train students to become skilled appellate advocates. As was pointed out in the American Bar Association Report on Appellate Litigation (1985), appellate practice has long been neglected as a separate field of study in law schools. While extensive programs have been developed to teach trial practice, somehow law schools seem to assume that through the study of appellate opinions students will, by osmosis perhaps, gain the necessary knowledge about handling an appeal. The Report noted, in particular, the lack of casebooks on appellate practice; several "Appellate Advocacy" books, put out by student moot court boards, simply consist of materials on brief writing and oral argument.

Finally, the book hopes to contribute to the improvement of students' experience in intermural moot court programs. As noted by Professor Robert Martineau, leader of the movement to put more "court" into moot court activities, most moot court competitions involve debates of abstract legal principles that have little or nothing to do with the actual world of appellate practice. The competitors, therefore, have no incentive to learn about that world. As the movement for change gains ground, however, and competitions use fuller, more realistic records, and revolve around issues that incorporate questions that come up frequently in appellate practice, such as the appropriate standard of review or the question of harmless error, students entering these competitions will need to become familiar with these aspects of appellate litigation.

In this second edition, we have updated the material, as well as significantly expanding Chapters 4 and 7. Colleagues who used the first edition in their classes confirmed our own sense that students have particular difficulty with standards of review, and that few texts deal with this subject in depth, so we have now provided more detailed treatment of the topic in Chapter 4. And although many books do discuss brief-writing, we were persuaded that, for the sake of completeness, a book on appellate practice should include the somewhat fuller exploration of the techniques of written advocacy now contained in Chapter 7. We have also added materials on discretionary appeals in Chapter 2, civil appeals in Chapter 5, and *pro se* appeals in Chapter 6.

While this book can be helpful in a variety of contexts, it is designed primarily for use in a comprehensive appellate practice course. It includes exercises revolving around the most important principles of appellate practice that can be used as assignments. Ideally, it would be supplemented by a full, actual trial transcript which would constitute the record on appeal for which the students would prepare an appellate brief and, if time permits, conduct an oral argument. Most appellate practitioners have access to trial transcripts suitable for that purpose; in addition, the American Bar Association's Committee on Appellate Practice of the Appellate Judges Conference in 1988 established an appellate record library for use in law schools.

The book does not cover in detail the rules of appellate practice in any particular jurisdiction; the practitioner must study those rules carefully before embarking on an appeal. The concept of the book is, rather, to provide a basic understanding of the most fundamental principles of appellate litigation, using examples from the federal system as well as several illustrative states. No attempt has been made to summarize the separate, rather complicated areas of appeals from decisions by administrative agencies or of collateral attack on judgments through writs of habeas corpus or other remedies. For convenience, the parties on appeal are referred to as appellant and respondent, regardless of the terms that might be used in any particular court for a specific kind of an appeal.

May, 1995   Ursula Bentele
                                                           Eve Cary

Acknowledgments

The authors express their deep appreciation to the following colleagues, who spent considerable time reviewing the manuscript and provided valuable suggestions that greatly improved this book: Joyce Adolfsen, Stacy Caplow, Mary R. Falk, Maryellen Fullerton, Joel M. Gora, Richard A. Greenberg and Stanley Neustadter. We take full responsibility, of course, for any flaws that remain. We also thank our research assistant Mark Koestler and our proofreader Jill Rosenthal, both Brooklyn Law School students. We are grateful, too, to Elizabeth Antoine, Deanna Handler and June Parris, who typed and retyped the manuscript.

We also wish to acknowledge with gratitude the support we received while writing this book from the Dean, faculty and students of Brooklyn Law School. Finally, we want to thank our alma mater, the Legal Aid Society Criminal Appeals Bureau, New York City, where we first acquired our interest in appellate practice.

Table of Cases

Principal cases are in italics. References are to pages.

Chapter 1

Introduction

Appellate review is almost universally available in the United States, by constitution or statute, both in state and federal courts, for civil as well as criminal matters. Some Justices of the Supreme Court have suggested that, in criminal cases, a state may be required by the Constitution to afford at least some opportunity for review of convictions, noting that there are few, if any, situations in our system of justice in which a single judge is given unreviewable discretion over matters concerning a person's liberty or property.[1] Although the Supreme Court has never held that a litigant is entitled, as a matter of right, to have the decision in a case reviewed by an appellate court, the American judicial system operates on the assumption that the losing party in litigation should have at least one forum in which to challenge the result of the proceeding below. Whether due process requires such an opportunity for appellate review or not, one tier of review is, in fact, generally afforded to dissatisfied litigants.

The fact that appellate review is available, however, merely provides a mechanism by which the litigant, usually with the professional assistance of an appellate attorney, *may* be able to have adverse decisions considered and reversed, *if* the required procedures are followed, *if* the decision falls within the appellate court's scope of review, and *if* the court finds that the error calls for reversal. For the appellate practitioner, an understanding of these provisos is at least as important as the ability to write a persuasive brief on the merits of a claim.

Moreover, in recent years, the increasingly heavy caseload of appellate courts, particularly in the federal system and in states with large, litigious populations, has interfered to some extent with the courts' abilities to fulfill their role. The sheer volume of appellate litigation creates a strong temptation to limit the amount of time a court spends on any given case. Therefore, the effective practitioner seeking a reversal on appeal recognizes this reality and pays close attention to trying to convince the court, not only that an error has been made below, and that it seriously prejudiced the client, but that it can be corrected without undue expenditure of time and energy. The effective attorney for respondent, on the other hand, will try to capitalize on the court's workload by convincing the judges that the case can be affirmed summarily.

---

[1] *See Jones v. Barnes,* 463 U.S. 745, 756 n.1 (1983) (Brennan, J., and Marshall, J., dissenting).

The materials in this book are designed first to give law students and lawyers a foundation in the principles underlying appellate practice, so that they will be equipped to convince the court that a client's case is worthy of consideration, that the client's position is correct, and the client deserves a remedy. Second, the book seeks to provide appellate practitioners, in courts both real and moot, with practical information on handling a case on appeal.

The cases discussed in Chapter 2 should help the appellate lawyer make sure that a case is properly before the court, for the fastest way that courts dispose of a case is simply to dismiss the appeal on procedural grounds before ever looking at the merits of the claim, *i.e.* whether the decision below was right or wrong. Another way a court may avoid deciding the merits of a case is to decide that the issue it raises is not within the court's review powers, either because of the nature of the question or because it was never presented to the court below. The materials in Chapter 3 provide guidance for finding appropriate issues to present to particular appellate courts as well as giving some ideas about how to obtain review of an issue, even if trial counsel could have done a better job of preserving it for appeal.

Two other obstacles to obtaining a reversal in an appellate court are discussed in Chapters 4 and 5. Chapter 4 provides an overview of the standards used by appellate courts in reviewing different kinds of claims. In light of the great deference granted to the decision-maker below on some types of questions, appellate counsel must be prepared to formulate issues so as to increase the court's willingness to engage in a probing review. Chapter 5 discusses the final hurdle appellate counsel must overcome on the way to obtaining a reversal of the judgment below: the harmless error claim. Appellate counsel must know how to respond to the assertion that, even if error was committed, and properly objected to, the error was harmless in light of the strong evidence supporting the correctness of the judgment on the merits.

Chapter 6 includes materials on the right to the effective assistance of appellate counsel, as well as the particular obligations of assigned appellate counsel. Chapter 7 provides suggestions on brief-writing, with specific practical examples of how best to persuade the court, given the kind of issues presented by the case and the functions of the particular court being addressed. Finally, Chapter 8 focuses on how to make the most effective use of the shrinking time available for oral argument in today's overburdened appellate courts.

The Structure of the Appellate Court System

Every appellate practitioner needs to understand the structure and a bit of the history of the appellate court system. This understanding is not purely a matter of intellectual interest. It is also of considerable practical significance because the functions, powers and practices of different appellate courts vary significantly. The attorney who does not grasp these differences and act accordingly may find a poorly formulated appeal quickly dismissed.

Most jurisdictions have by now divided their appellate courts into at least two tiers, partly to accommodate increasing caseloads. A major difference between the two tiers is that the lower level, generally known as the intermediate appellate court, is usually available to litigants as of right. In contrast, appeals as of right to the highest court in any jurisdiction are permitted only in a small class of cases, while in most cases permission to appeal to the court must be requested and is sparingly granted.[2]

More important, the primary functions of the two tiers of appellate courts differ. Some background in the history of appellate procedure can help to illustrate these different functions. Two distinct approaches to appellate review were used in England, one for actions at law and one for suits in equity. At law, the courts used the "writ of error" procedure, which was a separate, semi-criminal action brought by the losing party in a law suit charging the trial judge in the case with having made a legal error that resulted in a "false verdict" having been rendered. The purpose of the proceeding was not to determine who should have won the original case, but rather to determine whether the judge had acted properly. The review procedure employed on the equity side served a very different function. Rather than a new action, this was a continuation of the original case which allowed the appellate court to review both the law and the facts presented at trial and, if appropriate, to render an entirely new decision.

American courts, for the most part, followed the writ of error model. Thus, as a rule, an appeal became first and foremost a search for judicial error in the trial record rather than a reconsideration of the result in the case, particularly in the higher-level appellate courts. The equity model of an appeal as a procedure for reviewing the overall outcome of a lawsuit is, however, also evident in the American system at the intermediate level.

In the two-tier appellate system, the higher courts in most jurisdictions are likely to focus on the correction of judicial errors. Indeed, these high courts' powers of review tend to be strictly limited, often by statute, to purely legal issues that have first been raised in the trial court. The only time such a court will review the facts in a case is when the legal sufficiency, as opposed to simply the weight, of the evidence has been challenged. The most important goal of the higher appellate courts is not simply to ensure that litigants in the particular case received a fair, error-free trial, but to develop a clear, consistent, coherent body of law that can be followed and applied by the lower courts. Thus, the highest state appeals courts, like the United States Supreme Court, choose cases in which important issues of constitutional law, issues of first impression, and questions of statutory interpretation are raised. Cases raising an issue over which the lower courts are split may also be considered.

---

[2] In New York, for example, the New York Court of Appeals, the state's highest court, agrees to hear approximately 4% of the criminal cases in which leave to appeal is sought.

While intermediate appellate courts are also concerned with the correction of legal errors occurring at trial, they generally have, in addition, the broad equity power denied to the higher appellate courts to review the entire case to ensure that justice was done to the parties and to correct legal errors that were not raised in the trial court when to do so would serve the interests of justice. Moreover, intermediate courts, unlike high courts, can review the facts in a case and make new factual findings based on the record below. Finally, they can reverse a judgment if, in their opinion, a verdict is against the weight of the evidence even though the evidence may be legally sufficient.

A. The Federal Court System

The federal courts of appeals, including both the numbered circuits and the specialized federal circuit, are technically intermediate appellate courts under the Supreme Court. Because of the extremely limited jurisdiction of Supreme Court, however, the circuit courts engage in both the correcting-error and doing-justice functions that tend to be divided in the state courts. It is not always clear which issues these courts will be willing to review because they do not act consistently, either from circuit to circuit or from case to case within a particular circuit.

The following chart shows the basic structure of the federal court system.

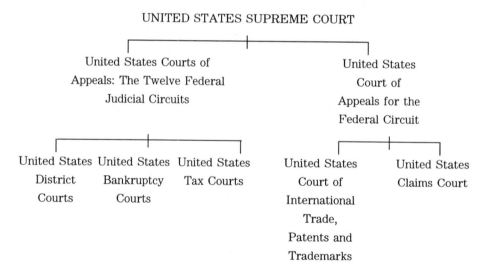

UNITED STATES SUPREME COURT

United States Courts of Appeals: The Twelve Federal Judicial Circuits

United States Court of Appeals for the Federal Circuit

United States District Courts

United States Bankruptcy Courts

United States Tax Courts

United States Court of International Trade, Patents and Trademarks

United States Claims Court

B. State Court Systems

Each state has its own system of organizing its courts and its own rules governing the powers of its various appellate courts. Although each jurisdiction operates in a somewhat different way, examination of three state court systems — Illinois, New York, and California — will illustrate the typical hierarchy and functions of state appellate courts.

Illinois has adopted a streamlined structure of one set of trial courts, a single level of intermediate courts, and finally the Supreme Court:

ILLINOIS STATE COURT SYSTEM
Supreme Court
|
Appellate Courts
|
Circuit Courts

The statutory powers of review of all appellate courts in Illinois are quite broad, extending both to review of the weight of the evidence and correction of any legal error that might have affected the judgment.[3] Nonetheless, because appeal to the Supreme Court is in most instances discretionary, plenary review tends to occur in the Appellate Courts, with the Supreme Court performing the function of correcting legal error and furthering the development of the law.

In New York, this division of functions has been codified, so that the review powers of the Court of Appeals[4] are limited by statute to particular kinds of questions, while the three different intermediate courts are permitted to engage in full review of an entire case.[5]

NEW YORK STATE COURT SYSTEM

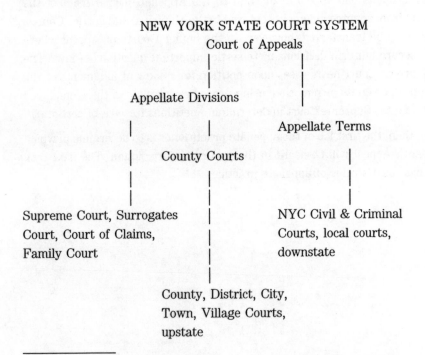

_____

[3] *See* Illinois Supreme Court Rule 366.

[4] The names given to various courts in New York are unique. In most states, as in California and Illinois, the highest appellate court is the Supreme Court, which in New York is a trial court. The highest appellate court in New York is the Court of Appeals, a name used by many states for their intermediate appellate courts.

[5] *See* N.Y.C.P.L.R. §5501 and N.Y.C.P.L. §§470.15 and 470.35.

Some appeals from trial courts go as of right to the lower intermediate County Courts and Appellate Terms, but may proceed to the Appellate Divisions by permission. Others, from the Supreme Courts, go directly to the Appellate Divisions as of right. In most cases, review can be had by the Court of Appeals only by permission, and the high court's scope of review is restricted largely to questions of law that were properly raised below.

California, like New York, has more than one intermediate appellate court to review cases from the specialized trial courts.

CALIFORNIA STATE COURT SYSTEM
Supreme Court

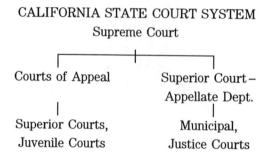

In California, litigants can appeal as of right to the Appellate Department of the Superior Court from adverse judgments entered in the Municipal and Justice Courts. Such appeals may be transferred, however, to the higher Courts of Appeal where necessary to secure uniform decisions or to settle important questions of law.[6] The California Supreme Court hears cases upon petition for review of judgments of the Courts of Appeal, or on its own motion, using procedures similar to those employed by the United States Supreme Court in determining petitions for writ of certiorari.[7]

Obviously, then, the first job of the appellate practitioner is to determine in which court the client's appeal will be heard in the particular jurisdiction. The next task is to learn that court's rules of appellate practice.

---

[6] *See* California Appellate Rules, Rule 62.
[7] *See* California Appellate Rules, Rule 28.

Chapter 2

Getting the Court's Attention

Introduction

In order to have a decision in a trial court reversed at the appellate level, counsel must begin by taking all procedural steps necessary to invoke the court's jurisdiction. The first step in every case is to ascertain whether an automatic right to appeal exists or whether permission to appeal is required. This is governed by statute and generally depends first on whether the court to which the appeal is sought is an intermediate appellate court or a court of last resort. Additional considerations may include whether the case is civil or criminal, whether the appeal is from a final judgment or an interlocutory order and, in a criminal case, whether the party seeking to appeal is the defense or the prosecution. Because the precise rules and the procedure required vary somewhat from court to court, counsel must ascertain the rules in the particular jurisdiction.

A. Appeals as of Right: The Notice of Appeal

Where an automatic right to appeal is guaranteed, the necessary procedural step could not be easier. Counsel must simply file a notice of appeal with the appropriate clerk within the time specified in the court's rules for taking an appeal. The example provided here shows that this notice is one of the simplest drafting tasks a lawyer will have to perform.

UNITED STATES DISTRICT COURT FOR THE
EASTERN DISTRICT OF NEW YORK

Wanna Peal,
    Plaintiff,   Docket No. 1234/95
    v.   NOTICE OF APPEAL
Haddad Wright,
    Defendant.

Notice is hereby given that Wanna Peal, plaintiff above named, hereby appeals to the United States Court of Appeals for the Second Circuit from the final judgment entered in this action on the 15th day of May, 1995.

May 23, 1995

/S/_____

Attorney for Plaintiff
246 Justice Court
Brooklyn, New York 98765
(333) 123-1234

B. Appeals by Permission

1. Request for Leave to Appeal in State Court

While filing a notice of appeal may be simplicity itself, the drafting of an effective request for leave to appeal to an appellate court requires careful thought and considerable work. Generally, in state court, the request is made by letter or motion to either the higher court to which counsel hopes to appeal or to the intermediate court which rendered the decision that counsel seeks to overturn. Following is New York's statute governing the method by which criminal cases are appealed to the Court of Appeals:

New York Criminal Procedure Law § 460.20

Certificate granting leave to appeal to court of appeals

1. A certificate granting leave to appeal to the court of appeals from an order of an intermediate appellate court is an order of a judge granting such permission and certifying that the case involves a question of law which ought to be reviewed by the court of appeals.

2. Such certificate may be issued by the following judges in the indicated situations:

(a) Where the appeal sought is from an order of the appellate division, the certificate may be issued by (i) a judge of the court of appeals or (ii) a justice of the appellate division of the department which entered the order sought to be appealed.

(b) Where the appeal sought is from an order of an intermediate appellate court other than the appellate division, the certificate may be issued only by a judge of the court of appeals.

3. An application for such a certificate must be made in the following manner:

(a) An application to a justice of the appellate division must be made upon reasonable notice to the respondent;

(b) An application seeking such a certificate from a judge of the court of appeals must be made to the chief judge of such court by submission thereof, either in writing or first orally and then in writing, to the clerk of the court of appeals. The chief judge must then designate a judge of such court to determine the application. The clerk must then notify the respondent of the application and must inform both parties of such designation.

4. A justice of the appellate division to whom such an application has been made, or a judge of the court of appeals designated to determine such an application, may in his discretion determine it upon such papers as he may request the parties to submit, or upon oral argument, or upon both.

5. Every judge or justice acting pursuant to this section shall file with the clerk of the court of appeals, immediately upon issuance, a copy of every certificate granting or denying leave to appeal.

Note that while New York's statute gives a choice of courts to which a leave-to-appeal request may be made, there is no second chance. Therefore, an attorney must consider carefully which court is more likely to grant the request. Generally, this will be the higher court, since the intermediate court is unlikely to think that its own decision requires review. If, however, there was a dissent in the intermediate court, the dissenting judge may be eager to have his or her view of the law prevail in the state's highest court.

Once the addressee of the leave-to-appeal letter has been chosen, the next step is to formulate the arguments designed to convince the court that the case is worthy of further review. At this point, it is important to keep in mind that the basic function of appellate courts of last resort is to decide issues of public importance and to formulate uniform rules that will guide lower courts in making decisions, rather than simply to give the parties in a particular case another hearing. Therefore, a leave-to-appeal request should not be simply a rehash of the issues raised on appeal in the intermediate court. Instead, it should be an explanation of the substantial reasons why the case is worthy of review by the state's highest court.

While these courts may, on occasion, be willing to consider a particularly serious denial of justice to an individual litigant, it is more likely that leave to appeal will be granted if counsel is able to convince the court that a case has broader public significance. For example, counsel might argue that the case raises an important issue of first impression, or that the intermediate court's opinion conflicts with prior opinions of the state's highest court or the Supreme Court of the United States or of other intermediate appellate courts within the jurisdiction.

The New York Court of Appeals recently granted a criminal defendant leave to appeal his judgment of conviction in a case in which it was revealed, after trial, that the prosecution had failed to turn over exculpatory evidence, a *per se* reversible error under a case called *People v. Rosario*, 9 N.Y. 2d 286, 173 N.E.2d 881, 213 N.Y.S.2d 448 (1961) and under state statute. The intermediate appellate court nevertheless upheld the conviction on several counts of the indictment and the defendant sought leave to appeal to the New York Court of Appeals in the letter excerpted below:

> This case raises novel and monumental issues of state-wide importance involving the *Rosario* rule. Stated broadly, the issue is the appropriate remedy for a conceded *Rosario* violation discovered after trial on a multi-count indictment. Should a *Rosario* violation vitiate conviction on all counts, particularly when the prosecutor has successfully argued to the factfinder that all of the counts are interrelated. . .or should the extent of the vacatur turn on the number of counts on which the defendant was tried, regardless of the "relatedness" of the counts, as the Appellate Division held?
>
> Before now, the Court of Appeals has never held, nor even hinted, that there may be circumstances in which one or more counts of conviction can be upheld despite a *Rosario* violation directly affecting some counts of conviction. Indeed, parsing the evidence to determine which counts of the indictment have been "tainted" by a *Rosario* violation seems inconsistent with the

per se error rule of *Rosario,* and the Court has consistently resisted creating any new exceptions to that rule. *See People v. Banch,* 80 N.Y.2d 610 (1992).

The Appellate Division entered new *Rosario* waters, uncharted by the Court of Appeals, by reinstating [the defendant's] conviction on eight counts of selling prescriptions for controlled substances, notwithstanding a *Rosario* violation, while upholding the trial court's vacatur of the conviction on two counts because of the *Rosario* violation. . . . Even assuming that the Court of Appeals might be inclined to hold, for the first time, that there can be cases in which a *Rosario* violation does not vitiate all counts of conviction, the Appellate Division went much further than required by the facts of this case. In the process, it not only created another new and unsanctioned exception to the *Rosario* rule, but one that is ultimately confusing and completely illogical, and ultimately dangerous. . . .

The Appellate Division's new *Rosario* exception is illogical because there is no reason why the number of counts of conviction should determine the scope of *Rosario* relief. . . . The new rule is dangerous because it is an inducement to prosecutorial abuse and will undermine judicial economy. Under the Appellate Division's numbers-based rule, a prosecutor can insulate a conviction from *Rosario* challenge by the simple expedient of bringing lengthy and repetitive multi-count indictments, secure in the knowledge that if he manages to obtain a conviction on 10 or more counts charging identical transactions he is free to disregard his *Rosario* obligations. Not only would such a rule confront the court system with longer trials, but it threatens to undermine *Rosario* itself.

In short, the Appellate Division's decision raises new and profound questions of the meaning, scope and vitality of *Rosario.* If left undisturbed, the Appellate Division's decision will unsettle the law in virtually every criminal trial. Win or lose, the issues raised by this case are plainly leave-worthy and ought to be reviewed by the Court of Appeals.

2. Petition for Writ of Certiorari to the United States Supreme Court

In a very small class of cases appeal may be had to the United States Supreme Court as of right.[1] The vast majority of cases heard by the Supreme Court, however, are reviewed on petitions for a writ of certiorari. A "cert. petition" resembles an appellate brief in form and a letter requesting leave to appeal in content. Its purpose,

---

[1] S. 952 amended 28 U.S.C. §§ 1252, 1254 and 1257 to all but eliminate the mandatory jurisdiction of the Supreme Court (effective June 27, 1988). Thus virtually all review by the Supreme Court is discretionary, obtained by petition for writ of certiorari. Before this amendment, appeals as of right to the Supreme Court had been available, at least in theory, in civil cases in which the United States was a party and where a federal court had declared a federal law unconstitutional; in cases in which a federal court had held a state statute unconstitutional; and in cases where a state court had held a federal statute unconstitutional or a state statute constitutional as against federal challenge.

like the purpose of a leave letter, is to convince the Supreme Court that a particular case is worthy of its review. The granting of *cert.* petitions is, however, purely discretionary, and approximately 95% of all petitions are denied. That is, out of approximately 5,000 petitions for a writ of certiorari each term, approximately 180 are granted. It is therefore crucial that the attorney seeking Supreme Court review understand the factors the Court considers when deciding whether to grant a petition.

The Court has stated on many occasions that its jurisdiction to review cases by way of certiorari was not conferred "merely to give the defeated party in the Circuit Court of Appeals another hearing." *Magnum Co. v. Coty,* 262 U.S. 159, 163 (1923). As Chief Justice Vinson explained in a 1949 speech:

> The Supreme Court is not, and never has been, primarily concerned with the correction of errors in lower court decisions. In almost all cases within the Court's appellate jurisdiction, the petitioner has already received one appellate review of his case. The debates in the Constitutional Convention make clear that the purpose of the establishment of one supreme national tribunal was, in the words of John Rutledge of South Carolina, 'to secure the national rights & uniformity of Judgmts.' The function of the Supreme Court is, therefore, to resolve conflicts of opinion on federal questions that have arisen among lower courts, to pass upon questions of wide import under the Constitution, laws, and treaties of the United States, and to exercise supervisory power over lower federal courts. If we took every case in which an interesting legal question is raised, or our *prima facie* impression is that the decision below is erroneous, we could not fulfill the Constitutional and statutory responsibilities placed upon the Court. To remain effective, the Supreme Court must continue to decide only those cases which present questions whose resolution will have immediate importance far beyond the particular facts and parties involved. Those of you whose petitions for certiorari are granted by the Supreme Court will know, therefore, that you are, in a sense, prosecuting or defending class actions; that you represent not only your clients, but tremendously important principles, upon which are based the plans, hopes and aspirations of a great many people throughout the country.

Stern and Gressman, *Supreme Court Practice* (BNA Books, Washington, D.C.) at 190.

Rule 17 of the Rules of the Supreme Court outlines the factors the Supreme Court may consider when deciding whether to grant review in a particular case.

> 1. A review on writ of certiorari is not a matter of right, but of judicial discretion, and will be granted only when there are special and important reasons therefor. The following, while neither controlling nor fully measuring the Court's discretion, indicate the character of reasons that will be considered.

(a) When a federal court of appeals has rendered a decision in conflict with the decision of another federal court of appeals on the same matter; or has decided a federal question in a way in conflict with a state court of last resort; or has so far departed from the accepted and usual course of judicial proceedings, or so far sanctioned such a departure by a lower court, as to call for an exercise of this Court's power of supervision.

(b) When a state court of last resort has decided a federal question in a way in conflict with the decision of another state court of last resort or of a federal court of appeals.

(c) When a state court or a federal court of appeals has decided an important question of federal law which has not been, but should be, settled by this Court, or has decided a federal question in a way in conflict with applicable decisions of this Court.

In addition to the presence of conflicting decisions, the importance of the issues involved in a case is a significant consideration in the granting of review. The Court has made clear, however, that "importance" means importance "to the public as distinguished from importance to the particular parties involved in the case." One situation in which the importance of a case may result in the grant of review is where a lower court holds a federal statute unconstitutional or where a federal statute is given an unwarranted construction in order to save its constitutionality. The correct construction and application of acts of Congress and federal administrative regulations is often considered important enough to warrant Supreme Court review on *certiorari,* as are important federal jurisdictional and procedural issues. The fact that similar issues are already pending before the Supreme Court indicates that the issues are important and therefore the Supreme Court may review in a case raising the same issues. It also may, in such a situation, postpone consideration of the petition until the first case has been decided and then dispose of the new case summarily in accordance with the decision in the first case.

While the presence of the above factors in a particular case will not guarantee that the Supreme Court will agree to review it, neither will their absence necessarily doom its chances of review by the Court. The Court does not always act consistently. Moreover, the Court almost never gives its reasons for either granting or denying *certiorari* in a particular case. It simply announces "*cert.* granted" or "*cert.* denied." Unsurprisingly, a virtual cottage industry has grown up of scholars who analyze decisions on *cert.* petitions to spot trends and to predict the areas of law in which the Court is likely to grant review. In any event, the attorney who seeks Supreme Court review should keep the above considerations in mind when deciding whether to seek *certiorari.*

Exercise

Madsen v. Women's Health Center, 114 S.Ct. 2516 (1994), a case decided by the Supreme Court in June, 1994 was one of many cases arising out of the attempts of Operation Rescue and several other anti-abortion groups and their members to shut down abortion clinics around the country. In *Madsen,* a clinic in Melbourne, Florida sought an injunction prohibiting Operation Rescue and others from engaging in harassment of patients and employees of the clinic. After extensive hearings, a Florida state court determined that Operation Rescue members had engaged in a variety of unlawful acts and the court issued an injunction placing a number of restrictions on demonstrations in the area surrounding the clinic. For purposes of the injunction, persons expressing a "pro-life" viewpoint, but not a "pro-choice" viewpoint, were considered to be acting in concert with Operation Rescue. Operation Rescue challenged the injunction in Florida Supreme Court on two grounds. First, it argued that the injunction was content-based because it restricted the speech of "pro-life" but not of "pro-choice" demonstrators. Second, it argued that several of the provisions of the injunction were over-broad because they placed impermissible prior restraints on peaceful expressive activity in addition to prohibiting unlawful conduct. The Florida Supreme Court upheld the injunction, stating:

> Operation Rescue claims that the time, place and manner restrictions at issue here are content-based. . . We disagree. The restrictions regulate when, where, and how Operation Rescue may speak, not what it may say. The restrictions make no mention whatsoever of abortion or any other political or social issue; they address only the volume, timing, location and violent or harassing nature of Operation Rescue's expressive activity.

While *Madsen* was wending its way through the state court system, another individual anti-abortion plaintiff sought to challenge the same injunction in federal court. The plaintiff argued that she was an opponent of abortion, but had no connection with Operation Rescue and simply wished to engage in protected First Amendment activity in the vicinity of the clinic. She feared, however, that should she do so, she would be arrested for acting in concert with Operation Rescue. She relied, in part, on *NAACP v. Claiborne Hardware,* 458 U.S. 886 (1982), in which the Supreme Court held that the First Amendment right of free speech and association restricted the ability of the state to outlaw an entire civil rights boycott simply because some of the boycotters engaged in acts of violence.

The Court of Appeals for the Eleventh Circuit came to the opposite conclusion from that of the Florida Supreme Court:

> That the speech restrictions at issue here are viewpoint based cannot seriously be doubted. The order enjoins Operation Rescue, Operation Rescue America, Operation Goliath, their officers, agents, members, employed and

servants and Ed Martin, Bruce Cadle, Pat Mahoney, Randall Terry, Judy Madsen, and Shirley Hobbs and all persons acting in concert or participation with them or on their behalf. . . .

Such a restriction is no more viewpoint neutral than one restricting the speech of "the Republican Party, George Bush, Bob Dole, Jack Kemp and all persons acting in concert or participation with them or on their behalf." The practical effect of this section of the injunction was to assure that while "pro-life" speakers would be arrested, pro-choice demonstrators would not.

The court noted, however, that the Court of Appeals for the Ninth Circuit had upheld an injunction in Portland, Oregon which prohibited "demonstrating or distributing literature. . ., shouting, screaming, chanting or yelling" by anti-abortion organizations and those acting in concert in the vicinity of an abortion clinic. *Cheffer v. McGregor,* 6 F.3d 705 (11th Cir. 1993).

If you were representing the losing party in either *Madsen* or *Cheffer,* what arguments would you make to convince the Supreme Court to review the case?

Hurry! Hurry! Timely Filing

While different courts have different rules of appellate procedure most, if not all, appellate courts impose rigid limits on the time within which the notice of appeal must be filed or leave to appeal sought. The following case shows the disastrous results that can follow from a failure to file a notice of appeal in a timely fashion.

United States v. Avendano-Camacho

786 F.2d 1392 (9th Cir. 1986)

KENNEDY, Circuit Judge:

Appellant Avendano-Camacho was convicted of conspiracy to possess and distribute heroin and aiding and abetting the distribution of heroin. The judgment of conviction was entered on April 10, 1985. On May 30, 1985, appellant attempted to file a notice of appeal which was rejected as untimely. Appellant contends that his failure to file the notice within the time prescribed by Federal Rule of Appellate Procedure 4(b) was the result of the incompetency of his trial counsel. On June 4, 1985, appellant sought from the district court an extension of time to file the notice, a request denied by order docketed June 6, 1985. Appellant timely appealed this order

on June 14, 1985. On appeal it is argued that Federal Rule of Appellate Procedure 4(b) denies appellant the equal protection of the laws since it permits the government thirty days in which to perfect an appeal while providing an individual defendant only ten days. Appellant also argues the district court erred in not finding that the alleged incompetency of his trial counsel in not filing the notice constituted "excusable neglect" warranting extension of the time for filing an appeal. We reject appellant's equal protection argument and, because we find ourselves without jurisdiction to hear the appeal, affirm the order of the district court.

While the equal protection clause of the

Fourteenth Amendment does not by its terms apply to federal enactments, equal protection claims may be brought under the Fifth Amendment due process clause and are approached in the same manner as are claims under the Fourteenth Amendment. See *Weinberger v. Wiesenfeld,* 420 U.S. 636, 638 n. 2 (1975). Classifications challenged as denying the equal protection of the laws are generally sustained if they rationally further a legitimate governmental interest. Only if the classification operates to the peculiar disadvantage of a suspect class, or interferes with a fundamental right, will it be subjected to strict scrutiny by the courts. *Massachusetts Board of Retirement v. Murgia,* 427 U.S. 307, 312 (1976). In this case there is no allegation that the classification disadvantages a suspect class. At least where the classification at issue is not based on wealth, the right to appeal is not considered a fundamental right. *Bell v. Hongisto,* 501 F.2d 346, 353-54 (9th Cir. 1974), *cert. denied,* 420 U.S. 962 (1975). Consequently, we apply the rational relation test to judge the classification here.

Applying this test, we have no difficulty finding that the different periods provided the government and criminal defendants for filing an appeal do not deny defendants the equal protection of the laws. It is reasonable to presume that it takes a large, bureaucratic organization such as the government, responsible for prosecuting thousands of cases across the country, a greater time to assess the merits of an appeal than it does an individual defendant. In reaching its decision whether or not to appeal, the government must be concerned, moreover, with the consistency of its position and the future impact of the case, considerations that do not weigh as heavily, if at all, in the decision of the defendant.

Having resolved defendant's constitutional challenge, we observe that courts have consistently viewed the filing deadlines of Federal Rule of Appellate Procedure 4(b) as "both mandatory and jurisdic-

tional." *Smith v. United States,* 425 F.2d 173, 174 (9th Cir. 1970) (citing *United States v. Robinson,* 361 U.S. 220, 229 (1960)). Here the appellant has missed the initial ten-day filing period, as well as the thirty additional days provided for seeking an extension of time due to "excusable neglect." While an exception to the rule that filing periods are jurisdictional has been recognized where an appellant has done "all he could under the circumstances" to perfect an appeal within the time permitted by the rule, *see, e.g., Fallen v. United States,* 378 U.S. 139, 143-44 (1964), this exception has been narrowly construed, and attorney neglect has not been seen as providing a basis for relief. Compare *id.* (prisoner mailed notice within ten-day period without knowing that prison mail was not picked up everyday) with *Berman v. United States,* 378 U.S. 530 (1964) (*per curiam*) (affirming dismissal of appeal where notice was one day late because counsel failed to file notice due to illness). Furthermore, the defendant does not claim that the district court failed to inform him of his right to appeal as provided by Federal Rule of Criminal Procedure 32(a)(2), thus perhaps preventing running of the time for filing a notice of appeal. Consequently, we lack jurisdiction to hear the appeal.

We are aware that this result seems harsh. We emphasize, however, that we do not here decide whether, in light of defendant's apparent lack of education or understanding of the English language, his counsel may not in fact have sufficiently informed him of his right to appeal and whether any such failure might constitute ineffective assistance of counsel. At this time the proper avenue for raising this claim is to file a petition under 28 U.S.C. §2255. While this circuit has not had occasion to address what remedy under section 2255 might be available to a federal prisoner who establishes that he was in fact denied the right to appeal as a result of ineffective counsel, we note that in at least one other circuit such a petitioner has been granted the right to file an out-of-time appeal. See *Mack v. Smith,* 659 F.2d 23, 25-26 (5th Cir. 1981); *Atilus v. United States,* 406 F.2d 694 (5th Cir. 1969).

The order of the district court is AFFIRMED.

Notes

1. Judge (now Supreme Court Justice) Kennedy suggests at the end of his opinion that the defendant may have another possible way to get his appeal heard. In other words, faced with the same record, reflecting a sequence of events in the past during which a critical necessary step was neglected, an appellate attorney might find a different route to the desired result. This situation is not uncommon in appellate practice, and the creative attorney may be able to achieve success in overcoming obstacles regarded as insurmountable by most practitioners.

2. Filing deadlines for the notice of appeal vary, both among the different jurisdictions and according to the kind of decision being appealed. The ten-day period allowed for appeal from a judgment in a federal criminal case is among the shortest; thirty-day periods are common. Counsel must, of course, determine the appropriate time period, and be sure to file the notice within that period.

3. What must be done to accomplish the "filing" of a notice of appeal has been the subject of litigation. As a general rule, the notice must actually be *received* by the clerk of the court before it is considered to have been properly filed. The Supreme Court has created an exception, however, for a prisoner filing a notice of appeal *pro se,* that is, without the assistance of counsel. *Houston v. Lack,* 487 U.S. 266 (1988). The prisoner had deposited his notice to the prison authorities for mailing three days before the end of the filing period, but the clerk had not marked it "filed" until one day after the time had elapsed. The Court, noting that the prisoner has no choice but to deliver the notice to prison authorities for mailing, declared that a *pro se* prisoner's notice of appeal would be considered "filed" at the time it was given to the prison authorities. The closeness of the decision (5 to 4), and the vehemence of the dissent, should give some idea of how critical compliance with filing deadlines is to getting the court to hear the case.

Some courts have promulgated rules by which documents are deemed filed at the time they are deposited, with the proper postage and addressed correctly, in an official United States mailbox. *See, e.g.,* Supreme Court Rule 28.2. Counsel must then generally submit an affidavit stating that the document was mailed within the required time period.

But Be Patient! The Finality Rule

The materials that follow explore the consequences, not of arriving too late at the appellate court, but of getting there too early.

The federal courts, as well as most states (with some notable exceptions),[1] limit the jurisdiction of their appellate courts largely to appeals from final judgments entered in the trial courts. The general rule about when an appeal to the court of appeals may be taken from a federal district court is stated in 28 U.S.C. § 1291:

> The courts of appeals . . . shall have jurisdiction of appeals from all final decisions of the district courts of the United States. . . .

The requirement that parties to a lawsuit must wait until a final judgment is entered before filing an appeal is based on several considerations. The most compelling factor is efficiency: the appellate court will only have to look at the case once, after all relevant decisions have been made by the trial court, and will not need to review many interim determinations that have become irrelevant by the time the case is finally concluded. The finality rule also gives control over the case to the trial judge in a way that would be undermined if attorneys could run to the appellate court every time the trial court made an adverse decision. In addition, an unscrupulous attorney might try to use numerous, expensive appeals to harass the opposing side, thereby creating a chilling effect on the litigation of meritorious claims.

The Federal Rules of Civil Procedure set forth the technical requirements for rendering a judgment "final" for purposes of appealability to the federal circuit courts: According to Rule 58, the judgment must be set forth separately, and according to Rule 79(a), it must be entered in the docket by the court clerk. Under Rule 54(b), the finality requirement can be met as to less than the whole lawsuit. Thus a district court can enter final judgment as to one of multiple parties, or as to one of several claims between two parties. The Supreme Court has defined a "separate" claim rather broadly for these purposes; the claim need not be based on a different transaction or occurrence, but could simply be based on a different legal theory.

The finality rule serves well the interests of efficiency and orderly procedure, but at times strict application of the rule would work injustice to the parties. Several exceptions have thus been developed, by statute and case law, to enable a losing party to obtain an immediate, or interlocutory, appeal of certain types of trial court decisions, before judgment becomes final.

A. Statutory Exceptions to the Finality Rule

Most jurisdictions have, by statute, provided appellate courts with review power over certain types of non-final orders.

---

[1] The intermediate appellate courts in New York are the most liberal in permitting immediate appeals of virtually all types of orders in civil cases. *See* p. 43, *infra.*

1. Interlocutory Appeals

28 U.S.C. §1292 contains the most important federal statutory exceptions to the finality rule:

§1292. Interlocutory decisions

(a) Except as provided in subsections (c) and (d) of this section, the courts of appeals shall have jurisdiction of appeals from:

(1) Interlocutory orders of the district courts of the United States, the United States District Court for the District of the Canal Zone, the District Court of Guam, and the District Court of the Virgin Islands, or of the judges thereof, granting, continuing, modifying, refusing or dissolving injunctions, or refusing to dissolve or modify injunctions, except where a direct review may be had in the Supreme Court;

(2) Interlocutory orders appointing receivers, or refusing orders to wind up receiverships or to take steps to accomplish the purposes thereof, such as directing sales or other disposals of property;

(3) Interlocutory decrees of such district courts or the judges thereof determining the rights and liabilities of the parties to admiralty cases in which appeals from final decrees are allowed.

(b) When a district judge, in making in a civil action an order not otherwise appealable under this section, shall be of the opinion that such order involves a controlling question of law as to which there is substantial ground for difference of opinion and that an immediate appeal from the order may materially advance the ultimate termination of the litigation, he shall so state in writing in such order. The Court of Appeals which would have jurisdiction of an appeal of such action may thereupon, in its discretion, permit an appeal to be taken from such order, if application is made to it within ten days after the entry of the order: *Provided, however,* That application for an appeal hereunder shall not stay proceedings in the district court unless the district judge or the Court of Appeals or a judge thereof shall so order.

[Subdivisions (c) and (d) deal with the jurisdiction of the United States Court of Appeals for the Federal Circuit.]

a. Injunctions

The provision concerning injunctions has its roots in the historic division between law and equity. In England, traditionally, immediate appeals could be taken from orders entered by courts sitting in equity; in law courts, however, litigants had to await the final judgment before obtaining appellate review.

To understand the rationale behind allowing interlocutory appeals from orders concerning injunctions, it is useful to look at the problems that might result from strict application of the final order doctrine. Consider the consequences of awaiting final judgment in the following situation:

> The district court has granted an injunction ordering a company to discontinue emitting wastes into a navigable stream. This means that the company must halt production in its factory, which employs 1000 workers; if production is stopped for more than two weeks, the local competitor will have gained an insuperable edge in the market. The trial is scheduled to start in a month.

What might have happened by the time the trial was completed?

Appellate attorneys have at times obtained immediate review of non-final orders by arguing that a given order, while not technically an injunction, shared some of the same characteristics as injunctions, and therefore should be subject to interlocutory appeal. The Supreme Court has construed the provision permitting interlocutory appeals from injunctive orders narrowly, however, in keeping with the policy against piecemeal appeals. Immediate appeal is generally limited to circumstances where awaiting final judgment would have "serious, and perhaps irreparable" consequences. *Gardner v. Westinghouse Broadcasting Co.*, 437 U.S. 478, 480 (1978).

In keeping with this restrictive interpretation of §1292(a), the Supreme Court finally, in 1988, closed the door to interlocutory appeals in one situation in which they had been permitted for more than fifty years. Before the adoption of the Federal Rules of Civil Procedure, federal courts maintained the distinction between actions at law and proceedings in equity. Even though the same judge was presiding over the entire case, technically a judge sitting as a chancellor in equity could stay an action at law pending resolution of an equitable defense. For example, if a widow sued at law to recover on a life insurance policy, and the insurance company raised the equitable defense that the policy had been obtained by fraud, the judge could stay trial of the law action while resolving the validity of the defense. Plaintiff, seeking immediate appeal of the court's decision to stay her trial, could argue that the stay was tantamount to an injunction issued by an equity court to restrain an action at law.

In the first case presenting such a situation, the Supreme Court found the analogy persuasive, and permitted an immediate appeal, despite the fact that the judge was, in one sense, simply organizing his docket by deciding which of several issues would be resolved first. *Enelow v. New York Life Ins. Co.*, 293 U.S. 379 (1935). Even after the merger of law and equity, the Court continued to permit immediate appeals from orders granting or denying stays of "legal" proceedings on "equitable" grounds. *See Ettelson v. Metropolitan Life Ins. Co.*, 317 U.S. 188 (1942). In *Gulfstream Aerospace Corp. v. Mayacamas Corp.*, 485 U.S. 271, 108 S.Ct. 1133 (1988), however, the Court finally decided that the so-called *Enelow-Ettelson* doctrine had long outlived any reasonable justification, and discarded it.

b. Controlling Questions of Law

The rationale behind the exception contained in §1292(b) is illustrated by the following situation:

> The district judge is faced with a novel question of law concerning whether certain allegations state a valid claim; she is inclined to deny the defendant's motion to dismiss, but thinks the appellate court may disagree. Defendant's counsel is convinced that the motion should be granted.

What, if anything, can counsel do? What procedures would have to be followed?

Since this provision requires the approval of both the district court and the court of appeals, either of which may withhold certification for any reason, the party seeking an interlocutory appeal would be well advised to explore other avenues described in this chapter in attempting to secure review before final judgment.

2. Writs of Mandamus and Prohibition

Most jurisdictions give parties another way of obtaining appellate review of particular kinds of orders in exceptional circumstances. For example, the federal All Writs Act, 28 U.S.C. §1651(a) provides:

> The Supreme Court and all courts established by Act of Congress may issue all writs necessary or appropriate in aid of their respective jurisdictions and agreeable to the usages and principles of law.

This power does not confer additional jurisdiction on appellate courts, but rather aids them in preventing district courts from exceeding their jurisdiction or requiring them to adhere to the clear dictates of the law. Prohibition and Mandamus are generally restricted to situations where the party is clearly entitled to the relief sought, and where no other adequate means are available to obtain that relief. At times, circuit courts in granting mandamus will point to the fact that the issue is one of first impression, or that the error is a recurring one not correctable by appeal after final judgment. These extraordinary writs are not, in other words, to be used as a substitute for appeal; they tend to be reserved for protection of rights that are fundamental to a fair hearing or that could not be effectively protected if the party had to await a final judgment. In the first category are denials of the right to jury trial and determinations by a judge that recusal is not warranted under circumstances where disqualification is required by statute. *See e.g., Dairy Queen v. Wood,* 369 U.S. 469, 472 (1962); *In re Cooper,* 821 F.2d 833 (lst Cir. 1987); *In re Beard,* 811 F.2d 818 (4th Cir. 1987). Even when the issue is whether a judge should be disqualified, however, a writ of mandamus will not be issued unless the appellate court finds that petitioner is indisputably entitled to relief; the court must be convinced that the trial court's decision "cannot be defended as a rational conclusion supported by a reasonable reading of the record." *In re United States,* 666 F.2d 690, 695 (1st Cir. 1981).

In the second category, some courts have granted mandamus to correct discovery orders requiring the production of documents claimed to be privileged. *See, e.g., In re Burlington Northern, Inc.,* 810 F.2d 601 (7th Cir. 1986); *Bogosian v. Gulf Oil Corp.,* 738 F.2d 587 (3d Cir. 1984). Mandamus was justified in these situations because, once the information was disclosed, appeal from final judgment would fail to provide an adequate remedy.

B. Judicial Interpretations of the Finality Requirement

Faced with situations that would seem to make it advisable to permit an appeal before entry of final judgment, courts have on occasion defined the finality requirement so as to permit immediate appeal from decisions that are "final" only in a very special sense. In the following case, the Supreme Court developed the so-called *Cohen* doctrine, or collateral order doctrine, permitting immediate appeal of a pretrial order that does not finally dispose of the litigation.

Cohen v. Beneficial Industrial Loan Corp.
337 U.S. 541 (1949)

Mr. Justice JACKSON delivered the opinion of the Court.

The ultimate question here is whether a federal court, having jurisdiction of a stockholder's derivative action only because the parties are of diverse citizenship, must apply a statute of the forum state which makes the plaintiff, if unsuccessful, liable for the reasonable expenses, including attorney's fees, of the defense and entitles the corporation to require security for their payment.

Petitioners' decedent, as plaintiff, brought in the United States District Court for New Jersey an action in the right of the Beneficial Industrial Loan Corporation, a Delaware corporation doing business in New Jersey. The defendants were the corporation and certain of its managers and directors. The complaint alleged generally that since 1929 the individual defendants engaged in a continuing and successful conspiracy to enrich themselves at the expense of the corporation. Specific charges of mismanagement and fraud extended over a period of eighteen years and the assets allegedly wasted or diverted thereby were said to exceed $100,000,000. The stockholder had demanded that the corporation institute proceedings for its recovery but, by their control of the corporation, the individual defendants prevented it from doing so. This stockholder, therefore, sought to assert the right of the corporation. One of 16,000 stockholders, he owned 100 of its more than two million shares, so that his holdings, together with 150 shares held by the intervenor, approximated 0.0125% of the outstanding stock and had a market value that had never exceeded $9,000.

The action was brought in 1943, and various proceedings had been taken therein when, in 1945, New Jersey enacted the statute which is here involved. Its general effect is to make a plaintiff having so small an interest liable for all expenses and attorney's fees of the defense if he fails to make good his complaint and to entitle the corporation to indemnity before the case can be prosecuted. These conditions are made applicable to pending actions. The corporate defendant therefore moved to require security, pointed to its by-laws by which it might be required to indemnify the individual defendants, and averred that a bond of $125,000 would be appropriate.

The District Court was of the opinion that the state enactment is not applicable to such an action when pending in a federal court. The Court of Appeals was of a contrary opinion and reversed, and we granted certiorari.

APPEALABILITY

At the threshold we are met with the question whether the District Court's order refusing to apply the statute was an appealable one. Title 28 U.S.C. 1948 ed § 1291 provides, as did its predecessors, for appeal only "from all final decisions of the district courts," except when direct appeal to this Court is provided. Section 1292 allows appeals also from certain interlocutory orders, decrees and judgments, not material to this case except as they indicate the purpose to allow appeals from orders other than final judgments when they have a final and irreparable effect on the rights of the parties. It is obvious that, if Congress had allowed appeals only from those final judgments which terminate an action, this order would not be appealable.

The effect of the statute is to disallow appeal from any decision which is tentative, informal or incomplete. Appeal gives the upper court a power of review, not one of intervention. So long as the matter remains open, unfinished or inconclusive, there may be no intrusion by appeal. But the District Court's action upon this application was concluded and closed and its decision final in that sense before the appeal was taken.

Nor does the statute permit appeals, even from fully consummated decisions, where they are but steps towards final judgment in which they will merge. The purpose is to combine in one review all stages of the proceeding that effectively may be reviewed and corrected if and when final judgment results. But this order of the District Court did not make any step toward final disposition of the merits of the case and will not be merged in final judgment. When that time comes, it will be too late effectively to review the present order and the rights conferred by the statute, if it is applicable, will have been lost, probably irreparably. We conclude that the matters embraced in the decision appealed from are not of such an interlocutory nature as to affect, or to be affected by, decision of the merits of this case.

This decision appears to fall in that small class which finally determine claims of right separable from, and collateral to, rights asserted in the action, too important to be denied review and too independent of the cause itself to require that appellate consideration be deferred until the whole case is adjudicated. The Court has long given this provision of the statute this practical rather than a technical construction. . . .

We hold this order appealable because it is a final disposition of a claimed right which is not an ingredient of the cause of action and does not require consideration with it. But we do not mean that every order fixing security is subject to appeal. Here it is the right to security that presents a serious and unsettled question. If the right were admitted or clear and the order involved only an exercise of discretion as to the amount of security, a matter the statute makes subject to reconsideration from time to time, appealability would present a different question. . . .

Notes

1. The Court went on to hold that the statute requiring the shareholder to post bond as security did not violate the federal Constitution, that its application to pending litigations did not render it unconstitutionally retroactive, and that, since it was not merely a regulation of procedure, it was applicable in the federal courts under the *Erie* doctrine.

2. Almost thirty years after the decision in *Cohen,* the Supreme Court explicitly set forth the requirements that must be met to satisfy the collateral order doctrine. "To come within the 'small class' of decisions excepted from the final-judgment rule by *Cohen,* the order must conclusively determine the disputed question, resolve an important issue completely separate from the merits of the action, and be effectively unreviewable on appeal from a final judgment." *Coopers & Lybrand v. Livesay,* 437 U.S. 463, 468 (1978).

3. It may be useful in trying to understand the collateral order doctrine, or *Cohen* rule, to think about what would have happened if the order had been held *not* to have been appealable. What might have been lost had no interlocutory appeal been permitted? In reading the following materials, try to determine what arguments were likely to have been made by the attorneys for the parties seeking interlocutory appeal to try to fit within the collateral order doctrine. What were the likely responses by the parties seeking dismissal of the appeal? What does it take to get a federal appellate court's attention before judgment is entered?

Flanagan v. United States

465 U.S. 259 (1984)

Justice O'CONNOR delivered the opinion of the Court.

In *Firestone Tire & Rubber Co. v. Risjord,* 449 U.S. 368 (1981), the Court held that a pretrial denial of a motion to disqualify counsel in a civil case is not appealable prior to trial under 28 U.S.C. § 1291 as a final collateral order. The Court reserved the questions of the immediate appealability of pretrial denials of disqualification motions in criminal cases and of pretrial grants of disqualification motions in both criminal and civil cases. *Id.,* at 372, n. 8. We decide today that a District Court's pretrial disqualification of defense counsel in a criminal prosecution is not immediately appealable under 28 U.S.C. § 1291.

I

Petitioners are four police officers who formed a "grandpop" decoy squad in the Philadelphia Police Department. Petitioner Flanagan would pose as an aged derelict, a likely target for street criminals. When Flanagan gave the standard alarm, the other members of the decoy team would move in to make an arrest.

A federal grand jury in the Eastern District of Pennsylvania indicted petitioners in September 1981. The indictment alleged that petitioners had conspired to make arrests without probable cause and had unlawfully arrested and abused eight people. One count of the indictment charged petitioners with conspiring to deprive citizens of their civil rights in violation of 18 U.S.C. § 241. The remaining 12 counts charged petitioners, in various combinations, with committing substantive civil rights offenses in violation of 18 U.S.C. § 242.

Prior to the return of the indictment, petitioners had retained the law firm of Sprague and Rubenstone to act as joint counsel. Petitioners decided to continue the joint representation after the indictment was handed down, even though the indictment did not make the same allegations against all petitioners. Petitioners Keweshan, Landis, and McNamee, however, moved to sever their case from petitioner Flanagan's, arguing that the government's evidence against Flanagan alone was so much greater than the evidence against them that severance was necessary to avoid prejudicial spillover. In addition, based on the asserted differences in their involvement in the activities alleged in the substantive counts of the indictment, petitioners moved to dismiss the conspiracy count. The Government responded by moving to disqualify Sprague and Rubenstone from its multiple representation of petitioners and by asking the court to inquire into the representation as required by Federal Rule of Criminal Procedure 44(c).

In early December 1981, following a hearing and briefing on the Government's motion, the District Court disqualified the law firm from participation in the case. The court found that no actual conflict of interest had yet developed but that there was a clear potential for conflict. Most notably, the severance motion and supporting papers showed that petitioner Flanagan's interests were likely to diverge from the other petitioners' interests. The District Court also found that petitioners had voluntarily, knowingly, and intelligently waived their right to conflict-free representation. The court concluded, however, that it had the authority and, indeed, the obligation under Rule 44(c) to disqualify counsel when "the

likelihood is great that a potential conflict may escalate into an actual conflict." The court presumed that Sprague and Rubenstone had obtained privileged information from each of the petitioners and therefore disqualified the law firm from representing any of them.

Petitioners appealed to the United States Court of Appeals for the Third Circuit, which affirmed the decision of the District Court in June 1982. Although jurisdiction was not challenged, the Court of Appeals noted that it had jurisdiction under 28 U.S.C. § 1291 because the disqualification order was appealable prior to trial as a collateral order within the meaning of *Cohen v. Beneficial Industrial Loan Corp.*, 337 U.S. 541 (1949). The court went on to hold that the disqualification order was proper because an actual conflict of interest was very likely to arise. In July 1982, the court denied rehearing but stayed issuance of the mandate to permit filing of a petition for a writ of certiorari in this Court.

Petitioners filed their petition in September 1982, one year after the grand jury had returned the indictment against them. They contended that disqualification of counsel of their choice after they had knowingly waived conflict-free representation deprived them of their Sixth Amendment right to assistance of counsel and of their Fifth Amendment due process right to present a common defense through joint counsel. We granted certiorari in January 1983. The parties briefed and argued both the merits and the jurisdictional question – whether the disqualification order was immediately appealable under 28 U.S.C. § 1291. We now reverse the judgment of the Court of Appeals because we conclude that the court had no jurisdiction to review the disqualification order prior to entry of final judgment in the criminal case.

II

"Finality as a condition of review is an

historic characteristic of federal appellate procedure." *Cobbledick v. United States,* 309 U.S. 323, 324 (1940). Thus, the jurisdictional statute applicable to this case limits the jurisdiction of the Courts of Appeals to appeals from "final decisions of the district court." 28 U.S.C. § 1291. This final judgment rule requires "that a party must ordinarily raise all claims of error in a single appeal following final judgment on the merits." *Firestone Tire & Rubber Co. v. Risjord,* 449 U.S., at 374. In a criminal case the rule prohibits appellate review until conviction and imposition of sentence. *Berman v. United States,* 302 U.S. 211, 212 (1937).

The final judgment rule serves several important interests. It helps preserve the respect due trial judges by minimizing appellate-court interference with the numerous decisions they must make in the prejudgment stages of litigation. It reduces the ability of litigants to harass opponents and to clog the court through a succession of costly and time-consuming appeals. It is crucial to the efficient administration of justice. For these reasons "[t]his Court has long held that the policy of Congress embodied in [section 1291] is inimical to piecemeal appellate review of trial court decisions which do not terminate the litigation. . . ." *United States v. Hollywood Motor Car Co.,* 458 U.S. 263, 265 (1982).

The Court has also long held that "this policy is at its strongest in the field of criminal law." *Ibid.* More than 40 years ago the Court noted that the reasons for the final judgment rule are "especially compelling in the administration of criminal justice." *Cobbledick v. United States,* 309 U.S., at 325. Promptness in bringing a criminal case to trial has become increasingly important as crime has increased, court dockets have swelled, and detention facilities have become overcrowded.

As the Sixth Amendment's guarantee of a Speedy Trial indicates, the accused may have a strong interest in speedy resolution of the charges against him. In addition, "there is a societal interest in providing a speedy trial which exists separate from, and at times in opposition to, the interests of the accused." *Barker v. Wingo,* 407 U.S. 514, 519 (1972). As time passes, the prosecution's ability to meet its burden of proof may greatly diminish: evidence and witnesses may disappear, and testimony becomes more easily impeachable as the events recounted become more remote. Delay increases the cost of pretrial detention and extends "the period during which defendants released on bail may commit other crimes." *United States v. MacDonald,* 435 U.S. 850, 862 (1978). Delay between arrest and punishment prolongs public anxiety over community safety if a person accused of a serious crime is free on bail. It may also adversely affect the prospects for rehabilitation. Finally, when a crime is committed against a community, the community has a strong collective psychological and moral interest in swiftly bringing the person responsible to justice. Prompt acquittal of a person wrongly accused, which forces prosecutorial investigation to continue, is as important as prompt conviction and sentence of a person rightly accused. Crime inflicts a wound on the community, and that wound may not begin to heal until criminal proceedings have come to an end.

The importance of the final judgment rule has led the Court to permit departures from the rule "only when observance of it would practically defeat the right to any review at all." *Cobbledick v. United States,* 309 U.S. at 324-325 (footnote omitted). The Court has allowed a departure only for the "limited category of cases falling within the 'collateral order' exception delineated in *Cohen.* . . ." *United States v. Hollywood Motor Car Co.,* 458 U.S., at 265. To come within this "narrow exception," a trial court order must, at a minimum, meet three conditions. First, it "must conclusively determine the disputed question"; second, it must "resolve an important issue completely separate from the merits of the action"; third, it must "be effectively unreviewable on appeal from a final judgment." *Coopers & Lybrand v. Livesay,* 437 U.S. 463, 468 (1978) (footnote omitted).

Because of the compelling interest in prompt trials, the Court has interpreted the requirements of the collateral-order exception to the final judgment rule with the utmost strictness in criminal cases. The Court has found only three types of pretrial orders in criminal prosecutions to meet the requirements. *See United States v. Hollywood Motor Car Co.,* 458 U.S., at 265. Each type involves "'an asserted right the legal and practical value of which would be destroyed if it were not vindicated before trial.'" *Id.,* at 266.

An order denying a motion to reduce bail may be reviewed before trial. The issue is finally resolved and is independent of the issues to be tried, and the order becomes moot if review awaits conviction and sentence. *Stack v. Boyle,* 342 U.S. 1 (1951). Orders denying motions to dismiss an indictment on double jeopardy or Speech or Debate grounds are likewise immediately appealable. Such orders finally resolve issues that are separate from guilt or innocence, and appellate review must occur before trial to be fully effective. The right guaranteed by the Double Jeopardy Clause is more than the right not to be convicted in a second prosecution for an offense: it is the right not to be "placed in jeopardy" – that is, tried for the offense. *Abney v. United States,* 431 U.S. 651 (1977). Similarly, the right guaranteed by the Speech or Debate Clause is more than the right not to be convicted for certain legislative activities: it is the right not to "be questioned" about them – that is, not to be tried for them. *Helstoski v. Meanor,* 442 U.S. 500 (1979). Refusals to dismiss an indictment

for violation of the Double Jeopardy Clause or of the Speech or Debate Clause, like denials of bail reduction, are truly final and collateral, and the asserted rights in all three cases would be irretrievably lost if review were postponed until trial is completed.

An order disqualifying counsel lacks the critical characteristics that make orders denying bail reduction or refusing to dismiss on double jeopardy or Speech or Debate grounds immediately appealable. Unlike a request for bail reduction, a constitutional objection to counsel's disqualification is in no danger of becoming moot upon conviction and sentence. Moreover, it cannot be said that the right petitioners assert, whether based on the Due Process Clause of the Fifth Amendment or on the Assistance of Counsel Clause of the Sixth Amendment, is a right not to be tried. Double jeopardy and Speech or Debate rights are *sui generis* in this regard. *See United States v. MacDonald,* 435 U.S., at 860, n. 7. Rather, just as the speedy trial right is merely a right not to be convicted at an excessively delayed trial, the asserted right not to have joint counsel disqualified is, like virtually all rights of criminal defendants, merely a right not to be convicted in certain circumstances. Unlike a double jeopardy or Speech or Debate claim, petitioners' claim "would be largely satisfied by an acquittal resulting from the prosecution's failure to carry its burden of proof." *Id.,* at 859. *See also United States v. Hollywood Motor Car Co.,* 458 U.S., at 268 (vindictive prosecution rightfully protected by post-conviction review). "Bearing the discomfiture and cost of a prosecution for crime even by an innocent person is one of the painful obligations of citizenship." *Cobbledick v. United States,* 309 U.S., at 325.

A disqualification order thus is not analogous to any of the three types of interlocutory orders that this Court has found immediately appealable in criminal cases. Accordingly, *Stack, Abney,* and

Helstoski provide no authority for petitioners' assertion that a disqualification order satisfies the three necessary conditions for coverage by the collateral order exception. Nor does petitioners' jurisdictional assertion gain support from a direct inquiry into whether a disqualification order satisfies the three *Coopers & Lybrand* conditions. This is so regardless of the nature of the right to joint representation claimed by petitioners.

Petitioners correctly concede that post-conviction review of a disqualification order is fully effective to the extent that the asserted right to counsel of one's choice is like, for example, the Sixth Amendment right to represent oneself. *See Faretta v. California,* 422 U.S. 806 (1975). Obtaining reversal for violation of such a right does not require a showing of prejudice to the defense, since the right reflects constitutional protection of the defendant's free choice independent of concern for the objective fairness of the proceeding. Similarly, post-conviction review is concededly effective to the extent that petitioners' asserted right is like the Sixth Amendment rights violated when a trial court denies appointment of counsel altogether, *see Gideon v. Wainwright,* 372 U.S. 335 (1963), or denies counsel's request to be replaced because of conflict of interest, *see Holloway v. Arkansas,* 435 U.S. 475 (1978). No showing of prejudice need be made to obtain reversal in these circumstances because prejudice to the defense is presumed. In sum, as petitioners concede, if establishing a violation of their asserted right requires no showing of prejudice to their defense, a pretrial order violating the right does not meet the third condition for coverage by the collateral order exception: it is not "effectively unreviewable on appeal from a final judgment."

If, on the other hand, petitioners' asserted right is one that is not violated absent some specifically demonstrated prejudice to the defense, a disqualification order still falls outside the coverage of the collateral order exception. We need not consider, however, whether the third *Coopers & Lybrand* condition is satisfied – that is, whether post-conviction review is plainly ineffective. It is sufficient to note that the second *Coopers & Lybrand* condition – that the order be truly collateral – is not satisfied if petitioners' asserted right is one requiring prejudice to the defense for its violation.

On this assumption, a disqualification order, though final, is not independent of the issues to be tried. Its validity cannot be adequately reviewed until trial is complete. The effect of the disqualification on the defense, and hence whether the asserted right has been violated, cannot be fairly assessed until the substance of the prosecution's and defendant's cases is known. In this respect the right claimed by petitioners is analogous to the speedy trial right. In *United States v. McDonald, supra,* the Court concluded that because impairment of the defense is an important factor in judging whether a speedy trial violation has occurred, a denial of a motion to dismiss on speedy trial grounds is not separable from the issues at trial. The same conclusion applies to a disqualification order if prejudice to the defense is a necessary element of petitioners' claim. In these circumstances, the second *Coopers & Lybrand* condition for immediate appealability as a collateral order is not satisfied: the disqualification order does not resolve an "issue completely separate from the merits of the action."

In short, whether or not petitioners' claim requires a showing of prejudice, a disqualification order does not qualify as an immediately appealable collateral order in a straightforward application of the necessary conditions laid down in prior cases. Further, petitioners' claim does not justify expanding the small class of criminal case orders covered by the collateral order exception to the final judgment rule – either by eliminating any of the *Coopers & Lybrand* conditions or by interpreting them less strictly than the Court's cases have done. The costs of such expansion are great, and the potential rewards are small.

Unlike an appeal of a bail decision, *see Stack v. Boyle*, 342 U.S., at 12 (opinion of Jackson, J.), an appeal of a disqualification order interrupts the trial. In criminal cases such interruption exacts a presumptively prohibitive price. Moreover, an appellate court's reversal of a disqualification order would not result in dismissal of the prosecution. The prosecution would continue, though only after long delay. The potential rewards of an immediate appeal are thus even smaller than they were in *United States v. MacDonald, supra,* and *United States v. Hollywood Motor Car Co., supra,* where the Court rejected claims of immediate appealability for orders denying motions to dismiss on speedy trial and vindictive prosecution grounds even though reversal of the orders would have led to dismissal of all or some charges. *See also Roche v. Evaporated Milk Ass'n,* 319 U.S. 21 (1943) (no pretrial review of order denying motion to dismiss indictment for lack of jurisdiction); *Heike v. United States,* 217 U.S. 423, 430-431 (1910) (no pretrial review of order rejecting claim of statutory immunity from prosecution). Here, a delayed trial is a certain result of interlocutory appellate review. Allowing immediate appeal of a disqualification order thus would severely undermine the policies behind the final judgment rule.

III

"'[T]he final judgment rule is the dominant rule in federal appellate practice.' 6 MOORE FEDERAL PRACTICE (2d ed. 1953), 113. Particularly is this true of criminal prosecutions." *DiBella v. United States,* 369 U.S. 121, 126 (1962). Nothing about a disqualification order distinguishes it from the run of pretrial judicial decisions that affect the rights of criminal defendants yet must await completion of trial-court proceedings for review. Such an order fails to satisfy the stringent conditions for qualification as an immediately appealable collateral order, and the overriding policies against interlocutory review in criminal cases apply in full. The exceptions to the final judgment rule in criminal cases are rare. An order disqualifying counsel is not one.

The judgment of the Court of Appeals is accordingly reversed. On remand the appeal should be dismissed.

Notes

1. In the *Flanagan* opinion, what kinds of orders, in criminal cases, were found immediately appealable, before final judgment? How did each of these orders satisfy the three *Cohen* or *Coopers & Lybrand* requirements?

2. Suppose a trial judge arbitrarily refused to assign counsel to represent an indigent defendant who was clearly entitled, under the Sixth Amendment, to the assistance of counsel. Could the defendant appeal that order denying assignment of counsel before trial? The order would finally determine the counsel issue, which is separate from the merits. But the order fails the third test, since it is effectively reviewable on appeal from the final judgment. The appellate court would simply reverse the judgment and order a new trial, with counsel to be assigned to the defendant. Unlike the protection against double jeopardy, the defendant has no "right not to be tried" without the aid of counsel; the right, rather, is not to suffer a judgment obtained in the absence of counsel.

3. The *Flanagan* Court also refused to place orders disqualifying defense counsel into the category justifying immediate appeal. Which of the three requirements was found lacking? As the Court noted, the answer to that question depends on how the right to counsel of one's choice is defined. If the right is an absolute one, such that no showing of prejudice is required, then it is indeed separate from the merits. Such a right, however, is effectively reviewable on appeal, just like the order denying counsel altogether. If, on the other hand, the right to counsel of one's choice is not absolute, but only available to avoid the prejudice suffered by the defendant from disqualification of a particular attorney, then it may indeed be effectively unreviewable on appeal from final judgment, since it is impossible to tell what other counsel would have done differently. Under these circumstances, however, the disqualification order fails the second prong of the *Cohen* test, because it is not separate from the merits.

4. As the *Flanagan* Court observed, the availability and effectiveness of an appeal after final judgment is one of the considerations to be taken into account when deciding whether to permit immediate appeal from a pre-trial order. An appeal after final judgment will be based, however, on all the evidence adduced at trial. If that evidence amounts to overwhelming proof of the defendant's guilt, an appellate court will be inclined to disregard any pre-trial irregularity as harmless error. (*See* Chapter 5, *infra*). Does the defendant, denied the opportunity of an interlocutory appeal, have a real remedy for such violations of his rights as, for example, an indictment obtained pursuant to improper grand jury proceedings?

In *United States v. Mechanik,* 475 U.S. 66 (1986), the Supreme Court held that a certain kind of grand jury abuse, namely allowing two witnesses to appear together in violation of Federal Rule of Criminal Procedure 6(d), was "cured" by the defendant's subsequent conviction after trial. This ruling formed the basis of appellate counsel's argument in a subsequent case, involving improper disclosure of matters occurring before the grand jury in violation of Rule 6(e)(2), that an immediate appeal should be permitted from a district court's order denying defendant's motion to dismiss the indictment because of this violation. Counsel in *Midland Asphalt v. United States,* 489 U.S. 794 (1989), asserted that, since this kind of a violation would be "cured" in the event of a conviction, the defendant's right to an appeal after final judgment was ineffective as a way of reviewing the grand jury error.

The Court, without deciding whether *Mechanik* would indeed apply to violation of grand jury secrecy, set up two possible scenarios: First, if the rule in *Mechanik* were *not* found to apply to grand jury secrecy violations, such violations could effectively be reviewed on appeal from a conviction. Second, if *Mechanik would* prevent reversal based on this kind of grand jury abuse after a conviction, then, as in *Mechanik,* the danger sought to be avoided has been prevented – obviously proof of guilt beyond a reasonable doubt would incorporate proof sufficient to establish probable cause. Justice Scalia seemed to assume that Rule 6(d), the Rule at issue in *Mechanik* prohibiting unauthorized persons from being present in the grand jury, has the same purpose as Rule 6(e), requiring secrecy of grand jury proceedings, that is to prevent issuance of an indictment on less than probable cause. Do the two rules really perform the same functions? Judge Pierce, writing for the Court of Appeals for the Second Circuit in *Midland Asphalt*, found that, unlike the prohibition against the presence of unauthorized persons, which protects only the interest of the defendant, the secrecy requirement protects society's interest in keeping confidential the identity of witnesses and persons under investigation, as well the interest in ensuring a fair trial. *United States v. Midland Asphalt*, 840 F.2d 1040, 1046 (2d Cir. 1988). The lower court found that the order was not immediately appealable only because it was likely that these interests could be protected by review on appeal after final judgment. *Id.*

Neither the Second Circuit nor the Supreme Court expressed particular concern about a third possible scenario, that of the defendant who, after having his motion to dismiss the indictment on the ground of grand jury abuse denied, is acquitted at trial. Surely that defendant's right not to be tried except upon a valid indictment has not been secured. Allowing immediate appeal of pretrial motions to dismiss indictments out of concern for defendants who are ultimately acquitted would, however, greatly increase the number of appealable orders, and result in the very problem of piecemeal appeals that the final order doctrine is designed to avoid. The relative infrequency of acquittals may justify refusal to expand significantly the right to interlocutory appeals of such pretrial orders.

5. Nonetheless, the Supreme Court did not, in *Midland Asphalt*, close the door to all interlocutory appeals of orders refusing to dismiss indictments. What argument might be made on behalf of a defendant facing trial on an indictment by a grand jury consisting of only two persons? In a recent case in New York, defense counsel moved to dismiss a federal indictment on the ground that the grand jury had been selected in accordance with a racially discriminatory plan. The motion was denied and the attorneys, albeit unsuccessfully, sought to bring an interlocutory appeal. The excerpt from the brief that follows not only provides a summary of the collateral order doctrine, but presents a good example of a creative and cogent written argument advocating a position known to be looked on with disfavor in the appellate court.

It is against [a] backdrop of a serious and probably meritorious constitutional challenge to the District's Plan that the Court is asked to decide a preliminary jurisdictional question: whether racial discrimination in the selection of a federal grand jury is subject to interlocutory appellate review. That question itself presents a new issue of exceptional importance. We know of no case that has decided the issue, and neither the government nor the Panel has cited such a case. In view of the important constitutional and statutory rights implicated by the underlying appeal, and the ramifications of those underlying issues for numerous other cases, we respectfully submit that the Court must and does have appellate jurisdiction to review those underlying issues immediately and on an interlocutory basis.

Under the "collateral order" exception to the "final judgment" rule for appellate jurisdiction, district court "decisions" are "final" for purpose of 28 U.S.C. § 1291 when they

> finally determine claims of right separate from, and collateral to, rights asserted in the action, too important to be denied review and too independent of the cause itself to require that appellate jurisdiction be deferred until the whole case is adjudicated.

Cohen v. Beneficial Industrial Loan Corp., 337 U.S. 541, 546 (1949). To satisfy the "collateral order" doctrine, an order must "(1) conclusively determine the disputed question, (2) resolve an important issue completely separate from the merits of the action, and (3) be effectively unreviewable on appeal from a final judgment." *Midland Asphalt Corp. v. United States,* 489 U.S. 794, 799 (1989), *quoting Coopers & Lybrand v. Livesay,* 437 U.S. 463, 468 (1978). The Supreme Court has interpreted the third ("Reviewability") prong of the "collateral order" test as satisfied only by orders that involve "an asserted right the legal and practical value of which would be destroyed if it were not vindicated before trial." *Midland Asphalt,* 489 U.S. at 800-802. In other words, the asserted right must implicate "the right not to be tried at all." *Id.*

The Supreme Court has so far recognized only three types of motions in criminal cases the denial of which is immediately appealable: bail, double jeopardy and Speech and Debate Clause motions. *Id.* at 799. It has, however, plainly left open the possibility that other types of asserted rights will satisfy the "collateral order" test, particularly in the grand jury context. For example, in *Midland Asphalt,* the Court wrote that a defect in the grand jury "so fundamental that it causes the grand jury no longer to be a grand jury, or the indictment no longer to be an indictment" implicates the Fifth Amendment right not to be tried except upon grand jury indictment and thereby satisfies the "collateral order" test. *Id.* at 802.

Based on that formulation, the 10th Circuit has recently held that a pre-trial order denying a defendant's motion for access to grand jury voting or quorum records is immediately appealable as a "collateral order." *United States v. Deffenbaugh Industries, Inc.,* 957 F.2d 749 (10th Cir. 1992).

Moreover, in *Vasquez v. Hillery,* 474 U.S. 254 (1986), the Supreme Court granted *habeas* relief to a state murder defendant 24 years after his indictment by a grand jury from which blacks had been excluded, even though the defendant had been convicted on sufficient evidence after trial before a fairly composed petit jury and the discriminatory practices had long since ceased. The *Vasquez* court rejected the state's "harmless error" argument and reaffirmed the principle that "discrimination on the basis of race in the selection of grand jurors 'strikes at the fundamental values of our judicial system and our society as a whole.'" *Id.* at 262.

Here, the essence of appellants' claim is that, as a result of the constitutional and statutory shortcomings in the District's Plan, they were indicted by a grand jury selected in a racially discriminatory manner, in violation of their rights under the Sixth and Fifth Amendments and the Act. In denying that motion [the lower court] conclusively determined those claims so far as appellants' rights were concerned, and those claims raised obviously important issues separate from and collateral to the merits of the prosecution.

Thus, the real issue here is whether the right asserted in this case would be "effectively unreviewable on appeal from a final judgment" or, in other words, implicates the right not to be tried at all. We submit that, win or lose after trial, no defendant should be required to defend himself against an indictment returned by a grand jury selected pursuant to a process infected by racial discrimination. A grand jury composed in such a prohibited manner is not a true grand jury and any indictment it returns is not a true indictment within the meaning of *Midland Asphalt*. The right not to be tried on such an indictment returned by such a grand jury is lost forever if not reviewed before trial, just as the rights protected by the Double Jeopardy Clause are lost if not reviewed pre-trial.

If denial of access to grand jury voting or quorum records is immediately appealable because an indictment returned by too few grand jurors is not a true indictment, as *Deffenbaugh Industries* holds, and if the "harmless error" doctrine cannot save a state indictment returned decades earlier by a grand jury selected in a racially discriminatory manner because such discrimination "strikes at the fundamental values of our judicial system and our society," as *Vasquez* holds, then surely a pretrial motion to dismiss a federal indictment returned by a grand jury from which racial minorities are systematically and unjustifiably excluded should also be immediately appealable. We submit that this Court would not hesitate to assume interlocutory appellate jurisdiction to review a jury selection plan that expressly excluded racial minorities from serving on grand juries. That is our case, except that the Plan's disproportionate exclusion of racial minorities is not explicit, but is its ineluctable effect.

In fact, the government as well as the courts would benefit from interlocutory appellate review in cases like this one where appellants have raised a concededly substantial claim of racial discrimination in the grand jury selection process. It makes little sense to defer appellate review of such a serious and substantial claim for months or even years, when the likely outcome in the event of a conviction – reversal, reindictment and retrial – will prejudice the government as much as appellants.[1] Appellate review at this early stage is particularly prudent in view of the great number of other pending grand jury investigations and trials put at risk so long as the issues raised by appellants remain unresolved.

In short, the lower court's order denying appellant's jury challenge – a challenge that has already contributed importantly to changing the face of the District's jury selection system – satisfies the "collateral order" doctrine and should be immediately appealable.

6. The Supreme Court has been just as strict about adherence to the finality rule in civil cases. In *Van Cauwenberghe v. Biard,* 486 U.S. 517 (1988), the Court upheld the Ninth Circuit's dismissal of an immediate appeal from an order denying a motion to dismiss on the ground that the extradited defendant was immune from civil process, or, in the alternative, on the basis of *forum non conveniens.* The following year, in *Lauro Lines S.R.L. v. Chasser,* 490 U.S. 495 (1989), the Court was similarly unmoved by the argument that an important right would be lost by failure to grant an interlocutory appeal. In the *Lauro Lines* case, involving the cruise ship hijacked by terrorists in the Mediterranean, the Italian ship owner moved to dismiss a suit brought by passengers in a New York court, citing a clause on each passenger's ticket requiring any suit to be brought only in the courts of Naples, Italy. The district court denied the motion. The Supreme Court affirmed the court of appeals' decision finding that the order did not fall within the *Cohen* collateral order doctrine:

> *Lauro Lines* argues here that its contractual forum-selection clause provided it with a right to trial before a tribunal in Italy, and with a concomitant right not to be sued anywhere else. This "right not to be haled for trial before tribunals outside the agreed forum," petitioner claims, cannot effectively be vindicated by appeal after trial in an improper forum. There is no obviously correct way to characterize the right embodied in petitioner's forum-selection provision: "all litigants who have a meritorious pretrial claim for dismissal can reasonably claim a right not to stand trial." *Van Cauwenberghe,* 486 U.S. at 524. The right appears most like that to be free from trial if it is characterized – as by petitioner – as a right not to be sued at all except in a Neapolitan forum. It appears less like a right not to be subjected to suit if characterized – as by the Court of Appeals – as "a right to have the binding adjudication of claims occur in a certain

---

[1] The United States Attorney has recognized that the Plan creates the "perception that there is a strong, race-based, outcome-determinative" effect on jury selection in the District. Removing that well-founded public "perception" is surely an important additional ground for immediate review of the Plan and its defects.

forum." 844 F.2d at 55. Even assuming that the former characterization is proper, however, petitioner is obviously not entitled under the forum-selection clause of its contract to avoid suit altogether, and an entitlement to avoid suit is different in kind from an entitlement to be sued only in a particular forum. Petitioner's claim that it may be sued only in Naples, while not perfectly secured by appeal after final judgment, is adequately vindicable at that stage – surely as effectively vindicable as a claim that the trial court lacked personal jurisdiction over the defendant – and hence does not fall within the third prong of the collateral order doctrine.

Lauro Lines, 490 U.S. at 500-501. Justice Scalia, in his concurring opinion, agreed with petitioners that their right not to be sued except in Naples would be destroyed by permitting the trial to go forward in New York, but asserted that this "right" was "not sufficiently important to overcome the policies militating against interlocutory appeals." *Id.* at 503. Given these policies, the ship owners would have to be content with reversal of any judgment obtained in New York, if a court ultimately agreed that the contractual forum selection clause must be upheld.

Similarly, in the following case, the Court was unpersuaded that a so-called "right not to stand trial altogether" provided a basis for an interlocutory appeal.

Digital Equipment Corp. v. Desktop Direct, Inc.

114 S. Ct. 1992 (1994)

Justice SOUTER delivered the opinion of the Court.

Section 1291 of the Judicial Code confines appeals as of right to those from "final decisions of the district courts." 28 U.S.C. § 1291. This case raises the question whether an order vacating a dismissal predicated on the parties' settlement agreement is final as a collateral order even without a district court's resolution of the underlying cause of action. *See Cohen v. Beneficial Loan Corp.,* 337 U.S. 541, 546 (1949). We hold that an order denying effect to a settlement agreement does not come within the narrow ambit of collateral orders.

I

Respondent, Desktop Direct, Inc. (Desktop) sells computers and like equip-

ment under the trade name "Desktop Direct." Petitioner, Digital Equipment Corporation is engaged in a similar business and in late 1991 began using that trade name to market a new service it called "Desktop Direct from Digital." In response, Desktop filed this action in the United States District Court for the District of Utah, charging Digital with unlawful use of the Desktop Direct name. Desktop sent Digital a copy of the complaint, and negotiations between officers of the two corporations ensued. Under a confidential settlement reached on March 25, 1992, Digital agreed to pay Desktop a sum of money for the right to use the "Desktop Direct" trade name and corresponding trademark, and for waiver of all damages and dismissal of the suit. That same day, Desktop filed a notice of dismissal in the District Court.

Several months later, Desktop moved to vacate the dismissal and rescind the settlement agreement, alleging misrepresentation of material facts during settlement negotiations. The District Court granted the motion, concluding "that a fact finder could determine that [Digital] failed to disclose material facts to [Desktop] during settlement negotiations which would have resulted in rejection of the settlement offer." After the District Court declined to reconsider that ruling or stay its order vacating dismissal, Digital appealed.

The Court of Appeals for the Tenth Circuit dismissed the appeal for lack of jurisdiction, holding that the District Court order was not appealable under § 1291, because it neither "ended the litigation on the merits" nor "[fell] within the long-recognized 'collateral order' exception to the final judgment requirement." Applying the three-pronged test for determining when "collateral order" appeal is allowed, *see Cohen, supra; Coopers & Lybrand v. Livesay,* 437 U.S. 463 (1978), the Court of Appeals concluded that any benefits claimed under the settlement agreement were insufficiently "important" to warrant the immediate appeal as of right. Although Digital claimed what it styled a "right not to go to trial," the court reasoned that any such privately negotiated right as Digital sought to vindicate was different in kind from an immunity rooted in an explicit constitutional or statutory provision or "compelling public policy rationale," the denial of which has been held to be immediately appealable.

II

A

The collateral order doctrine is best understood not as an exception to the "final decision" rule laid down by Congress in § 1291, but as a "practical construction" of it. We have repeatedly held that the statute entitles a party to appeal not only from a district court decision that "ends the litigation on the merits and leaves nothing more for the court to do but execute the judgment," *Catlin v. United States,* 324 U.S. 229, 233 (1945), but also from a narrow class of decisions that do not terminate the litigation, but must, in the interest of "achieving a healthy legal system," nonetheless be treated as "final." The latter category comprises only those district court decisions that are conclusive, that resolve important questions completely separate from the merits, and that would render such important questions effectively unreviewable on appeal from final judgment in the underlying action. Immediate appeals from such orders, we have explained, do not go against the grain of § 1291, with its object of efficient administration of justice in the federal courts.

But we have also repeatedly stressed that the "narrow" exception should stay that way and never be allowed to swallow the general rule, that a party is entitled to a single appeal, to be deferred until final judgment has been entered, in which claims of district court error at any stage of the litigation may be ventilated. We have accordingly described the conditions for collateral order appeal as stringent, and have warned that the issue of appealability under § 1291 is to be determined for the entire category to which a claim belongs, without regard to the chance that the litigation at hand might be speeded, or a "particular injustice" averted by a prompt appellate court decision.

B

Here, the Court of Appeals accepted Digital's claim that the order vacating dismissal (and so rescinding the settlement agreement) was the "final word on the subject addressed," 993 F. 2d, at 757 (citation omitted) and held the second *Co-*

hen condition, separability, to be satisfied, as well. Neither conclusion is beyond question,[2] but each is best left untouched here, both because Desktop has made no serious effort to defend the Court of Appeals judgment on those points and because the failure to meet the third condition of the *Cohen* test, that the decision on an "important" question be "effectively unreviewable" upon final judgment, would in itself suffice to foreclose immediate appeal under § 1291. Turning to these dispositive factors, we conclude, despite Digital's position that it holds a "right not to stand trial" requiring protection by way of immediate appeal, that rights under private settlement agreements can be adequately vindicated on appeal from final judgment.

C

The roots of Digital's argument that the settlement with Desktop gave it a "right not to stand trial altogether" (and that such a right *per se* satisfies the third *Cohen* requirement) are readily traced to *Abney v. United States*, 431 U.S. 651 (1977), where we held that § 1291 entitles a criminal defendant to appeal an adverse ruling on a double jeopardy claim, without waiting for the conclusion of his trial. After holding the second *Cohen* requirement satisfied by the distinction between the former jeopardy claim and the question of guilt to be resolved at trial, we

---

[2] It might be argued that given the District Court's "somewhat cryptic" reference to what "a trier of fact could determine," its recision order here was merely "tentative," and thus inadequate under the first *Cohen* test, or that the basis for vacating, Digital's alleged misrepresentations about when it first learned of Desktop's use of the trade name, was so "enmeshed in the factual and legal issues comprising the plaintiff's cause of action," i.e., whether Digital (wilfully) misappropriated the name, as to elude *Cohen's* second requirement for collateral order appeal. Indeed, it is possible that the District Court phrased its order here in equivocal terms precisely because it assumed that this lack of separability would preclude any immediate appeal under § 1291.

emphasized that the Fifth Amendment not only secures the right to be free from multiple punishments, but by its very terms embodies the broader principle, "'deeply ingrained . . . in the Anglo-American system of jurisprudence,'" that it is intolerable for "'the State, with all its resources . . . [to] make repeated attempts to convict an individual [defendant], thereby subjecting him to embarrassment, expense and ordeal and compelling him to live in a continuing state of anxiety and insecurity.'" We found that immediate appeal was the only way to give "full protection" to this constitutional right "not to face trial at all."

Abney's rationale was applied in *Nixon v. Fitzgerald*, 457 U.S. 731, 742 (1982), where we held to be similarly appealable an order denying the petitioner absolute immunity from suit for civil damages arising from actions taken while petitioner was President of the United States. Seeing this immunity as a "functionally mandated incident of the President's unique office, rooted in the . . . separation of powers and supported by our history," we stressed that it served "compelling public ends," and would be irretrievably lost if the former President were not allowed an immediate appeal to vindicate this right to be free from the rigors of trial.

Next, in *Mitchell v. Forsyth*, 472 U.S. 511 (1985), we held that similar considerations supported appeal under § 1291 from decisions denying government officials qualified immunity from damages suits. An "essential attribute" of this freedom from suit for past conduct not violative of clearly established law, we explained, is the "entitlement not to stand trial or face the other burdens of litigation," one which would be "effectively lost if a case [were] erroneously permitted to go to trial." Echoing the reasoning of *Nixon v. Fitzgerald*, we explained that requiring an official with a colorable immunity claim to defend a suit for damages would be "peculiarly disruptive of effective government," and would work the very "distraction . . . from . . . duty, inhibition of discretionary action, and deterrence of able people from public service" that qualified immunity was meant to avoid.

D

Digital puts this case on all fours with *Mitchell*. It maintains that it obtained dual rights under the settlement agreement with Desktop, not only a broad defense to liability but the "right not to stand trial," the latter being just like the qualified immunity held immediately appealable in *Mitchell*. As in *Mitchell*, that right must be enforceable on collateral order appeal, Digital asserts, or an adverse trial ruling will destroy it forever.

While Digital's argument may exert some pull on a narrow analysis, it does not hold up under the broad scrutiny to which all claims of immediate appealability under § 1291 must be subjected. To be sure, *Abney* and *Mitchell* are fairly cited for the proposition that orders denying certain immunities are strong candidates for prompt appeal under § 1291. But Digital's larger contention, that a party's ability to characterize a district court's decision as denying an irreparable "right not to stand trial" altogether is sufficient as well as necessary for a collateral order appeal, is neither an accurate distillation of our case law nor an appealing prospect for adding to it.

Even as they have recognized the need for immediate appeals under § 1291 to vindicate rights that would be "irretrievably lost" if review were confined to final judgments only, our cases have been at least as emphatic in recognizing that the jurisdiction of the courts of appeals should not, and cannot, depend on a party's agility in so characterizing the right asserted. This must be so because the strong bias of § 1291 against piecemeal appeals almost never operates without

some cost. A fully litigated case can no more be untried than the law's proverbial bell can be unrung, and almost every pretrial or trial order might be called "effectively unreviewable" in the sense that relief from error can never extend to rewriting history. Thus, erroneous evidentiary rulings, grants or denials of attorney disqualification, and restrictions on the rights of intervening parties may burden litigants in ways that are only imperfectly reparable by appellate reversal of a final district court judgment; and other errors, real enough, will not seem serious enough to warrant reversal at all, when reviewed after a long trial on the merits. In still other cases, an erroneous district court decision will, as a practical matter, sound the "death knell" for many plaintiffs' claims that might have gone forward if prompt error correction had been an option. But if immediate appellate review were available every such time, Congress's final decision rule would end up a pretty puny one, and so the mere identification of some interest that would be "irretrievably lost" has never sufficed to meet the third *Cohen* requirement.

Nor does limiting the focus to whether the interest asserted may be called a "right not to stand trial" offer much protection against the urge to push the § 1291 limits. We have, after all, acknowledged that virtually every right that could be enforced appropriately by pretrial dismissal might loosely be described as conferring a "right not to stand trial," *see, e.g., Midland Asphalt*, 489 U.S., at 501. Allowing immediate appeals to vindicate every such right would move § 1291 aside for claims that the district court lacks personal jurisdiction, that the statute of limitations has run, that the movant has been denied his Sixth Amendment right to speedy trial, that an action is barred on claim preclusion principles, that no material fact is in dispute and the moving party is entitled to judgment as a matter of law, or merely that the complaint fails to state a claim. Such motions can be made in virtually every case, and it would be no consolation that a party's meritless summary judgment motion or res judicata claim was rejected on immediate appeal; the damage to the efficient and congressionally mandated allocation of judicial responsibility would be done, and any improper purpose the appellant might have had in saddling its opponent with cost and delay would be accomplished. Thus, precisely because candor forces us to acknowledge that there is no single, "obviously correct way to characterize" an asserted right, we have held that § 1291 requires courts of appeals to view claims of a "right not to be tried" with skepticism, if not a jaundiced eye.

In *Midland Asphalt,* for example, we had no trouble in dispatching a defendant's claim of entitlement to an immediate appeal from an order denying dismissal for alleged violation of Federal Rule of Criminal Procedure 6(e), forbidding disclosure of secret grand jury information. Noting "'a crucial distinction between a right not to be tried and a right whose remedy requires the dismissal of charges,'" we observed that Rule 6(e) "contains no hint" of an immunity from trial, and we contrasted that Rule with the Fifth Amendment's express provision that "no person shall [be] held to answer" for a serious crime absent grand jury indictment. Only such an "explicit statutory or constitutional guarantee that trial will not occur," we suggested, could be grounds for an immediate appeal of right under § 1291. . . .

E

As Digital reads the cases, the only things standing in the way of an appeal to perfect its claimed rights under the settlement agreement are the lone statement in *Midland Asphalt,* to the effect that only explicit statutory and constitutional immunities may be appealed immediately under § 1291, and language (said

to be stray) repeated in many of our collateral order decisions, suggesting that the "importance" of the right asserted is an independent condition of appealability. The first, Digital explains, cannot be reconciled with *Mitchell's* holding, that denial of qualified immunity (which we would be hard-pressed to call "explicitly . . . guaranteed" by a particular constitutional or statutory provision) is a collateral order under § 1291; as between *Mitchell* and the *Midland Asphalt* dictum, Digital says, the dictum must give way. As for the second obstacle, Digital adamantly maintains that "importance" has no place in a doctrine justified as supplying a gloss on Congress's "final decision" language.

1

These arguments miss the mark. First, even if *Mitchell* could not be squared fully with the literal words of the *Midland Asphalt* sentence, (*but cf. Lauro Lines,* 490 U.S., at 499, noting that *Midland Asphalt* was a criminal case and *Mitchell* was not), that would be only because the qualified immunity right is inexplicit, not because it lacks a good pedigree in public law. Indeed, the insight that explicitness may not be needed for jurisdiction consistent with § 1291 only leaves Digital with the unenviable task of explaining why other rights that might fairly be said to include an (implicit) "right to avoid trial" aspect are less in need of protection by immediate review, or more readily vindicated on appeal from final judgment, than the (claimed) privately negotiated right to be free from suit. It is far from clear, for example, why § 1291 should bless a party who bargained for the right to avoid trial, but not a party who "purchased" the right by having once prevailed at trial and now pleads res judicata; or a party who seeks shelter under the statute of limitations, which is usually understood to secure the same sort of "repose" that Digital seeks to vindicate here; or a party not even subject to a claim on which relief could be granted.

Digital answers that the status under § 1291 of these other (seemingly analogous) rights should not give us pause, because the text and structure of this particular settlement with Desktop confer what no *res judicata* claimant could ever have, an express right not to stand trial. But we cannot attach much significance one way or another to the supposed clarity of the agreement's terms in this case. To ground a ruling here on whether this settlement agreement in terms confers the prized "right not to stand trial" (a point Desktop by no means concedes) would flout our own frequent admonitions that availability of collateral order appeal must be determined at a higher level of generality. Indeed, just because it would be the rare settlement agreement that could not be construed to include (at least an implicit) freedom-from-trial "aspect," we decide this case on the assumption that if Digital prevailed here, any district court order denying effect to a settlement agreement could be appealed immediately. . . .

2

The more fundamental response, however, to the claim that an agreement's provision for immunity from trial can distinguish it from other arguable rights to be trial-free is simply that such a right by agreement does not rise to the level of importance needed for recognition under § 1291. This, indeed, is the bone of the fiercest contention in the case. In disparaging any distinction between an order denying a claim grounded on an explicit constitutional guarantee of immunity from trial and an order at odds with an equally explicit right by private agreement of the parties, Digital stresses that the relative "importance" of these rights, heavily relied upon by the Court of Appeals, is a rogue factor. No decision of this Court, Digital maintains, has held an

order unappealable as "unimportant" when it has otherwise met the three *Cohen* requirements, and whether a decided issue is thought "important," it says, should have no bearing on whether it is "final" under § 1291.

If "finality" were as narrow a concept as Digital maintains, however, the Court would have had little reason to go beyond the first factor in *Cohen*. And if "importance" were truly aberrational, we would not find it featured so prominently in the *Cohen* opinion itself, which describes the "small class" of immediately appealable prejudgment decisions in terms of rights that are "too important to be denied review" right away. To be sure, Digital may validly question whether "importance" is a factor "beyond" the three *Cohen* conditions or whether it is best considered, as we have sometimes suggested it should be, in connection with the second, "separability," requirement; but neither enquiry could lead to the conclusion that "importance" is itself unimportant. To the contrary, the third *Cohen* question, whether a right is "adequately vindicable" or "effectively reviewable," simply cannot be answered without a judgment about the value of the interests that would be lost through rigorous application of a final judgment requirement.

While there is no need to decide here that a privately conferred right could never supply the basis of a collateral order appeal, there are surely sound reasons for treating such rights differently from those originating in the Constitution or statutes. When a policy is embodied in a constitutional or statutory provision entitling a party to immunity from suit (a rare form of protection), there is little room for the judiciary to gainsay its "importance." Including a provision in a private contract, by contrast, is barely a prima facie indication that the right secured is "important" to the benefitted party (contracts being replete with boilerplate), let alone that its value exceeds that of other rights not embodied in agreements (*e.g.,* the right to be free from a second suit based on a claim that has already been litigated), or that it qualifies as "important" in *Cohen's* sense, as being weightier than the societal interests advanced by the ordinary operation of final judgment principles. Where statutory and constitutional rights are concerned, "irretrievable loss" can hardly be trivial, and the collateral order doctrine might therefore be understood as reflecting the familiar principle of statutory construction that, when possible, courts should construe statutes (here § 1291) to foster harmony with other statutory and constitutional law. But it is one thing to say that the policy of § 1291 to avoid piecemeal litigation should be reconciled with policies embodied in other statutes or the Constitution, and quite another to suggest that this public policy may be trumped routinely by the expectations or clever drafting of private parties.[7]

Indeed, we do not take issue with the Tenth Circuit's observation that this case shares more in common with *Lauro Lines* than with *Mitchell.* It is hard to see how, for purposes of § 1291, the supposedly explicit "right not to be tried" element of

_____

[7] This is not to say that rights originating in a private agreement may never be important enough to warrant immediate appeal. To the contrary, Congress only recently enacted a statute, 102 Stat. 4671, see 9 U.S.C. § 16 (1988 ed., Supp. IV), essentially providing for immediate appeal when a district court rejects a party's assertion that, under the Arbitration Act, a case belongs before a commercial arbitrator and not in court, a measure predicted to have a "sweeping impact," 15B C. Wright, A. Miller, & E. Cooper 17 § 3914, Federal Practice and Procedure p. 11 (1992); see generally, id., pp. 7-38. That courts must give full effect to this express congressional judgment that particular policies require that private rights be vindicable immediately, however, by no means suggests that they should now be more ready to make similar judgments for themselves. Congress has expressed no parallel sentiment, to the effect that settlement-agreement rights are, as a matter of federal policy, similarly "too important" to be denied immediate review.

the settlement agreement in this case differs from the unarguably explicit, privately negotiated "right not to be tried in any forum other than Naples, Italy," in that one. There, no less than here (if Digital reads the settlement agreement correctly), one private party secured from another a promise not to bring suit for reasons that presumably included avoiding the burden, expense, and perhaps embarrassment of a certain class of trials (all but Neapolitan ones or, here, all prompted by Desktop). The losing argument in *Lauro Lines* should be a losing argument here.

Nor are we swayed by Digital's last-ditch effort to come within *Cohen's* sense of "importance" by trying to show that settlement-agreement "immunities" merit first-class treatment for purposes of collateral order appeal, because they advance the public policy favoring voluntary resolution of disputes. It defies common sense to maintain that parties' readiness to settle will be significantly dampened (or the corresponding public interest impaired) by a rule that a district court's decision to let allegedly barred litigation go forward may be challenged as a matter of right only on appeal from a judgment for the plaintiff's favor.

III

A

Even, finally, if the term "importance" were to be exorcized from the *Cohen* analysis altogether, Digital's rights would remain "adequately vindicable" or "effectively reviewable" on final judgment to an extent that other immunities, like the right to be free from a second trial on a criminal charge, are not. As noted already, experience suggests that freedom from trial is rarely the sine qua non (or "the essence," see *Van Cauwenberghe,* 486 U.S., at 525) of a negotiated settlement agreement. Avoiding the burden of a trial is no doubt a welcome incident of out-of-court dispute resolution (just as it is for parties who prevail on pretrial motions), but in the run of the mill cases this boon will rarely compare with the "'embarrassment'" and "'anxiety'" averted by a successful double jeopardy claimant, see *Abney*, 431 U.S., at 661-662, or the "'distraction from . . . duty,'" *Mitchell*, 472 U.S., at 526, avoided by qualified immunity. Judged within the four corners of the settlement agreement, avoiding trial probably pales in comparison with the benefit of limiting exposure to liability (an interest that is fully vindicable on appeal from final judgment). In the rare case where a party had a special reason, apart from the generic desire to triumph early, for having bargained for an immunity from trial, *e.g.*, an unusual interest in preventing disclosure of particular information, it may seek protection from the district court.

The case for adequate vindication without immediate appeal is strengthened, moreover, by recognizing that a settling party has a source of recompense unknown to trial immunity claimants dependent on public law alone. The essence of Digital's claim here is that Desktop, for valuable consideration, promised not to sue, and we have been given no reason to doubt that Utah law provides for the enforcement of that promise in the same way that other rights arising from private agreements are enforced, through an action for breach of contract. See, *e.g., Van-Dyke v. Mountain Coin Machine Distributors, Inc.*, 758 P. 2d 962 (Utah App. 1988) (upholding compensatory and punitive damages award against party pursuing suit in the face of settlement agreement). And as for Digital's suggestion that Desktop is using this proceeding not to remedy a fraud but merely to renege on a promise because it now thinks it should have negotiated a better deal, when a party claims fraud or otherwise seeks recision of a settlement for such improper purposes, its opponent need not rely on a court of appeals for protection. See Fed. Rule Civ.

Proc. 11 (opponent may move for sanction when litigation is motivated by an "improper purpose, such as . . . unnecessary delay or needless increase in the cost of litigation").

B

In preserving the strict limitations on review as of right under § 1291, our holding should cause no dismay, for the law is not without its safety valve to deal with cases where the contest over a settlement's enforceability raises serious legal questions taking the case out of the ordinary run. While Digital's insistence that the District Court applied a fundamentally wrong legal standard in vacating the dismissal order here may not be considered in deciding appealability under § 1291, it plainly is relevant to the availability of the discretionary interlocutory appeal from particular district court orders "involving a controlling question of law as to which there is substantial ground for difference of opinion," provided for in § 1292(b) of Title 28. Indeed, because we suppose that a defendant's claimed entitlement to a privately negotiated "immunity from suit" could in some instances raise "a controlling question of law . . . [which] . . . may materially advance the ultimate termination of the litigation," the discretionary appeal provision (allowing courts to consider the merits of individual claims) would seem a better vehicle for vindicating serious contractual interpretation claims than the blunt, categorical instrument of § 1291 collateral order appeal. See *Van Cauwenberghe*, 486 U.S., at 529-530; *Coopers & Lybrand*, 437 U.S., at 474-475.[9]

---

[9] We recognize that § 1292 is not a panacea, both because it depends to a degree on the indulgence of the court from which review is sought and because the discretion to decline to hear an appeal is broad, see, *e.g., Coopers & Lybrand*, 437 U.S., at 475, (serious docket congestion may be adequate reason to support denial of certified appeal). On the other hand, we find nothing in the text or purposes of either statute to justify

IV

The words of § 1291 have long been construed to recognize that certain categories of pre-judgment decisions exist for which it is both justifiable and necessary to depart from the general rule, that "the whole case and every matter in controversy in it [must be] decided in a single appeal." But denying effect to the sort of (asserted) contractual right at issue here

is far removed from those immediately appealable decisions involving rights more deeply rooted in public policy, and the rights Digital asserts may, in the main, be vindicated through means less disruptive to the orderly administration of justice than immediate, mandatory appeal. We accordingly hold that a refusal to enforce a settlement agreement claimed to shelter a party from suit altogether does not supply the basis for immediate appeal under § 1291. The judgment of the Court of Appeals is therefore *Affirmed.*

---

the concern, expressed here by Digital, that a party's request to appeal under § 1292(b) might operate, practically or legally, to prejudice its claimed right to immediate appeal under § 1291.

Note

At the end of his opinion, Justice Souter notes, as the Court had observed in prior cases, that rejection of a judicially created exception to the finality rule does not leave prospective appellants entirely without the possibility of an immediate appeal. The "safety valve" of a discretionary interlocutory appeal pursuant to 28 U.S.C. § 1292(b) is available for cases involving controlling questions of law as to which there is substantial disagreement among the courts.

Other Approaches

As we have seen, the federal courts generally, and with increasing strictness, insist on entry of a final judgment as a condition to granting appellate review. Not all jurisdictions so limit the appellate process, however. New York is probably the most liberal in allowing interlocutory appeals to the intermediate appellate courts in civil cases. As is demonstrated by the pertinent section of the Civil Practice Law and Rules reproduced below, virtually anything that is reduced to a judgment or order can be appealed, as of right, to the Appellate Division; within the small category of orders not so appealable, most orders may be appealed by permission.

§5701. Appeals to Appellate Division From Supreme and County Courts

(a) Appeals as of right. An appeal may be taken to the appellate division as of right in an action, originating in the supreme court or a county court:

1. from any final or interlocutory judgment except one entered subsequent to an order of the appellate division which disposes of all the issues in the action; or

2. from an order not specified in subdivision (b), where the motion it decided was made upon notice and it:

(i) grants, refuses, continues or modifies a provisional remedy; or

(ii) settles, grants or refuses an application to resettle a transcript or statement on appeal; or

(iii) grants or refuses a new trial; except where specific questions of fact arising upon the issues in an action triable by the court have been tried by a jury, pursuant to an order for that purpose, and the order grants or refuses a new trial upon the merits; or

(iv) involves some part of the merits; or

(v) affects a substantial right; or

(vi) in effect determines the action and prevents a judgment from which an appeal might be taken; or

(vii) determines a statutory provision of the state to be unconstitutional, and the determination appears from the reasons given for the decision or is necessarily implied in the decision; or

3. from an order, where the motion it decided was made upon notice, refusing to vacate or modify a prior order, if the prior order would have been appealable as of right under paragraph two had it decided a motion made upon notice.

(b) Orders not appealable as of right. An order is not appealable to the appellate division as of right where it:

1. is made in a proceeding against a body or officer pursuant to article 78; or

2. requires or refuses to require a more definite statement in a pleading; or

3. orders or refuses to order that scandalous or prejudicial matter be stricken from a pleading.

(c) Appeals by permission. An appeal may be taken to the appellate division from any order which is not appealable as of right on an action originating in the supreme court or a county court by permission of the judge who made the order granted before application to a justice of the appellate division; or by permission of a justice of the appellate division in the department to which the appeal could be taken, upon refusal by the judge who made the order or upon direct application.

Note

New York's highest court takes a much more restrictive view of interlocutory appeals, and will generally review only final judgments, with limited exceptions to serve purposes similar to those served by deviations from the final judgment rule in federal court. In other jurisdictions, the rules concerning appellate jurisdiction over non-final orders vary considerably. The practitioner seeking to appeal from an order that may not fall within the court's review powers must first research that question in an effort to get the court's attention.

Appeals by the Prosecution

A. Appeals from Final Judgments

Appeals by the government in criminal cases, even when final judgments have been entered, are limited by the constitutional prohibition against double jeopardy. Appellate courts accordingly will not review a judgment of acquittal at the behest of the government, since further prosecution would be barred by the double jeopardy clause. By statute, 18 U.S.C. § 3731, federal appeals from final judgments in criminal cases are permitted only when they do not run afoul of the double jeopardy prohibition. As the following case suggests, this means, in general, that no further proceedings would be required in the trial court if the judgment were reversed.

United States v. Wilson

420 U.S. 332 (1975)

Mr. Justice MARSHALL delivered the opinion of the Court.

Respondent George J. Wilson, Jr., was tried in the Eastern District of Pennsylvania for converting union funds to his own use, in violation of § 501(c) of the Labor-Management Reporting and Disclosure Act of 1959, 73 Stat. 536, 29 U.S.C. § 501(c). The jury entered a guilty verdict, but on a postverdict motion the District Court dismissed the indictment. The court ruled that the delay between the offense and the indictment had prejudiced the defendant, and that dismissal was called for under this Court's decision in *United States v. Marion*, 404 U.S. 307 (1971). The Government sought to appeal the dismissal to the Court of Appeals for the Third Circuit, but that court held that the Double Jeopardy Clause barred review of the District Court's ruling. We granted certiorari to consider the applicability of the Double Jeopardy Clause to appeals from postverdict rulings by the trial court. We reverse.

I

In April 1968 the FBI began an investigation of respondent Wilson, the business manager of Local 367 of the International Brotherhood of Electrical Workers. The investigation focused on Wilson's suspected conversion in 1966 of $1,233.15 of union funds to pay part of the expenses of his daughter's wedding reception. The payment was apparently made by a check drawn on union funds and endorsed by the treasurer and the president of the local union. Respondent contended at trial that he had not authorized the two union officials to make the payment on his behalf and that he did not know the bill for the reception had been paid out of union funds. In June 1970 the FBI completed its investigation and reported to the Organized Crime Strike Force and the local United States Attorney's Office. There the matter rested for some 16 months until, three days prior to the running of the statute of limitations, respondent was indicted for illegal conversion of union funds.

Wilson made a pretrial motion to dismiss the indictment on the ground that the Government's delay in filing the action had denied him the opportunity for a fair trial. His chance to mount an effective defense was impaired, Wilson argued, because the two union officers who had signed the check for the reception were unavailable to testify. One had died in 1968, and the other was suffering from a terminal illness. After a hearing, the court denied the pretrial motion, and the case proceeded to trial. The jury returned a verdict of guilty, after which the defendant filed various motions including a motion for arrest of judgment, a motion for a judgment of acquittal, and a motion for a new trial.

The District Court reversed its earlier ruling and dismissed the indictment on the ground that the preindictment delay was unreasonable and had substantially prejudiced the defendant's right to a fair trial. The union treasurer had died prior to 1970, the court noted, so the loss of his testimony could not be attributed to the preindictment delay. The union president, however, had become unavailable during the period of delay. The court ruled that since he was the only remaining witness who could explain the circumstances of the payment of the check, the preindictment delay violated the respondent's Fifth Amendment right to a fair trial. This disposition of the *Marion* claim made it unnecessary to rule on the defendant's other postverdict motions.

The Government sought to appeal the District Court's ruling pursuant to the Criminal Appeals Act, 18 U.S.C. §3731, but the Court of Appeals dismissed the appeal in a judgment order, citing our decision in *United States v. Sisson,* 399 U.S. 267 (1970). On the Government's petition for rehearing, the court wrote an opinion in which it reasoned that since the District Court had relied on facts brought out at trial in finding prejudice from the preindictment delay, its ruling was in effect an acquittal. Under the Double Jeopardy Clause, the Court of Appeals held, the Government could not constitutionally appeal the acquittal, even though it was rendered by the judge after the jury had returned a verdict of guilty.

II

The Government argues that the Court of Appeals read the Double Jeopardy Clause too broadly and that it mischaracterized the District Court's ruling in terming it an acquittal. In the Government's view, the constitutional restriction on governmental appeals is intended solely to protect against exposing the defendant to multiple trials, not to shield every determination favorable to the defendant from appellate review. Since a new trial would not be necessary where the trier of fact has returned a verdict of guilty, the Government argues that it should be permitted to appeal from any adverse postverdict ruling. In the alternative, the Government urges that even if the Double Jeopardy Clause is read to bar appeal of any judgment of acquittal, the District Court's order in this case was not an acquittal and it should therefore be appealable. The respondent argues that under our prior cases the Double Jeopardy Clause prohibits appeal of any order discharging the defendant when, as here, that order is based on facts outside the indictment. Because we agree with the Government that the constitutional protection against Government appeals attaches only where there is a danger of subjecting the defendant to a second trial for the same offense, we have no occasion to determine whether the ruling in Wilson's favor was actually an "acquittal" even though the District Court characterized it otherwise.

A

This Court early held that the Government could not make an appeal in a criminal case without express statutory authority. *United States v. Sanges,* 144 U.S. 310 (1892). Not reaching the underlying constitutional issue, the Court held only that the general appeals provisions of the Judiciary Act of 1891, 26 Stat. 827, 828, were not sufficiently explicit to overcome the common-law rule that the State could not sue out a writ of error in a criminal case unless the legislature had expressly granted it that right. 144 U.S., at 318, 322-323.

Fifteen years later, Congress passed the first Criminal Appeals Act, which conferred jurisdiction on this Court to consider criminal appeals by the Government in limited circumstances. 34 Stat. 1246. The Act permitted the Government to take an appeal from a decision dismissing an indictment or arresting judgment where the decision was based on "the invalidity, or construction of the statute upon which the indictment is founded," and from a decision sustaining a special plea in bar, when the defendant had not been put in jeopardy. The Act was construed in accordance with the common-law meaning of the terms employed, and the rules governing the conditions of appeal became highly technical. . . .

Congress finally disposed of the statute in 1970 and replaced it with a new Criminal Appeals Act intended to broaden the Government's appeal rights. While the language of the new Act is not dispositive, the legislative history makes it clear that Congress intended to remove all statutory barriers to government appeals and to allow appeals whenever the Constitution would permit. . . .

B

The statutory restrictions on Government appeals long made it unnecessary for this Court to consider the constitutional limitations on the appeal rights of the prosecution except in unusual circumstances. Even in the few relevant cases, the discussion of the question has been brief. Now that Congress has removed the statutory limitations and the Double Jeopardy Clause has been held to apply to the States, see *Benton v. Maryland,* 395 U.S. 784 (1969), it is necessary to take a closer look at the policies underlying the Clause in order to determine more precisely the boundaries of the Government's appeal rights in criminal cases.

As has been documented elsewhere, the idea of double jeopardy is very old. The early development of the principle can be traced through a variety of sources ranging from legal maxims to casual references in contemporary commentary. Although the form and breadth of the prohibition varied widely, the underlying premise was generally that a defendant should not be twice tried or punished for the same offense. Writing in the 17th century, Lord Coke described the protection afforded by the principle of double jeopardy as a function of three related common-law pleas: *autrefois acquit, autrefois convict,* and pardon. With some exceptions, these pleas could be raised to bar the second trial of a defendant if he could prove that he had already been convicted of the same crime. Blackstone later used the ancient term "jeopardy" in characterizing the principle underlying the two pleas of *autrefois acquit* and *autrefois convict.* That principle, he wrote, was a "universal maxim of the common law of England, that no man is to be brought into jeopardy of his life more than once for the same offense." 4 W. Blackstone, COMMENTARIES *335-336.

The history of the adoption of the Double Jeopardy Clause sheds some light on what the drafters thought Blackstone's "universal maxim" should mean as applied in this country. . . .

In the course of the debates over the Bill of Rights, there was no suggestion that the Double Jeopardy Clause imposed any general ban on appeals by the prosecution. The only restriction on appeal rights mentioned in any of the proposed versions of the Clause was in Maryland's suggestion that "there shall be . . . no appeal from matter of fact," which was apparently intended to apply equally to the prosecution and the defense. Nor does the common-law background of the Clause suggest an implied prohibition against state appeals. Although in the late 18th century the King was permitted to sue out a writ of error in a criminal case under certain circumstances, the principles of *autrefois acquit* and *autrefois convict* imposed no apparent restrictions on this right. It was only when the defendant was indicted for a second time after either a conviction or an acquittal that he could seek the protection of the common-law pleas. The development of the Double Jeopardy Clause from its common-law origins thus suggests that it was directed at the threat of multiple prosecutions, not at Government appeals, at least where those appeals would not require a new trial. . . .

The policy of avoiding multiple trials has been regarded as so important that exceptions to the principle have been only grudgingly allowed. Initially, a new trial was thought to be unavailable after appeal, whether requested by the prosecution or the defendant. It was not until 1896 that it was made clear that a defendant could seek a new trial after conviction, even though the Government enjoyed no similar right. *United States v. Ball,* 163 U.S. 662. Following the same policy, the Court has granted the Government the right to retry a defendant after a mistrial only where "there is a manifest necessity for the act, or the ends of public justice would otherwise be defeated." *United States v. Perez,* 9 Wheat. 579, 580, 6 L.Ed. 165 (1824).

By contrast, where there is no threat of either multiple punishment or successive prosecutions, the Double Jeopardy Clause is not offended. In various situations where appellate review would not subject the defendant to a second trial, this Court has held that an order favoring the defendant could constitutionally be appealed by the Government. Since the 1907 Criminal Appeals Act, for example, the Government has been permitted without serious constitutional challenge to appeal from orders arresting judgment after a verdict has been entered against the defendant. . . . Since reversal on appeal would merely reinstate the jury's verdict, review of such an order does not offend the policy against multiple prosecution.

Similarly, it is well settled that an appellate court's order reversing a conviction is subject to further review even when the appellate court has ordered the indictment dismissed and the defendant discharged. *Forman v. United States,* 361 U.S. 416, 426 (1960). If reversal by a court of appeals operated to deprive the Government of its right to seek further review, disposition in the court of appeals would be "tantamount to a verdict of acquittal at the hands of the jury, not subject to review by motion for rehearing, appeal, or certiorari in this Court." *Ibid.*

It is difficult to see why the rule should be any different simply because the defendant has gotten a favorable postverdict ruling of law from the District Judge rather than from the Court of Appeals, or because the District Judge has relied to some degree on evidence presented at trial in making his ruling. Although review of any ruling of law discharging a defendant obviously enhances the likelihood of conviction and subjects him to continuing expense and anxiety, a defendant has no legitimate claim to benefit from an error of law when that error could be corrected without subjecting him to a second trial before a second trier of fact. . . .

III

Applying these principles to the present case is a relatively straightforward task. The jury entered a verdict of guilty against Wilson. The ruling in his favor on the *Marion* motion could be acted on by the Court of Appeals or indeed this Court without subjecting him to a second trial at the Government's behest. If he prevails on appeal, the matter will become final, and the Government will not be permitted to bring a second prosecution against him for the same offense. If he loses, the case must go back to the District Court for disposition of his remaining motions. We therefore reverse the judgment and remand for the Court of Appeals to consider the merits of the Government's appeal.

Reversed and remanded.

Notes

1. In order to preserve the prosecution's right to appellate review, a trial judge who agrees with the defendant that the evidence produced at trial is insufficient as a matter of law may reserve decision on the defendant's motion for a judgment of acquittal until after the jury renders its verdict. The judge's order setting aside a guilty verdict would then be appealable by the government, since the verdict could simply be reinstated if the prosection prevails on appeal. *See, e.g., People v. Marin,* 102 A.D.2d 14, 15, 478 N.Y.S.2d 650 (N.Y. App. Div. 1984), *aff'd,* 65 N.Y.2d 741, 481 N.E.2d 556, 492 N.Y.S.2d 16 (1985).

2. By a 5 to 4 vote, the Supreme Court, in *United States v. Scott,* 437 U.S. 82 (1978), approved the government's appeal of an order dismissing two counts of an indictment on the ground that preindictment delay had prejudiced the defendant's ability to present his defense. The order was entered, upon motion of the defendant, at the close of all the evidence, before the case was submitted to the jury. The majority relied primarily on two reasons for allowing the appeal, despite the fact that reversal of the order would permit further proceedings on the indictment. First, the Court found significant that it was the *defendant's* decision not to have those counts submitted to the jury. The prohibition of the double jeopardy clause is designed to prevent repeated attempts by the *government* to present a case to the factfinder. The Court analogized the situation to one in which the defendant moves for a mistrial; a trial court's granting of such a motion generally does not bar a retrial. Second, the Court made the distinction, over the vehement objections of the dissenters, between dismissal of counts on legal grounds and dismissal on grounds related to factual guilt or innocence. The majority found that dismissal of charges on the grounds of preindictment delay constituted "a legal judgment that a defendant, although criminally culpable, may not be punished because of a supposed constitutional violation." *Id.* at 98. Since, by securing such a judgment, the defendant has avoided a decision on his guilt or innocence, the double jeopardy clause does not prevent further proceedings to obtain a verdict, should the government prevail on its appeal.

3. As the dissenters predicted, *id.* at 103, the *Scott* decision led to considerable litigation about what constitutes dismissal on "legal" versus "factual" grounds. Prosecutors tried to pursue appeals from judgments that had previously been thought to be tantamount to acquittal, and therefore not subject to appeal by the government. In one such case, the Pennsylvania Supreme Court permitted an appeal from a trial court's dismissal, at the close of the prosecution's case in chief, of certain charges on the ground that the evidence was legally insufficient

to support a conviction. Relying on *Scott,* the Pennsylvania Supreme Court found that the decision was not a factual determination, but rather one of whether the evidence, if believed by the factfinder, was sufficient as a matter of law. Since, as in *Scott,* the defendant sought this dismissal on grounds unrelated to actual guilt or innocence, the decision should not be regarded as an acquittal, and consequently the government's appeal could proceed.

The United States Supreme Court reversed. In a brief, unanimous opinion relying on pre-*Scott* precedents, the Court held that a ruling at the close of the prosecution's case finding the state's evidence insufficient as a matter of law to establish the defendant's guilt amounts to an acquittal. Accordingly, the prosecution's appeal was barred by the double jeopardy clause. *Smalis v. Pennsylvania,* 476 U.S. 140, 144 (1986).

4. The prosecution can generally appeal from a sentence only if it is illegal, that is below the minimum sentence allowed by statute. In the 1980's, several jurisdictions, including the federal government, adopted mandatory sentencing guidelines in order to reduce the disparity among sentences meted out by different judges. These guidelines provide for appeals by the government from sentences that depart from the range set forth by the guidelines. *See, e.g.,* 18 U.S.C. § 3742(b).

B. Interlocutory Appeals by the Prosecution

1. Suppression Orders

While the interest in speedy and orderly disposition of criminal cases operates to discourage immediate appeals by the government of pre-trial orders, just as it severely limits interlocutory appeals by defendants, the decision about whether the prosecution should be permitted to appeal from certain kinds of pre-trial orders in criminal cases must take into consideration the constraints, discussed above, inherent in the prohibition against double jeopardy.

If, for example, a trial court erroneously suppresses or excludes evidence critical to the government's case, and as a result the jury acquits the defendant, the government has no right to appeal the trial court's determination. For this reason, most jurisdictions have, by statute, authorized interlocutory appeals by the government when the order sought to be reviewed effectively prevents the government from proceeding with its case. Jurisdictions vary in how devastating the order must be to the government's case. In federal court, the government may appeal from

> a decision or order of a district court suppressing or excluding evidence . . . not made after the defendant has been put in jeopardy and before the verdict or finding on an indictment or information, if the United States attorney certifies to the district court that the appeal is not taken for

purpose of delay and that the evidence is a substantial proof of a fact material in the proceeding.

18 U.S.C. § 3731. Similarly, in Illinois a prosecutor may obtain an interlocutory appeal of an order suppressing evidence by certifying that suppression substantially impairs the prosecution. *See People v. Hatfield,* 112 Ill.Dec. 909, 161 Ill. App.3d 401, 514 N.E.2d 572 (1987).

In New York, on the other hand, the prosecutor, in order to be permitted to appeal a suppression order, must file a statement that deprivation of use of the evidence ordered suppressed has left the prosecution without adequate proof to proceed with the case. *See* N.Y.C.P.L. § 450.50(1). The government is barred from further prosecution of the case unless the suppression order is reversed. N.Y.C.P.L. § 450.50(2).

2. Orders Setting Bail

As the Court indicated in *Flanagan v. United States,* pre-trial orders setting or denying bail do fall within the collateral order doctrine so as to permit interlocutory appeal by a defendant. By federal statute, a parallel right to appeal the *granting* of bail has been afforded to the prosecution. *See* 18 U.S.C. § 3731.

Chapter 3

Scope of Review and the Preservation Requirement

Scope of Review

"Scope of Review" refers to the questions that a court has the power to decide. Not every issue that arises in a lower court can be reviewed by an appellate court. On the contrary, in addition to such considerations as the "case or controversy" requirement, mootness, ripeness and the standing of the parties to raise an issue, the scope of review of appellate courts is further restricted by decisional law, court rules and statutes to specific kinds of questions. As we have seen in Chapters 1 and 2, however, not all courts are subject to the same limitations. The appellate lawyer's first task when choosing which issues to raise on appeal is therefore to ascertain the scope of review of the court that will be hearing the appeal.

At all levels of appellate review, it is a fundamental rule that the appellate court is bound strictly by the record of the evidence adduced in the trial court. An appellate court has no power to consider new evidence on appeal. In those relatively rare cases in which important new evidence has been discovered post-trial, the case must be remanded to the lower court for a determination of its significance; the appellate court cannot perform that function in the first instance. Indeed, any attempt by counsel to introduce a new fact in an appellate argument may be viewed as a serious infraction and will at least result in the new material's being stricken from the brief by the court.

The Preservation Requirement

In addition to the requirement that all appellate arguments must be based on facts reflected in the record of the trial court, the next most important limitation on an appellate court's scope of review is the general rule that any legal issue raised on appeal must have been "preserved." That is, the issue must first have been presented to the trial court. This rule stems directly from the old writ of error procedure, since, as a matter of common sense, a judge could not have erred with respect to an issue that had never been presented at trial.

Despite the disappearance today of the original rationale underlying the preservation requirement, there remain some substantial modern reasons for its continuing application. First, if a party who objects to a ruling of the trial court voices its disagreement at the time the ruling is made, the court has the opportunity to consider the objection, hear the views of the opposing party and, if necessary, to correct the error or arrive at a mutually agreeable alternative. In this way, the need for any appeal at all can be avoided, with the consequent saving of valuable judicial resources. Second, the rule avoids the danger of sandbagging by trial counsel, who, knowing full well that reversible error is being committed, fails to call the error to the attention of the trial court so as to ensure an appealable issue in the event of an adverse verdict. Third, by making it likely that under all but the most exceptional circumstances it is the trial that will determine the final outcome of the case, the preservation rule also encourages trial lawyers to prepare carefully and to perform competently, rather than to assume that any omissions or mistakes can always be remedied on appeal. Finally, the rule recognizes the unfairness of snatching a judgment from the prevailing party on the basis of arguments that it never had the opportunity to meet at trial.

For all of these reasons, the failure of trial counsel to object to an erroneous ruling will result in the inability of some appellate courts and the unwillingness of others to consider the issue. The New York Court of Appeals is an example of a court that simply does not have the power to review non-preserved errors. In New York, the Court of Appeals' jurisdiction is limited to issues of law, and issues of law are defined by statute as legal errors that have been preserved at trial. *See* N.Y.C.P.L. § 470.05(2). Judges of the New York Court of Appeals therefore require attorneys seeking leave to appeal to indicate the place in the record where the issue sought to be raised has been preserved. If the issue has not been preserved, the Court has no choice but to deny leave to appeal.

In the following case, the Pennsylvania Supreme Court came to the conclusion, over two vigorous dissents, that, although it was not precluded from considering unpreserved errors, the reasons for the preservation doctrine are sufficiently strong to warrant its refusal ever to consider alleged errors that were not objected to at trial.

Dilliplaine v. Lehigh Valley Trust Company

457 Pa. 255, 322 A.2d 114 (1974)

ROBERTS, Justice.

On April 23, 1966, automobiles driven by Wayne F. Dilliplaine and James A. Burdette collided. Subsequently Burdette died of causes unrelated to the accident. Dilliplaine then brought this trespass action against the executor of Burdette's estate, Lehigh Valley Trust Company, for injuries suffered in the accident.

The jury found for defendant and Dilliplaine's motion for a new trial was denied. The Superior Court affirmed. We granted the petition for allowance of appeal. The sole issue is whether the trial court erred by instructing the jury that the deceased was presumed to have exercised due care at the time the accident occurred.

Appellant Dilliplaine frankly concedes that he neither offered a point for charge nor took specific exception to the due care instruction actually given. In his motion for

a new trial and again on appeal, he argued that in giving the presumption of due care instruction the trial judge committed basic and fundamental error.

Appellant espouses the theory that an appellate court must consider trial errors claimed to be basic and fundamental despite the absence of any objection or specific exception at trial. This theory has been applied primarily to asserted infirmities in a trial court's instructions to the jury.

We believe that two practical problems with basic and fundamental error make it an unworkable appellate procedure. Initially, appellate court recognition of alleged errors not called to the trial court's attention has a deleterious effect on the trial and appellate process. Also, despite its repeated articulation, the theory has never developed into a principled test, but has remained essentially a vehicle for reversal when the predilections of a majority of an appellate court are offended.

Appellate court consideration of issues not raised in the trial court results in the trial becoming merely a dress rehearsal. This process removes the professional necessity for trial counsel to be prepared to litigate the case fully at trial and to create a record adequate for appellate review. The ill-prepared advocate's hope is that an appellate court will come to his aid after the fact and afford him relief despite his failure at trial to object to an alleged error. The diligent and prepared trial lawyer – and his client – are penalized when an entire case is retried because an appellate court reverses on the basis of an error opposing counsel failed to call to the trial court's attention. Failure to interpose a timely objection at trial denies the trial court the chance to hear argument on the issue and an opportunity to correct error. It also tends to postpone unnecessarily disposition of other cases not yet tried for the first time.

The notion of basic and fundamental error not only erodes the finality of the trial court holdings, but also encourages unnecessary appeals and thereby further burdens the decisional capacity of our appellate courts. Trial counsel, though he may not have claimed error at trial, is inspired after trial and an adverse verdict by the thought that an appellate court may seize upon a previously unclaimed error and afford relief on a ground not called to the trial court's attention.

Perhaps at an earlier stage of our jurisprudential development his practice could be justified. Today, however, there is no excuse for and appellate courts should not encourage less than alert professional representation at trial. Virtually all active practitioners at our bar have had a formal legal education at a law school accredited by the American Bar Association. The Pennsylvania Bar Institute, Pennsylvania Trial Lawyers Association, and local bar associations as well as the American Bar Association and the American Law Institute provide programs of continuing legal education for members of the bar.

Requiring a timely specific objection to be taken in the trial court will ensure that the trial judge has a chance to correct alleged trial errors. This opportunity to correct alleged errors at trial advances the orderly and efficient use of our judicial resources. First, appellate courts will not be required to expend time and energy reviewing points on which no trial ruling has been made. Second, the trial court may promptly correct the asserted error. With the issue properly presented, the trial court is more likely to reach a satisfactory result, thus obviating the need for appellate review on this issue. Or if a new trial is necessary, it may be granted by the trial court without subjecting both the litigants and the courts to the expense and delay inherent in appellate review. Third, appellate courts will be free to more expeditiously dispose of the issue properly preserved for appeal.[8] Finally, the exception requirement will remove the advantage formerly enjoyed by the unprepared trial lawyer who looked to the appellate court to compensate for his trial omissions.

The other major weakness of the basic and fundamental error theory is its *ad hoc* nature. The theory has been formulated in terms of what a particular majority of an appellate court considers basic or fundamental. Such a test is unworkable when neither the test itself nor the case law applying it develop a predictable, neutrally-applied standard.

We conclude that basic and fundamental error has no place in our modern system

---

[8] When only properly preserved issues are considered on appeal, a full transcript of the trial will often be unnecessary. The trial court on post-trial motions (and the appellant court) will require transcripts of only those portions of the trial which are in issue. Reduction of the number of complete transcripts required for appeal will minimize both the expense and delay which now make an appeal so costly.

of jurisprudence. This doctrine, which may in the past have been acceptable, has become an impediment to the efficient administration of our judicial system. Basic and fundamental error will therefore no longer be recognized as a ground for consideration on appeal of allegedly erroneous jury instructions; a specific exception must be taken.

Because appellant failed to specifically object to the trial court's instruction on presumption of due care, we will not consider this allegation of error. The order of the Superior Court is affirmed.

POMEROY, J., filed a concurring and dissenting opinion in which EAGEN, J., joined.

MANDERINO, Justice (concurring).

I join in the majority opinion by Mr. Justice Roberts holding that the rule of basic and fundamental error is a rule without specific standards and should be abolished. The abolition of the rule, I should like to add, does not leave an aggrieved party without a remedy.

Issues not raised in the trial court because of ineffective assistance of counsel may be reviewable on appeal in a criminal case. *Commonwealth ex rel. Washington v. Maroney*, 427 P. 599, 235 A.2d 349 (1967), sets forth specific standards which are applicable in determining whether counsel was effective in a criminal case.

An aggrieved party in a civil case, involving only private litigants unlike a defendant in a criminal case, does not have a constitutional right to the effective assistance of counsel. The remedy in a civil case, in which chosen counsel is negligent, is an action for malpractice.

POMEROY, Justice (concurring and dissenting).

While I concur in the result reached by the majority in the case before us, I cannot agree that the time has come to discard the doctrine of basic and fundamental error as it applies to erroneous jury instructions. However limited its scope and rare the occasions for its application, I believe the doctrine has a useful role to play in protecting the constitutional rights of litigants in our courts.

The doctrine of basic and fundamental error has been long established in this and other jurisdictions. The doctrine is not confined to errors in jury instructions but can embrace any trial error which deprives a litigant of his fundamental right to a fair and impartial trial. This right is an integral part of due process law, guaranteed to all litigants by the Fifth and Fourteenth Amendments. Obviously it is only an unusual trial error that will amount to a denial of due process, and in my view, the doctrine should be available to remedy only those trial errors so contrary to fundamental fairness as to reach the dimensions of a constitutional violation.

I am not persuaded that the doctrine of basic and fundamental error encourages careless or cynical disregard of orderly trial procedure by trial lawyers. The very uncertainty, indeed the unlikelihood, of the doctrine's application argues against any such consequence. Attorneys have everything to gain and nothing to lose from timely objection to errors at trial. We have applied the doctrine so sparingly that surely it is a rare lawyer indeed who would risk a charge of malpractice or incompetence on the speculation that an appellate court will find a particular error to be basic and fundamental.

The majority suggests that, whatever justification may once have existed for the fundamental error concept, it may now be safely discarded in view of the high quality of formal education which most trial attorneys receive today, and the various opportunities for continuing legal education. This complacency is not shared by other observers of the workings of our legal system. As Chief Justice Warren E. Burger has remarked but recently:

"Many judges in general jurisdiction trial courts have stated to me that fewer than 25 percent of the lawyers appearing before them are genuinely qualified; other judges go as high as 75 percent. I draw this from conversations extending over the past twelve to fifteen years at judicial meetings and seminars, with literally hundreds of judges and experienced lawyers. It would be safer to pick a middle ground and accept as a working hypothesis that from one-third to one-half of the lawyers who appear in the serious cases are not really qualified to render fully adequate representation." W. E. Burger, *The Special Skills of Advocacy: Are Specialized Training and Certification of Advocates Essential to Our System of Justice?* 42 Ford. L. Rev. 227, 234 (1973) (footnotes omitted).

While in Pennsylvania we have what I consider a generally high degree of competence in the trial bar, the fact remains that there has been in recent decades, here as elsewhere, phenomenal change in both substantive and procedural law, accompanied by a tremendous increase in the volume of litigation. As Chief Justice Burger suggests, there is evidence that, at the same time, the quality of trial advocacy in our nation's courts has been declining. We must strive to reverse this trend, to be sure, but I do not think we should do so at the expense of litigants who are not to blame for their attorneys' shortcomings. There are other, more direct and less costly ways of raising standards of trial advocacy than discarding the doctrine of basic and fundamental error.

Nor do I believe that the fundamental error doctrine adds significantly to admittedly overcrowded appellate dockets. It is the nature of humankind to be ever hopeful in the face of the most discouraging odds, and I fear that as long as there are appellate courts there will be litigants pursuing frivolous appeals. This is particularly true in the area of criminal law, where most defendants receive legal representation at no personal cost, and where all state remedies must be exhausted to pave the way for possible relief in the federal courts. A truly egregious criminal trial error which we decline to consider on appeal because not preserved below is almost certain to resurface in a post-conviction proceeding in the form of a charge of ineffectiveness of counsel. Considerations of judicial economy argue in favor of dealing with errors of this sort on direct appeal from the judgment of sentence.

Finally, it bears emphasizing that the rule now being discarded has existed not for the benefit of lazy and incompetent lawyers, but for the protection of litigants who may have been denied the essential elements of a fair and impartial trial. The considerations of judicial convenience and efficiency cited by the majority, important as they are, should give way in the rare situation where basic rights of this sort are in the balance. I believe that, in repudiating the doctrine as it applies to erroneous jury instructions, the majority has taken a step which is both unnecessary and unwise.

Notes

1. Few courts have followed the lead of the Pennsylvania Supreme Court in doing away entirely with exceptions to the preservation requirement. Many are nevertheless stringent in applying the general principle. An appellate lawyer must simply research carefully the preservation requirements in the particular jurisdiction. In many cases, the court's view of the preservation requirement will determine whether it is worth raising an issue at all.

2. Even courts that have the power to reach unpreserved errors may hesitate to exercise that power. For example, the Appellate Division of the New York Supreme

Court is one of those intermediate appellate courts having explicit statutory authority under New York's Criminal Procedure Law to reach unpreserved issues "in the interest of justice." Nevertheless, as the following case shows, the New York intermediate appellate courts, too, refuse to consider unpreserved errors in all but the most exceptional cases.

People v. Udzinski

146 A.D.2d 245, 541 N.Y.S.2d 9 (N.Y. App. Div. 1989)

BRACKEN, Justice.

The principal question in this case is whether an error in a jury charge, which the defendant claims constituted a violation of his constitutional right to be tried only upon theories charged in the indictment, is reviewable as a matter of law in the absence of a timely objection. We hold that it is not, and affirm the conviction.

"A person is guilty of sexual abuse in the first degree when he subjects another person to sexual contact . . . by forcible compulsion" (Penal Law § 130.65[1]). The meaning of the term "forcible compulsion" embraces both the concept of actual force and the concept of the threat of force (Penal Law § 130.00[8][a], [b]). However, when an indictment specifies that an accused committed sodomy in the first degree through the use of actual force alone, it is error for the Trial Judge to instruct the jury, over objection, that the crime may also be committed by the use of the threat of force.

The defendant in this case argues that a new trial is necessary as to that count of the indictment which charged him with sexual abuse in the first degree, because by allowing the jury to convict him of this charge based upon a finding that the crime was accomplished by the use of the threat of force, where the indictment specifies that actual force was used, the Trial Judge, in effect, altered the theory of the prosecution.

Assuming that . . . [prior case law] lends validity to this argument, we find that modification of the judgment on this ground would nonetheless be unwarranted, because any error in this regard was not properly preserved for appellate review as a matter of law and would, in any event, be harmless.

It is conceded that defense counsel did not object or except to the Trial Judge's definition of the term "forcible compulsion" in its jury charge. . . . The defendant argues that a question of law is nonetheless presented, since "no objection is necessary to preserve a deprivation of a fundamental constitutional right." The defendant contends that the alleged . . . error in this case deprived him of a constitutional right to be tried only upon theories presented in the indictment so that such error must be considered reviewable as a matter of law. This court has recently held, in a case decided after the argument of this appeal, that such an error is not reviewable as a matter of law in the absence of an objection. . . .

Before proceeding to address this contention, it will be helpful to recall the rationale underlying the doctrine of preservation. . . . This doctrine precludes appellate review, as a matter of law, of any ruling made by the court of original instance unless a protest was made to the ruling "at any . . . time when the court had an opportunity of effectively changing the same" (CPL 470.05[2]). By limiting a litigant's right to have a particular error corrected on appeal where no protest was voiced at the time the error was committed, the doctrine of preservation encourages all parties to be vigilant in the protection of their substantive and procedural rights throughout the course of a litigation. "Abandonment of the [preservation doctrine] actually increases [the prospect of] trial error. Absent the finality rule, judges, prosecutors and defense counsel need not carefully watch for errors during trial because errors can be corrected on appeal though not preserved for review" (29 DePaul L. Rev. 753, 760). . . .

The Supreme Court of the United States has repeatedly emphasized that appellate review of claims of error which were not properly raised in the court of original instance (*see*, Fed. Rules of Crim. Pro. 52[b]) provides the accused with an "extravagant protection" to be exercised only in exceptional cases. . . . The refusal to afford appellate review of arguments raised for the first time in the appellate court "encourage[s] all trial participants to seek a fair and accurate trial the first time around."
. . .

At trial, "the accused is in the courtroom, the jury is in the box, the judge is on the bench, and the witnesses, having been subpoenaed and duly sworn, await their turn to testify. Society's resources have been concentrated at that time and place in order to decide, within the limits of human fallibility, the question of guilt or innocence of one of its citizens. Any procedural rule which encourages the result that those proceedings be as free of error as possible is thoroughly desirable, and the contemporaneous-objection rule surely falls within this classification" (*Wainwright v. Sykes*, 433 U.S. 72, 90, 97 S.Ct. 2497, 2508, 53 L.Ed.2d 594). The doctrine of preservation, therefore, should not be viewed as a pretext by which appellate courts may overlook those errors which are inevitable at any trial . . . but instead should be regarded as an indispensable means of avoiding such errors in the first instance.

The preservation doctrine applies, in general, to all but an extremely narrow class of error. While it is possible to derive from prior decisional law sweeping statements such as "no exception is necessary to preserve for appellate review a deprivation of a fundamental constitutional right," it is now clear that such *obiter dictum* no longer reflects sound law. For example, the Court of Appeals has stated that "the rule requiring a defendant to preserve his points for appellate review applies generally to claims of error involving Federal constitutional rights."

The preservation doctrine has been applied so as to preclude appellate review of a wide variety of arguments relating to errors which clearly affected fundamental rights (*see, e.g., People v. Fernandez*, 72 N.Y.2d 827, *People v. Fleming*, 70 N.Y.2d 947 [right to confront adverse witnesses]; *People v. Ruz*, 70 N.Y.2d 942 [ex post facto punishment]; *People v. Iannelli*, 60 N.Y.2d 684, *People v. Dozier*, 52 N.Y.2d 781 [unconstitutionality of criminal statute, due process]; *People v. Thomas*, 50 N.Y.2d 467 [Sandstrom error]; *People v. Miguel*, 53 N.Y.2d 920 [Dunaway error]; *People v. Cedeno*, 52 N.Y.2d 847 [due process violation based on delay in prosecution]; *People v. Martin*, 50 N.Y.2d 1029 [Payton error]; *People v. Booker*, 49 N.Y.2d 989, *People v. Tutt*, 38 N.Y.2d 1011 [Miranda error]; *People v. Lieberman*, 47 N.Y.2d 931 [violation of constitutional right to speedy trial]). As a matter of Federal constitutional law, state appellate courts may properly decline to review claims of Federal constitutional error on the basis that such claims were not raised in a procedurally correct manner (*see, e.g., Wainwright v. Sykes*, 433 U.S. 72 [Florida procedure, consistent with Federal constitution, required Miranda claim to be raised at trial or not at all]; *Engle v. Isaac*, 456 U.S. 107 [defendant's failure to except to jury instruction which unconstitutionally shifted burden of proof on defense of justification constituted valid basis for state appellate court's refusal to entertain argument]). A defendant in a state criminal prosecution who forfeits his right to state appellate review of a constitutional argument because of a procedural default on his part may not avoid the consequences of such forfeiture by resorting to an application for a writ of habeas corpus in the Federal courts, and it is now settled that Federal habeas corpus review of a question of constitutional law which was resolved against the defendant in the state courts on procedural grounds generally is not permitted.

The preservation doctrine has been extended so far as to preclude appellate review, as a matter of law, of what could convincingly be said to be the most fundamental of all possible defects in a criminal proceeding, that is, the failure of the People to adduce legally sufficient evidence of the crime of which the defendant is convicted. In *People v. Colavito*, 70 N.Y.2d 996 and *People v. Bynum*, 70 N.Y.2d 858, it was held that a defendant may not raise, for the first time on appeal, arguments concerning the legal sufficiency of the prosecution's evidence; such arguments could be advanced only if they had been raised with specificity in the trial court. The Appellate Division, of course, may entertain such arguments in the interest of justice (CPL 470.15[6][a]), as may the Federal appellate courts pursuant to the "plain error" rule (Fed. Rules of Crim. Pro. 52[b]). . . .

Similarly, by failing to assert the appropriate objection at trial, a defendant may forfeit his right to argue on appeal that the Trial Judge's instructions to the jury did not properly define the elements of the crime. . . . Thus, if the Trial Judge in this case had entirely failed to define the term "forcible compulsion," the error would not have been reviewable as a matter of law in the absence of an appropriate objection. However, such an error would be reviewable in this court as an aspect of our interest of justice jurisdiction, and such an error in the Federal courts may also be considered so fundamental as to be properly reviewable as a matter of discretion.

Considering the scope and number of the truly fundamental errors to which the preservation doctrine does apply, one encounters difficulty in deriving from precedent a rigid standard by which to ascertain those errors to which the doctrine does not apply (*see, e.g., People v. Michael*, 48 N.Y.S.2d 1 [double jeopardy]; *People v. Samuels*, 49 N.Y.S.2d 218 [State constitutional right to counsel]). In *People v. Patterson*, 39 N.Y.2d 288, the Court of Appeals stated that errors which " 'would affect the organization of the court or the mode of proceedings prescribed by law' " are reviewable as a matter of law even in the absence of an objection. . . . Appellate review of errors of law, in the absence of an objection, was held to be permitted "where a question of jurisdiction or fundamental rights is involved and public injury would result."

The rule that certain fundamental irregularities in a criminal prosecution may not be waived or even consented to by the defendant derives from the concept that neither the defendant nor the prosecutor nor the court has the right to deprive the public of its interest in preserving the basic fairness of our judicial system. "The State, the public, have an interest in the preservation of . . . liberties." While the defendant, by consent, may alter the substantive and procedural rules by which a criminal case is prosecuted, this power does not "extend so far as to work radical changes in great and leading provisions as to the organization of the tribunals or the mode of proceeding prescribed by the constitution and the laws." Thus, the most basic components of a fair trial – a fair judge, a fair jury, and a court of competent jurisdiction – are generally held to be so important that the defendant cannot, through application of the preservation doctrine on appeal, forfeit his right to object to their absence; *People v. Parisi*, 276 N.Y. 97 [absence of trial judge]; *Cancemi v. People*, 18 N.Y. 128 [jury of less than 12]. In holding such fundamental irregularities to be reviewable even in the absence of an objection, it is the interest of society at large, and not the personal interest of the defendant, which the courts protect.

The unpreserved error allegedly present in the Trial Judge's charge in the present case, far from working a radical change "in great and leading provisions as to . . . the mode of proceeding prescribed by the constitution and the laws" constituted, at worst, an instruction which conveyed to the jury the correct definition of the elements of the crime with which the defendant was charged, in an instance where the indictment against the defendant purportedly led him to believe that the People would limit their "theory" so as to, in effect, narrow the definition of the crime. While we recognize the fundamental place that a properly drawn indictment has in our criminal justice system, we cannot consider the error in this case to be jurisdictional, or otherwise fundamental. . . .

A. Recognizing a Preserved Error

1. Objections to Rulings and Orders

a. Adequacy of Objection

Because the absence of an objection at trial to an erroneous ruling will, in most cases, result in the refusal of the appellate court to review the issue, it is obviously not enough for appellate counsel simply to locate a trial error in the record and to show that it was prejudicial (*See* Chapter 5 on harmless error). Counsel's first task is to demonstrate to the court that the error was adequately preserved for appellate review. Sometimes, if trial counsel was competent, this may not be a difficult task; there, on the record, will appear the words "I object, Your Honor" accompanied by counsel's clear and correct explanation of the grounds for the objection. In such cases, counsel for appellant need do no more than refer to the page in the record on which the objection appears and can then proceed to discuss the merits of the case. Counsel for respondent will not mention preservation at all.

As a result of the fast pace and high pressure of trial, however, in many cases even skilled trial counsel will fail to make well-formulated, articulate objections. Nevertheless, the attorney may have made noises of some sort to communicate dissatisfaction with the trial court's ruling. In such cases the threshold issue on appeal will be whether the error was adequately preserved for the appellate court's review. Counsel for appellant will, of course, attempt to convince the appellate court that the error was preserved, while counsel for respondent will argue vigorously that it was not. Rule 46 of the Federal Rules of Civil Procedure and Rule 51 of the Federal Rules of Criminal Procedure provide that in order to preserve an objection to a ruling or order of court, it is sufficient that a party "makes known to the court the action which he desires the court to take or his objection to the action of the court and his grounds therefor." It is not necessary now in federal court, as it once was, for an attorney to take a formal exception after the court overrules an objection, nor is any particular formal language necessary to preserve an error for appellate review. The test is simply whether the record makes clear that all parties and the court understood what the objecting lawyer wanted done and why. Most state courts follow this modern rule, although some still require that formal exceptions be taken.

Because an appellate lawyer's job is so much easier if an error was preserved, it is worth combing the trial record for indications that some type of objection was made and understood by the court and the opposing parties. The following case gives an example of an imperfectly preserved issue that nonetheless received appellate consideration.

Stone v. Morris

546 F.2d 730 (7th Cir. 1976).

STECKLER, District Judge.[1]

This is an appeal from a jury verdict and judgment adverse to plaintiff-appellant's civil rights claim under 42 U.S.C. § 1983.

The issues presented are whether the district court erred in refusing to permit the plaintiff-appellant, Jeff T. Stone, to attend the trial of his civil rights claim, and whether the court committed reversible error in refusing to admit into evidence a memorandum authorized by a prison correctional counselor.

The action was brought in the United States District Court for the Northern District of Illinois. At that time plaintiff Stone was an inmate in the Joliet Branch of the Illinois State Penitentiary serving a one-hundred to two-hundred year sentence for murder. Prior to the trial he was transferred from Joliet in the Northern District of Illinois to the Menard Correctional Center in the Eastern District of Illinois.

Plaintiff's principle [sic] contention is that the district court deprived him of a fair trial and of his constitutional right of access to the courts and counsel by ex-

cluding him from the jury trial of his prison-connected civil rights claim.

The defendants-appellees argue that the plaintiff waived any objection to his exclusion from the trial because no objection was made until the motion for a new trial was filed ten days after the jury returned its verdict. Defendants contend that the plaintiff was not prejudiced by his exclusion because his case was fully presented through his disposition and the introduction of exhibits. It is also the defendant's position that a prisoner-plaintiff has no constitutional right to be present at his civil rights trial, and that the trial judge properly excluded the prison memorandum from evidence as hearsay.

The issues before the trial court involved principally questions of fact. We therefore have carefully examined the record, and particularly the trial proceedings, to determine whether the plaintiff's claim was fairly submitted to the jury.

Stone commenced his action by filing a lengthy and detailed *pro se* complaint naming as defendants Ernest E. Morris, the Assistant Superintendent and later Warden at Joliet, and three other members of the staff of Joliet: John Gentry, Lieutenant, Virdeen Willis, a Captain, and H. B. McElroy, an Officer.

The complaint alleged that on October

---

[1] Honorable William E. Steckler, Chief District Judge for the Southern District of Indiana, is sitting by designation.

16, 1972, defendants Gentry, Willis, and McElroy, and two other prison guards, Officers Moland and Hinch, subjected the plaintiff to a brutal beating with various weapons for which he was hospitalized and from which he continued to suffer. . . .

The defendants filed a motion to dismiss or for summary judgment accompanied by a memorandum of law and separate affidavits of Willis, Gentry, McElroy, and Morris. In their affidavits the defendants denied that any such incident as alleged by Stone occurred on October 16, 1972, and stated that on October 18, 1972, Stone had been transferred from cell 109 to cell 702 without any particular incident.

The district court denied the motion to dismiss, ruled that the *pro se* complaint stated a good cause of action, and ordered the defendants to answer. The court then appointed counsel to represent the plaintiff. By leave of court plaintiff's court-appointed counsel filed an amended complaint, abbreviating the lengthy allegations of the *pro se* complaint, limiting the relief sought, and adding Officers Moland and Hinch as parties defendant. On March 28, 1974, the defendants filed their answer to the amended complaint in which they renewed their denials of the allegations of the complaint.

Pursuant to an order of the court issued on March 27, 1974, plaintiff's counsel on May 1, 1974, more than a year prior to the trial, filed a designation of the witnesses he intended to call at trial. Plaintiff's counsel stated in the designation that he intended to base his case entirely on the plaintiff's own testimony and that he would call no other witnesses at trial. On February 14, 1975, defendants' counsel took plaintiff's discovery deposition with plaintiff's counsel present. For the purpose of the deposition plaintiff was transported to the Stateville Correctional Center in Joliet from the Menard Correc-

tional Center, to which he had been transferred from Joliet in late 1973.

On March 24, 1975, at a conference to fix a trial date the district court ruled *sua sponte* that the court would not secure plaintiff's attendance at the trial. The court stated that as far as the plaintiff was concerned the court would try the case by deposition. . . .

The case was tried to a jury from May 27 through May 30, 1975. At the trial plaintiff's testimonial evidence consisted solely of the reading of plaintiff's discovery deposition. . . .

The first question presented on review is whether the action of the district judge in summarily excluding Stone from his civil rights trial infringed upon his constitutional right of access to the courts and to counsel. . . .

Defendants point out that plaintiff's counsel did not make a formal objection to the district court's *sua sponte* ruling on March 24, 1975, which excluded the plaintiff from the trial of his claim. We do not believe that the failure of plaintiff's counsel to register a formal objection after the court made its ruling serves as a waiver of the issue. Inasmuch as counsel had filed a designation of witnesses naming only the plaintiff himself, we feel that the purpose of Rule 46 of the Federal Rules of Civil Procedure was satisfied, although it would have been the better course for plaintiff's counsel to have registered a formal objection. The purpose of Rule 46 is to inform the trial judge of possible errors so that he may have the opportunity to consider his rulings and to correct them if necessary. Normally that purpose can be adequately served only by the making of an objection on the record, but if the court and the other litigants know what action a party desires the court to take, the purpose of the rule is served. In such circumstances a formal objection is not required, and the failure of the court to take the desired action may be asserted as error on appeal. We therefore hold that under the circumstances of this case the failure of counsel to enter a formal objection to the *sua* *sponte* ruling of the district court excluding the plaintiff from the trial does not amount to a waiver of the issue. . . .

Note

In *Stone v. Morris* the court referred to the failure to preserve an error as a "waiver." Although this word is frequently used to describe the actions of the trial lawyer who fails to object, the characterization has frequently been criticized on the ground that "waiver" in law most precisely refers to a knowing and voluntary giving up of rights rather than to mere inadvertence or incompetence that results in a forfeiture of a right.

b. Theory of Objection

Frequently appellate courts find that an issue was not adequately preserved, despite a clear objection to a ruling made at trial, if, on appeal, counsel argues that the ruling was erroneous for a reason different from the one advanced by trial counsel. The following case is an example of an instance in which a New York appellate court found that an issue was unpreserved because the argument on appeal concerning a particular error did not closely match the argument made to the trial judge concerning the same error.

People v. Tutt

38 N.Y.2d 1011, 348 N.E.2d 920, 384 N.Y.S.2d 444 (1976).

MEMORANDUM

The order of the Appellate Division should be affirmed.

We reach our conclusion on a very narrow ground. We do not suggest that at the time defendant made the statement and surrendered the car keys, both of which are sought to be suppressed, he then waived any aspect of the full preinterrogation admonitions to which he was constitutionally entitled. We agree with the dissenters that the record here would not support any such finding. Rather, we conclude that there should be an affirmance because of the failure of defendant at the suppression hearing to preserve the error on which reliance is now placed for a reversal.

At that hearing defendant advanced but a single, categorical contention – that he had been given none of the constitutionally mandated admonitions before interrogation. There was then no intimation either in his own testimony or in the recorded argument of counsel on his behalf that it would be claimed that that portion of the admonitions covering the right to counsel was deficient in its extent and explicitness. Thus, the People were afforded no opportunity to meet the theory first put forward on appeal, namely, that the preinterrogation statements made by the police did not go far enough explicitly to advise defendant that his right to counsel included the right to have counsel present at his on-the-scene questioning.

There can, of course, be no doubt that the right to counsel extends to representation during any interrogation by the police and that the defendant is entitled to advice to such effect. Where, however, the defendant fails at the suppression hearing to challenge a narrow aspect of the sufficiency of the admonitions given him, at a time when the People would have an evidentiary opportunity to counter his assertion, he may not then be heard to complain on appeal. . . .

COOKE, Judge (dissenting).

I dissent and vote to reverse the order of the Appellate Division.

The failure of the arresting officer to adequately inform defendant of his right to the assistance of counsel prior to and during custodial interrogation violated the principles articulated in *Miranda v. Arizona*. Absent a knowing and voluntary waiver of this right, incriminating statements made by defendant after his arrest should have been suppressed.

The only issue at the suppression hearing was whether defendant had waived his *Miranda* rights. . . .

The error arising from the conceded deficiencies in the *Miranda* warnings was preserved at the conclusion of the suppression hearing by the motion of defendant's attorney to suppress "on the grounds there was no *proper* warning, required by the Constitution and the doctrine of *Miranda v. Arizona*." After said attorney argued in support of the motion, the court inquired of the Assistant District Attorney if he wished to be heard. The prosecutor spoke at some length but did not request an opportunity to submit additional proof. No further formalism should have been required of defendant's attorney in order that the right to review the error be preserved.

Notes

1. New York's Criminal Procedure Law provides that an objection is sufficient to preserve an error for appellate review if, in response to a protest by a party, the court expressly decided the question raised on appeal. Thus, the theory of the trial judge for overruling an objection can take the place of the theory of the trial lawyer who made it for purposes of appeal.

2. Federal courts can also be strict about refusing to consider new theories on appeal. For example, in *Snapp v. United States Postal Service-Texarkana*, 664 F.2d 1329 (5th Cir. 1982) the plaintiff, Richard Snapp, brought suit in federal district court to enjoin the United States Postal Service from complying with a writ of garnishment issued by a Tennessee court. The district court dismissed the case for lack of federal subject matter jurisdiction. It rejected Snapp's argument that his case came under both 28 U.S.C. § 1337, which provides for federal court jurisdiction over suits arising under acts of Congress that regulate commerce; and under 28 U.S.C. § 1346(a)(2), which gives the district courts jurisdiction over an action against the United States for less than $10,000 when the action is based on federal constitutional, statutory or regulatory law or on a contract with the United States.

On appeal to the Court of Appeals for the Fifth Circuit, Snapp argued additionally for the first time that the Postal Service's garnishment of his wages deprived him of property without due process in violation of the Fifth Amendment because he never received notice of the institution of garnishment proceedings from the Tennessee court. The Court of Appeals refused to consider this theory, however, because Snapp had failed to present it to the court below. The court concluded that the district court had properly dismissed the action for want of federal jurisdiction.

Example

In the following case a defendant was charged with the sexual abuse of six teenage boys. On summation the prosecutor argued that the testimony of each of the complainants corroborated the testimony of all of the other complainants. The defendant argued that the prosecutor's cross-corroboration arguments deprived defendant of a fair trial. The prosecutor countered that this issue had not been preserved for appellate review. Defense counsel replied that the issue had been preserved.

The People's Summation

THE PROSECUTOR: Ladies and gentlemen, you heard the defense say, at the outset of counsel's summation, that this case was not about dates. It was about credibility. Well, I submit to you, ladies and gentlemen, you've been hearing about dates and children's abilities and inabilities to remember dates since jury selection. In fact, it was probably the one issue that you were asked about over and over.

DEFENSE COUNSEL: I object to that.

THE COURT: It's a question for the jury to determine what effect the evidence has had on you with regard to the People's burden of proof to prove the charges. You may consider the evidence in accordance with the Court's instructions on the law.

DEFENSE COUNSEL: Thank you, Judge.

THE PROSECUTOR: You begin to see a course of conduct here. A pattern which emerges. I'm going to ask you to look at that, look at that closely. The individual facts in the testimony of each of those boys adds up to something much bigger.

Some years ago, this defendant took an oath, a Hippocratic oath to be a doctor. For reasons that we can only surmise, he strayed from that oath. And the six boys that you saw come in here and testify before you, are the result of that. Not for any other reason.

We're going to go through each of their testimony, and I'm going to ask you, look for a consistent pattern that emerges from the individual facts that six different young boys told you, six boys who have never met. At no time have they ever discussed their testimony with each other. They came in here, each of them, and told you their individual stories. Take a close look at that.

* * *

These boys were each testifying independently on their own memory as to what was done to them. And I submit to you that that testimony is corroborative.

DEFENSE COUNSEL: Objection.

THE COURT: With regard to counsel's opinion as to what the evidence should suggest to you, I've told you previously . . . That you may accept their suggestions if you feel that they're well-founded, if you feel that they reflect the evidence as you heard it, and as you believe it was adduced. If you don't, you may reject it.

THE PROSECUTOR: Thank you, Judge.

* * *

Ladies and gentlemen, these boys wouldn't know each other if they bumped into each other on the street. They have never met, and never discussed their testimony. And, again, look at the pattern. This is no coincidence.

* * *

Consider these things in determining the credibility of the People's witnesses: First, they're six separate victims that didn't know each other. They never talked to each other about this; there is no conspiracy. Look at the similarities in each of their testimonies.

* * *

At the end of the summation defense counsel moved for a mistrial based on the prosecutor's comments.

Defense Brief

In his summation, the prosecutor's principal theme was that the facts pertaining to each complainant "add up to something much bigger," that is, that the jury should find appellant guilty because of the cumulative effect of the evidence pertaining to each of the six complainants. Thus, over objection, the prosecutor repeatedly told the jury that "[t]he testimony of each of these six boys corroborates each other," to "look for a consistent pattern that emerges from the individual facts that six different young boys have told you," and that "six separate victims that didn't know each other" would not have "put themselves through the embarrassment" of testifying and could not all be wrong or lying. . . .

Prosecutor's Brief

Appellant . . . advances two related but distinct claims, concerning the "cross-corroboration" argument by the prosecutor in summation and the alleged commingling of evidence relating to separate crimes by the jury, in support of his main contention that consolidation denied him a fair trial. Neither of these issues was properly preserved for review by a contemporaneous objection.

The first time the prosecutor referred to the fact that the "testimony of each of the victims corroborates each other," the trial court *sustained* defense counsel's general objection with the following curative instruction:

THE COURT: It's a question for the jury to determine what effect the evidence has had on you with regard to the People's burden of proof to prove the charges. *You may consider the evidence in accordance with the court's instructions on the law.*

A subsequent similar remark by the prosecutor again provoked a general objection from defense counsel, followed by a curative instruction from the court. Since defense counsel neither requested any additional curative instruction nor moved for a mistrial at that time on the basis of the prosecutor's remarks, no error of law was preserved for appellate review. The additional comments of the prosecutor suggesting the existence of a pattern in the testimony of six complainants and the similarities in the testimony of the victims provoked no defense objection at all.

Defense Reply Brief

The People claim that the prosecutor's "cross-corroboration" argument was not preserved for review. The record belies the People's contention. The People contend that the first time appellant objected to the People's "cross-corroboration" argument the court "*sustained*" the objection and gave a "curative" instruction, which the People quote. The People further contend that, in later asking for a mistrial at the end of the People's summation because of the "cross-corroboration" argument, an objection that the People characterize as "untimely," appellant "acknowledged that the court had sustained his objection."

Here is what the record actually shows:

THE PROSECUTOR: The testimony of these six boys corroborates each other.

DEFENSE COUNSEL: I object to that.

THE COURT: *It's a question for the jury to determine what effect the evidence has had on you* with regard to the People's burden of proof to prove the charges. You may consider the evidence in accordance with the Court's instructions on the law.

THE PROSECUTOR: *Thank you, Judge* [emphasis added].

The foregoing colloquy plainly shows that the court did not "sustain" appellant's objection, contrary to the People's contention. The court never said the word "sustained" or any word like it. Nor was the court's instruction "curative," as the People claim. On the contrary, in stating that "it's a question for the jury to determine what effect the evidence had on you with regard to the People's burden of proof," the court *overruled* appellant's objection because it permitted the jury to adopt the People's "cross-corroboration" argument. In fact, the prosecutor, himself, understood the court to have overruled the objection, not "sustained" it, since he thanked the court after the instruction.

At the end of the summation, defense counsel renewed his objection to the People's "cross-corroboration" argument, and asked for a mistrial on that ground as well as for other remarks in the People's summation. While the record reflects defense counsel's statement that "the Court *did* sustain my first objection," the statement is undoubtedly the stenographer's typographical error in view of the context in which the statement was made, that is, defense counsel actually stated that the court "did not" sustain his first objection. If the record accurately reflects counsel's statement after the People's summation, he misspoke, because the record plainly demonstrates that the court did *not* sustain his first objection to the "cross-corroboration" argument.[2]

The People contend that appellant's second objection to the People's "cross-corroboration" argument did not preserve the issue for review because the objection was "followed by a curative instruction." Again, here is what the record actually shows:

> THE PROSECUTOR: . . .These boys were each testifying independently on their own memory as to what was done to them. *And I submit to you that that testimony is corroborative.*
>
> DEFENSE COUNSEL: Objection.
>
> THE COURT: With regard to counsel's opinion as to what the evidence should suggest to you, *I've told you previously . . . that you may accept their suggestions if you feel that they're well-founded, if you feel that they reflect the evidence as you heard it, and as you believe it was adduced.* If you don't, you may reject it.
>
> THE PROSECUTOR: *Thank you, Judge.*

The court's instruction represents another *overruling* of appellant's objection because the court told the jury that they were entitled to accept and adopt the People's cross-corroboration argument. The prosecutor's "thank you" reflects that he understood the court's instruction the same way. Moreover, since the court handled the second objection in a manner virtually identical to the first, the second objection is further proof that the first was not "sustained" or "cured."

The People also contend that the prosecutor's repeated "pattern" argument in summation "provoked no defense objection at all." The "pattern" argument, however, was part and parcel of, and subsumed by, the "cross-corroboration" argument. An argument that the jury should look at the "consistent pattern that emerges from the individual facts that six different young boys told you" is no different from an argument that each boy's testimony "cross-corroborated" the testimony of the others. That is what defense counsel meant when, in moving for mistrial at the end of the People's summation, he told the court that:

> I don't believe in rising every time to object. I think it's rude and unprofessional and inappropriate . . . Most of the prosecutor's objectionable remarks I raised objection to. *Then when it was repeated, I didn't make the same objection, understanding that the Court is always consistent, and makes the same rulings.* It has been my experience, on the basis of this highly inflammatory summation, I ask for . . . a mistrial. The Prosecutor stated on *at least three occasions* that the

---

[2] Even if the record can somehow be read as reflecting that the court sustained counsel's first objection, although it plainly cannot be, a protest to the People's summation voiced at the end of the summation is not "untimely," particularly when defense counsel courteously refrained from interrupting the People's summation because of his view that contemporaneous objections can be "rude and unprofessional and inappropriate."

testimony of each boy should be used to corroborate the other.

In other words, counsel unsuccessfully objected on two or three occasions to the People's "cross-corroboration" argument, and was entitled to refrain from further antagonizing the jury and disrupting the People's summation by needlessly repeating the objection when the People made the same argument in other terms, the "consistent pattern" argument. Thus, both the "cross-corroboration" and "pattern" arguments are preserved for this Court's review as a matter of law.

2. Objections to Jury Charge Errors

Many appellate courts are particularly strict about requiring contemporaneous objections to erroneous jury instructions before permitting them to be challenged on appeal. Rule 51 of the Federal Rules of Civil Procedure and Rule 30 of the Federal Rules of Criminal Procedure both provide that no party may raise as error on appeal any portion of the charge or omission from the charge to which no objection was distinctly made before the jury retired to deliberate.

The reasoning underlying the special rules regarding preservation of charge errors is that the charge is a crucial part of every trial for which an attorney has an opportunity to prepare carefully. Moreover, it is very easy for the trial court to remedy charge errors if they are brought to its attention at the time the charge is given. As with rulings and orders, a question is often raised about whether counsel at trial adequately preserved a charge error for appellate review. In the following case, trial counsel no doubt believed that he had preserved an objection to the court's charge. A majority of the appellate court, however, thought otherwise. The dissenting opinion describes some of the problems in determining whether an adequate objection has been made to a jury charge error.

People v. Hoke
62 N.Y.2d 1022 (1984)

MEMORANDUM

The appeal should be dismissed.

Although the Appellate Division order states that reversal of defendant's conviction was on the law, the opinion reveals that it was in fact based upon an exercise of discretion. After the trial court had denied defendant's requested alibi charge and, in its place, given a different alibi charge, defendant did not specify why the charge as given was inadequate. Thus, while there was preservation as to the court's refusal to charge in accordance with defendant's request, there was no preservation with respect to error in the alibi charge as given.[4] The Appellate Division reversal was not grounded in the failure to charge as requested, but in its conclusion that the trial court's alibi instructions as given were bur-

---

[4] Far from carrying "the concept of preservation much too far" (dissent), the requirement of specific objection in these circumstances serves a salutary purpose. Defense counsel, having heard the charge as given and knowing best how it fails to satisfy his request, by objection at that point gives the court the opportunity to correct any error.

den-shifting. Accordingly, its determination rested on an exercise of its interest of justice jurisdiction, and does not satisfy the jurisdictional predicate for review by this court (CPL 450.90, subd 2). (*See People v. Dercole*, 52 N.Y.2d 956.)

Chief Judge Cooke (dissenting). The majority's conclusion, that the Appellate Division acted in its discretion, is based upon the invalid assumption that defendant did not preserve his objection to the court's failure to charge that the People had the burden of disproving the alibi beyond a reasonable doubt. The majority carries the concept of preservation much too far. Therefore, respectfully, I must dissent.

Defendant was prosecuted for attempted robbery and asserted an alibi defense. Prior to the jury charge, defendant requested an instruction on alibi that provided in part: "I further charge you that alibi is not an affirmative defense under the law of New York, but is a defense other than an affirmative defense and, hence, is a defense as to which the People have the burden of disproving beyond a reasonable doubt. In layman's terms, this means that the defendant has no burden of proving the alibi defense. It is the burden on the prosecution to disprove the alibi defense beyond a reasonable doubt."

The trial judge expressly denied defendant's request, stating, "I have examined it. I refuse to so charge." The judge did not state that he was planning to give a different alibi charge or that he would give a charge which substantially comported with defendant's request. The judge did, however, charge on alibi: "The defendant claims he was not present at the scene of the crime and has offered evidence to show that he was elsewhere. In the law, this is known as an alibi defense. As I have previously charged you, the People have the burden of establishing the guilt of the defendant beyond a reasonable doubt. The defendant is not required to prove his innocence. If the evidence as to alibi, if believed by you, the jury, when taken into consider-

ation with all of the other evidence, raises reasonable doubt as to the defendant's guilt, he is entitled to an acquittal."

After the charge, when asked by the trial judge if there were any requests, defense counsel replied, "Yes, Your Honor. I have already mentioned them previously." Counsel did not offer to explain why the judge's charge was erroneous or how it differed from the requested charge.

The Appellate Division reversed defendant's conviction on the ground that the alibi charge improperly shifted the burden of proof to defendant. It reached its decision "on the law," without any discussion of the preservation issue.

The Legislature has already prescribed what is necessary for a party to preserve an error for appellate review. CPL 470.05 (subd 2) provides in part: "a question of law with respect to a ruling or instruction . . . is presented when a protest thereto was registered, by the party claiming error, at the time of such ruling or instruction. . . . Such protest need not be in the form of an 'exception' but is sufficient if the party made his position with respect to the ruling or instruction known to the court. In addition, a party who without success has either expressly or impliedly sought or requested a particular ruling or instruction, is deemed to have thereby protested the court's ultimate disposition of the matter or failure regardless of whether any actual protest thereto was registered."

Here, defendant requested an alibi charge which properly stated the law in writing, prior to the jury charge. This request was expressly denied. Under these circumstances, the purported error is fully preserved for review by the terms of CPL 470.05 (subd 2). The statute does not require the party "without success" to proffer any further explanation why the refusal to charge as requested is incorrect or how the charge, as given, fails to comport with the law as espoused in a defendant's request.

Indeed, this court has not, until today,

required such an explanation in order to preserve an objection to a jury charge in situations where the request to charge is denied (compare *People v. Le Mieux,* 51 N.Y.2d 981, 982-983, with *People v. Whalen,* 59 N.Y.2d 273, 279-280). In *Le Mieux,* defendant made a timely written request that the trial court charge the jury on an aspect of corroboration. The judge did not grant the request or give any other similar charge. This court stated, "[b]y this submission, the written form of which in this case lessened the possibility of judicial oversight, defendant must be deemed to have thereby protested the court's ultimate . . . failure to . . . instruct sufficiently to raise a question of law . . . regardless of whether any actual protest thereto was registered (CPL 470.05). Therefore, no additional or literal 'exception' was required to preserve the point" (*People v. Le Mieux, supra, see People v. Victor,* 62 N.Y.2d 374, *supra* [defendant, whose request to charge was denied, made no further objection after the jury charge and issue was preserved]). Nor did this court view defendant's failure to make a further specific objection after the charge, other than the blanket renewal of all his prior requests, as a waiver of his "position already preserved with respect to a request on which the verdict could very well have turned" (*People v. Le Mieux,* 51 N.Y.2d 981, 983, *supra*). Indeed, even the dissent agreed that "the request was by itself sufficient to raise an issue that is cognizable in our courts under the limited review powers conferred upon us by CPL 470.35 (subd 1), and no further exception or renewal of the request was necessary" [Gabrielli, J., dissenting]).

This preservation rule yields a different result when the trial judge informs a defendant that a request will be granted, but then delivers an altered charge that is not to defendant's satisfaction. For example, in *People v. Whalen,* 59 N.Y.2d 273, the trial court granted the defendant's request but then failed to charge in the precise terms desired. After the charge, defendant

asked for the original language without, however, explaining how the judge had deviated from it. This court first reviewed the rule under the CPL and cited the holding in *Le Mieux* with approval. It held that, in the "different circumstances" present, a specific objection as to why the given charge was inadequate was required to provide an opportunity for the trial judge to correct the obvious discrepancy between the actual charge and the defendant's granted request. Thus, in that situation, the failure to point out the error was fairly considered a waiver of any objection to the instruction.

The rule that can be culled from *Le Mieux* and *Whalen* is that if the individual circumstances indicate that defendant's request has been denied, there is no need to make any further objection or explanation to avoid waiving the error but if the judge has effectively granted the request, any failure to adhere to that ruling must be brought to the judge's attention either before or after the charge.

The situation here is closer to that in *Le Mieux,* where the judge refused the request to charge, than in *Whalen,* where the judge inadvertently deviated from the language of the granted request. Once the request is denied, no purpose will be served by any further objection to the actual charge, which is expected to differ. The battle over the correct jury charge has been fought and lost.

This holds true whether a judge rejects a defendant's request and then delivers no charge on the subject, as in *Le Mieux,* or proceeds to instruct on the topic in terms different from those requested, as here. In either event, the understanding between a judge and a defendant has been made clear by the judge's denial of the defendant's request. Where, as here, the charge given related to the exact same legal point covered in defendant's request for an alibi charge, there is no reason to distinguish between an objection to the judge's refusal to charge as requested and an objection to the charge as given. It must be remembered that a jury charge is an instruction on the relevant legal principles. A request to charge is inherently a party's statement of the proper controlling law. Thus, a judge is on notice that denial of a requested instruction or any substantial deviation from the language of that request is a rejection of defendant's view of the law and will be viewed by defendant as error. Accordingly, the defendant is under no further burden to bring the matter to the court's attention for corrective action (CPL 470.05, subd 2) and defendant here has preserved his objection to both the failure to charge as requested and the erroneous charge that was given on the subject of his request. This result would change, of course, if the charge as given included statements beyond the scope of a defendant's request. In that situation, the judge would never have been put on notice that defendant viewed the statement as error and, therefore, an objection would be required.

The approach set forth herein is consistent with that taken in *Whalen*. A judge who grants a request has acceded to the sponsoring party's statement of the pertinent legal principles. Thus, a deviation from this language in the actual charge cannot be assumed to be a decision that the party's request is erroneous. Indeed, the lapse will be deemed inadvertent and the party is compelled to point out the discrepancy. This will allow the court either to make the correction itself or to reject the party's request on the record.

Under this view, defendant successfully preserved his objection to the jury charge and a question of law is properly presented before this court. The charge given failed to state, as defendant properly requested, that the People had the burden of disproving the alibi beyond a reasonable doubt. Also, the language "if believed by you, the jury," implied that defendant bore some burden of proving the alibi. These improperly shifted the burden of proof requiring a reversal of the conviction and a new trial (*see People v. Victor,* 62 N.Y.2d 374, *supra*).

Accordingly, the order of the Appellate Division should be affirmed.

Note

Appellate courts occasionally excuse the failure to preserve an issue where it is clear from the record that an objection to a ruling of the lower court would have been futile. *Mays v. Dealers Transit, Inc.,* 441 F.2d 1344 (7th Cir. 1971) was an appeal from a judgment in favor of the defendants following a jury verdict in a diversity action in which the plaintiff sought to recover damages for the alleged wrongful death of her husband Daniel Mays in a motor vehicle accident. The plaintiff contended that the district court committed reversible error in instructing the jury on the claimed contributory negligence of the decedent in failing to fasten his seat belt. The court's instructions 4, 18 and 21 dealt with this issue. Instruction 4 stated that the jury should decide:

> whether or not Daniel Mays failed to use and to fasten about his person the seat belt which was then provided for his use in the vehicle in which he was riding?

Id. at 1346.

> Instruction 18 stated:

> If you find that Daniel Mays violated such [common law duty as set forth in Instruction number four (4)] . . . then I instruct you that you would be war-

ranted in finding that Daniel Mays as you may determine was negligent.
Id. at 1347.

Instruction 21 stated:

You will weigh all of the evidence to ascertain whether or not a reasonably prudent passenger, under all of the facts and circumstances in evidence, would have been using the vehicle's seat belt and determine in accordance with these instructions whether or not Daniel Mays was negligent.

As explained elsewhere in these instructions, the Defendants raising this defense must also prove that Daniel Mays would not have been killed had he used the seat belt, or stated another way, that Daniel Mays' failure to use the seat belt proximately contributed to his death.

Id. at 1350.

Plaintiff objected to Instruction 4 and 18 but failed to object to 21. Nevertheless, on appeal she argued for the first time that the lower court had committed reversible error in giving that charge as well. Despite the lack of objection, the Court of Appeals agreed to review the claimed error.

The failure of plaintiff to object to Instruction No. 21 presents the question of whether plaintiff can now be heard to complain of the giving of the other instructions pertaining to the seat belt matter.

A troublesome aspect of the matter is whether in the interest of fairness of trial, since if No. 4 and No. 18 were bad, No. 21 would also have been, plaintiff should be allowed to preserve her error and yet have the favorable aspects of the issue to which objection was being made. . . .

Rule 51, Fed. R. Civ. P., is quite explicit on the matter: "No party may assign as error the giving or the failure to give an instruction unless he objects thereto before the jury retires to consider its verdict, stating distinctly the matter to which he objects and the grounds of his objection."

In the case before us we are not unmindful that in sequence, Instruction No. 21 was the third instruction dealing with the matter of the seat belt defense and the court had already clearly indicated its intention to let the jury consider the matter. Counsel had already explicitly stated objections to the prior instructions and no doubt it would have appeared a fruitless exercise to have again advanced the same objections.

As is pointed out in *Sweeney v. United Feature Syndicate, Inc.,* 129 F.2d 904, 906 (2d Cir. 1942), the purpose of the exceptions is to inform the trial judge of possible errors so that he may have an opportunity to reconsider his rulings and, if necessary, correct them. In *Sweeney* the court pointed out that there was full discussion of the point raised which adequately informed the court as to what the plaintiff contended the law was and the entry of a formal exception thereafter would have been a mere technicality. The court points out that the cases construing Rule 51, Fed. R. Civ. P., strictly all involved situations where no indication was given to the judge that error would be assigned to his ruling.

We are also not unmindful of cases where notwithstanding an analysis reflecting that the issue of an instruction was not properly preserved on appeal, the court nevertheless would not rest the decision solely on that basis.

In *Richfield Oil Corp. v. Karseal Corp.,* 271 F.2d 709, 722 (9th Cir. 1959), *cert. denied,* 361 U.S. 961 (1960), going further than some courts, the court recognized that even though objections have been stated distinctly, it would have been unlikely to have caused the court to change its previously announced position, nevertheless, "to preserve the question, on appeal, not only should the objection have been made but the grounds thereof should have been distinctly stated." (Citations omitted.) The court then irrespective of this pronouncement stated that while the objections were not available to the appellant on appeal, the court would still consider the question as to whether the giving of the instruction was error.

We therefore consider whether the giving of Instructions Nos. 4, 18 and 21 constituted reversible error. . . .

Mays, 441 F.2d at 1351-52.

B. Unpreserved Errors Warranting Appellate Review

Except in courts like Pennsylvania's which refuse to review unpreserved errors under any circumstances, most courts have recognized that in most cases, trial attorneys do not fail to object to legal errors for improper strategic reasons, but rather through ignorance or inexperience or simply nervousness and confusion in the heat of trial. In such situations, completely barring a party from any chance to appeal a significant legal error because counsel has blundered seems unduly harsh. Accordingly, though strict preservation requirements are the rule, exceptions have been carved out both by statute and case law in certain situations. For the most part, these exceptions are made *ad hoc* with little discussion of the reason for granting the exception in the particular case. The United States Supreme Court has approved this procedure, stating that "[t]he matter of what questions may be taken up and resolved for the first time on appeal is one left primarily to the discretion of the Court of Appeals to be exercised on the facts of individual cases." *Singleton v. Wulff,* 428 U.S. 106, 121 (1976). Exceptions to preservation requirements, then, vary not only from court to court but from case to case, and the best advice for a lawyer faced with a substantial unpreserved error is not to abandon it as lost. Instead, appellate counsel should be prepared to spend time researching the preservation requirements of the particular court to determine whether the error is one that may be raised for the first time on appeal.

1. The Plain Error Rule

The major exception to the preservation requirement is the provision for reviewing for the first time on appeal "plain error" that affects substantial rights. Fed. R. Crim. P. 52(b) provides specifically that "[p]lain errors or defects affecting substantial rights may be noticed although they were not brought to the attention of the court." Fed. R. Evid. 103(d) contains a similar exception to the requirement of objections to evidentiary rulings in federal courts. Some states have also adopted plain error statutes. Even though no parallel rule exists in the Federal Rules of Civil Procedure, and many states provide no specific authorization, both state and federal appellate courts have developed the "plain error" doctrine in civil as well as criminal cases. This doctrine allows them "[i]n exceptional circumstances, . . . in the public interest" to "notice errors to which no exception has been taken, if the errors are obvious, or if they otherwise seriously affect the fairness, integrity or public reputation of judicial proceedings." *United States v. Atkinson,* 297 U.S. 157, 160 (1936).

Different courts have different views of what sort of errors "seriously affect the fairness" of a trial. In the following case, for example, the Supreme Court took a very narrow view of plain error in a case involving prosecutorial misconduct.

United States v. Young

470 U.S. 1 (1985)

Chief Justice BURGER delivered the opinion of the Court.

[The defendant was charged with a scheme to defraud an oil refinery. On summation, defense counsel made several remarks concerning the prosecutor's "reprehensible" conduct in the case. The prosecutor responded by giving his personal opinion as to the defendant's lack of veracity and guilt. Defense counsel failed to object to these remarks.]

On appeal, respondent alleged that he was unfairly prejudiced by the prosecutor's remarks made during closing rebuttal argument. In per curiam opinion, the Court of Appeals, one judge dissenting without opinion, reversed the conviction and remanded for retrial. The Court of Appeals held that the prosecutor's statements constituted misconduct and were sufficiently egregious to constitute plain error. In short, respondent's failure to ob-

ject at trial was held not to preclude appellate review. Rejecting the Government's contention that the statements were invited by the defense counsel's own closing argument, the Court of Appeals stated that "the rule is clear in this Circuit that improper conduct on the part of opposing counsel should be met with an objection to the court, not a similarly improper response." . . .

The principal issue to be resolved is not whether the prosecutor's response to defense counsel's misconduct was appropriate, but whether it was "plain error" that a reviewing court could act on absent a timely objection. Our task is to decide whether the standard laid down in *United States v. Atkinson,* 297 U.S. 157 (1936) and codified in Federal Rule of Criminal Procedure 52(b), was correctly applied by the Court of Appeals.

Nearly a half century ago this Court

counseled prosecutors "to refrain from improper methods calculated to produce a wrongful conviction. . . ." The Court made clear, however, that the adversary system permits the prosecutor to "prosecute with earnestness and vigor." In other words, "while he may strike hard blows, he is not at liberty to strike foul ones." . . .

It is clear that counsel on both sides of the table share a duty to confine arguments to the jury within proper bounds. Just as the conduct of prosecutors is circumscribed, "[t]he interests of society in the preservation of courtroom control by the judges are no more to be frustrated through unchecked improprieties by defenders." Defense counsel, like the prosecutor, must refrain from interjecting personal beliefs into the presentation of his case. Defense counsel, like his adversary, must not be permitted to make unfounded and inflammatory attacks on the opposing advocate.

The kind of advocacy shown by this record has no place in the administration of justice and should neither be permitted nor rewarded; a trial judge should deal promptly with any breach by either counsel . . . .

We emphasize that the trial judge has the responsibility to maintain decorum in keeping with the nature of the proceeding; "the judge is not a mere moderator, but is the governor of the trial for the purpose of assuring its proper conduct." The judge "must meet situations as they arise and [be able] to cope with . . . the contingencies inherent in the adversary process." Of course, "hard blows" cannot be avoided in criminal trials; both the prosecutor and defense counsel must be kept within appropriate bounds.

The situation brought before the Court of Appeals was but one example of an all too common occurrence in criminal trials – the defense counsel argues improperly, provoking the prosecutor to respond in kind, and the trial judge takes no corrective action. Clearly two improper arguments – two apparent wrongs – do not make for a right result. Nevertheless, a criminal conviction is not to be lightly overturned on the basis of a prosecutor's comments standing alone, for the statements or conduct must be viewed in context; only by so doing can it be determined whether the prosecutor's conduct affected the fairness of the trial. To help resolve this problem, courts have invoked what is sometimes called the "invited response" or "invited reply" rule, which the Court treated in *Lawn v. United States*, 355 U.S. 339 (1958).

The petitioners in *Lawn* sought to have the Court overturn their criminal convictions for income tax evasion on a number of grounds, one of which was that the prosecutor's closing argument deprived them of a fair trial. In his closing argument at trial, defense counsel in *Lawn* had attacked the Government for "persecuting" the defendants. He told the jury that the prosecution was instituted in bad faith at the behest of federal revenue agents and asserted that the Government's key witnesses were perjurers. The prosecutor in response vouched for the credibility of the challenged witnesses, telling the jury that the Government thought those witnesses testified truthfully. In concluding that the prosecutor's remarks, when viewed within the context of the entire trial, did not deprive petitioners of a fair trial, the Court pointed out that defense counsel's "comments clearly invited the reply." . . .

In order to make an appropriate assessment, the reviewing court must not only weigh the impact of the prosecutor's remarks, but must also take into account defense counsel's opening salvo. Thus the import of the evaluation has been that if the prosecutor's remarks were "invited," and did no more than respond substantially in order to "right the scale," such comments would not warrant reversing a conviction.

Courts have not intended by any means to encourage the practice of zealous counsel's going "out of bounds" in the manner of defense counsel here, or to encourage prosecutors to respond to the "invitation." Reviewing courts ought not to be put in the position of weighing which of two inappropriate arguments was the lesser. "Invited responses" can be effectively discouraged by prompt action from the bench in the form of corrective instructions to the jury, and when necessary, an admonition to the errant advocate.

Plainly, the better remedy in this case, at least with the accurate vision of hindsight, would have been for the District Judge to deal with the improper argument of the defense counsel promptly and thus blunt the need for the prosecutor to respond. Arguably defense counsel's misconduct could have warranted the judge to interrupt the argument and admonish him, thereby rendering the prosecutor's response unnecessary. Similarly, the prosecutor at the close of defense summation should have objected to the defense counsel's improper statements with a request that the court give a timely warning and curative instruction to the jury. Defense counsel, even though obviously vulnerable, could well have done likewise if he thought that the prosecutor's remarks were harmful to his client. Here neither counsel made a timely objection to preserve the issue for review. However, interruptions of arguments, either by an opposing counsel or the presiding judge, are matters to be approached cautiously. At the very least, a bench conference might have been convened out of the hearing of the jury once defense counsel closed, and an appropriate instruction given.

Here the Court of Appeals was not unaware of our holdings and those of other Circuits, but seemingly did not undertake to weigh the prosecutor's comments in context. The court acknowledged defense counsel's obvious misconduct, but it does not appear that this was given appropriate weight in evaluating the situation.
. . .

As we suggested earlier, the dispositive issue under the holdings of this Court is not whether the prosecutor's remarks amounted to error, but whether they rose to the level of "plain error" when he responded to defense counsel. In this setting and on this record the prosecutor's response – although error – was not "plain error" warranting the court to overlook the absence of any objection by the defense.

The plain error doctrine of Federal Rule of Criminal Procedure 52(b) tempers the blow of a rigid application of the contemporaneous-objection requirement. The Rule authorizes the Courts of Appeals to correct only "particularly egregious errors," *United States v. Frady,* 456 U.S. 152 (1982), those errors that "seriously affect the fairness, integrity or public reputation of judicial proceedings," *United States v. Atkinson,* 297 U.S. at 160. In other words, the plain-error exception to the contemporaneous-objection rule is to be "used sparingly, solely in those circumstances in which a miscarriage of justice would otherwise result." *United States v. Frady, supra,* at 163, n.14. Any unwarranted extension of this exacting definition of plain error would skew the Rule's "careful balancing of our need to encourage all trial participants to seek a fair and accurate trial the first time around against our insistence that obvious injustice be promptly redressed." Reviewing courts are not to use the plain-error doctrine to consider trial court errors not meriting appellate review absent timely objection – a practice which we have criticized as "extravagant protection."

Especially when addressing plain error, a reviewing court cannot properly evaluate a case except by viewing such a claim against the entire record. We have been reminded:

"In reviewing criminal cases, it is particularly important for appellate courts to relive the whole trial imaginatively and not to extract from episodes in isolation abstract questions of evidence and procedure. To turn a criminal trial into a quest for error no more promotes the ends of justice than to acquiesce in low standards of criminal prosecution." *Johnson v. United States,* 318 U.S. 189, 202 (1943) (Frankfurter, J., concurring).

It is simply not possible for an appellate court to assess the seriousness of the claimed error by any other means. As the Court stated in *United States v. Socony-Vacuum Oil Co.,* 310 U.S. at 240, "each case necessarily turns on its own facts."

When reviewed with these principles in mind, the prosecutor's remarks cannot be said to rise to the level of plain error. Viewed in context, the prosecutor's statements, although inappropriate and amounting to error, were not such as to undermine the fundamental fairness of the trial and contribute to a miscarriage of justice.[14]

---

[14] The Court of Appeals held that the prosecutor's improper remarks constituted "plain error" solely because the prosecutor ignored that court's rule prohibiting such responses. A *per se* approach to plain-error review is flawed. An error, of course, must be more than obvious or readily apparent in order to trigger appellate review under Federal Rule of Criminal Procedure 52(b). Following decisions such as *United States v. Frady, United States v. Socony-Vacuum Oil Co.,* and *United States v. Atkinson,* federal courts have consistently interpreted the plain-error doctrine as requiring an appellate court to find that the claimed error not only seriously affected "substantial rights," but that it had an unfair prejudicial impact on the jury's deliberations. Only then would the court be able to conclude that the error undermined the fairness of the trial and contributed to a miscarriage of justice. To do otherwise could well lead to having appellate courts indulge in the pointless exercise of reviewing "harmless plain errors" – a practice that is contrary to the draftsmen's intention behind Rule 52(b), and one that courts have studiously avoided and commentators have properly criticized. It should be noted that the Tenth Circuit seems to have retreated from its position

The prosecutor responded with his "personal impressio[n]" that respondent intended to commit a fraud to answer defense counsel's accusation that no member of the prosecution team believed that respondent intended to defraud Apco. Indeed, the prosecutor made a point to preface his statement by summarizing defense counsel's acerbic charge and candidly told the jury that he was giving his "personal impressions" because defense counsel had asked for them.

Notwithstanding the defense counsel's breach of ethical standards, the prosecutor's statement of his belief that the evidence showed Apco had been defrauded should not have been made; it was an improper expression of personal opinion and was not necessary to answer defense counsel's improper assertion that no one on the prosecution team believed respondent intended to defraud Apco. Nevertheless, we conclude that any potential harm from this remark was mitigated by the jury's understanding that the prosecutor was countering defense counsel's repeated attacks on the prosecution's integrity and defense counsel's argument that the evidence established no such crime.

Finally, the prosecutor's comments that respondent had not acted with "honor and integrity," and his calling attention to the jury's responsibility to follow the court's instructions were in response to defense counsel's rhetoric that respondent alone was the sole honorable actor in "this whole affair," and that the jury should not find respondent guilty simply because he could not understand applicable, but complex, federal regulations. The prosecutor was also in error to try to exhort the jury to "do its job"; that kind of pressure, whether by the prosecutor or defense counsel, has no place in the administration of criminal justice, *see,*

---

that improper prosecutorial remarks are *per se* "plain error." *Mason v. United States,* 719 F.2d 1485, 1489-90 (1983).

e.g., ABA Standard for Criminal Justice, 3-5.8(c) and 4-7.8(c). Given the context of the prosecutor's remarks and defense counsel's broadside attack, however, we conclude that the jury was not influenced to stray from its responsibility to be fair and unbiased.[15]

The concerns underlying our reactions against improper prosecutorial arguments to the jury are implicated here, but not to the extent that we conclude that the jury's deliberations were compromised. The prosecutor's vouching for the credibility of witnesses and expressing his personal opinion concerning the guilt of the accused pose two dangers: such comments can convey the impression that evidence not presented to the jury, but known to the prosecutor, supports the charges against the defendant and can thus jeopardize the defendant's right to be tried solely on the basis of the evidence presented to the jury; and the prosecutor's opinion carries with it the imprimatur of the Government and may induce the jury to trust the Government's judgment rather than its own view of the evidence.

The prosecutor's statement of his belief that respondent intended to commit a fraud contained no suggestion that he was relying on information outside the evidence presented at trial. He supported his comment by referring to respondent's own testimony that Compton received 85 cents a barrel for its deliveries to Apco and that respondent personally received a bonus of one percent of Compton's net profits; he then summarized portions of the evidence adduced at trial before suggesting to the jury that the record established the fraud charged. Although it was improper for the prosecutor to express

---

[15] The jury acquitted respondent of the most serious charge he faced, interstate transportation of stolen property. This reinforces our conclusion that the prosecutor's remarks did not undermine the jury's ability to view the evidence independently and fairly.

his personal opinion about respondent's guilt, when viewed in context, the prosecutor's remarks cannot be read as implying that the prosecutor had access to evidence outside the record. The jury surely understood the comment for what it was - a defense of his decision and his integrity - in bringing criminal charges on the basis of the very evidence the jury had heard during the trial.

Finally, the overwhelming evidence of respondent's intent to defraud Apco and submit false oil certifications to the Government eliminates any lingering doubt that the prosecutor's remarks unfairly prejudiced the jury's deliberations or exploited the Government's prestige in the eyes of the jury. Not a single witness supported respondent's asserted defense that fuel oil mixed with condensate could be certified and sold as crude oil, and several witnesses flatly rejected such a proposition. Indeed, respondent's crude oil trader testified that he had never heard of a firm legally blending fuel oil with condensate and stating that the mixture was crude oil. It was undisputed that respondent failed to advise Apco of what he was actually supplying and that the oil supplied did not meet the contract requirements.

Moreover, the evidence established beyond any doubt whatever that respondent deliberately concealed his scheme to defraud Apco. Apart from enlisting the aid of an oil brokerage firm to "recertify" the fuel oil as crude oil, respondent on three separate occasions, when questioned by two Apco officials and by FBI agents, falsely denied that he was supplying fuel oil instead of crude oil. Under these circumstances, the substantial and virtually uncontradicted evidence of respondent's willful violation provides an additional indication that the prosecutor's remarks, when reviewed in context, cannot be said to undermine the fairness of the trial and contribute to a miscarriage of justice.

Notes

1. Appellate courts in the various jurisdictions have formulated the plain error rule in many different ways. The Illinois courts, for example, permit first-time consideration on appeal "when the question of guilt is close and the evidence in question might have significantly affected the outcome of the case or where error alleged is so substantial as to reflect on the fairness or impartiality of the trial regardless of how closely balanced the evidence is." *People v. Sanders*, 99 Ill.2d 262, 457 N.E.2d 1241, 1246, 75 Ill. Dec. 682 (1983). In New York, fundamental constitutional errors, most importantly denial of the right to counsel, may be raised for the first time on appeal. *People v. Arthur*, 22 N.Y.2d 325, 239 N.E.2d 537, 292 N.Y.S.2d 663 (1968). The willingness of a court to review unpreserved "plain errors" depends in part on whether it perceives its primary duty to be to correct legal errors or to reach a just result in a particular case.

2. In criminal cases, an attorney who finds a serious unpreserved error may have the option of arguing that the defendant was deprived of his constitutional right to effective representation of counsel. This is a difficult argument to win because an attorney's conduct has to be very bad indeed before a court will find that it was ineffective as a matter of law. Nevertheless, the issue both substantively and procedurally may be worth investigating.

3. Some courts that acknowledge the plain error rule are nevertheless reluctant to apply it in civil cases. The Supreme Court of North Carolina, for example, has held that the plain error doctrine does not apply at all to appeals in civil cases. *Durham v. Quincy Mut. Fire Ins. Co.*, 317 S.E.2d 372 (N.C. 1984). The Court of Appeals for the Seventh Circuit has also distinguished between civil and criminal cases as a basis for deciding whether to review plain errors. *Parrett v. City of Connersville, Inc.*, 737 F.2d 690 (7th Cir. 1984).

2. Interest Of Justice Jurisdiction

Some appellate courts, usually intermediate state courts, have explicit statutory authority to reach unpreserved issues "in the interest of justice." For example, New York's Criminal Procedure law provides:

§470.15 Determination of appeals by intermediate appellate courts; scope of review

1. Upon an appeal to an intermediate appellate court from a judgment, sentence or order of a criminal court, such intermediate appellate court may consider and determine any question of law or issue of fact involving error or defect in the criminal court proceedings which may have adversely affected the appellant.

* * *

3. A reversal or a modification of a judgment, sentence or order must be based upon a determination made:

(a) Upon the law; or

(b) Upon the facts; or

(c) As a matter of discretion in the interest of justice; or

(d) Upon any two or all three of the bases specified in paragraphs (a), (b) and (c).

* * *

6. The kinds of determinations of reversal or modification deemed to be made as a matter of discretion in the interest of justice include, but are not limited to, the following:

(a) That an error or defect occurring at a trial resulting in a judgment, which error or defect was not duly protested at trial . . . so as to present a question of law, deprived the defendant of a fair trial. . . .

Under this provision, a New York attorney finding an unpreserved error in a criminal case can make the same arguments to the Appellate Division that would have been made had there been an objection. Instead of asking the court to decide the issue "as a matter of law," however, legal error being defined as one to which an objection has been lodged, the lawyer would request the court to reverse the judgment "in the interest of justice."

Although a court may have interest of justice jurisdiction it is still preferable to raise an issue as a matter of law whenever possible and to invoke interest of justice jurisdiction only as a fall-back position. The reason for this strategy is simply that, as a practical matter, the attorney who calls upon a court to exercise its interest of justice jurisdiction must be prepared with a convincing argument that a reversal will in fact be in the interest of justice, which is often a difficult task. While an appellate court, even in an obviously correctly decided case, may be willing to reverse for a sufficiently serious legal error, it is unlikely to find that justice requires it to grant a new trial to a clearly guilty defendant who never bothered to object to a claimed error at trial. Moreover, a decision of the intermediate appellate court "in the interest of justice" precludes further appeals to a higher court which can consider only legal issues. The following case illustrates the typical response of a court asked to act in the interest of justice.

People v. Cornish

43 A.D.2d 103, 349 N.Y.S.2d 694 (N.Y. App. Div. 1973)

STEUER, Justice.

Defendant was convicted after trial of possession of a weapon as a felony and prohibited use of weapons. Proof at the trial left no doubt whatever of defendant's guilt and there is no claim on this appeal that it did. However, it appears that defendant testified on his own behalf. The Assistant District Attorney's cross-examination is claimed to be prejudicial as to three aspects of inquiry. As to the first, defendant's em-

ployment, the defendant had testified on direct and the cross-examination was not improper. As to the two others, involving falsification of an income tax return and an assault, for neither of which the defendant was indicted, his categorical denials should have concluded inquiry. However, the matter was pressed and the defendant confronted with documentary evidence.

But as to these, not only was there no objection, but the court invited objection from defense counsel and the invitation was refused. We are asked to reverse nevertheless in "the interests of justice." This naturally raises the question of just what are the interests of justice in such a situation. If justice is more interested in a technically perfect trial than in one in which a proper result is reached, then the interests of justice would indicate a reversal. Here we have no way of knowing what prompted counsel to allow the improper testimony to pass without objection. He might well, in the absence of any other viable contention, have hoped to capitalize on the District Attorney's over zealousness to obtain a sympathetic response from the jury. But, whatever may be the reason, we cannot see that an appellate court is required to overlook the omission where guilt is clear.

The judgment should be affirmed.

Notes

1. One issue that can always be raised for the first time on appeal is a challenge to the subject matter jurisdiction of the trial court. The theory behind this exception to the preservation requirement is that if the trial court lacked jurisdiction, then it had no power to act regardless of the wishes of the parties, and any judgment it rendered was a nullity. An issue may therefore have a better chance of success if it is framed as a challenge to a court's jurisdiction than if it is argued simply as an error on the part of the trial judge. In *People v. Caban*, 129 A.D.2d 721, 514 N.Y.S.2d 483 (N.Y.App.Div. 1987), the appellate lawyer may have hoped in this manner to get around trial counsel's failure to move to dismiss the indictment. The court was unpersuaded:

> The defendant waived his objection that the indictment was duplicitous by failing to raise the issue before the trial court. While a claim that an indictment is jurisdictionally defective may be raised for the first time on appeal "an indictment is jurisdictionally defective only if it does not effectively charge the defendant with the commission of a particular crime." A claim that an indictment is duplicitous (CPL 200.30[1]) is not directed to the failure of any count to effectively charge the defendant with the commission of a crime, but rather to the fact that it effectively charges him with the commission of more than one crime. Thus, the defendant's failure to raise the issue of duplicity at the trial level precludes him from raising it on appeal.

2. Some courts have allowed some "quasi-jurisdictional" issues to be raised for the first time on appeal, such as, for example, the state's immunity from suit under the Eleventh Amendment. *Della Grotta v. Rhode Island*, 781 F.2d 343 (1st Cir. 1986). In addition, a number of appellate courts make an exception allowing "purely legal issues" requiring no fact development to be raised for the first time on appeal. In *United States v. Dann*, 706 F.2d 919 (9th Cir. 1983), for example, the Court of Appeals agreed to review the statutory interpretation of a provision of the Indian Claims Act.

The court said:

> We acknowledge that the Danns did not contest in the district court the government's assertion that payment was now "automatic." The Government first

raised this "automatic payment" argument in its third supplemental memorandum to the district court, long after the district court had taken the parties' cross-motions for summary judgment under advisement. Normally an appellant may not present arguments in this court that it did not properly raise below, but application of that rule is discretionary. It is well settled in this circuit that where the new issue is purely a legal one, the injection of which would not have caused the parties to develop new or different facts, we may resolve it on appeal. The question here is purely one of statutory construction that is both central to this case and important to the public.

Exercise

Following is an excerpt from a criminal trial of a defendant charged with assault. On direct examination, the prosecutor elicited from the complainant that he had seen the defendant once before, two weeks prior to the assault, when the defendant had tried to sell a watch on the street. Over defense objection, the prosecutor then elicited the details of the previous encounter as follows:

A.   My friend was at a corner grocery store talking with some other guys and he come up, the accused, he come up with a black watch, a battery watch.

[Following an off-the-record discussion, defense counsel's objection was overruled.]

Q.   Please continue describing the encounter . . .

A.   Okay. He come up with a black watch in his hand. He asked a guy if he wanted to buy it.

Q.   If he wanted to what?

A.   To buy the watch. He wanted to know from this guy if he wanted to buy the watch.

The guy said no.

My friend took the watch and said, how much do you want for it?

DEFENSE COUNSEL: Objection. I think it is irrelevant, the exact conversation that occurred two weeks prior to the incident.

If he's going into it for the purpose of identification –

THE COURT: If there was a discussion, I tend to agree with defense counsel that the details at this point are irrelevant . . .

On appeal, defendant made the following argument that this cross-examination was improper:

First, on direct examination of the complainant, the prosecutor specifically elicited the details of an incident unrelated to the crime at issue, which occurred some two weeks earlier, in which defendant had tried to sell a watch. The court eventually recognized that the details of this encounter were irrelevant to identification or any other issue in the case. Yet, it initially overruled defense counsel's objection, with the result that the jurors heard enough about the watch incident to create the clear impression that defendant – who had apparently approached a group of relative strangers on the street and tried to sell them a watch – was selling stolen property.

In *People v. Rivera,* 82 A.D.2d 892 (1st Dept. 1982), the First Department found improper the admission of evidence that a defendant charged with a robbery threw away a bag containing a watch unrelated to the crime when the police approached him. The court found that the evidence "could only have had the effect of leaving the jury with the impression that defendant had committed a similar but uncharged crime." Although the jury had been told to disregard the evidence, the court reversed the conviction.

Similarly here, the suggestion that defendant was selling a stolen watch only two weeks before his purported theft of money and a watch from the complainant could only have left the jury with the impression that appellant had committed a similar uncharged crime. The prejudice to appellant was obvious. Moreover, in the instant case, the jurors were never even told to disregard this testimony.

If you were the prosecutor what argument would you make that the issue was not preserved?

Chapter 4

Standards of Review

Introduction

The attorney who has followed the procedures described in Chapter 2 has established a right to be in the appellate court. The attorney has neither forfeited the right by tardy filings, nor jumped the gun by appealing from a non-final order that is not immediately appealable. By paying attention to the materials in Chapter 3, counsel has identified an issue or issues within the appellate court's review powers. In order to obtain the desired relief for the client, however, the appellate attorney must do more than be in the right court at the right time with an issue properly before the court. Simply presenting the client's substantive arguments to the court may not suffice to secure a favorable outcome. Counsel must carefully examine the often critical issue of what standard of review the appellate court will use in evaluating the claims brought before it. In extreme cases the applicable standard can affect the decision about whether to take the appeal at all, and it should have a profound impact on the attorney's decisions about which issues to concentrate on and how to frame the arguments in the brief.

One way of looking at the question of what standard of review will be used on appeal is to focus on the degree of deference to be given to the initial decision-maker. On questions of law, the decisions of the trial judge are generally given no deference whatever; the appellate court will determine these issues _de novo,_ or independently. On questions of fact, on the other hand, the decisions of the trial judge or jury are given considerable deference. On decisions that have been committed to the trial court's discretion, the degree of deference will vary according to the issue presented.

These different standards of review reflect the appropriate functions of appellate courts, which are often entirely different from those of trial courts. The primary function of appellate courts is correction of legal error, or in some cases development of the law in light of changing conditions. Thus an appellate court is most likely to reverse a decision below if the trial court made erroneous rulings of law that may have had a significant impact on the outcome. Appellate courts are unlikely, on the other hand, to reverse factual determinations, especially when trial is by jury. Decisions about questions of fact, as long as they are made in the proper legal framework, will generally be considered to have been properly determined by the trial court.

Apart from decisions concerning the law and determinations of fact, judges make countless determinations before, during and after a trial that fall within their discretion. As to such determinations, the appellate court's assessment of whether a decision falling within a range of discretion warrants reversal will depend on the type of issue being reviewed, as well as on the factors entering into the trial judge's exercise of, or failure to exercise, discretion.

The situations at the extremes give clear signals to the appellate advocate about how to approach the case – or whether to advise the client against the appeal altogether. The attorney seeking a reversal is in the best position when raising a question of law; by contrast, the appellate standard of review for questions of fact is extremely limited. The vast majority of issues, however, are somewhere in the middle, and here the attorney's task of ascertaining the proper standard of review, and framing the issues so as best to take advantage of the likely standard, is much more difficult.[1] The rest of the materials in this Chapter are designed to provide an introduction to the language and principles applicable to the standards of review most likely to be encountered by appellate lawyers.

De Novo Review of Questions of Law

In order to determine the appropriate standard of review, the advocate must first correctly classify the decision below. As the following case shows, if the judge's determination was a ruling based on the law, it is subject to *de novo* review.

---

[1] Not only is it sometimes tricky to determine whether an issue presents a pure question of law, or whether it is mixed with questions of fact as to which a different standard may apply, but the terminology used by courts in assessing the relevant standard can be inconsistent and confusing. And to add to the problems, one gets the distinct impression that discussions of the standard of review may at times be window dressing – a way for the court to arrive at the desired outcome without grappling with the substantive issue.

Schoenbein v. Board of Trustees of Police Pension Fund

65 Ill. App. 2d 379, 212 N.E.2d 380 (1965)

STOUDER, Justice.

This is an appeal from a judgment of the Circuit Court of Tazewell County reversing an order of the Board of Trustees of the Police Pension Fund of the Village of Morton.

The Conservator of the estate of Bruce Schoenbein, incompetent, hereinafter referred to as Appellee, commenced this action by filing a petition for a pension with the Board of Trustees of the Police Pension Fund of the Village of Morton, hereinafter referred to as Appellant. The facts as shown by the petition and evidence are not in dispute. Likewise no question of procedure is involved.

Appellee was appointed policeman by the Village of Morton in 1956 and served as such until December, 1962. In 1960 the Village of Morton by ordinance provided for a "Police Pension Fund System" as authorized by statute. All policemen then employed became entitled to participate in the pension program regardless of age at first appointment and regardless of physical condition. Appellee being a policeman at the time of the adoption of the ordinance became entitled to its benefits without examination or further qualification. Appellee made regular contributions to the pension fund until March, 1963. In December, 1962 Appellee, by reason of mental illness, was unable to perform his duties as a policeman. Thereafter in January, 1963 he was committed to a state hospital for treatment. . . . On June 10, 1963, Appellee filed his petition for pension and a hearing was held thereon in September, 1963. The evidence of four witnesses was considered by the Board in behalf of Appellee. Three of the witnesses were doctors and they each testified that Appellee was mentally ill to the extent that he was incompetent to perform his duties as a policeman. No evidence was presented concerning any other condition affecting Appellee's state of health. The fourth witness, the Appellee's brother and conservator, testified that Appellee had been gainfully employed as a hod carrier and farm laborer since his release from the hospital on March 7, 1963, until the time of the hearing, the doctors at the hospital having recommended physical labor as treatment for Appellee's mental illness. At the conclusion of the hearing the Board found that Appellee had failed to prove that he was "physically disabled" as required by statute and denied his claim for a pension.

Appellee filed a complaint in the Circuit Court of Tazewell County under the provisions of the Administrative Review Act seeking to reverse the order of the Board. The Court, after reviewing the record, found that Appellee was not mentally fit to perform the duties of a policeman and therefore became physically disabled to an extent necessitating his suspension from the police force. The Court thereupon reversed the order of the Board and granted Appellee's pension and it is from this judgment that Appellant appeals.

Appellant in seeking to reverse the decision of the Court below contends that the Court erroneously interpreted the statutory requirement that a policeman be "physically disabled" in order to be entitled to a pension under section 10-8-7, Chapter 24, Illinois Revised Statutes 1961 which is as follows: "Whenever any member of a regularly constituted police force in any such city, village or incorporated town, becomes physically disabled to such an extent as to necessitate the suspending of performance of his duty on such police force, or retirement from the police force, he shall be paid from the fund a pension of one half of the salary attached to the rank he held on the police force for one year immediately prior to the time of his so suspending performance of his duty or retirement. Whenever such disability ceases and the policeman resumes the performance of his duty on the police force such pension shall cease. . . ." Appellant contends that this provision is clear and unambiguous and does not include a policeman who is "mentally unfit" or "mentally disabled."

The sole question before us is what meaning shall be ascribed to the phrase "physically disabled." The facts not being in dispute, their legal effect becomes a matter of law and the rule as to the power of the court to set aside the decision only when it was made against the manifest weight of the evidence has no application. . . .

In determining the meaning of a statute a primary rule of construction is that words are to be given their plain ordinary meaning. Where the legislature has expressed itself in clear unambiguous language the plain meaning of the words so employed cannot be disregarded.

Dictionaries define "physical" as "of or pertaining to the body" and "mental" as "of or pertaining to the mind," the words are therefore words of distinction or opposition. The words physical or mental are used in ordinary language to refer to distinct and different parts or aspects of a person. The language of the witnesses for Appellee is of especial pertinence in this respect. Each of the . . . witnesses by their language recognized the distinction and differences between "physical disability" and "mental disability" and each concluded that Appellant was not "physically disabled" and was not physically impaired. . . .

The provisions of a police pension act are necessarily the function of the legislature. It is not within the province of the courts to determine what the legislature might have done or should have done, but only what it has done.

It is our conclusion that the legislature has expressed itself clearly and unambiguously in requiring that a policeman become "physically disabled" before he is entitled to a pension. We find nothing in the letter, spirit or intent of the statutes applicable to or supporting Appellee's contentions. Appellee has failed to prove that he was physically disabled and accordingly the order of the Trustees of the Police Pension Fund of the Village of Morton denying Appellee's pension was correct and should have been sustained by the Court below. Finding error in the judgment of the Circuit Court of Tazewell County the judgment is reversed.

CORYN, Justice (dissenting).

I do not agree with the majority opinion in this case, as I am of the opinion that their interpretation of the words "physical disability" as used in the Police Pension Fund Act, Ch. 24 § 10-8-7, Ill. Rev. Stat. 1961, is too narrow and not within the spirit and intent of said statute. Some emphasis has been placed on dictionary definitions of these words in the majority opinion. The correct definition, in my opinion, is to be found in Black's Law Dictionary, Fourth Edition, on page 548, which states: "A physical disability is a disability or incapacity caused by physical defect or infirmity, or mental weakness or alienation. . . ." This definition recognizes that the human mind, limbs, organs, etc., are all parts of the whole, that is, the body, and that physical disability means impairment of any part of the body. That this broader definition of the term "physical disability" was intended by the legislature is even more evident when we consider that mental incapacity often results from illness or injury to parts of the body other than the brain. . . . In my opinion, mental illness or injury, and resulting disability, is within the meaning and intent of that section of the Police Pension Fund Act providing for disability benefits to a policeman who is "physically disabled to such an extent as to necessitate the suspending of performance of his duty on such police force."

The order of the Circuit Court of Tazewell
County granting the plaintiff a disability
pension should be affirmed.

Notes

1. The United States Supreme Court again confirmed that all questions of law must be reviewed *de novo* by appellate courts in *Salve Regina College v. Russell,* 111 S. Ct. 1217 (1991). The case involved a decision by a district court, sitting in diversity jurisdiction, that rested on a particular interpretation of the relevant Rhode Island state law. The court of appeals had granted some deference to the district court's determination of Rhode Island's substantive law, apparently on the basis that district judges are better arbiters of unsettled state law because of their greater exposure to the judicial system of the state. The Supreme Court rejected that reasoning, and remanded the case to the court of appeals for *de novo* review. The Court reiterated the rationale for the rule that questions of law are to be decided independently by appellate courts: promotion of doctrinal coherence and economy of judicial administration. The Court noted that courts of appeals, with multi-judge panels, are structurally suited to the collaborative process that promotes accuracy in decision-making, devote their primary attention to legal issues, and benefit from more detailed briefing and argument focused on the particular questions before the court than is customary in trial courts.

2. It is the province of the appellate court to decide whether a particular finding is factual or legal, regardless of how the trial court might have characterized the issue. The Supreme Court of California, in *Bennett v. Forrest,* 24 Cal.2d 485, 150 P.2d 416 (1944), rejected a party's attempt to bind the appellate court to the trial judge's finding, which was phrased in factual terms, that a probate decree was not *res judicata*:

> As we have seen all of the factors necessary to make the decree of distribution available as a bar were found. The ultimate conclusion of whether it was *res judicata* was one of law rather than fact. . . . [I]t is nothing more than a legal conclusion from the facts found, a matter upon which this court is at liberty to draw the correct conclusion to support the judgment.

150 P.2d at 420.

3. An appellate court may disagree, not only with the trial court's characterization of an issue as either factual or legal, but with the characterization of appellate counsel. Counsel will not help the client's cause by mislabeling a legal question as a question of fact, or vice versa, and thereby adopting an inappropriate standard of review. The court's attitude towards appellant's argument may well be affected by such a mistake:

> Initially, we note that while plaintiffs assert that the decision of the Director of Labor was against the manifest weight of the evidence, the relevant facts

here which concern the question as to whether a lockout includes a "constructive lockout" are not disputed and, by reason thereof, their legal effect becomes a matter of law.

Local 7-641, Oil, Chemical & Atomic Workers v. Dept. of Labor, 106 Ill. App. 3d 476, 435 N.E.2d 1192, 1194 (1982).

4. It is not always obvious, however, whether the judge's decision amounted to an interpretation of the law, or whether it involved a finding of fact so as to place it in a category in which some deference should be granted to the trial court. For example, in *Icicle Seafoods, Inc. v. Worthington,* 475 U.S. 709 (1986), a district court had determined that engineers working on board a nonself-propelled fish-processing barge are "seamen" for purposes of the Fair Labor Standards Act. The Court of Appeals for the Ninth Circuit reversed, finding that the judge had made an erroneous legal ruling in defining the term "seamen." The United States Supreme Court, in turn, reversed the Ninth Circuit, holding that the ruling was a factual finding about what work the engineers actually performed on the barge. The Supreme Court chided the Court of Appeals for applying the wrong standard of review when, using a *de novo* standard, it determined that the engineers were *not* seamen. Justice Stevens, dissenting, saw the issue as a legal question – what is the proper definition of "seamen" under the statute – which the Court of Appeals had properly decided and then applied to the undisputed facts.

If it is unclear how a question will be categorized, the best course is to be forthright with the court. Appellant's counsel, in trying to persuade the court to review the issue *de novo,* will likely be more successful by including an argument that the case indeed presents a question of law than by simply assuming that the court will necessarily see it that way.

Appellate Review of the Facts

When faced with disputed factual issues, appellate courts give substantial deference to the decision made in the trial court. The trier of the facts, whether judge or jury, who saw and heard the witnesses in person, is in the best position to assess their credibility. In addition, the judge or jury received the trial evidence in a relatively short, concentrated period, providing the opportunity to integrate the various pieces in a coherent way. Appellate courts, faced only with the transcript of the trial, are therefore generally hesitant to substitute their own interpretation of the facts for that arrived at by the trial judge or jury.

A. Jury Trials

1. Civil Cases

When the trial is held before a jury, considerable deference is granted to the necessary factual components of any verdict rendered. In federal court, the constitutional provision contained in the Seventh Amendment that "no fact tried by a jury shall be otherwise re-examined in any court of the United States, than according to the rules of the common law" operates to place substantial constraints on reversal of a jury's decision. In most states, a similar constitutional or statutory guarantee of a jury trial protects jury decisions on factual issues from reversal by appellate courts.

Even jury verdicts are not sacrosanct, however. If the verdict is unsupported by *any* evidence, an appellate court is empowered, and indeed may be obligated, to reverse.[2] The courts will not protect a judgment secured from an irrational jury despite the absence of any evidence to support the verdict.

Where there is *some* evidence supporting the verdict, the appellate court's review of the facts can be more probing only if trial counsel made timely and appropriate motions to challenge the sufficiency of the evidence. Generally, to obtain appellate review of the weight of the evidence, or of the question whether the verdict was supported by substantial evidence, counsel must have made a motion for a directed verdict at the close of all the evidence in the case, *see e.g.* Fed. R. Civ. P. 50(a), along with a post-trial motion for judgment notwithstanding the verdict (j.n.o.v.), *see e.g.* Fed. R. Civ. P. 50(b), or a post-trial motion for a new trial on the grounds that the verdict was against the weight of the evidence, *see e.g.* Fed. R. Civ. P. 59(a).[3] Although the trial court's decision on motions directed at the factual support for a particular verdict is said to be within the trial judge's discretion, subject to review only for abuse of that discretion (see the discussion of Review of Matters Within Trial Court's Discretion, *infra*), appellate courts scrutinize carefully orders *granting* such motions in order to preserve the parties' right to a jury trial. *See e.g. Spurling v. General Motors Corp.,* 528 F.2d 612 (5th Cir. 1976). If the trial court grants any of the motions challenging the evidentiary basis for the verdict, the appellate court must examine the evidence to decide whether interference with the jury's verdict was warranted. The appellate court's review will be more probing if the trial judge has directed a verdict or granted j.n.o.v. than if a new trial has been ordered, since the former deprives the party of a decision by any jury, while the latter gives the losing party an opportunity to persuade another set of jurors. The test for review of a directed verdict or j.n.o.v., stated in different ways by different courts, is often described as a reasonableness test: could a rational trier of facts, taking the evidence in the light most favorable to the verdict, have arrived at that conclusion? Review of the grant of a motion for a new trial has been described as an inquiry into whether the verdict was against the *great* weight of the evidence.[4] If the motions are denied, the appellate court's review will be even more deferential,

---

[2] *See Little v. Bankers Life & Casualty Co.,* 426 F.2d 509, 511 (5th Cir. 1970).

[3] Such motions can, of course, also be made on the ground that legal error occurred during the trial that infected the verdict. For the purposes of the present discussion of review of facts, only motions attacking the adequacy of the *factual* basis for the jury's verdict are pertinent.

[4] *See, e.g.,* Shows v. Jamison Bedding, Inc., 671 F.2d 927, 930 (5th Cir. 1982).

since the trial judge's decision was in harmony with the verdict of the jury.

In the following cases, the two circuit courts treat quite differently the orders of the district courts that had set aside jury verdicts. In *Connell,* the Federal Circuit affirmed the granting of a motion for judgment notwithstanding the verdict despite objections based on Seventh Amendment grounds. In the *Jacobs Manufacturing* case, on the other hand, the Eighth Circuit was unpersuaded that the trial court's refusal to give effect to the jury's decision was appropriate.

Connell v. Sears, Roebuck & Co.

722 F.2d 1542 (Fed. Cir. 1983)

MARKEY, Chief Judge.

[The jury in this patent infringement action had found Connell's patent for a hair "teasing and unsnarling implement" to be valid, despite defendant's claim that the patent was invalid for obviousness considering several prior art patents in the field. The trial court, in granting j.n.o.v., as well as the reviewing appellate court, found that "the jury's conclusion of nonobviousness was without factual foundation supported by substantial evidence."]

Jury verdicts must be treated with great deference. The Seventh Amendment to the Constitution preserves the right to trial by jury in suits at common law and also provides that United States Courts shall not reexamine facts tried by jury except under the rules of common law. With the merger of law and equity, denial of the right in certain types of cases ceased. Permitting the jury to draw legal conclusions based on the jury's fact findings and reached in light of instructions on the law has been preserved as part of the right. The court, though it remains ultimately responsible for upholding the law applicable to the facts found, cannot substitute its view for that of the jury when to do so would be an effective denial of the right to trial by jury.

Deference due a jury's fact findings in a civil case is not so great, however, as to require acceptance of findings where, as here, those findings are clearly and unquestionably not supported by substantial evidence. To so hold would be to render a trial and the submission of evidence a farce.

Following a civil jury trial, a jury may return a naked general verdict for one of the parties. That verdict involves a presumption that the jury found the facts and reached the legal conclusions undergirding its verdict. That practice leaving a wide area of uncertainty on review, appellate judges have expressed grave concern over use of the general verdict in civil cases. Still, there are safeguards and alternatives. Rule 49(a) Fed. R. Civ. P., provides for special verdicts in which the jury answers specific fact questions. Rule 49(b) provides for general verdicts accompanied by the jury's answers to interrogatories. Rule 50(a) provides for a directed verdict at the close of the case presented by one side. Rule 50(b) provides for a judgment notwithstanding the jury's verdict such as that with which we here deal. Rule 51 provides for instructions to the jury on the law to guide its conclusions on legal questions. Rule 52 makes clear that the court must make its own fact findings and reach its own conclusions of law when sitting with an advisory jury. Rule 59(a) provides for a new trial on many grounds, including a determination that a jury had reached its verdict as a result of passion and prejudice. In sum, the right to trial by jury in a civil case carries with it a number of procedural safeguards insuring the parties and the system against an improper outcome that might result from a posited unruly or "rogue elephant" jury. The rules have thus strengthened the right by insuring the reliability of jury verdicts.

Jacobs Manufacturing Co. v. Sam Brown Co.

19 F.3d 1259 (8th Cir. 1994)

FAGG, Circuit Judge.

This lawsuit arises from the breakdown of a distributor relationship between the Jacobs Manufacturing Company (Jacobs), a manufacturer of truck engine brakes, and Sam Brown Company (Brown), its largest distributor. After the relationship ended, Jacobs brought this diversity action for its unpaid account balance, and Brown counterclaimed asserting Jacobs made fraudulent and negligent misrepresentations. Brown appeals the district court's order granting judgment as a matter of law (JAML) to Jacobs. We affirm in part and reverse in part.

I

In 1976 Jacobs's representatives approached Brown's chief executive officer (CEO) to solicit Brown as a Jacobs distributor. Brown's CEO expressed concern about the distributorship agreement's one-year term and Jacobs's right to sell directly to original equipment manufacturers. The representatives responded the agreement would last a "lifetime" if Brown performed well, the only original equipment manufacturer integrating Jacobs's products in Brown's territory would be Brown's account, and Jacobs would refer to Brown all original equipment manufacturer inquiries from Brown's exclusive territory. Assured this oral understanding was also part of the agreement, Brown's CEO signed the annual distributorship agreement. Brown became Jacobs's top distributor in North America. Each year after 1976, Jacobs sent Brown a new agreement with a letter from Jacobs's general sales manager stating that he was "sure [their] continued association [would] be long term and mutually beneficial." Brown signed the agree-

ments each year until 1984. Jacobs repeatedly reassured Brown it would be a long-term distributor and promised to inform Brown about any developments affecting Brown's distributorship and expansion effort. With borrowed money, Brown invested more than one million dollars in developing its Jacobs distributorship to comply with Jacobs request that Brown have suitable physical facilities and trained service personnel available around the clock.

Contrary to its representations to Brown, Jacobs was considering changes to its distribution system. As early as 1974, Jacobs's five-year marketing plan called for an analysis of the advantages of directly marketing and servicing its products. In 1979, Jacobs hired a consultant to develop alternative distribution plans. Without disclosing this purpose, Jacobs's vice president asked Brown to give the consultant unlimited access to Brown's premises and business records. The vice president told Brown the reason for the consultant's visit was to allow the consultant to find out how a Jacobs distributor operated. With Brown's cooperation, the consultant obtained knowledge of Brown's production and marketing practices and other confidential information, but assured Brown the information would not be disclosed.

Later, in June 1981, Jacobs received a commissioned report from a different consulting firm, Bain and Company. The Bain report stated that "with a very carefully staged, time-phased program, Jacobs could gradually eliminate almost all of the distributors." The Bain report recommended that Jacobs pursue the fleet program, eliminate the original equipment manufacturer distributor segment first, bring the distributor role in-house, and fully eliminate all external distributor segments by 1984. The report warned that to avoid loss of sales, goodwill, and image, distributors would have to be kept in place until Jacobs had its own direct sales system ready. A few days after receiving the Bain report, Jacobs executives studied the report at a hotel.

In July 1981, a month after receiving the Bain report, Jacobs encouraged Brown to continue financially supporting its Jacobs distributorship through a trucking industry recession that began in May 1980, promising Brown would be rewarded by future business when the recession ended. Jacobs's regional representative also assured Brown that their relationship was "like a marriage" and the distributorship would "go on and on." In September 1981, however, Jacobs's in-house counsel sent a written inquiry to a Jacobs executive asking whether Jacobs was "still considering a change in its distribution system [that] will enable Jacobs to go direct and eliminate all distributors and middlemen."

Behind its false front of assurances to Brown, Jacobs began to implement the Bain report's recommendations. In 1982 Jacobs started a program of direct sales to Brown's truck fleet customers. After Brown sent Jacobs a letter complaining about the program, Jacobs responded that the new program was merely a special promotion. Jacobs reassured Brown that Jacobs's short-range and long-range marketing strategies were not affected and that distributors would continue as the backbone of Jacobs's sales effort. Despite its assurances, however, Jacobs was analyzing a "Single Price Strategy" under which Jacobs would sell its products directly to any customer at the same price Jacobs charged its distributors, destroying the value of the distributorships. Nonetheless, Jacobs continued to urge Brown to maintain its distribution efforts through the recession, claiming both companies would benefit when the market rebounded. Jacobs's general sales manager admitted he knew about the Bain report and that Jacobs was considering changing its basic method of distribution as early as 1974, but never disclosed this information to Brown.

Consistent with the Bain report, when the recession ended in 1983 Jacobs unveiled its "Single Price Strategy," which Jacobs implemented by changing the annual distributorship agreements. Jacobs informed Brown in September 1983 that effective January 1, 1984, Jacobs would accept direct orders from original equipment manufacturers at the same prices offered to distributors, eliminate the distributors' exclusive territories, and reserve the right to sell directly to anyone at one price. Jacobs expanded its own sales and service force and in November 1983 directly solicited Brown's original equipment manufacturer and truck fleet customers, which together constituted 90% of Brown's customers for Jacobs's brakes. Jacobs fully realized the consequences of the distribution changes: Jacobs's 1983 Eastern Regional Annual Report declared, "[Jacobs's] announcement . . . of the 1984 Single Price Strategy irrevocably has changed the traditional role of our distributors. [They] must either change or die. Most will probably die."

In December 1983 Brown sent Jacobs a letter complaining that Jacobs's new policy would effectively destroy Brown's distributorship, and reminding Jacobs that Brown had incurred heavy losses during the recession based on Jacobs's assurances Brown would benefit when the market improved. Brown also stated it would be unable to recover the one million dollars it had invested in facilities and marketing for Jacobs's brakes. Jacobs did not respond to Brown's letter in writing, but a Jacobs manager noted on the letter that Jacobs should send "someone with rapport [to] visit [Brown's CEO and] give him a crumb." Because Brown could not profitably sell Jacobs's products to customers who could buy directly from Jacobs at the same price, Brown refused to sign Jacobs's 1984 distributorship agreement.

II

Jacobs filed this diversity action against Brown for the unpaid account balance owing for products sold to Brown when the distributor relationship ended. Brown denied liability and counterclaimed, alleging Jacobs made several fraudulent misrepresentations: (1) Jacobs's statements in and after 1976 that it was not considering any plans to change its existing distribution method; (2) Jacobs's assurance in July 1981 that it had no plans to change its existing distribution method; and (3) Jacobs's statements in and after July 1981 that, if Brown remained a Jacobs distributor during the market recession, Brown's distributorship would continue when the market rebounded. Following a fifteen-day trial, the district court granted Jacobs's JAML motion on its claim against Brown, and submitted Brown's counterclaims to the jury. The jury found all three Jacobs representations were fraudulent and the third representation was also negligent. The jury awarded Brown almost $ 2.5 million in actual damages, consisting of out-of-pocket losses and lost future profits, and $ 2.7 million in punitive damages.

Sixteen months after the jury returned its verdict, the district court granted Jacobs's renewed JAML motion on Brown's counterclaims. Without the benefit of the trial transcript, the district court concluded there was no evidence from which the jury could reasonably infer that the second and third representations were false when made, and as a matter of law, Brown could not justifiably rely on any of Jacobs's representations. . . . The district court also granted Jacobs's alternative motion for a new trial on Brown's counterclaims.

III

Brown contends the district court erroneously granted Jacobs's JAML motion on Brown's fraudulent misrepresentation counterclaims. To establish fraudulent mis-

representation, Brown had to show, among other things, that Jacobs's representations were false when made and that Brown had a right to rely on the representations. Brown contends that, contrary to the district court's view, the evidence supports the jury's findings that Jacobs's second and third representations were false when made and that Brown justifiably relied on all three representations. We agree.

In reviewing the district court's grant of JAML, we apply the same standard that governed the district court. We consider the evidence and the reasonable inferences that may be drawn from the evidence in the light most favorable to Brown. JAML should not have been granted unless all the evidence points one way and is susceptible of no reasonable inferences sustaining Brown's position. The standard of review for JAML is the same under Missouri and federal law.

Under Missouri law, fraud may be inferred from facts and circumstances and need not be shown by direct evidence. Whether the facts and circumstances justify a conclusion that a defendant knows a representation is false when made is a question for the jury. When a fraudulent misrepresentation claim is based on a statement of intent, the plaintiff establishes falsity by showing that when the speaker made the statement, the speaker did not intend to perform consistently with the statement. Although intent not to perform cannot be shown solely by the speaker's nonperformance, intent can be shown by other evidence.

In our view, a rational jury could find the second and third representations were false when made. This is so because, viewing the evidence in the light most favorable to Brown, the jury could reasonably infer Jacobs had decided to eliminate external distributors when it made these statements to Brown. Before 1981, Jacobs concealed distribution studies and deceived Brown about the purpose of a consultant's visit. The June 1981 Bain report recommended a carefully staged, time-phased program to eliminate Jacobs's distributors by 1984. Jacobs's later conduct and timing neatly coincided with the Bain report's recommendations. We believe the jury could reasonably infer that in June 1981 Jacobs secretly adopted the Bain report's recommendation to eliminate the traditional distributors. Thus, a reasonable jury could find the second representation – Jacobs's assurances in and after July 1981 that it had no plans to change its distribution system – was untrue when made. A reasonable jury could also find that when Jacobs made the third representation, Jacobs did not intend that Brown would benefit from increased sales after the recession's end.

This leaves the issue of Brown's reliance on the three representations. Evidence that Brown continued to incur expenses to maintain its distributorship until Jacobs announced the changes in the distributorship agreement shows Brown relied on Jacobs's representations. A rational jury could also find that Brown's reliance was justified. The district court held that even assuming all three representations were false, Brown's reliance on the verbal representations was not justified as a matter of law because the verbal representations conflicted with the express terms of the written distributorship agreements. This view is unsupported by Missouri law, however.

In a Missouri fraud case, it is for the jury to decide whether a party is entitled to rely on verbal representations that conflict with a written agreement. Thus, Brown's reliance on Jacobs's verbal representations could be justified, even though the verbal representations contradicted the distributorship agreements' one-year terms and reservation to Jacobs of the right to sell directly to original equipment manufacturers. Although Brown also knew Jacobs was selling products directly to Brown's truck fleet customers, Brown could justifiably rely on Jacobs's assurances that the program was temporary and Jacobs's distributors would continue as the backbone of Jacobs's sales effort. It was for the jury to decide whether Brown's reliance on Jacobs's verbal representations was justified.

Because the jury's finding that all three representations were fraudulent supports the damages awarded, we need not consider whether Brown's negligent misrepresentation counterclaim was properly submitted to the jury.

* * *

VI

Having decided the district court erroneously granted JAML on the liability issue, we must also consider the district court's conditional grant of a new trial. The district court held Jacobs is entitled to a new trial on the third representation because the verdicts of fraud and negligence were inconsistent. We agree with Brown that Jacobs waived the right to a new trial based on inconsistent verdicts, and failed to preserve the issue for our review, when Jacobs failed to object and move for resubmission before the jury's discharge. In any event, because the first and second representations were properly submitted to the jury on the fraud theory alone and these representations support the jury's awards of compensatory and punitive damages, any inconsistency with respect to the third representation was harmless error.

The district court also granted a new trial on the ground the punitive damages award was not supported by "substantial evidence." Although this is an imprecise statement of the evidentiary standard for granting a new trial, the district court also correctly stated it could disturb the jury's verdict only if the verdict was against the "great weight" of the evidence, so that granting a new trial would prevent a miscarriage of justice. Instead of explaining reasons for concluding a new trial should be granted on the weight of the evidence, however, the district court merely stated, "For all of the reasons previously discussed, there was not substantial evidence supporting the award of punitive damages."

Because the "previously discussed" reasons could only refer to the district court's analysis of the evidentiary basis for the punitive damages award when considering Jacobs's motion for JAML, it is less than clear that the district court applied the new trial standard rather than the JAML standard in granting Jacobs a new trial. If the district court applied the JAML standard, the court could not grant a new trial because "[JAML] principles have no application to the consideration of a motion for new trial on the ground that the verdict is against the weight of the evidence." Regardless of whether the district court considered its earlier analysis of the evidence under the JAML standard or the new trial standard, however, the evidentiary analysis was infected by the district court's legally incorrect view that Brown could not justifiably believe Jacobs's verbal representations over the written agreement's terms, as we have already pointed out. Further, if the district court used the new trial standard, the court misapplied it. The district court did not properly weigh Brown's testimony about Jacobs's verbal representations, find Brown's testimony unworthy of belief, or find a significant weight factor favoring Jacobs. Rather, because Brown's testimony was at odds with the written agreements, the district court concluded that "a reasonable jury could not fairly conclude [Jacobs's] conduct was either outrageous or . . . reckless." Putting the district court's misconception of Missouri law aside, this case simply involves diametrically opposed credible evidence, and it is the jury's function to choose between plausible versions of the evidence. *Pence,* 961 F.2d at 781. *Pence* makes clear that when, as in this case, reasonable persons can differ in evaluating credible evidence and the district court has not diminished the credible evidence by finding witnesses unworthy of belief or otherwise properly rejecting some of the testimony, a new trial on the ground of weight of the evidence should not be granted. The district court could not properly grant a new trial in this case. We thus need not remand, but simply reverse the district court's conditional grant of a new trial.

Brown also contends the district court committed error in considering the jury's responses to special interrogatories that the district court submitted after the jury returned unambiguous verdicts. We agree. Special interrogatories are inappropriate after the jury has returned an unambiguous verdict because "there is no reason to ask the same question a second time in a different form" or to question the jury's reasoning. Postverdict interrogatories may imply the jury's verdict is unjustified and cause the jury to answer the interrogatories in a manner inconsistent with the verdict. Thus, the district court should not have considered the jury's answers to postverdict interrogatories in deciding whether to grant a new trial. At any rate, the district court recognized the postverdict interrogatory answers alone would not warrant a new trial.

VII

Accordingly, we affirm the district court's grant of JAML on Jacobs's claim and reverse the district court's grant of JAML or a new trial on Brown's fraudulent misrepresentation counterclaim. We remand to the district court with instructions to enter judgment in favor of Brown in accordance with the jury's verdict on Brown's fraudulent misrepresentation counterclaim.

Notes

1. In reviewing judgments or orders that set aside jury verdicts, the appellate court must balance the party's right to trial by jury against the deference due to

the trial court that, having observed the proceedings, saw fit to reject the jury's conclusion. *See Perricone v. Kansas City Southern Ry. Co.*, 704 F.2d 1376 (5th Cir. 1983). The effective appellate attorney should be aware of these conflicting values, and emphasize the importance of whichever principle will benefit the client.

2. Although the *Jacobs* court criticized the district judge's use of interrogatories *after* the jury's verdict had been rendered, the use of written interrogatories in civil cases, when posed in advance of, or in conjunction with, receipt of a verdict is quite common in civil cases. When the responses to those interrogatories are inconsistent with each other, and cannot be reconciled, the appellate court has the power to set aside a jury verdict based on inconsistent responses, and remand for a new trial. *See Gallick v. Baltimore and Ohio R.R. Co.*, 372 U.S. 108, 119 (1963).

3. Not all appellate review of facts found by a jury will necessarily bring into play the Seventh Amendment prohibition against re-examination of facts. For example, if a state legislature enacts a damage cap on recovery for a given type of injury, may the court reduce a jury award above that maximum without offending the Seventh Amendment? How could the defendant's attorney characterize the issue so as to provide the appellate court with a standard of review that would give no deference to the jury's verdict? Would the reduction of damages result from a reexamination of the facts found by the jury, or from a legislative mandate? *See Davis v. Omitowoju*, 883 F.2d 1155 (3d Cir. 1989).

2. Criminal Cases

Special considerations regarding the standard of review come into play when appellate courts review judgments in criminal cases. In addition to the right to trial by jury, the constitutional requirements that no one may be deprived of life or liberty without due process of law, and that one may not be twice placed in jeopardy for the same offense, have particular ramifications for the appellate review of criminal cases.

a. Legal Sufficiency

The due process clauses of the Fifth and Fourteenth Amendments to the United States Constitution have been construed to impose the obligation on appellate courts of ensuring that criminal convictions are based on sufficient evidence adduced by the prosecution. Thus the reasonable doubt standard applies not only at the trial level, but obligates an appellate court to review a conviction to ensure that it rests on sufficient evidence. In the landmark case of *Jackson v. Virginia*, 443 U.S. 307 (1979), the Supreme Court set forth the federal constitutional standard of legal sufficiency.

Jackson v. Virginia

443 U.S. 307 (1979)

Mr. Justice STEWART delivered the opinion of the Court.

The Constitution prohibits the criminal conviction of any person except upon proof of guilt beyond a reasonable doubt. *In re Winship,* 397 U.S. 358. The question in this case is what standard is to be applied in a federal habeas corpus proceeding when the claim is made that a person has been convicted in a state court upon insufficient evidence.

I

The petitioner was convicted after a bench trial in the Circuit Court of Chesterfield County, Va., of the first-degree murder of a woman named Mary Houston Cole. Under Virginia law, murder is defined as "the unlawful killing of another with malice aforethought." Premeditation, or specific intent to kill, distinguishes murder in the first from murder in the second degree; proof of this element is essential to conviction of the former offense, and the burden of proving it clearly rests with the prosecution.

That the petitioner had shot and killed Mrs. Cole was not in dispute at the trial. The State's evidence established that she had been a member of the staff at the local county jail, that she had befriended him while he was imprisoned there on a disorderly conduct charge, and that when he was released she had arranged for him to live in the home of her son and daughter-in-law. Testimony by her relatives indicated that on the day of the killing the petitioner had been drinking and had spent a great deal of time shooting at targets with his revolver. Late in the afternoon, according to their testimony, he had unsuccessfully attempted to talk the victim into driving him to North Carolina. She did drive the petitioner to a local diner. There the two were observed by several police officers, who testified that both the petitioner and the victim had been drinking. The two were observed by a deputy sheriff as they were preparing to leave the diner in her car. The petitioner was then in possession of his revolver, and the sheriff also observed a kitchen knife in the automobile. The sheriff testified that he had offered to keep the revolver until the petitioner sobered up, but that the latter had indicated that this would be unnecessary since he and the victim were about to engage in sexual activity.

Her body was found in a secluded church parking lot a day and a half later, naked from the waist down, her slacks beneath her body. Uncontradicted medical and expert evidence established that she had been shot twice at close range with the petitioner's gun. She appeared not to have been sexually molested. Six cartridge cases identified as having been fired from the petitioner's gun were found near the body.

After shooting Mrs. Cole, the petitioner drove her car to North Carolina, where, after a short trip to Florida, he was arrested several days later. In a post arrest statement, introduced in evidence by the prosecution, the petitioner admitted that he had shot the victim. He contended, however, that the shooting had been accidental. When asked to describe his condition at the time of the shooting, he indicated that he had not been drunk, but had been "pretty high." His story was that the victim had attacked him with a knife when he resisted her sexual advances. He said that he had defended himself by firing a number of warning shots into the ground, and had then reloaded his revolver. The victim, he said, then attempted to take the gun from him, and the gun "went off" in the ensuing struggle. He said that he fled without seeking help for the victim because he was afraid. At the trial, his position was that he had acted in self-defense. Alternatively, he claimed that in any event the State's own evidence showed that he had been too intoxicated to form the specific intent necessary under Virginia law to sustain a conviction of murder in the first degree.[2]

The trial judge, declaring himself convinced beyond a reasonable doubt that the petitioner had committed first-degree murder, found him guilty of that offense.[3] The petitioner's motion to set aside the judgment as contrary to the evidence was denied, and he was sentenced to serve a term of 30 years in the Virginia state penitentiary. A petition for writ of error to the Virginia Supreme Court on the ground that the evidence was insufficient to support the conviction was denied.

The petitioner then commenced this habeas corpus proceeding in the United States District Court for the Eastern District of Virginia, raising the same basic claim. Applying the "no evidence" criterion of *Thompson v. Louisville*, 362 U.S. 199, the District Court found the record devoid of evidence of premeditation and granted the writ. The Court of Appeals for the Fourth Circuit reversed the judgment. . . . The court was of the view that some evidence that the petitioner had intended to kill the victim could be found in the facts that the petitioner had reloaded his gun after firing warning shots, that he had had time to do so, and that the victim was then shot not once but twice. The court also concluded that the state trial judge could have found that the petitioner was not so intoxicated as to be incapable of premeditation.

We granted certiorari to consider the

petitioner's claim that under *In re Winship, supra,* a federal habeas corpus court must consider not whether there was *any* evidence to support a state-court conviction, but whether there was sufficient evidence to justify a rational trier of the facts to find guilt beyond a reasonable doubt.

II

Our inquiry in this case is narrow. The petitioner has not seriously questioned any aspect of Virginia law governing the allocation of the burden of production or persuasion in a murder trial. As the record demonstrates, the judge sitting as factfinder in the petitioner's trial was aware that the State bore the burden of establishing the element of premeditation, and stated that he was applying the reasonable-doubt standard in his appraisal of the State's evidence. The petitioner, moreover, does not contest the conclusion of the Court of Appeals that under the "no evidence" rule of *Thompson v. Louisville, supra,* his conviction of first-degree murder is sustainable. And he has not attacked the sufficiency of the evidence to support a conviction of second-degree murder. His sole constitutional claim, based squarely upon *Winship,* is that the District Court and the Court of Appeals were in error in not recognizing that the question to be decided in this case is whether any rational factfinder could have concluded beyond a reasonable doubt that the killing for which the petitioner was convicted was premeditated. The question thus raised goes to the basic nature of the constitutional right recognized in the *Winship* opinion.

III

A

This is the first of our cases to expressly consider the question whether the due process standard recognized in *Winship* constitutionally protects an accused against conviction except upon evidence that is sufficient fairly to support a conclusion that every element of the crime has been estab-

---

[2] Under Virginia law, voluntary intoxication – although not an affirmative defense to second-degree murder – is material to the element of premeditation and may be found to have negated it.

[3] When trial without a jury is had on a not guilty plea in Virginia, the court is to "have and exercise all the powers, privileges and duties given to juries. . . " Va. Code § 19.2-257 (1975).

lished beyond a reasonable doubt. Upon examination of the fundamental differences between the constitutional underpinnings of *Thompson v. Louisville, supra,* and of *In re Winship, supra,* the answer to that question, we think, is clear.

It is axiomatic that a conviction upon a charge not made or upon a charge not tried constitutes a denial of due process. *Cole v. Arkansas,* 333 U.S. 196. These standards no more than reflect a broader premise that has never been doubted in our constitutional system: that a person cannot incur the loss of liberty for an offense without notice and a meaningful opportunity to defend. A meaningful opportunity to defend, if not the right to a trial itself, presumes as well that a total want of evidence to support a charge will conclude the case in favor of the accused. Accordingly, we held in the *Thompson* case that a conviction based upon a record wholly devoid of any relevant evidence of a crucial element of the offense charged is constitutionally infirm. The "no evidence" doctrine of *Thompson v. Louisville* thus secures to an accused the most elemental of due process rights: freedom from a wholly arbitrary deprivation of liberty.

The Court in *Thompson* explicitly stated that the due process right at issue did not concern a question of evidentiary "sufficiency." The right established in *In re Winship,* however, clearly stands on a different footing. *Winship* involved an adjudication of juvenile delinquency made by a judge under a state statute providing that the prosecution must prove the conduct charged as delinquent – which in *Winship* would have been a criminal offense if engaged in by an adult – by a preponderance of the evidence. Applying that standard, the judge was satisfied that the juvenile was "guilty," but he noted that the result might well have been different under a standard of proof beyond a reasonable doubt. In short, the record in *Winship* was not totally devoid of evidence of guilt.

The constitutional problem addressed in *Winship* was thus distinct from the stark problem of arbitrariness presented in *Thompson v. Louisville.* In *Winship,* the Court held for the first time that the Due Process Clause of the Fourteenth Amendment protects a defendant in a criminal case against conviction "except upon proof beyond a reasonable doubt of every fact necessary to constitute the crime with which he is charged." In so holding, the Court emphasized that proof beyond a reasonable doubt has traditionally been regarded as the decisive difference between criminal culpability and civil liability. The standard of proof beyond a reasonable doubt, said the Court, "plays a vital role in the American scheme of criminal procedure," because it operates to give "concrete substance" to the presumption of innocence to ensure against unjust convictions, and to reduce the risk of factual error in a criminal proceeding. At the same time by impressing upon the factfinder the need to reach a subjective state of near certitude of the guilt of the accused, the standard symbolizes the significance that our society attaches to the criminal sanction and thus to liberty itself.

The constitutional standard recognized in the *Winship* case was expressly phrased as one that protects an accused against a conviction except on "*proof* beyond a reasonable doubt. . . ." In subsequent cases discussing the reasonable doubt standard, we have never departed from this definition of the rule or from the *Winship* understanding of the central purposes it serves. In short, *Winship* presupposes as an essential of the due process guaranteed by the Fourteenth Amendment that no person shall be made to suffer the onus of a criminal conviction except upon sufficient proof – defined as evidence necessary to convince a trier of fact beyond a reasonable doubt of the existence of every element of the offense.

B

Although several of our cases have intimated that the factfinder's application of the reasonable-doubt standard to the evidence may present a federal question when a state conviction is challenged, the Federal Courts of Appeals have generally assumed that so long as the reasonable-doubt instruction has been given at trial, the no-evidence doctrine of *Thompson v. Louisville* remains the appropriate guide for a federal habeas corpus court to apply in assessing a state prisoner's challenge to his conviction as founded upon insufficient evidence. We cannot agree.

The *Winship* doctrine requires more than simply a trial ritual. A doctrine establishing so fundamental a substantive constitutional standard must also require that the factfinder will rationally apply that standard to the facts in evidence.[8] A "reasonable doubt," at a minimum, is one based upon "reason." Yet a properly instructed jury may occasionally convict even when it can be said that no rational trier of fact could find guilt beyond a reasonable doubt, and the same may be said of a trial judge sitting as a jury. In a federal trial, such an occurrence has traditionally been deemed to require reversal of the conviction. *Glasser v. United States,* 315 U.S. 60, 80. Under *Winship,* which established proof beyond a reasonable doubt as an essential of Fourteenth Amendment due process, it follows that when such a conviction occurs in a state trial, it cannot constitutionally stand.

. . .

After *Winship* the critical inquiry on review of the sufficiency of the evidence to support a criminal conviction must be not simply to determine whether the jury was properly instructed, but to determine whether the record evidence could reasonably support a finding of guilt beyond a reasonable doubt. But this inquiry does not require a court to "ask itself whether *it*

_____

[8] The trier of fact in this case was a judge and not a jury. But this is of no constitutional significance. The record makes clear that the judge deemed himself "properly instructed."

believes that the evidence at the trial established guilt beyond a reasonable doubt." Instead, the relevant question is whether, after viewing the evidence in the light most favorable to the prosecution, *any* rational trier of fact could have found the essential elements of the crime beyond a reasonable doubt. This familiar standard gives full play to the responsibility of the trier of fact fairly to resolve conflicts in the testimony, to weigh the evidence, and to draw reasonable inferences from basic facts to ultimate facts. Once a defendant has been found guilty of the crime charged, the factfinder's role as weigher of the evidence is preserved through a legal conclusion that upon judicial review *all of the evidence* is to be considered in the light most favorable to the prosecution. The criterion thus impinges upon "jury" discretion only to the extent necessary to guarantee the fundamental protection of due process of law.[13]

That the *Thompson* "no evidence" rule is simply inadequate to protect against misapplication of the constitutional standard of reasonable doubt is readily apparent. "[A] mere modicum of evidence may satisfy a 'no evidence' standard . . . ." *Jacobellis v. Ohio,* 378 U.S. 184, 202 (Warren, C.J., dissenting). Any evidence that is relevant—that has any tendency to make the existence of an element of a crime slightly more probable than it would be without the evidence, cf. Fed. Rule Evid. 401—could be deemed a "mere modicum." But it could not seriously be argued that such a "modicum" of evidence could by itself rationally support a conviction beyond a reasonable doubt. The *Thompson* doctrine simply fails to supply a workable or even a predictable

_____

[13] The question whether the evidence is constitutionally sufficient is of course wholly unrelated to the question of how rationally the verdict was actually reached. Just as the standard announced today does not permit a court to make its own subjective determination of guilt or innocence, it does not require scrutiny of the reasoning process actually used by the factfinder—if known.

standard for determining whether the due process command of *Winship* has been honored.[14]

C

Under 28 U.S.C. § 2254, a federal court must entertain a claim by a state prisoner that he or she is being held in "custody in violation of the Constitution or laws or treaties of the United States." Under the *Winship* decision, it is clear that a state prisoner who alleges that the evidence in support of his state conviction cannot be fairly characterized as sufficient to have led a rational trier of fact to find guilt beyond a reasonable doubt has stated a federal constitutional claim. Thus, assuming that state remedies have been exhausted, *see* 28 U.S.C. § 2254(b), and that no independent and adequate state ground stands as a bar, it follows that such a claim is cognizable in a federal habeas corpus proceeding. The respondents have argued, nonetheless, that a challenge to the constitutional sufficiency of the evidence should not be entertained by a federal district court under 28 U.S.C. § 2254.

In addition to the argument that a *Winship* standard invites replication of state criminal trials in the guise of § 2254 proceedings—an argument that simply fails to recognize that courts can and regularly do gauge the sufficiency of the evidence without intruding into any legitimate domain of the trier of fact—the respon-

dents have urged that any departure from the *Thompson* test in federal habeas corpus proceedings will expand the number of meritless claims brought to the federal courts, will duplicate the work of the state appellate courts, will disserve the societal interest in the finality of state criminal proceedings, and will increase friction between the federal and state judiciaries. In sum, counsel for the State urges that this type of constitutional claim should be deemed to fall within the limit on federal habeas corpus jurisdiction identified in *Stone v. Powell,* 428 U.S. 465, with respect to Fourth Amendment claims. We disagree.

First, the burden that is likely to follow from acceptance of the *Winship* standard has, we think, been exaggerated. Federal-court challenges to the evidentiary support for state convictions have since *Thompson* been dealt with under § 2254. A more stringent standard will expand the contours of this type of claim, but will not create an entirely new class of cases cognizable on federal habeas corpus. Furthermore, most meritorious challenges to constitutional sufficiency of the evidence undoubtedly will be recognized in the state courts, and, if the state courts have fully considered the issue of sufficiency, the task of a federal habeas court should not be difficult. And this type of claim can almost always be judged on the written record without need for an evidentiary hearing in the federal court.

Second, the problems of finality and federal-state comity arise whenever a state prisoner invokes the jurisdiction of a federal court to redress an alleged constitutional violation. A challenge to a state conviction brought on the ground that the evidence cannot fairly be deemed sufficient to have established guilt beyond a reasonable doubt states a federal constitutional claim. Although state appellate review undoubtedly will serve in the vast majority of cases to vindicate the due process protection that follows from *Winship,* the same could also

---

[14] Application of the *Thompson* standard to assess the validity of a criminal conviction after *Winship* could lead to absurdly unjust results. Our cases have indicated that failure to instruct a jury on the necessity of proof of guilt beyond a reasonable doubt can never be harmless error. Thus a defendant whose guilt was actually proved by overwhelming evidence would be denied due process if the jury was instructed that he could be found guilty on a mere preponderance of the evidence. Yet a defendant against whom there was but one slender bit of evidence would not be denied due process so long as the jury has been properly instructed on the prosecution's burden of proof beyond a reasonable doubt. Such results would be wholly faithless to the constitutional rationale of *Winship.*

be said of the vast majority of other federal constitutional rights that may be implicated in a state criminal trial. It is the occasional abuse that the federal writ of habeas corpus stands ready to correct.

The respondents have argued nonetheless that whenever a person convicted in a state court has been given a "full and fair hearing" in the state system – meaning in this instance state appellate review of the sufficiency of the evidence – further federal inquiry – apart from the possibility of discretionary review by this Court – should be foreclosed. This argument would prove far too much. A judgment by a state appellate court rejecting a challenge to evidentiary sufficiency is of course entitled to deference by the federal courts, as is any judgment affirming a criminal conviction. But Congress in § 2254 has selected the federal district courts as precisely the forums that are responsible for determining whether state convictions have been secured in accord with federal constitutional law. The federal habeas corpus statute presumes the norm of a fair trial in the state court and adequate state postconviction remedies to redress possible error. See 28 U.S.C. § 2254(b), (d). What it does not presume is that these state proceedings will always be without error in the constitutional sense. The duty of a federal habeas corpus court to appraise a claim that constitutional error did occur – reflecting as it does the belief that the "finality" of a deprivation of liberty through the invocation of the criminal sanction is simply not to be achieved at the expense of a constitutional right – is not one that can be so lightly abjured.

The constitutional issue presented in this case is far different from the kind of issue that was the subject of the Court's decision in *Stone v. Powell, supra.* The question whether a defendant has been convicted upon inadequate evidence is central to the basic question of guilt or innocence. The constitutional necessity of proof beyond a reasonable doubt is not confined to those defendants who are morally blameless. *E.g., Mullaney v. Wilbur,* 421 U.S. at 697-698 (requirement of proof beyond a reasonable doubt is not "limit[ed] to those facts which, that if not proved, would wholly exonerate" the accused). Under our system of criminal justice even a thief is entitled to complain that he has been unconstitutionally convicted and imprisoned as a burglar.

We hold that in a challenge to a state criminal conviction brought under 28 U.S.C. § 2254 – if the settled procedural prerequisites for such a claim have otherwise been satisfied – the applicant is entitled to habeas corpus relief if it is found that upon the record evidence adduced at the trial no rational trier of fact could have found proof of guilt beyond a reasonable doubt.[16]

IV

Turning finally to the specific facts of this case, we reject the petitioner's claim that under the constitutional standard dictated by *Winship* his conviction of first degree murder cannot stand. A review of the record in the light most favorable to the prosecution convinces us that a rational factfinder could readily have found the petitioner guilty beyond a reasonable doubt of first-degree murder under Virginia law.

There was no question at the trial that the petitioner had fatally shot Mary Cole. The crucial factual dispute went to the sufficiency of the evidence to support a finding that he had specifically intended to kill her. This question, as the Court of Appeals recognized, must be gauged in the light of applicable Virginia law defining the element of premeditation. Under that law it is well settled that premeditation need not

---

[16] The respondents have suggested that this constitutional standard will invite intrusions upon the power of the States to define criminal offenses. Quite to the contrary, the standard must be applied with explicit reference to the substantive elements of the criminal offense as defined by state law. Whether the State could constitutionally make the conduct at issue criminal at all is, of course, a distinct question.

exist for any particular length of time, and that an intent to kill may be formed at the moment of the commission of the unlawful act. From the circumstantial evidence in the record, it is clear that the trial judge could reasonably have found beyond a reasonable doubt that the petitioner did possess the necessary intent at or before the time of the killing.

The prosecution's uncontradicted evidence established that the petitioner shot the victim not once but twice. The petitioner himself admitted that the fatal shooting had occurred only after he had first fired several shots into the ground and then reloaded his gun. The evidence was clear that the two shots that killed the victim were fired at close, and thus predictably fatal, range by a person who was experienced in the use of the murder weapon. Immediately after the shooting, the petitioner drove without mishap from Virginia to North Carolina, a fact quite at odds with his story of extreme intoxication. Shortly before the fatal episode, he had publicly expressed an intention to have sexual relations with the victim. Her body was found partially unclothed. From these uncontradicted circumstances, a rational factfinder readily could have inferred beyond a reasonable doubt that the petitioner, notwithstanding evidence that he had been drinking on the day of the killing, did have the capacity to form and had in fact formed an intent to kill the victim.

The petitioner's calculated behavior both before and after the killing demonstrated that he was fully capable of committing premeditated murder. His claim of self-defense would have required the trial judge to draw a series of improbable inferences from the basic facts, prime among them the inference that he was wholly uninterested in sexual activity with the victim but that she was so interested as to have willingly removed part of her clothing and then attacked him with a knife when he resisted her advances, even though he was armed with a loaded revolver that he had just demonstrated he knew how to use. It is evident from the record that the trial judge found this story, including the petitioner's belated contention that he had been so intoxicated as to be incapable of premeditation, incredible.

Only under a theory that the prosecution was under an affirmative duty to rule out every hypothesis except that of guilt beyond a reasonable doubt could this petitioner's challenge be sustained. That theory the Court has rejected in the past. We decline to adopt it today. Under the standard established in this opinion as necessary to preserve the due process protection recognized in *Winship,* a federal habeas corpus court faced with a record of historical facts that supports conflicting inferences must presume—even if it does not affirmatively appear in the record—that the trier of fact resolved any such conflicts in favor of the prosecution and must defer to that resolution. Applying these criteria, we hold that a rational trier of fact could reasonably have found that the petitioner committed murder in the first degree under Virginia law.

For these reasons, the judgment of the Court of Appeals is affirmed.

It is so ordered.

Mr. Justice POWELL took no part in the consideration or decision of this case.

Mr. Justice STEVENS, with whom THE CHIEF JUSTICE and Mr. Justice REHNQUIST join, concurring in the judgment.

The Constitution prohibits the criminal conviction of any person except upon proof *sufficient to convince the trier of fact* of guilt beyond a reasonable doubt. This rule has prevailed in our courts "at least from our early years as a Nation." *In re Winship,* 397 U.S. 358, 361.

Today the Court creates a new rule of law—one that has never prevailed in our jurisprudence. According to the Court, the Constitution now prohibits the criminal conviction of any person—including, apparently, a person against whom the facts have already been found beyond a reasonable doubt by a jury, a trial judge, and one or more levels of state appellate judges—except upon proof sufficient to convince a federal judge that a "rational trier of fact could have found the essential elements of the crime beyond a reasonable doubt."

The adoption of this novel constitutional rule is not necessary to the decision of this case. Moreover, I believe it is an unwise act of lawmaking. Despite its chimerical appeal as a new counterpart to the venerable principle recognized in *Winship,* I am persuaded that its precipitous adoption will adversely affect the quality of justice administered by federal judges. . . . [N]either the record in this case, nor general experience with challenges to the sufficiency of the evidence supporting criminal convictions, supports, much less compels, the conclusion that there is any need for this new constitutional precept.

* * *

Notes

1. The concurring Justices asserted that the new standard set forth in *Jackson v. Virginia* was unnecessary. While reversals of state court convictions based on this standard have by no means been common, federal courts have, in a significant number of cases, found the evidence so lacking that "no rational trier of fact could have found proof of guilt beyond a reasonable doubt." As you read the cases that follow, consider what factors may have led to convictions, and appellate affirmance of convictions, despite such slender reeds of evidence. What do these cases, and others you may discover in your own research, suggest about the need for federal habeas corpus review of the sufficiency of criminal convictions?

2. In the next two cases excerpted below, two different panels of the Court of Appeals for the Ninth Circuit dealt with convictions obtained solely on the basis of fingerprints of the defendant found at the scene of the crime. With technological advances, such convictions are likely to become more common. Are the two cases truly distinguishable? Which has the better analysis?

Mikes v. Borg

947 F.2d 353 (9th Cir. 1991)

REINHARDT, Circuit Judge.

Melvin Mikes, a California state prisoner, appeals the district court's order dismissing his petition for a writ of habeas corpus pursuant to 28 U.S.C. § 2254. Following a trial by jury, Mikes was convicted of murder in the first degree and commission of an offense with the use of a deadly or dangerous weapon, and was sentenced to state prison for 25 years to life. The California Court of Appeal affirmed the judgment and the California Supreme Court denied Mikes' petition for review without explanation or citation of authorities. Mikes contends on habeas review that the inculpatory evidence, which consisted exclusively of fingerprint evidence, was insufficient to support his conviction. We agree.

I. Facts

On March 10, 1980, Harold Hansen was found dead in the basement of his fix-it shop, with the pockets of his clothing turned inside out. The shop, which was located on the main floor of the building, had been burglarized. Near Hansen's body, police investigators found three chrome posts – a three-foot post, a six-foot post, and a "turnstile" post – all of which constituted portions of a disassembled turnstile unit. Hansen had purchased the turnstile (in assembled or disassembled form) at a hardware store's going-out-of-business sale, approximately four months prior to his death. The investigators determined that the assailant used the three-foot post to murder Hansen.

The government's case against Mikes rested exclusively upon the fact that his fingerprints were among those found on the posts that lay adjacent to the victim's body. The officers lifted a total of 46 fingerprints from the area designated as the crime scene. Of the 16 fingerprints that were identifiable, the police determined that six belonged to Mikes and ten did not. Thirty were not sufficiently clear to permit identification of the source. In particular, the government introduced evidence that five "consecutive" prints were found on the three-foot post – the murder weapon. The prosecution's expert testified that he identified the first and fourth of the consecutive prints as Mikes' right forefinger and right little finger, respectively. The remaining three prints on the murder weapon were unidentifiable. Three of fifteen prints found on the six-foot post, and one of two prints from the "turnstile" post belonged to Mikes. Other unidentifiable prints were also found on these posts. None of the prints taken from the fix-it shop area, where the police discovered a number of empty jewelry boxes strewn about, or from the jewelry boxes themselves, or from the stair rail leading to the basement, were identified as Mikes'. In fact, none of the fingerprints found anywhere on the premises except on the posts were identified as Mikes'.

II. Standard of Review

We review *de novo* a district court's decision to deny a petition for writ of habeas corpus. *Barker v. Estelle*, 913 F.2d 1433, 1437 (9th Cir. 1990). However, in reviewing the question whether the evidence was sufficient to sustain Mikes' conviction, we, like the district court, must view that evidence in the light most favorable to the government and determine whether on that basis any rational factfinder could have found the essential elements of the crime beyond a reasonable doubt. *Jackson v. Virginia*, 443 U.S. 307, 320 (1979). A conviction that fails to meet the *Jackson* standard violates due process and entitles the convicted defendant to habeas relief.

III. Analysis

The critical question presented by this case is whether the evidence of Mikes' fingerprints on three posts, one of which was identified as the murder weapon, is sufficient by itself to allow a rational trier of fact to convict him of murder. The prosecution's case rested exclusively on the theory that Mikes' fingerprints were impressed on these objects during the commission of the crime. We have held that fingerprint evidence alone may under certain circumstances support a conviction. *United States v. Scott*, 452 F.2d 660, 662 (9th Cir. 1971). However, in fingerprint-only cases in which the prosecution's theory is based on the premise that the defendant handled certain objects while committing the crime in question, the record must contain sufficient evidence from which the trier of fact could reasonably infer that the fingerprints were in fact impressed at that time and not at some earlier date. In order to meet this standard the prosecution must present evidence sufficient to permit the jury to conclude that the objects on which the fingerprints appear were inaccessible to the defendant prior to the time of the commission of the crime.[7]

------

[7] From a practical standpoint, this evidentiary showing is even more critical in cases, like the one before us, in which fingerprints other than the defendant's, or unidentifiable prints, also appear on the murder weapon; however, the showing is essential even when it is only the defendant's prints that appear on a particular item.

Here, the prosecution introduced no evidence placing the defendant at the scene of the crime – either on the day of the murder or on any other occasion. Nor did the prosecution find any items stolen from the deceased in Mikes' possession. Nor, unlike *Scott,* the one case in which we upheld a conviction based on fingerprint evidence alone, did the defendant's fingerprints appear on any recovered stolen property. Finally, none of the fingerprints found on any of the objects located in the area actually burglarized, the fix-it shop itself, were identified as Mikes'. The only evidence that the prosecution introduced to tie Mikes to the murder, or the burglary, was his fingerprints found on several posts of a disassembled turnstile – one of which posts served as the murder weapon – bought by the decedent four months prior to his death, and kept in the basement. The issue in this case is whether that fingerprint evidence, standing alone, is sufficiently probative to allow a reasonable juror to conclude beyond a reasonable doubt that Mikes committed the murder. While the government need not exclude all inferences or reasonable hypotheses consistent with innocence, the record must contain sufficient probative facts from which a factfinder could reasonably infer a defendant's guilt, under the beyond a reasonable doubt standard. In cases such as the one before us, there must, at the very least, be sufficient evidence in the record to permit the factfinder to determine when the fingerprints were impressed; otherwise, any conviction would be based on pure speculation. Here, the government's theory of the case rests on the premise that Mikes' fingerprints were placed on the posts at the time the crime was committed. Accordingly, we must examine the record to determine whether the fingerprint evidence is sufficiently probative to warrant the conclusion by a reasonable factfinder that the prints were placed on the posts at the time of the murder.

The government argues that the posts were inaccessible to the petitioner because they were kept in Hansen's basement, a location from which Hansen excluded the general public, and which Mikes did not have permission to enter. The government's argument falls far short of showing the inaccessibility of the posts to Mikes. Mikes' conviction cannot be upheld unless the record shows that the objects in question were inaccessible to him during the "relevant time." The "relevant time" is defined as the time prior to the commission of the crime during which the defendant reasonably could have placed his fingerprints on the object in question and during which such prints might have remained on that object. We must examine, in each case, the circumstances surrounding the custody or location of the object, as well as its function, the accessibility of the object to the defendant, and the extent to which the object was or could have been handled by others. As we consider whether the record is sufficient to warrant the inference that Mikes did not have access to the posts during the relevant period, our inquiry must center on the specific facts regarding these circumstances; in this connection, we must carefully examine both generally and specifically the nature and character of the fingerprint evidence at issue, particularly with respect to the question of durability.

While the prosecution did not offer any evidence regarding the age of the fingerprints found on the posts, the defense expert testified that fingerprints can last indefinitely. This is consistent with the testimony of government experts in other cases. Given that the undisputed record shows that fingerprints may last indefinitely, we must next examine the custody, location, and function of the objects involved – *i.e.,* the turnstile posts – to determine whether Mikes' prints, if impressed at an earlier date, reasonably could have remained intact until the time of the murder. Hansen purchased the posts at a hardware store's going-out-of-business sale, approximately four months before his murder. After the purchase, he placed the posts in his basement; the posts remained there until his death. The record shows that the basement area was inaccessible to the general public. The fact that Hansen did not allow the general public to enter into the basement area for the four month period preceding the commission of the crime does not, however, help the prosecution. To the contrary, it suggests that prints placed on the posts prior to Hansen's purchase of them and still on them at the time of the acquisition are likely to have remained undisturbed during the time the posts were in Hansen's possession. Therefore, the relevant period in this case is the time immediately preceding the four month period during which Hansen had custody of the posts. The question becomes, then, whether there is a reasonable possibility that Mikes could have impressed his prints on the posts in the period preceding their purchase by Hansen, or, to put it more accurately, whether the record contains sufficient evidence that the posts were inaccessible to Mikes during that period.

The testimony in the record establishes that Mikes' fingerprints were found on "ordinary" turnstile posts – the type often used in public places, such as a grocery or other commercial store. Immediately prior to Hansen's purchase, the posts were offered for sale in a hardware store as part of its going-out-of-business sale. For some indeterminate period prior to the store's offering them for sale, the posts presumably were used for their ordinary purpose and were accessible to the general public, as parts of an operating turnstile unit. The evidence in the record is wholly insufficient to preclude the reasonable possibility that Mikes' fingerprints were placed on the posts during the period prior to Hansen's acquisition of them. To the contrary, it establishes that the posts were fully accessible to the general public, including Mikes, during that period and that Mikes' fingerprints could well have been placed on the posts prior to Hansen's purchase of them. Specifically, Mikes could have handled the posts while they were in the hardware store, either in their assembled or disassembled form. Under the evidence presented, the fingerprints in question could have been placed on the posts by a person who disassembled the turnstile, a person who sold the turnstile to Hansen, or any person who considered buying the turnstile prior to Hansen's acquisition. It is also possible, though less likely, that the fingerprints could have been impressed on the posts on the last occasion on which the turnstile was in general use, either in the hardware store or elsewhere.[9]

In order to support a finding that Mikes is guilty beyond a reasonable doubt, the record must demonstrate that he in fact touched the posts at the time the crime was committed and not at some earlier point. Under our judicial system, the defendant has no duty to explain the presence of his fingerprints. Likewise, he is under no obligation to illuminate any inferences from the fingerprint evidence that are consistent with his innocence. To put it more directly, the defendant need not explain how or when his fingerprints were placed on the object in question; that burden lies elsewhere. On the basis of the record before us, a reasonable factfinder could not conclude beyond a reasonable doubt that Mikes' fingerprints were placed on the turnstile

---

[9] The government's expert also stated that the five consecutive prints were in a "grasping-type" pattern. The government contends that this evidence provides additional support for the conclusion that Mikes used the post to murder Hansen. The argument has little persuasive force, however, because only two of the five prints were identified as Mikes' and the police fingerprint experts did not find any palm or thumb prints belonging to Mikes on the post. More important, people generally grasp turnstile posts while using them for the purpose normally intended, or in connection with any of the functions discussed above. Therefore, the "grasp" does not tend to support the theory that the person whose fingerprints reflected the act of grasping used the post in a violent fashion.

posts at the time of the commission of the crime. There is insufficient evidence to warrant that conclusion rather than the conclusion that the fingerprints were impressed on the posts at an earlier time. There is, in short, a total failure of proof on the "accessibility" question.

The government argues that this case is similar to *United States v. Scott*, 452 F.2d 660 (9th Cir. 1971), the only reported case in which we have upheld a conviction that was based on fingerprint evidence alone. We find that case clearly distinguishable. Scott was convicted of one count of entering a federal savings and loan association with the intent to commit a felony therein, and one count of taking and carrying away with the intent to steal, certain money and property of a federal savings and loan association. We held that the combined fingerprint evidence presented at trial was sufficient to prove that the defendant had committed these crimes. The defendant's prints were found not only on a battery inside a flashlight left at the scene of the crime, but also on a blank check and travelers checks stolen from the association, both forms of checks having been inaccessible to the defendant prior to the offense. We observed that "the identification of the defendant's fingerprints upon one battery inside the flashlight might well have been insufficient circumstantial evidence to survive a motion for acquittal." However, we concluded that "when that evidence is combined with positive fingerprint evidence upon the Association's stolen check and its stolen travelers checks, the ring of circumstantial evidence tightens around the defendant." The facts that the defendant's prints were found on the flashlight left at the scene of the crime and that they were found on the previously inaccessible stolen property constituted more than sufficient proof that the defendant entered the savings and loan association and stole the checks.

Scott is obviously an entirely different case from the one before us. *Scott* does not depend upon a showing that the defendant's fingerprints were impressed upon the objects at the time of the commission of the crime. Indeed, in *Scott* the defendant may well have left his fingerprints on the battery long before entering the savings and loan institution; likewise, if the defendant wore gloves during the theft (or even if he did not but had co-conspirators), his fingerprints may have been impressed on the stolen checks some time after the crime was committed. The combination of the showing that defendant's property was found at the scene of the crime and that the defendant had handled checks stolen from the association during or after their theft provided a sufficient basis upon which a jury could reasonably have inferred that the accused committed the crimes. Unlike in *Scott*, the prosecution in the case before us presented no evidence that Mikes' prints were found on the allegedly stolen property. Nor did the prosecution in the case before us offer sufficient evidence that the property on which Mikes' fingerprints were found was previously inaccessible to him. Finally, none of the property containing Mikes' prints was property which was brought to and left at the crime scene during the commission of the offense. Thus, *Scott* is different from the case before us in almost every material respect.

On the basis of similar, and perhaps more probative, evidence than is presented here, other circuits have concluded that fingerprint evidence is insufficient to support a conviction in the absence of an adequate showing that the fingerprints could have been impressed only at the time of the crime. In *Borum v. United States*, 127 U.S. App. D.C. 48, 380 F.2d 595 (D.C. Cir. 1967), the prosecution introduced evidence that four fingerprints taken from empty jars that had contained a coin collection were the defendant's and that the defendant was within a mile and a half of the victim's home during at least a part of the time period within which the crime was committed. The D.C. Circuit concluded that this evidence was insufficient to sustain the defendant's conviction for housebreaking because there was no direct or circumstantial evidence indicating that the defendant touched the jars in the course of the housebreaking.

The clear principle arising from the cases decided by our fellow circuits is that, in a case resting upon the premise that the defendant impressed his fingerprints on an object at the time of the commission of the crime and supported solely by evidence that the defendant's fingerprints were found on that object, the record must contain sufficient evidence to permit a jury, applying the beyond a reasonable doubt standard, to draw the inference that the defendant touched the object during the commission of the crime. That is a principle that we have ourselves acknowledged on more than one occasion, and that we reiterate today. Accordingly, in the case before us, the evidence in the record must be sufficient to justify a reasonable factfinder's conclusion that the posts were not accessible to the defendant during the relevant period (here, the period shortly before Hansen's acquisition of them). The record falls far short of meeting that standard.

As the court said in *Borum*, "to allow this conviction to stand would be to hold that anyone who touches anything which is found later at the scene of a crime may be convicted." *Borum v. United States*, 127 U.S. App. D.C. 48, 380 F.2d 595, 597 (D.C.

Cir. 1967). Regardless of Mikes' actual guilt or innocence, we decline to establish a precedent that would permit such a result. Any determination that Mikes' fingerprints were left on the posts during the commission of the offense is unreasonably speculative.

CONCLUSION

We do not purport to set forth a rule specifying the precise quantum of fingerprint evidence needed to sustain a conviction. But, in a case in which the prosecution's theory is that the defendant's fingerprints were placed on the murder weapon at the time of the commission of the crime or were left at the scene of the crime during its commission, the record must show that the object was inaccessible to the defendant or that the defendant did not have access to the crime scene, during the relevant period prior to the crime's commission. The prosecution here rested its case upon the theory that Mikes' fingerprints were placed on the murder weapon at the time the crime was committed; however, the record fails to establish that the turnstile posts were inaccessible to him during the relevant period preceding the commission of the offense. We therefore hold that Mikes' conviction violated his right to due process. Accordingly, the judgment of the district court is reversed and the case is remanded to that court with instructions to grant the writ of habeas corpus.

REVERSED and REMANDED.

Taylor v. Stainer

31 F.3d 907 (9th Cir. 1994)

TROTT, Circuit Judge.

The Attorney General of California appeals the district court's grant of habeas corpus to Michael Taylor. Taylor was convicted of first-degree murder based solely on a fingerprint of his that police found on the victim's windowsill and the inferences drawn from that print. The district court

concluded that this fingerprint was not sufficient evidence to support the conviction and granted Taylor's petition. We have jurisdiction under 28 U.S.C. § 2253, and we reverse.

I

In December 1978, police found Mildred Jackson's body on the bedroom floor of her apartment. The medical examiner determined she died from head wounds sustained from a beating with a blunt or flat object. The police believed the killer had entered the apartment through an open kitchen window that was determined to be the "point of entry" in connection with the crime. The window's latch was broken and the screen was bent. All other windows were closed and the doors were locked. Ms. Jackson's television set was missing, and her bedroom had been ransacked.

The police collected a fingerprint from the bottom interior edge of the open window's windowsill and another from a cup in the bedroom. A fingerprint expert concluded the print under the windowsill could have been left by a person reaching over the sill from outside the window or by a person reaching under the sill from inside the apartment. Ten years after the murder, in 1988, the Los Angeles Police Department began using a new computer system for identifying fingerprints, and the police matched the print from the windowsill with Taylor's prints. The print from the cup did not match either Taylor or Ms. Jackson. No evidence, other than the fingerprint, connected Taylor to the crime.

Taylor was charged with felony murder based on a burglary homicide, and the jury convicted him of first-degree murder. He was sentenced to life in prison. After exhausting his remedies in California state court, he petitioned for habeas relief in district court. The district court, relying on this court's opinion in *Mikes v. Borg*, 947 F.2d 353 (9th Cir. 1991), *cert. denied*, 112 S. Ct. 3055 (1992), concluded that "the record does not contain sufficient evidence to permit the rational factfinder to determine when Mr. Taylor's print was impressed . . . [or] that the windowsill was inaccessible to Mr. Taylor before the crime." The court, therefore, held that Taylor's conviction violated due process and granted his petition for habeas corpus. We granted the government's motion for a stay of the district court's judgment pend-

ing resolution of this appeal. . . .

II

In the present case, the district court determined the evidence was insufficient to permit the factfinder to conclude that the windowsill was inaccessible to Taylor prior to the crime. The court observed:

> Three reasonable inferences remain that point to his innocence. He could have impressed the print earlier as an invited guest in the apartment. He could have left the print earlier while doing paid work on the windowsill. He could have left the print earlier while engaged in criminal activity. The burden for rebutting these inferences lies with the People. This burden the People have not met.

The State argues these "inferences" are pure speculation by the district court and points out that no evidence supports any of them.

We conclude the district court's reliance on *Mikes* is misplaced because the facts in that case are distinguishable from those before us today. The turnstile and the posts in *Mikes* had been in a store – a public place where anyone could have had access to them. The inside of Ms. Jackson's windowsill was not in a public place, and Taylor would not have had access to it absent some unusual circumstance. Moreover, the print was found precisely at the point of entry for this burglary-murder, and the location of the print under the sill strongly suggests it was left by someone crawling through the window. Thus, *Mikes* does not control here. To hold that the evidence against Taylor was insufficient, we would have to extend *Mikes* to cover fingerprints that are found in places or on objects that were never accessible to the general public and that can be explained in a manner consistent with innocence only through farfetched, unsupported speculation. This we decline to do.

The government is only required to rule

out any hypotheses of innocence that are sufficient to create reasonable doubt. The district court, in this case, suggested three hypotheses the government failed to rebut. Each of these could conceivably create some doubt as to Taylor's guilt. Yet, there is no evidence supporting any of these hypotheses. In order to grant the habeas petition, we must find, after considering the evidence in the light most favorable to the government, that no rational jury could have found guilt beyond a reasonable doubt. The existence of some small doubt based on an unsupported yet unrebutted hypothesis of innocence is not sufficient to invalidate an otherwise legitimate conviction. As the future Chief Justice Burger stated in his dissent in *Borum,* the district court "seems to assume that the prosecution's case must answer all questions and remove all doubts, which, of course, is not the law because that would be impossible; the proof need only satisfy reasonable doubt." 380 F.2d at 599 (Burger, J., dissenting). The jury in this case had sufficient evidence from which to find Taylor guilty beyond a reasonable doubt.

The district court's decision is reversed – Taylor's habeas corpus petition is DENIED.

Notes

1. The *Taylor* opinion quotes with seeming approval the dissenting opinion (written, as it notes, by the future Chief Justice Burger) in the *Borum* case from the District of Columbia Circuit. The *Mikes* opinion had relied rather heavily on the majority opinion in that case. What is the significance of this quotation, if any?

2. As you read the three cases that follow, *Stallings v. Tansy, Ticey v. Peters,* and *Evans-Smith v. Taylor,* try to categorize the evidence adduced to gain insight into what troubled these federal judges (a majority or just a dissenter) so much as to compel them to vacate convictions that had been arrived at after full trials and upheld on appeal through the state system.

Stallings v. Tansy

28 F.3d 1018 (10th Cir. 1994)

EBEL, Circuit Judge.

Petitioner, who was convicted on five counts of passing forged checks in violation of N.M. Stat. Ann. 30-16-10(B), seeks habeas relief pursuant to 28 U.S.C. § 2254 on the grounds that the trial court's examination of petitioner at trial deprived him of a fair trial and that insufficient evidence was adduced at trial to support petitioner's convictions. Petitioner raised both of these issues on direct appeal to the New Mexico Court of Appeals, which affirmed his convictions. Petitioner then presented the same issues to the district court, which denied petitioner habeas relief and dismissed his petition with prejudice. After a careful review of the state court record, we conclude that the evidence was not sufficient to support a finding of all the essential elements of the forgery charges and, therefore, we reverse.

The evidence clearly established that petitioner passed five forged checks made payable to him. Petitioner argued, however, that he did not know the checks were forged at the time he cashed them. Petitioner contended that the person who wrote the checks represented himself to be the named owner of the account and petitioner had seen the person's identification, which confirmed his representation. Petitioner maintained that he received the checks in payment for goods he sold and services he provided to the maker of the checks and that he negotiated the checks quite openly at a grocery store where he was well known.

The critical issue in this case, then, is whether the evidence established that petitioner knew the checks were forged when he cashed them. On that issue, the record is devoid of any evidence. Because petitioner's knowledge was an essential element of the State's case, we must conclude that the forgery convictions violated petitioner's due process rights. Having reached this conclusion, we need not consider whether the trial court's examination of petitioner also denied him a fair trial.

* * *

In its case-in-chief, the State adduced evidence that petitioner cashed each of the third-party checks, which were drawn on an Oklahoma bank account in the name of Randy Thacker, at a grocery store in Farmington, New Mexico, during late June and early July of 1984. The owner of the account testified that he discovered his checkbook was missing from his Farmington apartment in July 1984, that he did not write any of the five checks at issue, and that he had never met petitioner. The evidence established that petitioner was well known at the grocery store, that he presented proper identification when cashing the checks at issue, and that he had cashed third-party checks there in the past. Finally, the State adduced evidence that all of the checks petitioner negotiated were returned to the store unpaid and marked "forgery." When Jack Morrison, the store owner, told petitioner that one of the checks was returned unpaid, petitioner replied that he did not have any money to make good on the check.

At the conclusion of the State's case, petitioner moved for a judgment of acquittal, arguing that the State had produced

no evidence to show that he either knew the checks were forged or intended to injure or defraud the grocery store when he cashed them. The State argued that petitioner's knowledge and intent were established by his statement to Morrison that he did not have the money to make good on the returned check. The trial court denied petitioner's motion without comment. In so ruling, the trial court erred.

We must bear in mind that petitioner was not charged with forging the checks himself and there was no evidence to suggest that he had. In addition, these were third-party checks, *i.e.*, the checks were not drawn on an account that petitioner represented to be his own. Under these circumstances, the jury could not logically infer from petitioner's statement, that he did not have the money to make good on the check, that petitioner knew at the time he negotiated any of the checks that they were forged. Petitioner was in the same position as someone who innocently negotiates a third-party check that turns out not to be backed by sufficient funds; the person negotiating the check may or may not have sufficient funds of his own to make good on the check. Thus, the State presented no evidence in its case-in-chief on one of the essential elements of the crime: that petitioner knew the checks were forged when he passed them.

After the trial court denied petitioner's motion for judgment of acquittal, petitioner took the stand and testified in his defense. Petitioner thereby waived any claim he had based on the insufficiency of the State's evidence at the conclusion of its case-in-chief. Our review of petitioner's sufficiency claim, therefore, must take into account not only the evidence adduced during the State's case-in-chief, but also the evidence adduced by the defendant in his case and the rebuttal evidence.

We turn, then, to the evidence presented after the State rested. Petitioner admitted at the outset of his testimony that he had a prior felony conviction for attempted burglary and motorcycle theft. Petitioner then explained how he came to be in possession of the forged checks. In May 1984, petitioner became acquainted with a person who said his name was Randy Thacker, and with whom petitioner shared an interest in cars. Over the course of the summer, the two became friends and petitioner sold Thacker a number of personal items, including stereo and martial arts equipment, for which Thacker paid with the checks at issue. Thacker also gave petitioner a check for the expenses petitioner incurred when he drove Thacker to Iowa. Petitioner said he had no reason to believe the person with whom he was dealing was not Randy Thacker, because he had seen Thacker's identification. Petitioner did admit that, to assist him in cashing the checks at the grocery store, he asked Thacker to make notations in the memo sections of some of the checks indicating that petitioner received the checks in the course of his employment. Petitioner explained that he frequently received checks in connection with his employment and cashed them at the grocery store because he did not have a checking account at a bank. Petitioner presented no other witnesses in his defense.

On rebuttal, Morrison testified that sometime after the bank returned the checks unpaid, he told petitioner he did not get paid on one of them. Petitioner replied that he did not know why the check would have been returned, and, as far as he knew, the check was good. Petitioner told Morrison that he had only $ 400.00 in his savings account to pay on the check, which Morrison said was not enough. Petitioner did not pay Morrison any money on the checks.

At the close of all the evidence, petitioner moved again for a judgment of acquittal, arguing that the evidence did not establish that he knew any of the checks were forged at the time he cashed them or that he acted with intent to injure or defraud the grocery store. The trial court de-

nied petitioner's motion and sent the case to the jury, which convicted petitioner on all five counts of forgery.

"To be sufficient, the evidence supporting [a] conviction must be substantial; that is, it must do more than raise a mere suspicion of guilt." Knowledge can be proven by circumstantial evidence. "The proven circumstances from which an accused's state of mind or intent can be inferred are his acts, conduct and words."

In upholding petitioner's convictions on direct appeal, the New Mexico Court of Appeals concluded that the following circumstantial evidence established beyond a reasonable doubt that petitioner knew the checks were forged: (1) he failed to pay the store after being told that one of the checks was returned unpaid; (2) he had a prior felony conviction; and (3) he admitted that he asked the maker of the checks to put false notations on the checks indicating he received them in the course of his employment so the checks would be easier to cash. The district court relied on two additional factors in concluding the evidence was sufficient on habeas review: petitioner failed to question why the checks were drawn on an out-of-state checking account; and petitioner failed to ascertain anything about the purported Randy Thacker's ability to pay on the checks. On appeal, the State relies on the same evidence in arguing that the evidence was sufficient to convict.

We note at the outset that all the evidence relied on by the State and the previous reviewing courts, with the exception of petitioner's failure to make good on the checks after being told one of them was returned unpaid, was adduced during the defendant's case; practically none of the allegedly pertinent evidence of knowledge came in during the State's case-in-chief. We have previously determined that no inference of petitioner's knowledge could be drawn from the evidence about petitioner's conversation with Morrison that was adduced in the State's case-in-chief. The additional evidence about that conversation that was adduced on rebuttal does not provide any additional support for an inference that petitioner knew the checks were forged.

Morrison did not testify that he told petitioner any of the checks were forged; rather, he simply said that he did not get paid on one of them. Petitioner's response to Morrison was entirely compatible with his asserted ignorance of the forgery: petitioner said he did not know why the check had been returned and, as far as he knew, the check was good. In accordance with our previous discussion, petitioner's statement that he had only $ 400.00 in savings, which Morrison indicated was not sufficient to cover his loss, does not support an inference that petitioner knew at the time he cashed the checks that any of them were forged.

The most damaging evidence against petitioner was his admission that he told the maker of the checks to put false notations on them indicating that petitioner received the checks in the course of his employment, rather than for personal goods and services. Although the notations represent a misrepresentation upon the face of the checks and, therefore, cast doubt on petitioner's general truthfulness and moral character, they do not support a logical inference that petitioner knew the checks were forged. The purpose of the notations was to facilitate cashing the third-party checks. The notations served the same purpose regardless of whether the checks were good or were forged. Therefore, petitioner's actions in having the false notations placed on the checks do not increase the likelihood that petitioner knew the checks were forged.

We turn, then, to petitioner's failure to question why the checks he received were drawn on an out-of-state bank, which the jury could have concluded was unusual. We note at the outset that the true owner of the account testified that he lived in Farmington, New Mexico, yet maintained a checking account in Oklahoma. In our mobile society, maintenance of an out-of-state bank account is not particularly unusual. Moreover, while the nature of the out-of-state checks may have given petitioner reason to question the creditworthiness of the purported Randy Thacker, that fact does not give rise to an inference that petitioner knew the checks were forged, especially in light of petitioner's uncontradicted testimony that he saw the identification of the person who represented himself to petitioner as Randy Thacker. Under the circumstances, we do not see how petitioner's failure to question why the checks were drawn on an out-of-state bank is evidence of petitioner's guilt.

Nor is petitioner's failure to ascertain information about the purported Randy Thacker's ability to pay on the checks evidence of petitioner's guilt. Petitioner was charged with passing checks he knew were forged, not with passing checks he knew were not backed by sufficient funds. The purported Randy Thacker's ability to pay on the checks is not relevant to petitioner's knowledge that the checks were forged.

Finally, we consider the inferences that can be drawn from petitioner's past criminal record. Petitioner's prior conviction for attempted burglary and motorcycle theft does not support an inference that petitioner committed the forgeries charged here. Rather, the prior conviction is relevant only to the jury's determination of petitioner's credibility.

If we assume the jury completely disbelieved petitioner, and, therefore, disregarded petitioner's testimony, as the State suggests in its brief, we are left with the evidence adduced during the State's case-in-chief and on rebuttal. As we discussed earlier, however, this evidence was not sufficient to support an inference that petitioner knew the checks were forged when he cashed them.

An essential of the due process guaranteed by the Fourteenth Amendment [is] that no person shall be made to suffer the onus of a criminal conviction except upon sufficient proof – defined as evidence necessary to convince a trier of fact beyond a reasonable doubt of the existence of every element of the offense. *Jackson*, 443 U.S. at 316. Overturning a state court conviction for lack of sufficient evidence is not a step that we take lightly or often. Nonetheless, when we have concluded "that upon the record evidence adduced at the trial no rational trier of fact could have found proof of guilt beyond a reasonable doubt," we have not hesitated to grant the petitioner habeas relief, and we do not hesitate to do so here. . . .

Ticey v. Peters

8 F.3d 498 (7th Cir. 1993)

BAUER, Circuit Judge.

David Ticey filed a petition for a writ of habeas corpus pursuant to 28 U.S.C. § 2254. The district court granted Ticey's petition. We reverse.

I.

In habeas corpus actions, we presume as true the facts found by the state court. *Sumner v. Mata*, 449 U.S. 539 (1981); 28 U.S.C. § 2254(d). We draw the facts, therefore, from the Illinois Appellate Court decision reported as *People v. Ticey*, 214 Ill. App. 3d 1043, 574 N.E.2d 810, 158 Ill. Dec. 697 (1991).

Fifteen-year-old Sherry Johnson lived in Chicago with her mother, her brother David Ticey, and her infant. They were home the evening of November 12, 1987, but Ticey left at some point that night. At about 12:30 a.m., Johnson was in bed. Her bedroom was dark except for the illumination from a bathroom light that was outside her room. At approximately 12:30 a.m., a man entered her room. He choked her, stuck his fingernails in her neck, and raped her. He wore a condom.

Johnson was taken to the hospital during the early hours of November 13. An examination revealed sperm inside her vagina. She was bruised, frightened, and upset. Chicago Police Detective Thomas Ptak interviewed Johnson at the hospital. During their conversation, Johnson identified Ticey as her attacker. She told Ptak that she could see Ticey's face when he came in her room because of the light from the bathroom, and she recognized Ticey's voice. She also said she knew it was Ticey because her attacker had a peculiar odor that she recognized as Ticey's. Moreover, she told Ptak that she recognized Ticey's body height and weight. Ticey was arrested based on Johnson's statement.

Three days later on November 16, 1987, Johnson, her mother, Ptak, and an assistant state's attorney ("ASA") met to discuss the rape. Johnson again identified Ticey as her assailant. She was in a fragile emotional condition. During the course of the meeting, Johnson and her mother had a confrontation, after which Johnson broke down crying. Following the confrontation, Johnson claimed she could not be sure who attacked her. Johnson did not, however, deny that Ticey was her attacker.

Ticey remained in jail awaiting trial. Nearly every day, he telephoned his mother's home from prison to speak with his girlfriend. Johnson often answered the telephone when he called. At some point, Johnson left her mother's home and stayed with a friend. While she was living with her friend, Johnson changed her mind about identifying Ticey as her attacker. She wrote the ASA a letter asking that he drop the charges against Ticey. When Johnson met with the ASA on December 15, 1987, she told him that she was no longer sure who raped her and reiterated her desire that the ASA drop the charges against Ticey. Further, she told the ASA that a week after the attack she saw her assailant in a store and that she told her mother that she saw him. Despite Johnson's recantation of her identification of Ticey as her attacker, the ASA proceeded with Ticey's prosecution.

Ticey requested a bench trial rather than trial by jury. Ptak testified at trial to Johnson's statement at the hospital that identified Ticey as her attacker. Ptak stated that Johnson "was shaking, she was crying, she had noticeable bruises about her neck and swelling also." He further testified that Johnson said that "while laying in her bed she saw [Ticey] come into her room, there was a light on in the bathroom just across from the room, she saw his face, she knows his height and weight. She also said he has a peculiar body odor about him and she identified him from all of those, his face, the height, weight and the odor of him."

Johnson also testified at trial. She stated that she could not be sure who her attacker was. She then was given the opportunity to explain her earlier identification of Ticey as her attacker. She was asked: "Sherry, when you told Detective Ptak when you met him in the hospital that it was your brother, you were sure it was your brother on that date, weren't you?" Johnson answered, "Yes, and I was calling for my brother to help me, I was calling, I was scared, I was calling for him to help me and they asked, asking me all the questions at the same time, that's what happened, he was asking me questions and he was asking me questions so I just said David, I said, my brother's name."

The government argued that Johnson was pressured to change her story by her mother, Ticey, and other family members. Ticey argued that Johnson was lying about the rape because her attacker wore a condom but sperm was discovered in her vagina. He also argued that even if a rape occurred, he did not commit it. The trial judge found Ticey guilty and sentenced him to 10 years imprisonment.

Ticey appealed to the Illinois Appellate Court, arguing that the contemporaneous identification was not enough evidence to convict him in the face of Johnson's testimony. He acknowledged that one witness' testimony might be enough to convict if that testimony was credible, however, he claims that Ptak's testimony about Johnson's statement was unreliable and therefore could not be the sole basis for his conviction.

The Illinois Appellate Court held that Johnson's prior identification of Ticey, although inconsistent with her trial testimony, was sufficient to convict. The court relied on a similar Illinois case, [in which] the Illinois Appellate Court held constitutional a statutory hearsay exception that allowed substantive use at trial of a minor's prior inconsistent statement identifying her attacker. The appellate court . . . here . . . held that Johnson's prior inconsistent statement identifying Ticey was admissible as substantive evidence and was sufficient to uphold his conviction.

II.

The district court found that Johnson's prior inconsistent statement was unreliable, and because that was the only evidence against Ticey, the court granted the petition because insufficient evidence existed to convict. We review habeas corpus decisions looking at the evidence in the light most favorable to the government. Because habeas corpus petitions allege constitutional violations, we review the issues *de novo*. When considering a due process challenge to the sufficiency of the evidence to support a conviction, we determine whether a rational trier of fact could find the defendant guilty beyond a reasonable doubt. *Jackson v. Virginia*, 443 U.S. 307 (1979). This inquiry focuses on the quantity and the quality of the evidence.

Ticey argues that the quality of the evidence against him is of such a character that no reasonable trier of fact could find him guilty beyond a reasonable doubt. Ticey . . . argues that a witness' paraphrased statement of another person's prior inconsistent statement is inadequate to serve as the sole basis for conviction and offends due process. Although Ticey seems to attack the substantive admission of the prior inconsistent identification, he instead attacks the statement as unreliable because the identification was not made under oath and because the statement was delivered by a police officer who paraphrased Johnson's statement. At oral argument, Ticey's attorney specifically stated that Ticey was not challenging the admissibility of Johnson's prior inconsistent statement, because the statement was admissible under Illinois law.

The district court accurately set forth Ticey's habeas corpus challenge to his conviction. The court stated: "Ticey's challenge is not whether Ms. Johnson's prior inconsistent statements were permissibly admitted as substantive evidence, but whether those statements were sufficient evidence upon which to base his conviction." The district court identified the inquiry it would use: "whether these recanted statements provided sufficient evidence of guilt to comport with the guarantees of due process (i.e., on the basis of the recanted statements, could any rational finder of fact have found Ticey guilty beyond a reasonable doubt)."

The district court cited the appropriate inquiry and the appropriate sufficiency of the evidence standard, and it went on to analyze the quality of the evidence. It considered whether the prior inconsistent statement used as substantive evidence was reliable enough to sustain a conviction, relying on *Vogel v. Percy*, 691 F.2d 843 (7th Cir. 1982). . . .

The cases from which *Vogel* was drawn illustrate the due process concerns surrounding unreliable evidence. The petitioner in *Vogel* raised a due process challenge to the substantive admission at trial of a prior inconsistent statement by a witness. We applied the *Vogel* facts to a number of inquiries gleaned from a similar chal-

lenge in a Fifth Circuit case and held that the prior unsworn inconsistent statement by the witness was admissible for substantive purposes. We considered whether: 1) the declarant was available for cross-examination; 2) the statement was made shortly after the events related and was transcribed promptly; 3) the declarant knowingly and voluntarily waived the right to remain silent; 4) the declarant admitted making the statement; and 5) there was some corroboration of the statement's reliability. All the factors focus on the reliability of the statement and the fairness of the circumstances under which the statement was made.

* * *

Vogel offers a framework by which reliability of out-of-court statements is assessed. The district court strictly applied the *Vogel* factors and held that because Johnson's statements at the hospital were not transcribed (an element of the second *Vogel* factor), and because the substance of the statements were not independently corroborated (the fifth *Vogel* factor), Johnson's statement was not sufficiently reliable to be the sole evidence supporting a conviction. We do not believe that the district court's use of the *Vogel* admissibility factors to weigh the quality of the evidence was misplaced. Nevertheless, these factors serve only as guidelines and, under those guidelines, Johnson's prior inconsistent statement was reliable. We, too, use the *Vogel* factors as a framework to determine reliability.

The first inquiry in *Vogel* is whether the witness was available for cross-examination. In this case, Johnson was available for cross-examination about her testimony to Ptak that Ticey was her attacker. She explained that she gave Ptak Ticey's name because she was confused by the questions and wanted Ticey's help. She did not, however, explain away or deny telling Ptak that Ticey's height, weight, voice, and odor were how she knew it was Ticey who attacked her. At oral argument, Ticey's attorney admitted that Johnson's explanation was "lame." Johnson acknowledged the prior statement, and it was up to the factfinder to determine whether she was telling the truth at trial or when she made the statement to Ptak. In light of her weak and incomplete explanation, and in the face of evidence of outside pressure to change her testimony, the trial court could reasonably find that Johnson's recantation at trial was not credible.

The second *Vogel* factor is when the prior inconsistent statement was made. This reflects the concern that if a significant amount of time passes between a crime and a statement, a greater opportunity exists for a witness to fabricate a story and an identification. If the statement is proximate in time to the event, less opportunity for fabrication exists. In this case, Johnson made her statement at the hospital within hours of the rape. The closeness in time to the event in question minimizes the opportunity for fabrication. Johnson was still experiencing the emotional aftereffects of the attack and was not yet subject to the outside pressure that the Illinois courts found influenced her trial testimony. Johnson's hospital identification statement apparently was not transcribed, yet her acknowledgment of her prior statement vitiates the need for transcription.

The third factor is whether the witness made a knowing and intelligent waiver of her right to remain silent. No such concerns are implicated here because the witness was the victim, not the suspect, of a crime.

The fourth factor is whether the declarant admits to making the prior inconsistent statement. As we discussed, Johnson admitted to giving Ptak her brother's name in response to his question asking who attacked her. Moreover, Johnson stated that Ticey was her attacker three days later at the State's attorney's office. Her reiteration of Ticey's role in the crime lent reliability to her earlier identification and her acknowledgment of the statement provided an opportunity to question Johnson about why she twice identified Ticey as the rapist.

The final factor is whether the prior inconsistent statement was corroborated. Johnson's identification of Ticey was not corroborated by physical evidence. However, Johnson again identified Ticey as the rapist three days following the attack. Ticey acknowledged this identification at trial, and gave no explanation of why it was not accurate.

On the whole, and considered in the *Vogel* framework, we believe Johnson's prior inconsistent statement was reliable, and it is of the quality that may support a conviction. But we must now consider whether it alone is enough to support Ticey's conviction in the face of Johnson's contrary statements at trial. We believe it is.

We have held that evidence similar to that presented in Ticey's case is enough to sustain a conviction. *Wandick v. Chrans*, 869 F.2d 1084 (7th Cir. 1989). In *Wandick*, we stated that "we will not disturb the trial judge's determination that the petitioner was guilty beyond a reasonable doubt. Credible testimony of one identification witness is sufficient to support a conviction." In this case, the trial judge found that Ptak's testimony about Johnson's prior identification was credible. The trial judge also found that Johnson's recantation of her identification and explanation of her statement was incredible. This is in keeping with the judiciary's wary reception of recantations. Ticey claims that Johnson's incredibility at trial does not, *a fortiori*, lend credibility to her prior inconsistent statement. In isolation that is true. But here, the facts surrounding the hospital identification, Johnson's reiteration that Ticey was the rapist three days later, and the facts leading up to her recantation, support the trial court's finding that Johnson's prior inconsistent statement was more credible than her trial testimony. The trial court observed Johnson's demeanor, considered her incomplete and unsound explanation, and listened to a credible witness' (Ptak's) account of the prior statement. After weighing these considerations, the trial court could determine that given the facts, Johnson was more credible at the hospital than she was at trial.

The factfinder must resolve the problem posed by conflicting hypotheses. Here, the government offered a hypothesis that Johnson was pressured into changing her story. Ticey offered a hypothesis that if Johnson was raped, he did not commit the crime, and Johnson was confused when she said he did. The trial court judge resolved the conflicting hypotheses after observing the witnesses and hearing all the facts. The court's decision that the government hypothesis was correct was reasonable. We believe that a rational trier of fact could find Ticey guilty beyond a reasonable doubt and sufficient evidence exists to support his conviction.

III.

The district court decision is REVERSED.

CUDAHY, Circuit Judge, dissenting. I think the learned trial judge correctly granted the writ here. The case, of course, is extremely close, but an even-handed application of the *Vogel* factors seems to me to point toward an affirmance.

The issue in this habeas corpus action is not whether "Johnson was more credible at the hospital than she was at trial." The issue is whether a rational trier of fact could find Ticey guilty beyond a reasonable doubt based simply on Johnson's untranscribed, uncorroborated and unsworn prior inconsistent statements. In *Vogel v. Percy*, 691 F.2d 843, 846-47 (7th Cir. 1982), we adopted five guidelines for determining whether the use of a prior inconsistent statement comports with due process. As the majority correctly indicates, "we considered whether: 1) the declarant was available for cross-examination; 2) the statement was made shortly after the events

related and was transcribed promptly; 3) the declarant knowingly and voluntarily waived the right to remain silent; 4) the declarant admitted making the statement; and 5) there was some corroboration of the statement's reliability."

We intended the application of these guidelines to "safeguard due process by 'preventing convictions where a reliable evidentiary basis is totally lacking.' " Despite the importance of this purpose, however, the majority dilutes the corroboration prong of the guidelines. For one thing, the hypothesis of family pressure on Johnson sufficient to make her change her story is just that—a hypothesis. Evidence to support it was (in Judge Duff's words) "scanty" and in my view suggestive only. (There was some sort of "confrontation" and emotional outburst at one of Johnson's interviews and she had telephone contact with her brother while he was in jail.) Perhaps this explains why the trial judge "made no specific finding about whether Johnson had been pressured to recant her story." More importantly, the majority has not pointed to any corroboration of Johnson's earlier identification. The majority relies for "corroboration" on another statement by Johnson. This statement may in a minor way add something to the credibility of the first one, but it essentially piles one uncorroborated (unsworn and unrecorded) statement on another. This is not "corroboration" as the word is commonly understood. Cf. *People v. Winfield*, 160 Ill. App. 3d 983, 513 N.E.2d 1032, 1034, 112 Ill. Dec. 423 (Ill. App. Ct. 1987) (affirming trial court's specific finding that alleged sexual abuse victim had been pressured into recanting accusation of father based on the court's observation of the father in court and on the fact that the recanted statement was transcribed, given under oath, and similar to statements victim made to nurse treating her).

When this Court adopted the *Vogel* guidelines, we sought to determine whether a court violated due process by admitting prior inconsistent statements which were not the only basis for the conviction:

Additional witnesses for the state positively identified petitioner Vogel as having purchased a pair of nylon pantyhose the evening of the robbery; as having been in the vicinity of the robbery under suspicious circumstances at the time the market alarm was sounded; and as having asked a friend to dispose of certain clothing approximately two hours after the robbery.

Vogel then testified in his own behalf.

He admitted the substance of the statements against him, but offered exculpatory explanations for each of his acts on the night of the robbery.

If anything, the guidelines should be applied more stringently in a case like Ticey's where the inconsistent statements are the sole foundation for the conviction. Given the absence of truly corroborative evidence supporting Johnson's initial identification, the circumstances in this case do not foreclose a reasonable doubt. I therefore respectfully dissent.

Evans-Smith v. Taylor

19 F.3d 899 (4th Cir. 1994)

MURNAGHAN, Circuit Judge.

Appellant, William Evans-Smith, is serving a twenty-year sentence at Virginia's Staunton Correctional Center for the 1985 murder of his wife, Barbara Evans-Smith. He was first convicted after a jury trial and sentenced to five years imprisonment in August 1985. That conviction was overturned on appeal to the Virginia Court of Appeals on the ground that much of the evidence used to obtain the conviction was either improperly admitted hearsay evidence or evidence that was more prejudicial than probative.

A second trial was set and Evans-Smith moved for a change of venue on account of pretrial publicity; his motion was denied after an extensive hearing. During the course of the second trial, which began on April 17, 1989, nearly four years after the first trial, Evans-Smith filed a Motion to Strike, arguing that the solely circumstantial nature of the evidence presented by the Commonwealth was insufficient to establish guilt. His motion was denied. The jury found Evans-Smith guilty of second-degree murder and recommended the maximum twenty-year sentence. Evans-Smith then moved to set aside the verdict, again arguing that the evidence was insufficient, and also arguing, among other grounds,

that the court's prior denial of the motion to change venue deprived him of a fair trial. He also moved for a new trial based upon alleged juror misconduct. Both motions were denied. Bond was denied, and Evans-Smith was sentenced to twenty years imprisonment.

Evans-Smith appealed through the state system. His appeals were denied.

. . . The present action is a § 2254 habeas appeal. In the district court, both the Commonwealth and Evans-Smith moved for summary judgment. After a hearing, the district court granted the Commonwealth's motion and denied Evans-Smith's. Evans-Smith appeals . . .

FACTS

In obtaining Evans-Smith's conviction, the Commonwealth proceeded on the theory that Evans-Smith killed or rendered his wife unconscious in the kitchen of their farmhouse, then dragged her body upstairs and staged a rape/robbery scene before leaving for work. Evans-Smith asserted throughout that he is innocent, that the murder was committed by an unidentified third party or parties, and that the Commonwealth failed to investigate properly the possibility that someone other than Evans-Smith was the murderer.

The prosecution agrees that the evidence used to convict Evans-Smith was entirely circumstantial. According to Loudoun County Medical Examiner Dr. Hocker, Barbara Evans-Smith (hereinafter "the victim") died sometime between 4:00 and 8:00 a.m. on the morning of April 15, 1985. His calculation was based on the degree of rigor mortis (60%) he observed upon his arrival at the crime scene at approximately 1:00 p.m. that afternoon. Dr. Byer, the medical examiner who performed the autopsy, determined that the victim died by strangulation thirty to sixty minutes after eating. The contents of the victim's stomach were consistent with the breakfast that Evans-Smith stated he had shared with his wife.

The victim's body was found in her second-floor bedroom of the couple's Loudoun County farmhouse with a pair of pantyhose wrapped three times around her neck and knotted. She was clad in a nightshirt and robe which had been ripped open, leaving her bare from the waist down. While the condition of her clothing suggested the possibility of a sexual assault, Dr. Byer found no seminal fluid or genital abrasions on the victim. There was a small amount of unexplained blood in her vaginal cavity. A pair of white underwear had been stuffed into the victim's mouth. Dr. Byer stated that the underwear was loosely packed, a fact which could lead to the inference that the underwear had been placed in the mouth after death, since the loose packing would not have served as an effective gag. The Commonwealth urged the jury to consider the underwear as evidence that the murder had been staged as a sexual assault.

Dr. Byer identified internal injury and hemorrhaging to the back of the victim's head which could have been caused by her head hitting the wooden stairs, as she was dragged to the second floor. The doctor testified, however, that "any blunt force trauma" could have caused the injury. He also noted triangular-shaped abrasions on the victim's neck near her jaw line, which

he believed were the victim's fingernail scratches, created while she was trying to remove the ligature from around her neck. There was no blood on the hands of the victim.

The bedroom in which the victim was found looked as if it had been ransacked, with items from the closets and dresser drawers strewn around the room. Evans-Smith's bedroom, separated from the victim's bedroom by a shared bathroom, had a similar appearance, but the rest of the house was in order, with the exception of an overturned, downstairs hall table and slightly skewed furniture in the kitchen. The Commonwealth argued that since only a few pieces of furniture had been moved, and many valuables were left either untouched or "neatly" laid out on the beds upstairs, the crime scene was consistent with a staged crime and not a real robbery.

Evans-Smith's daughter, Leslie Cook, noted in testifying for the prosecution that the front door was ajar when she arrived at the scene at approximately 11:00 a.m., that one of the two dogs was closed up in the laundry room, and that the other was outside. Cook also testified that she observed only one set of tire tracks on the newly raked gravel driveway as she came onto the property. She and another prosecution witness, William Laycock, testified to the presence of another set of tire tracks running across the hayfield toward a second exit on the morning in question. This second set of tracks was not investigated by the police, and the defense argued at trial that their existence implied that someone other than Evans-Smith had been to the house that morning.

Special Agent Ritchie of the Virginia State Police, a key participant in the investigation of the crime scene, placed bags over the victim's hands and feet upon his arrival to preserve any evidence on them during transport, and collected several other items from the crime scene for analysis, including jewelry boxes which had been tampered with and which Ritchie believed could be fingerprinted. No fingerprints were taken from the furniture and the other items that were found out of place on the first floor. Nor was fingerprinting undertaken along the staircase. Ritchie also observed two parallel scratch marks, which were photographed, on the linoleum floor in the kitchen. Although the Commonwealth attempted to cite these scratch marks as evidence that the victim was killed in the kitchen, then dragged across the floor and upstairs, State Police Special Agent Schultze, testifying for the prosecution, stated that the scratch marks could not have been caused by the soft slippers the victim was apparently wearing at the approximate time of the murder. Her slippers were found in different rooms on the first floor. At oral argument, the Commonwealth asserted that its argument was that the victim's bare heels had created the marks.

Among the evidence collected by Ritchie were seventy-three individual hair samples from around and on the body of the victim and from the stairway leading to the second floor, tissues removed from the wastebasket in the shared bathroom, the victim's nightshirt and robe, and various other items.

Of the fourteen hair samples taken from the stairway, Forensic Scientist Deanna Dabbs found ten of them to be unidentifiable, three to be consistent with the hair of the victim (one of which had been forcibly removed), and one blond head hair to belong to neither the victim nor to Evans-Smith. Thirty-nine of the fifty-nine hair samples taken from the victim's body or bedroom were found to be consistent with the victim's hair, seven were unidentifiable, and seven were consistent with the hair of Evans-Smith. None of the hair attributed to Evans-Smith had been forcibly removed. Of the remaining hair, one brown Caucasian head hair taken from the bag enclosing the victim's clenched left hand was found to belong to neither the victim nor to Evans-Smith. Five hair samples

taken from a pubic combing of the victim were definitely not Evans-Smith's, and could not be identified as belonging to the victim.

Dabbs analyzed several small blood stains on the victim's robe and a blood-stained tissue from the shared bathroom's wastebasket. There was also a band-aid found in the wastebasket with an amount of blood on it too minute to test. Two of seven blood stains on the robe were consistent with the same type as Evans-Smith's blood. Blood of the same type as Evans-Smith's was also found on a tissue retrieved from a wastebasket in the shared bathroom.

Evans-Smith told the police that he and his wife had cleared limbs, thorny locusts, and other brush from parts of their farm on the Saturday and Sunday morning preceding Monday's murder. Commonwealth witnesses corroborated this statement. While clearing the brush, Evans-Smith allegedly acquired several scratches on his arm and hands. At about noon on Sunday, after patching up his scratches with large band-aids, Evans-Smith and his wife attended the Oatland Point-to-Point horse race. Upon their return that afternoon, Evans-Smith raked the gravel driveway with a york rake.

Evans-Smith stated to investigators that he arose on the morning of the murder at 5:00 a.m, as usual, and drove down the one-quarter mile lane to the mailbox to retrieve the newspaper. While at the mailbox, Evans-Smith claimed, he caught a glimpse of a dark-colored van parked on the road near a neighbor's driveway, but thought nothing of it. He returned to the house, placed the newspaper on the hood of his wife's truck—as was their custom—and completed some farm chores. Evans-Smith stated that he returned to the house to breakfast with his wife at approximately 6:00 a.m., and after signing a birthday card for their son-in-law at his wife's request, kissing his wife goodbye in the kitchen, and watching her wave to him from her upstairs bedroom, he began his one and one-half to two hour commute to American University's Foreign Area Studies Office in Washington, D.C. According to Evans-Smith, the traffic coming into the city was "extremely slow" that morning. The prosecution put on witnesses who testified that there had been nothing extraordinary, such as accidents, about the traffic that morning. The Commonwealth argued that Evans-Smith complained "bitterly" about the traffic, and that his reaction was inconsistent with the normal state of rush hour traffic.

The trial transcript suggests that Evans-Smith did complain, but perhaps not "bitterly." The testimony of a co-worker was that

> [Our conversation] was concerned with the traffic that morning, that it was exceptionally bad. The traffic was very often bad coming over the Cabin John Bridge and it was exceptionally bad that morning, yeah.
>
>   And Mr. Evans-Smith was upset . . . in a way that is not abnormal with the traffic.

Two investigators who interviewed Evans-Smith two days after the murder testified that Evans-Smith told them at that time he had not made any stops on his way to work. He later told someone else and testified at the first trial that he had stopped at the university president's office to drop off some books. The office, however, was closed, and he proceeded on to work. According to prosecution witness Mimi Tandler, who was writing a book on the case, Evans-Smith told her after the first trial that he had stopped at a car wash on the way to work.

Evans-Smith stated that he arrived at his office at approximately 8:15 a.m. or "some time before 8:30 a.m." Evans-Smith's co-worker, Dorothy Lohman, testified that Evans-Smith usually arrived at work between 7:30 or 8:00 a.m., but that he was not at his desk at 8:45 a.m. when

she went to his office. She had a meeting with Evans-Smith concerning edits of a manuscript later that morning, however, at which time he appeared completely normal. Prosecution witness and coworker James Rudolph testified that the office arrival time was flexible and that it was normal for people to arrive between 8:00 and 8:30 a.m. He further testified that he had spoken with Evans-Smith in the office parking lot at 8:30 or 8:35 on the morning in question. This conversation was the source of the comments about the traffic. A defense witness stated that Evans-Smith arrived at work on April 15 between 8:00 and 8:30 a.m. Yet another stated that he had spoken with Evans-Smith in the men's bathroom on the same floor as Evans-Smith's office at 8:30 a.m.

Evans-Smith was contacted by the police at his office and told of the murder that afternoon. Lieutenant Brown and Investigator Merchant testified that Evans-Smith then asked a series of questions about whether his wife had been raped or disfigured, whether she was clothed or not, where she was located, and who found her. Although such questions might reasonably be expected, the prosecution argued that such questions suggested he knew what the murder scene looked like, and, in any event, were odd reactions for someone told of the murder of his wife. Brown testified that as soon as he told Evans-Smith that a burglary had occurred, Evans-Smith gasped, "Oh my God, the van," and then provided a description of the van, as noted above.

The investigators and Evans-Smith then left Washington for Loudoun County. The investigators, who trailed him on the way back, testified that Evans-Smith, upon reaching stop lights, would put his head in his hands or, alternatively, look in his rear view mirror.

When they reached the farm in Loudoun County, Evans-Smith was not allowed to visit the crime scene to see his wife's body. He engaged in a physical tussle with the authorities, during which they first observed several scratches on his arms. The scratches on his arms were the source of much testimony at the trial. The prosecution's theory was that the scratches were caused by the victim's fingernails in the course of a violent struggle with Evans-Smith. The Commonwealth based its argument on the testimony of its witness, Dr. Solin, who had examined Evans-Smith's scratches and had determined that they could have been caused by the victim's fingernails. He testified that his knowledge of the fingernails was based on Commonwealth photographs. Dr. Solin did not himself examine the victim's fingernails. Two other prosecution witnesses, who saw only photographs of Evans-Smith's scratches but had made a careful inspection of the victim's fingernails, concluded that her fingernails could not possibly have caused the scratches. These two witnesses, Loudoun Medical Examiner George T. Hocker and Virginia Deputy Chief Medical Examiner Dr. James C. Byer, both testified that the victim's fingernails were too short and dull to have made the scratches. They opined that the scratches were more likely made, as Evans-Smith claimed, by his work clearing thorn bushes. Evans-Smith's daughter, who testified for the prosecution, stated that she had seen her parents clearing out thorn bushes the day before the murder. Moreover, the only debris found under the victim's fingernails was identified by the prosecution witnesses as having resulted from her attempts to release the ligature from around her neck. None of the debris was consistent with Evans-Smith's blood or skin; indeed, there was no blood on the victim's hands at all. Evans-Smith had stated that the blood found on the tissues and medicated band-aid in his bathroom had come from his and his wife's having treated his scratches from the thorns. Prosecution witness, Dabbs, testified that the spots on the victim's robe might have been placed there at different times, one stain having been on the robe as long as

eight weeks previously, and the other less than one month previously. The test was not capable of determining whether the blood had been placed on the victim's robe the day of the murder.

On the evening of the murder, after the day's investigation had concluded, Evans-Smith was asked by the authorities to make a list of any items he believed were missing from the house. Two days later Evans-Smith asked to speak with Investigators Brown and Merchant. During the ensuing interrogation, he mentioned that his wife kept her jewelry and hay money in an aqua jewelry box in her bedroom. Prosecution witness Joe Rogers, a farmer who leased and cultivated the land adjoining Evans-Smith's farm, testified that Evans-Smith had phoned him ostensibly to discuss that year's planting. During the course of the conversation, Evans-Smith asked him to keep an eye out for anything suspicious that he might find and report it. Shortly thereafter, an employee of Rogers, while discing the neighboring field, found the aqua box in the field, slightly covered by dirt. There were no fingerprints on the box, but its composition as well as the time it had been exposed to the elements made it unlikely that such fingerprints would still exist.

Several other facts bear mention. During the week following the murder, Evans-Smith called his coworker, Rudolph, who was then vacationing in New Mexico. During their conversation, Evans-Smith related that he had been indicted, and he believed the state had bungled the investigation. He then related to Rudolph his activities on the morning of the murder, telling him of the stop at the president's office and his late arrival at the office. He seemed concerned, however, that Rudolph remembered his arrival time to be approximately 8:35, because he had already told the police that he thought he had arrived at work at 8:15 a.m. According to Rudolph, Evans-Smith mentioned that "it would be nice if he and I recalled the same time of arrival that morning." The Commonwealth argued that the conversation was evidence that Evans-Smith was trying to make other people's stories consistent with his own. Rudolph testified, however, that Evans-Smith did not threaten him, and that "he was not noticeably angry. I'm sure he was upset, everybody was upset." Rudolph testified that Evans-Smith was not angry with him. In addition, he testified further that his watch often ran five minutes fast, and that he could have seen Evans-Smith at 8:30 rather than at 8:35 a.m.

Evans-Smith attempted, with no success, to have the police investigate the possibility that two horse trainers, Robert Rivera and Rudy Ruiz, who were working at a horse barn on adjacent property at the approximate time of the murder, may have been involved in the crime. In support of this theory, Evans-Smith pointed to the fact that Rivera was on a $ 100,000 bond for drug charges and that he had been ruled off of the Charles Town race track, after drugging horses. There was some suggestion that Rivera's whereabouts on the morning of the murder were inconsistent with his statements at trial. The Rivera theory suffers from incomplete development in the record. On the basis of the foregoing evidence, essentially all there is, William Evans-Smith was convicted of the second degree murder of his wife of over forty years.

DISCUSSION

The standard of review for a claim of insufficient evidence is whether, viewing the evidence in the light most favorable to the prosecution, and according the benefit of all reasonable inferences to the government, any rational trier of fact could have found the defendant guilty beyond a reasonable doubt. The standard is obviously rigorous. As the Supreme Court recently has reiterated, "the writ of habeas corpus has historically been regarded as an extraordinary remedy." *Brecht v. Abrahamson,* 123 L. Ed. 2d 353, 113 S. Ct. 1710, 1719 (1993). Nevertheless, however circumscribed, the writ remains a remedy, "a bulwark against convictions that violate fundamental fairness."

The very existence of the *Jackson* test presupposes that juries accurately charged on the elements of a crime and on the strict burden of persuasion to which they must hold the prosecution, nevertheless "may occasionally convict even when it can be said that no rational trier of fact could find guilt beyond a reasonable doubt." [The test] was adopted to provide an additional safeguard against that possibility, and was to give added assurance that guilt should never be found except on a rationally supportable "state of near certitude."

The question before us in the instant case, therefore, is whether the wholly circumstantial evidence, taken together, could allow any rational trier of fact to conclude beyond a reasonable doubt that Evans-Smith murdered his wife. In conducting such an inquiry we consider all the evidence presented in the record.

The prosecution's theory of the case was that Evans-Smith, the victim's husband, for whatever reason but probably in the heat of passion (of which there was no proof), murdered his wife or rendered her unconscious in the kitchen after the two had breakfast. No evidence of motive nor of heat of passion was introduced at trial. Indeed, the only evidence before the jury was that the Evans-Smiths had been seen the day before the murder enjoying one another's company. The prosecution's theory was that he then dragged his wife up the stairs, and placed her on the floor of her bedroom. Realizing, according to the prosecution, that he would be a primary suspect, Evans-Smith then supposedly staged a robbery/rape scene and drove to work, perhaps arriving a little later than usual. According to the Commonwealth, Evans-Smith's statements and behavior after the crime suggested to the prosecution an attempt to cast blame elsewhere, lending further supposed support to the conclusion that he in fact had committed the murder and then had attempted to cover it up.

* * *

At the outset, it is worth noting that circumstantial evidence need not exclude every reasonable hypothesis of innocence. Rather "circumstances altogether inconclusive, if separately considered, may, by their number and joint operation ... be sufficient to constitute conclusive proof."

Even allowing for this important caveat, we believe that a rational trier of fact could not determine that the evidence supports a finding of guilt beyond a reasonable doubt. Instead, what the evidence shows is that Evans-Smith was at his home the morning of the murder, a fact he does not dispute and would be his most customary behavior. In addition, according all reasonable inferences to the benefit of the prosecution,[29] we believe a rational trier of fact possibly could conclude beyond a reasonable doubt that the crime scene was staged. It is the next step — an inference that Evans-Smith was within "a state of near certitude" the perpetrator of this terrible crime – that the evidence simply cannot support.

"A determination in federal collateral review that a state court conviction by jury verdict was not supported by constitution-

ally sufficient evidence is one to be made with special caution and anxiety." *West v. Wright,* 931 F.2d at 270. As in *West,* the instant case requires not only the reversal of a federal district court, but also of the state trial and appellate courts.

We conclude, however, that the evidence assessed in its entirety and in the light most favorable to the prosecution is not sufficient to persuade any rational trier of fact of the petitioner's guilt beyond a reasonable doubt, that Evans-Smith's conviction on the evidence therefore violated his constitutional right to due process, and that he is entitled to the relief sought in this habeas corpus proceeding. Evans-Smith could no doubt have acted as the prosecution has contended he did. However, the suppositions are derived from acts of his consistent with a husband's perfectly proper behavior mixed with imaginations of behavior for which his presence has not been proven. To start with the assumption that the crime was committed and then to show that each piece of circumstantial evidence can be explained in a consistent manner is fundamentally different from examining each piece of evidence and finally concluding beyond a reasonable doubt that the defendant was guilty. The prosecution has attempted to accomplish only the first alternative, not the second. As the Supreme Court has long taught "it is the duty of the Government to establish ... guilt beyond a reasonable doubt." Such guilt has not been established, and, as a consequence, Evans-Smith's right to due process has been violated.

We are unable to conclude that any rational trier of fact could have found Evans-Smith guilty beyond a reasonable doubt. We therefore remand the proceeding to the district court with directions to issue the writ vacating Evans-Smith's conviction.

---

[29] It is essential to remember that *Jackson* requires that we review all the evidence and then determine whether a rational trier of fact could have found guilt beyond a reasonable doubt. *See Jackson,* 443 U.S. at 319 ("*all of the evidence* is to be considered in the light most favorable to the prosecution") (emphasis in original). Favoring the prosecution with all inferences does not mean that we must ignore evidence that is in the record, but which they ignore. So, for example, as mentioned in the facts section, the unidentified hair taken from the evidence bag enclosing the victim's left hand as well as the unidentified hair from the pubic combing suggest a view of the events contrary to the one provided by the Commonwealth.

Notes

1. Among these three cases, the one conviction that stands (Ticey) is the only one with direct evidence (albeit in the form of hearsay statements) by a victim

identifying the defendant as having committed the crime. Significant scientific studies have demonstrated that the single most common factor leading to wrongful convictions is mistaken eyewitness identification. Can the *Jackson v. Virginia* standard address this difficult problem? Why not?

2. The court in *Stallings* was willing to consider the defendant's own testimony in evaluating whether the evidence was sufficient to support the conviction. Although in this case the court still found the evidence lacking, its position was that the *Jackson* standard required assessment of *all* the evidence, viewed in the light most favorable to the prosecution. What concerns are raised by this approach?

3. The *Jackson v. Virginia* standard applies equally to convictions obtained in federal courts, and federal circuits are called upon to analyze those convictions for legal sufficiency as well. Here, too, reversals are not frequent, but they do occur. The following cases illustrate two different responses to appellants' arguments that the evidence of participation in a conspiracy was insufficient to sustain the convictions.

United States v. Soto

716 F.2d 989 (2d Cir. 1983)

JUDGES: Newman and Winter, Circuit Judges, and Maletz, Senior Judge.*
* Of the United States Court of International Trade, sitting by designation.

MALETZ, Senior Judge.

Defendant-appellant Evelyn Soto appeals from her conviction on two counts of conspiracy. The first count charged Soto with conspiracy to distribute narcotics in violation of 21 U.S.C. § 846; the second with conspiracy to use a firearm to commit a felony, a violation of 18 U.S.C. § 371.

Soto advances three arguments on this appeal. The first relates to an allegedly erroneous evidentiary ruling regarding co-conspirator hearsay statements, *see United States v. Geaney,* 417 F.2d 1116 (2d Cir. 1969). Another goes to a purported failure to correctly charge the jury on the elements of a conspiracy. Soto's primary claim, however, is that the evidence was insufficient as a matter of law to convict her of conspiracy. On this score, we agree and reverse the judgment of the district court.

I

The basic facts are not in dispute. At the trial the government presented the testimony of four Drug Enforcement Administration (DEA) special agents. In essence their testimony established that Soto resided in a Bronx apartment located at 2526 Bronx Park East, 5-B, which was used, in part, as a narcotics "cutting mill."[1]

The government's chief witness was DEA Agent Fred Marrero. Agent Marrero testified that in his role as an undercover agent he met the person in charge of the cutting mill—a man known as "Cheo"—on June 29, 1982. Marrero was invited up to the Bronx apartment by Cheo where a group of six persons, including Soto, gathered in the bedroom. During Marrero's half-hour visit Soto remained in the bedroom for approximately ten to fifteen minutes. The meeting was interrupted at one point by the building superintendent who came to the apartment to speak to Cheo. As Cheo got up to leave, he commented that he (Cheo) did not allow anyone into

---

[1] A "cutting mill" is a place where relatively pure drugs – usually heroin or cocaine – are diluted before being sold on the street.

the bedroom. At the time several handguns and drug paraphernalia were in plain view. There was no discussion or mention of either narcotics or weapons by anyone during Marrero's visit.

Following a tip from a confidential informant, DEA Agents Thomas Ward and Marrero made several arrests and seized a cache of guns and drugs at the apartment in the early morning hours of July 2, 1982. At the time of the agents' entry into the apartment, Agent Ward found Soto and her young child asleep in the bedroom. A search of that room uncovered drugs, drug paraphernalia and a weapon. A search of the rest of the apartment reaped a large quantity of drugs, drug paraphernalia, cash and more weapons. Although the apartment contained a substantial amount of contraband, it is equally clear that apartment 5-B was more than just a cutting mill – it was also a domicile for several individuals, including Soto,[2] being furnished with couches, sleeping cots and a television set.

Two stipulations were also made part of the record. The first provided that Soto arrived in New York from Puerto Rico on or about June 8, 1982; that she resided at 2526 Bronx Park East, apartment 5-B, from June 8, through July 2; and that apartment 5-B was leased in the name of Pablo Rodriguez but, in reality, was paid for and controlled by Cheo and his wife, Nancy Medina. The second stipulation specified that ledger books found during the search of the apartment were examined by government experts for fingerprints and handwriting; that Soto's fingerprints were not identified, but those of Cheo and his wife were; and that Soto's handwriting was not identified as appearing anywhere on the ledger sheets. In this connection, Marrero testified that the ledger books contained a list of Cheo's employees and

___

[2] At the time of her arrest Soto gave the arresting agent the 2526 Bronx Park East address as the place where she lived.

their salaries, but did not contain Soto's name.

Against this background, we address Soto's principal contention that the evidence was insufficient as a matter of law to convict her beyond a reasonable doubt.

II

It is established that a defendant advancing a claim based on insufficiency of the evidence bears a very heavy burden. *See, e.g., United States v. Carson,* 702 F.2d 351, 361 (2d Cir. 1983). As this court stated in *Carson:*

> Our inquiry is whether the jury, drawing reasonable inferences from the evidence, may fairly and logically have concluded that the defendant was guilty beyond a reasonable doubt. *Jackson v. Virginia,* 443 U.S. 307, 317 (1979). In making this determination, we must view the evidence in the light most favorable to the government, and construe all permissible inferences in its favor.

Id. at 361. Given that "[a] conspiracy by its very nature is a secretive operation," the "existence of and participation in a conspiracy . . . may be established . . . through circumstantial evidence."

The most significant circumstance relied on by the government in support of the jury's finding of guilt is the fact that Soto lived in apartment 5-B for three weeks prior to her arrest. Her sustained and regular presence in that apartment, the government contends, is circumstantial evidence from which the jury could infer defendant's membership in the narcotics and firearms conspiracies.

We are constrained to disagree. While it would not be accurate to characterize Soto's presence at the apartment as merely transitory, we nevertheless consider the total circumstances of how Soto came to reside there to be highly significant. For here we have an individual newly arrived from Puerto Rico, accompanied by a child of tender years, clearly in need of shelter. To this end, as soon as she arrived in New York defendant took up residence at the 2526 Bronx Park East apartment. Although the living arrangements there may not have been ideal, there is no indication that defendant had any other alternative.

As defendant correctly observes, and as the government necessarily concedes, Soto's mere presence at the apartment, even coupled with the knowledge that a crime was being committed there, is not sufficient to establish her guilt. Evidence tending to show knowing participation in the conspiracy is also needed. Absent some showing of purposeful behavior tending to connect defendant with the acquisition, concealment, importation, use or sale of drugs or firearms, participation in the conspiracies cannot be proven by presence alone.

The government stresses that on the morning of the July 2 arrests Soto was found sleeping in the room where the drugs were cut. But this fact demonstrates nothing more than that defendant, as a mere guest or invitee, did not enjoy exclusive dominion or control over the bedroom or, for that matter, over the apartment in general. The government further submits that based on the statement by Cheo to Marrero to the effect that Cheo did not want the building superintendent in the bedroom, the inference can be drawn that Cheo trusted Soto and that, therefore, Soto must have joined the conspiracy. In our view, however, even conceding the reasonableness of such an inference, Cheo's statement at most shows that he trusted Soto, a feeling any person would quite naturally have before inviting another to share living quarters. To conclude from this that Soto had joined the conspiracy would require an inference no jury could reasonably make. The fact that Soto was considered trustworthy, given the circumstances here, is a far cry from her participation in the conspiracies.

Finally, we find misplaced the government's reliance on those cases where members of a vessel's crew were held to be participants in a drug conspiracy. A distinguishing factor in those cases is the joint enterprise element between captain and crew. There, the existence of a joint enterprise is inferable in view of the close relationship among those on board, coupled with the foreknowledge of the vessel's illicit mission given the large quantities of contraband frequently involved.

Here, by contrast, there is no comparable showing or even the slightest suggestion that Soto had knowledge of the ongoing drug mill activities before moving into the Bronx apartment. Moreover, considering the absence of her name from the list maintained by Cheo of persons he employed in the furtherance of the drug operation, the inescapable inference to be drawn from the evidence is that she never joined the conspiracy.

In sum, while the evidence need not have excluded every possible hypothesis of innocence, nevertheless, "where the crime charged is conspiracy, a conviction cannot be sustained unless the Government establishes beyond a reasonable doubt that the defendant had the specific intent to violate the substantive statute[s]." The government here produced no evidence whatever linking defendant to the conspiracies. Instead, we believe that on the basis of association alone, the jurors "let their imaginations run rampant."

Because we decide that there was insufficient evidence to support a conviction, we need not address the other issues raised on appeal.

III

For the foregoing reasons, the judgment of the district court is reversed and remanded with direction to enter a judgment of acquittal.

United States v. Macklin and Swain

927 F.2d 1272 (2d Cir. 1991)

JUDGES: Lumbard, Miner, and Mahoney, Circuit Judges.

MAHONEY, Circuit Judge.

Defendants-appellants Calvin Macklin, Jr. ("Macklin") and Arthur Garfield Swain ("Swain") appeal from judgments of conviction entered in the United States District Court for the Western District of New York, Richard J. Arcara, Judge, after a jury convicted them of conspiring to manufacture a substance containing phencyclidine ("PCP")[3] in violation of 21 U.S.C. § 846 (1988). Macklin contends on appeal that the indictment provided him with inadequate notice of the charge against him. Swain challenges the sufficiency of the evidence against him. . . .

For the reasons that follow, we affirm the judgments of conviction.

Background

During the evening of April 20, 1988, Macklin traveled from Buffalo, New York to New York City with Robert Yanders and Yanders' girlfriend, Betty Kendrick, in Kendrick's van. A week earlier, Macklin had asked Yanders to join him on the trip. Kendrick accompanied them because she wished to see New York.

Yanders drove the van, receiving directions along the way from Macklin. The three arrived in New York the morning of April 21. They stopped for breakfast, then went to a hotel where Yanders and Kendrick checked into a room. Macklin gave Kendrick the money to pay for the room, but remained behind in the van.

Some time later, while Yanders and Kendrick were watching television in the room, Macklin entered. Eventually, Macklin and Yanders returned to the van and drove away. Once again, Yanders was

at the wheel, following Macklin's directions. After driving for fifteen to thirty minutes, they arrived in the vicinity of a collision shop, where Macklin told Yanders to park. Macklin got out, and Yanders waited in the van. Macklin returned with a man not known to Yanders. Each was carrying a white box, and they loaded the boxes in the back of the van. Macklin got back into the van, and he and Yanders returned to the hotel.

At the hotel, Macklin gave Yanders $ 80.00 for the trip back to Buffalo, then left in a cab. At an earlier point, however, Macklin had given Yanders a phone number, accompanied by the names "Shirley" and "Fats," and instructed Yanders to call that number upon returning to Buffalo. Some time later, Yanders and Kendrick checked out of the hotel and began their journey back to Buffalo. During the trip, Yanders noticed a heavy industrial smell inside the van; the smell, he later testified, was "kind of like Lackawanna." Although the weather was cool, he kept the windows open.

At approximately 1:00 a.m. on April 22, Yanders and Kendrick reached the Williamsville toll area on the New York State Thruway near Buffalo. There, agents of the Drug Enforcement Administration ("DEA") and police officers, who had information which caused them to be on the lookout for the van, stopped the van and asked Yanders and Kendrick to get out. The agents verified that Kendrick was the owner of the vehicle, and obtained her consent to a search.

In the course of executing the search, the agents found two white boxes marked "J. T. Baker," recognized by one of the agents to be the name of a chemical manufacturer. The boxes emitted a "strong smell of chemicals." The agents spoke with

---

[3] In street parlance, PCP is known as "angel dust."

both Yanders and Kendrick, and ultimately asked Yanders if he would "assist . . . in [the] investigation at that point, and continue with the delivery of the chemicals." Yanders agreed. The agents then formulated a plan for carrying out the controlled delivery. Pursuant to the plan, the agents followed Yanders and Kendrick to their residence, located at 55 Reed Street in Buffalo.

At the residence, Yanders permitted an agent to attach a tape recorder to the telephone in order to monitor conversations with Macklin. The agent instructed Yanders to try to get Macklin to agree that Yanders would deliver the boxes to Macklin that night. Yanders then phoned Macklin three times at Macklin's home telephone number. During the third conversation, Macklin agreed to have Yanders bring the boxes in the van to Macklin's house. By then it was approximately 3:00 a.m.

Yanders then drove the van to Macklin's residence at 520 Broadway, and knocked at the door. Macklin answered. After speaking briefly, the two men went to the van, retrieved the two white boxes, and placed them in the trunk of Macklin's car, a white Buick automobile parked nearby. Macklin went back inside 520 Broadway, and Yanders drove the van back to 55 Reed Street.

Several hours later, at approximately 7:00 a.m., Macklin came out of 520 Broadway and got into the Buick, which the agents had been surveilling. He then drove to 62 Fox Street in Buffalo, the residence of Swain, parked, and walked to the back of the building. Five to ten minutes later, Macklin returned to the car and drove to a restaurant. He stayed at the restaurant only a short time, then returned to 62 Fox Street and backed into the driveway.

Some time later, Macklin, accompanied by Swain, drove the Buick from 62 Fox Street to 880 Broadway, and went into the building at the latter address. When they emerged shortly thereafter, Swain was carrying a box. Swain and Macklin placed the box in the trunk, then drove back to 62 Fox Street. Macklin again backed into the driveway, the trunk of the Buick was opened, and one of the two men was observed by a surveilling Buffalo city detective carrying a box toward the rear of the house. Ten to fifteen minutes later, Macklin and Swain got back into the Buick, drove to 520 Broadway, and entered that building.

Within a few minutes, a man later identified as Dwayne King came out of 520 Broadway and drove the Buick to Fox Street. He parked near the intersection of Fox Street and Broadway, got out, and walked through several yards in a direction away from Fox Street. He returned approximately five minutes later carrying a green duffel bag, then drove up Fox Street to number 62.

Juanita Sebastian, who lived from time to time at 62 Fox Street with Swain, was standing in front of the house when King drove up. She flagged him down and asked him to give her a ride to work. King gave her the green bag, which she carried into the house and placed on the kitchen table. She returned to the car, and she and King began driving down Fox Street.

DEA agents then stopped the car and spoke with King and Sebastian. In response to questions concerning activity at 62 Fox Street, Sebastian confirmed that Macklin and Swain had carried some boxes into the house that morning. The agents told Sebastian that they believed those boxes contained dangerous chemicals to be used for the manufacture of drugs, and asked for her consent to search the house. She agreed, and let the agents into the house. Inside, Sebastian told the agents that she believed the boxes had been placed in the attic, which was the second floor of the house, and they proceeded to the attic.

The attic was a large, open room with several tables. It had a "very heavy chemical smell." There were four boxes on the floor, and a fifth sitting on one of the tables. Among these were the two white boxes that Yanders and Kendrick had transported from New York. On the tables and in the boxes, at least two of which were open, were containers of hydrochloric acid, bromobenzene, ether, ligrione, sodium bisulfite, sodium metabisulfite, sodium cyanide, and other chemicals. There was also in the attic a plastic bag holding various paraphernalia such as sifters, bowls, beakers, spoons, and a mask.

The agents found a large mason jar inside a bowl, in which there was also some white residue, in the kitchen of the house. They also found the green duffel bag there; it contained another mason jar and a scale.

While the agents were in the house, the telephone rang; apparently both Sebastian and King spoke with the caller. King told agents that the caller was Swain, and that Swain had instructed King to bring the Buick back to 520 Broadway. An agent got into the back of the Buick to accompany King, and other surveillance units followed in separate vehicles. When King arrived at 520 Broadway, Macklin and Swain emerged and were arrested. Both men were then driven back to 62 Fox Street, and then to the Buffalo office of the DEA. One agent sitting in a closed car with them noticed a "heavy chemical, ether-type smell in the vehicle . . . coming from Mr. Swain and Mr. Macklin."

At the DEA office, Macklin and Swain were placed in a room in the cell area. Several days later, an agent found two pieces of paper in the same room; the paper "contained the names of chemicals and . . . appeared to contain some type of formula for the manufacture of PCP." Macklin's fingerprint was found on one of the papers.

On May 4, 1988, a grand jury indicted Macklin and Swain for the offense of conspiracy to manufacture a substance containing PCP in violation of 21 U.S.C. § 846 (1988). After an eight-day trial before Judge Arcara and a jury, Macklin and Swain were convicted of the charged offense on January 31, 1989.

* * *

B. Sufficiency of the Evidence as to Swain.

A defendant who challenges the sufficiency of the evidence against him "bears a 'very heavy burden.'" On review, "'pieces of evidence must be viewed not in isolation but in conjunction.'" Furthermore, the evidence must be viewed "in the light most favorable to the government," and we "must credit every inference that could have been drawn in the government's favor." In addition, the government need not "preclude every reasonable hypothesis which is consistent with innocence." "If, from the evidence viewed in this light, 'any rational trier of fact could have found the essential elements of the crime beyond a reasonable doubt, the conviction must be sustained.'"

Where a conspiracy is alleged, the necessary elements "'may be established . . . through circumstantial evidence.'" "However, 'absent evidence of purposeful behavior, mere presence at the scene of a crime, even when coupled with knowledge that a crime is being committed, is insufficient to establish membership in a conspiracy; and mere association with conspirators is similarly insufficient.'" Thus, to prove membership in a conspiracy, there must be "evidence of purposeful behavior designed to further" that conspiracy.

Swain argues forcefully that the evidence at trial showed only that he assisted Macklin in carrying boxes of chemicals into Swain's attic. Swain urges that even when viewed in the light most favorable to the government, the evidence introduced at trial provides no basis to infer that he had "any independent information about the nature or uses of these items." Accordingly, he contends, the evidence demonstrated no more than mere presence, and was therefore insufficient to support his conviction. In support of his contention, Swain lays particular emphasis upon our prior decisions in *United States v. Di Stefano*, 555 F.2d 1094 (2d Cir. 1977), *Soto*, and *United States v. Nusraty*, 867 F.2d 759

(2d Cir. 1989). These cases, however, are clearly distinguishable.

In *Di Stefano,* Ronald Blanda and Patrick Edwards, who intended to rob a bank together, decided to make a final check of the bank before carrying out their plan. While riding in a car with Di Stefano, they asked the driver to stop at the bank in order for Di Stefano to get change. Their actual intent, however, was to have Di Stefano look for guards and camera locations. They did not say this, however, since they did not want the driver to know of their scheme. When Di Stefano emerged from the bank, according to Edwards' testimony, she gave a nod to indicate that the coast was clear. Di Stefano was convicted of bank robbery and conspiracy to rob a bank.

We reversed Di Stefano's convictions for insufficiency of the evidence, reasoning that there was no evidence that either Edwards or Blanda informed her of their intent to rob the bank, especially in light of (1) the fact that the two men "deliberately did not discuss the robbery with [Di Stefano] during their ride to the bank because of the presence of [the driver] in the car," and (2) the complete absence of evidence that Di Stefano had any prior knowledge of the plan to rob the bank. On the crucial question of any communication to Di Stefano of an instruction to case the bank, Edwards' testimony was: "I don't know exactly how we told her to do it. I don't remember. I'm trying to remember. I can't."

In *Soto,* the defendant was living in a Bronx apartment that was being used as a narcotics "cutting mill." When DEA agents raided the apartment and seized drugs and weapons, Soto was found asleep with her young child in the bedroom. She was arrested with several others and ultimately convicted on two counts of conspiracy. Because the evidence clearly established that the apartment was crucial to a narcotics distribution conspiracy, "the most significant circumstance relied on by the government in support of the jury's

finding of guilt [was] the fact that Soto lived in [the] apartment . . . for three weeks prior to her arrest."

We reversed the conviction, stating:

> While it would not be accurate to characterize Soto's presence at the apartment as merely transitory, we nevertheless consider the total circumstances of how Soto came to reside there to be highly significant. For here we have an individual newly arrived from Puerto Rico, accompanied by a child of tender years, clearly in need of shelter. To this end, as soon as she arrived in New York defendant took up residence at the 2526 Bronx Park East apartment. Although the living arrangements there may not have been ideal, there is no indication that defendant had any other alternative.
>
> * * *
>
> Here, . . . there is no . . . showing or even the slightest suggestion that Soto had knowledge of the ongoing drug mill activities before moving into the Bronx apartment. Moreover, considering the absence of her name from the list maintained by [the organizer of the conspiracy] of persons he employed in the furtherance of the drug operation, the inescapable inference to be drawn from the evidence is that she never joined the conspiracy.

In *Nusraty,* one Robert Detrich was arrested at John F. Kennedy International Airport in New York after Customs officials discovered packets of heroin hidden in a new suit Detrich had brought with him from India. Detrich told DEA agents that he carried the suit in his luggage as a favor to Nusraty's brother, who had asked Detrich to deliver the suit to Nusraty in the United States. Detrich claimed that he had no knowledge of the heroin. He told agents that he expected Nusraty to meet him outside Customs, and agreed to make a controlled delivery to Nusraty under DEA surveillance.

As Detrich had anticipated, Nusraty was at the airport. Detrich's attempt to effectuate the controlled delivery failed, however, when Nusraty declined to accept the suit and denied Detrich's suggestion that Nusraty's brother had told Nusraty that the suit would be arriving. When Nusraty began to walk away from Detrich, both were arrested.

Nusraty's position prior to and during his trial was that he was present at the airport in connection with his job as a cab driver, and that his encounter with Detrich, whom he had met previously, was pure happenstance. The jury evidently declined to believe this testimony, and convicted Nusraty of conspiring to possess heroin with intent to distribute it, importing heroin, or aiding and abetting importation, and possessing heroin with intent to distribute it, or aiding and abetting such possession. On appeal, we reversed on all counts, stating:

> Even accepting the government's argument that Nusraty was waiting for Detrich at the airport, that single circumstance and the context in which it occurred are not sufficient evidence to show Nusraty's knowing involvement in the conspiracy charged. Simply waiting for someone at an airport, even under such suspicious circumstances as exist here, is not, by itself, an act from which knowing guilty involvement can reasonably be inferred.

Noting that Nusraty's conviction "rest[ed] principally on his presence at the airport, and on his association with his uncle, his brother, and Detrich, some or all of whom may have been links in a chain of narcotics distribution," we concluded that "the circumstantial evidence here was simply too thin to warrant an inference of guilty knowledge on the part of Nusraty."

We do not regard these precedents as governing decision here. The proven relationship of the defendants to the alleged criminal conduct was tenuous and fleeting in both *Di Stefano* and *Nusraty.* The *Soto* defendant was merely present at a site of narcotics activity, had a thoroughly plausible explanation for her presence, and was not included in a list of operatives maintained by the ringleader of the narcotics operation.

Here, by contrast, the chemicals needed to manufacture PCP, which emitted a distinctive and considerable odor, were assembled in the attic of Swain's residence. There was no apparent use for this combination of assembled chemicals other than the manufacture of PCP. Further, the jury was clearly entitled to conclude that Swain played an active personal role in that assembly. Such a conclusion could be derived not only from the surveillance observations of the DEA agents, but also from the testimony of Sebastian, who shared the residence at 62 Fox Street with Swain and testified that Swain and Macklin carried the boxes of chemicals to the attic at 62 Fox Street the morning of April 22, 1988. In addition to this being Swain's permanent residence, rather than a temporary abode as in *Soto,* any contention that Swain engaged in an innocent storage of the chemicals for Macklin is undermined by the subsequent delivery that morning to 62 Fox Street by Dwayne King of a green bag containing various paraphernalia useful for the manufacture of PCP from the chemicals previously assembled. Further, one of the DEA agents who arrested Swain testified that Swain smelled of chemicals in the car that transported him to the DEA office after his arrest.

In addition, Sebastian testified that after she was served with a subpoena to appear before the grand jury investigating this matter, Swain attempted to rekindle their relationship and dissuade her from testifying. According to Sebastian, Swain promised her that if she did not testify "he would give me a paid vacation anywhere I want to go." Sebastian rejected both of his suggestions, the two then began to argue, and a physical altercation ensued.

As Swain correctly contends, and as the district court carefully instructed the jury when Sebastian gave this testimony, this evidence was admissible not as direct proof of Swain's guilt, but rather of consciousness of guilt on his part. So considered, and taken in conjunction with the other evidence against Swain, we conclude that there was sufficient evidence to sustain his conviction.

Note

If you were representing Swain on appeal, what arguments would you make to try to persuade the court that the evidence against him was legally insufficient?

Exercise

Assume that, in the *Stallings* case, the defendant had testified as follows:

I met Randy Thacker in a bar on Main Street. He had on a big Mexican hat, one of these string ties with an aqua stone to hold it together, and high leather boots with a fancy design. He told me that he was one of the last descendants of Wyatt Earp, having lived in New Mexico all his life. We started talking and drinking together, and had something to eat, too. When the bar was about to close, he told me he didn't have any money, but could give me a few checks to cover his share. The rest of the checks were to pay for a cigarette lighter I had, that he claimed was an antique that fit in perfectly with his collection of Navajo jewelry.

The defendant was convicted, and on appeal, the prosecution argues that the jury could have inferred petitioner's guilty knowledge regarding the forged status of the checks from its disbelief of the defendant's inherently incredible testimony, as well as his demeanor on the witness stand. You are a clerk for a judge in a fictional federal circuit that has not addressed the issue of whether a jury's disbelief of a defendant's testimony can ever give rise to a positive inference of guilt. Write a memorandum discussing the circumstances, if any, under which a conviction should be permitted to stand based on negative inferences drawn from either the implausibility of a defendant's testimony, or from his demeanor on the stand.

b. *Weight of the Evidence*

The standard of review by appellate courts of the facts in criminal cases must take into account, not only the obligation of ensuring that criminal cases are based on sufficient evidence, but the consequences of reversal given the particular standard employed. In general, reversal of a conviction on appeal simply results in a new trial. The Supreme Court decided in *United States v. Ball,* 163 U.S. 662 (1896), that the double jeopardy clause does not bar another trial if the judgment in the first trial was vacated at the behest of the defendant on appeal.

If an appellate court reverses a conviction as based on insufficient evidence, however, the prohibition against double jeopardy comes into play. The Supreme Court, in *Burks v. United States*, 437 U.S. 1 (1978), decided that the Fifth Amendment double jeopardy clause, applied to the states through the Fourteenth Amendment, bars the prosecution from a second chance to convict a defendant against whom it has once presented insufficient evidence. The Court found that when an appellate court's reversal is based on the insufficiency of the evidence, the result is comparable to an acquittal, thereby preventing the state from retrying the defendant.

In the following case, the Court was asked to extend the prohibition against a second trial to the situation where a defendant convinces the appellate court that his conviction, while not based on *insufficient* evidence, must be reversed as against the *weight* of the evidence. In the course of examining that issue, the case explores the difference between the two standards of review.

Tibbs v. Florida

457 U.S. 31 (1982)

Justice O'CONNOR delivered the opinion of the Court.

We granted certiorari to decide whether the Double Jeopardy Clause[1] bars retrial after a state appellate court sets aside a conviction on the ground that the verdict was against "the weight of the evidence." After examining the policies supporting the Double Jeopardy Clause, we hold that a reversal based on the weight, rather than the sufficiency, of the evidence permits the State to initiate a new prosecution.

I

In 1974, Florida indicted petitioner Delbert Tibbs for the first-degree murder of Terry Milroy, the felony murder of Milroy, and the rape of Cynthia Nadeau. Nadeau, the State's chief trial witness, testified that she and Milroy were hitchhiking from St. Petersburg to Marathon, Fla., on February 3, 1974. A man in a green truck picked them up near Fort Myers and, after driving

a short way, turned off the highway into a field. He asked Milroy to help him siphon gas from some farm machinery, and Milroy agreed. When Nadeau stepped out of the truck a few minutes later, she discovered the driver holding a gun on Milroy. The driver told Milroy that he wished to have sex with Nadeau, and ordered her to strip. After forcing Nadeau to engage in sodomy, the driver agreed that Milroy could leave. As Milroy started to walk away, however, the assailant shot him in the shoulder. When Milroy fell to the ground, pleading for his life, the gunman walked over and taunted, "Does it hurt, boy? You in pain? Does it hurt, boy?" Then, with a shot to the head, he killed Milroy.

This deed finished, the killer raped Nadeau. Fearing for her life, she suggested that they should leave together and that she "would be his old lady." The killer seemed to agree and they returned to the highway in the truck. After driving a short distance, he stopped the truck and ordered Nadeau to walk directly in front of it. As soon as her feet hit the ground, however, she ran in the opposite direction. The killer fled with truck, frightened perhaps by an

---

[1] "[N]or shall any person be subject for the same offence to be twice put in jeopardy of life or limb. . . ." U.S. Const, Amdt 5. The Clause applies to the States through the Due Process Clause of the Fourteenth Amendment. *Benton v. Maryland*, 395 U.S. 784 (1969).

approaching car. When Nadeau reached a nearby house, the occupants let her in and called the police.

That night, Nadeau gave the police a detailed description of the assailant and his truck. Several days later a patrolman stopped Tibbs, who was hitchhiking near Ocala, Fla., because his appearance matched Nadeau's description. The Ocala Police Department photographed Tibbs and relayed the pictures to the Fort Myers police. When Nadeau examined these photos, she identified Tibbs as the assailant. Nadeau subsequently picked Tibbs out of a lineup and positively identified him at trial as the man who murdered Milroy and raped her.[3]

Tibbs' attorney attempted to show that Nadeau was an unreliable witness. She admitted during cross-examination that she had tried "just about all" types of drugs and that she had smoked marihuana shortly before the crimes occurred. She also evidenced some confusion about the time of day that the assailant had offered her and Milroy a ride. Finally, counsel suggested through questions and closing argument that Nadeau's former boyfriend had killed Milroy and that Nadeau was lying to

---

[3] The State's remaining witnesses included law enforcement agents, a man who had driven Milroy and Nadeau to Fort Myers, the houseowner who had called the police for Nadeau, acquaintances of Milroy, a doctor who had examined Nadeau shortly after the crimes, and the doctor who had performed the autopsy on Milroy. The doctors confirmed that Nadeau had had intercourse on the evening of February 3 and that Milroy had died that evening from a bullet wound in the head. The other witnesses confirmed that Nadeau and Milroy had been hitchhiking through Fort Myers on February 3 and that Nadeau had arrived at a house, in a hysterical condition, that evening.

A Florida prisoner, sentenced to life imprisonment for rape, also testified for the State. This prisoner claimed that he had met Tibbs while Tibbs was in jail awaiting trial and that Tibbs had confessed the crime to him. The defense substantially discredited this witness on cross-examination, revealing inconsistencies in his testimony and suggesting that he had testified in the hope of obtaining leniency from the State.

protect her boyfriend. Nadeau flatly denied these suggestions.

In addition to these attempts to discredit Nadeau, Tibbs testified in his own defense. He explained that he was college educated, that he had published a story and a few poems, and that he was hitchhiking through Florida to learn more about how people live. He claimed that he was in Daytona Beach, across the State from Fort Myers, from the evening of February 1, 1974, through the morning of February 6. He also testified that he did not own a green truck, and that he had not driven any vehicle while in Florida. Finally, he denied committing any of the crimes charged against him.

Two Salvation Army officers partially corroborated Tibbs' story. These officers produced a card signed by Tibbs, indicating that he had slept at the Daytona Beach Salvation Army Transit Lodge on the evening of February 1, 1974. Neither witness, however, had seen Tibbs after the morning of February 2. Tibbs' other witnesses testified to his good reputation as a law-abiding citizen and to his good reputation for veracity.

On rebuttal, the State produced a card, similar to the one introduced by Tibbs, showing that Tibbs had spent the night of February 4 at the Orlando Salvation Army Transit Lodge. This evidence contradicted Tibbs' claim that he had remained in Daytona Beach until February 6, as well as his sworn statements that he had been in Orlando only once, during the early part of January 1974, and that he had not stayed at any Salvation Army lodge after February 1. After the State presented this rebuttal evidence, Tibbs took the stand to deny both that he had been in Orlando on February 4 and that the signature on the Orlando Salvation Army card was his.

The jury convicted Tibbs of first-degree murder and rape. Pursuant to the jury's recommendation, the judge sentenced Tibbs to death. On appeal, the Florida Supreme Court reversed. *Tibbs v. State*, 337 So.2d 788 (1976) (*Tibbs I*). A plurality of three justices, while acknowledging that "the resolution of factual issues in a criminal trial is peculiarly within the province of a jury," identified six weaknesses in the State's case.[5] First, except for Nadeau's testimony, the State introduced no evidence placing Tibbs in or near Fort Myers on the day of the crimes. Second, although Nadeau gave a detailed description of the assailant's truck, police never found the vehicle. Third, police discovered neither a gun nor car keys in Tibbs' possession. Fourth, Tibbs cooperated fully with the police when he was stopped and arrested. Fifth, the State introduced no evidence casting doubt on Tibbs' veracity.[6] Tibbs, on the other hand, produced witnesses who attested to his good reputation. Finally, several factors undermined Nadeau's believability. Although she asserted at trial that the crimes occurred during daylight, other evidence suggested that the events occurred after nightfall when reliable identification would have been more difficult. Nadeau, furthermore, had smoked marihuana shorly before the crimes and had identified Tibbs during a suggestive photograph session. These weaknesses left the plurality in "considerable doubt that Delbert Tibbs [was] the man who committed the crimes for which he ha[d] been convicted." Therefore, the plurality concluded that the "interests of justice" required a new trial.[8]

Justice Boyd concurred specially, noting that " '[t]he test to be applied in determining the adequacy of a verdict is whether a jury of reasonable men could have returned that verdict.' " Apparently applying that standard, Justice Boyd found the State's evidence deficient. He concluded that "the weakness of the evidence presented in the trial court might well require that [Tibbs] be released from incarceration without further litigation," but "reluctantly concur[red]" in the plurality's decision to order a new trial because he understood Florida law to permit retrial.

On remand, the trial court dismissed the indictment, concluding that retrial would violate the double jeopardy principles articulated in *Burks v. United States*, 437 U.S. 1 (1978), and *Greene v. Massey*, 437 U.S. 19 (1978).[10] An intermediate appellate court disagreed and remanded the case for trial. The Florida Supreme Court affirmed the latter decision, carefully elaborating the difference between a reversal stemming from insufficient evidence and one prompted by the weight of the evidence. 397 So.2d 1120 (1981) (*Tibbs II*). As the court explained, a conviction rests upon insufficient evidence when, even after viewing the evidence in the light most favorable to the prosecution, no rational factfinder could have found the defendant guilty beyond a reasonable doubt. A reversal based on the weight of the evidence, on the other hand, draws the appellate court into questions of credibility. The "weight of the evidence" refers to "a determination [by] the trier of fact that a greater amount of credible

---

[5] The plurality completely discounted the testimony of the convicted rapist who recounted Tibbs' alleged confession. See n. 3, *supra*. This testimony, the justices concluded, appeared "to be the product of purely selfish considerations."

[6] The plurality opinion summarily dismissed the effect of the rebuttal evidence showing that Tibbs was in Orlando on February 4. A "superficial comparison" of the signature on the Orlando transit card with Tibbs' own signature, the plurality found, supported Tibbs' claim that he had not signed the card. Moreover, evidence that Tibbs was in Orlando on February 4 still did not place him in Fort Myers on February 3.

[8] At the time of Tibbs' first appeal, Florida Appellate Rule 6.16(b) (1962) provided in part: "Upon an appeal from the judgment by a defendant who has been sentenced to death the appellate court shall review the evidence to determine

if the interests of justice require a new trial, whether the insufficiency of the evidence is a ground of appeal or not." The substance of this Rule has been recodified as Florida Appellate Rule 9.140(f).

[10] We decided *Burks* and *Greene* after the Florida Supreme Court reversed Tibbs' conviction, but before he could be retried. We have applied *Burks* to prosecutions that were not yet final on the date of that decision.

evidence supports one side of an issue or cause than the other." *Id.*, at 1123.[11]

The Florida Supreme Court then classified *Tibbs I* as a reversal resting on the weight of the evidence. Nadeau's testimony, if believed by the jury, was itself "legally sufficient to support Tibbs' conviction under Florida law." In deciding to upset Tibbs' conviction, the court in *Tibbs I* had stressed those "aspects of Nadeau's testimony which cast serious doubt on her believability," an approach that bespoke a reweighing of the evidence. "Only by stretching the point . . .," the court concluded in *Tibbs II*, "could we possibly use an 'insufficiency' analysis to characterize our previous reversal of Tibbs' convictions."[12]

---

[11] Other courts similarly have explained the difference between evidentiary weight and evidentiary sufficiency. In *United States v. Lincoln*, 630 F.2d 1313 (CA8 1980), for example, the court declared:

"The court reviewing the sufficiency of the evidence, whether it be the trial or appellate court, must apply familiar principles. It is required to view the evidence in the light most favorable to the verdict, giving the prosecution the benefit of all inferences reasonably to be drawn in its favor from the evidence. The verdict may be based in whole or in part on circumstantial evidence. The evidence need not exclude every reasonable hypothesis except that of guilt . . . ." *Id.*, at 1316.

"When a motion for new trial is made on the ground that the verdict is contrary to the weight of the evidence, the issues are far different . . . . The district court need not view the evidence in the light most favorable to the verdict; it may weigh the evidence and in so doing evaluate for itself the credibility of the witnesses. If the court concludes that, despite the abstract sufficiency of the evidence to sustain the verdict, the evidence preponderates sufficiently heavily against the verdict that a serious miscarriage of justice may have occurred, it may set aside the verdict, grant a new trial, and submit the issues for determination by another jury." *Id.*, at 1319.

[12] Elsewhere in its opinion, the Florida Supreme Court ruled that Florida appellate courts no longer may reverse convictions on the ground that the verdict was against the weight of the evidence. This ruling does not diminish the importance of the issue before us. Courts in other jurisdictions sometimes rely upon the weight of the evidence to overturn convictions. For example, some federal courts have interpreted Rule

Having found that it could not "fairly conclude . . . that Tibbs' convictions were reversed on the grounds of evidentiary insufficiency," the Florida Supreme Court held that *Greene* and *Burks* do not bar retrial. Those decisions, the court believed, as well as *United States v. DiFrancesco*, 449 U.S. 117 (1980), interpret the Double Jeopardy Clause to preclude retrial after reversal of a conviction only when the appellate court has set the conviction aside on the ground that the evidence was legally insufficient to support conviction. Other reversals, including those based on the weight of the evidence or made in the "interests of justice," do not implicate double jeopardy principles. We granted certiorari to review this interpretation of the Double Jeopardy Clause. . . .

[The Court agrees with the Florida Supreme Court that reversals based on the weight of the evidence do not implicate the same policies that supported the decision to prohibit retrial after reversal based on insufficient evidence. Instead, the Court found applicable the same considerations that allow retrial after a successful appeal based on trial errors.]

In sum, we conclude that the Double Jeopardy Clause does not prevent an appellate court from granting a convicted defendant an opportunity to seek acquittal through a new trial.[22]

---

33 of the Federal Rules of Criminal Procedure, which authorizes a new trial "if required in the interest of justice," to permit the trial judge to set aside a conviction that is against the weight of the evidence.

[22] We note that a contrary rule, one precluding retrial whenever an appellate court rests reversal on evidentiary weight, might prompt state legislatures simply to forbid those courts to reweigh the evidence. Rulemakers willing to permit a new trial in the face of a verdict supported by legally sufficient evidence may be less willing to free completely a defendant convicted by a jury of his peers. Acceptance of Tibbs' double jeopardy theory might also lead to restrictions on the authority of trial judges to order new trials based on their independent assessment of evidentiary weight. Although Tibbs limits his argu-

III

We turn, finally, to apply the above principles to the present case. A close reading of *Tibbs I* suggests that the Florida Supreme Court overturned Tibbs' conviction because the evidence, although sufficient to support the jury's verdict, did not fully persuade the court of Tibbs' guilt. The plurality based its review on a Florida rule directing the court in capital cases to "review the evidence to determine if the interests of justice require a

─────

ment to appellate reversals, his contentions logically apply to a trial judge's finding that a conviction was against the weight of the evidence. *Cf. Hudson v. Louisiana*, 450 U.S. 40 (1981) (applying *Burks v. United States*, 437 U.S. 1 (1978), to trial judge's postverdict ruling that evidence was insufficient to support conviction). Endorsement of Tibbs' theory, therefore, might only serve to eliminate practices that help shield defendants from unjust convictions.

[23] At one point, the opinion does refer to " 'evidence which is not sufficient to convince a fair and impartial mind of the guilt of the accused beyond a reasonable doubt.' " 337 So.2d, at 791. This reference, however, occurs in a lengthy quotation from an earlier Florida decision. When read in context, it does not appear that the plurality actually applied this standard to the evidence in Tibbs' case. Moreover, the quotation containing this sufficiency language also speaks of evidence that is "not satisfactory" to the appellate court and that is not "substantial in character." *Ibid.* This language, in line with the remainder of *Tibbs I*, evidences a weighing of the evidence.

new trial, whether the insufficiency of the evidence is a ground of appeal or not." *See* n. 8, *supra*. References to the "interests of justice" and the justices' own "considerable doubt" of Tibbs' guilt mark the plurality's conclusions.[23] Those conclusions, moreover, stem from the justices' determination that Tibbs' testimony was more reliable than that of Nadeau. This resolution of conflicting testimony in a manner contrary to the jury's verdict is a hallmark of review based on evidentiary weight, not evidentiary sufficiency.

Any ambiguity in *Tibbs I*, finally, was resolved by the Florida Supreme Court in *Tibbs II*. Absent a conflict with the Due Process Clause, that court's construction of its prior opinion binds this Court. In *Tibbs II*, of course, the court unequivocably held that *Tibbs I* was "one of those rare instances in which reversal was based on evidentiary weight." 397 So.2d, at 1126 (per curiam). Thus, we conclude that Tibbs' successful appeal of his conviction rested upon a finding that the conviction was against the weight of the evidence, not upon a holding that the evidence was legally insufficient to support the verdict. Under these circumstances, the Double Jeopardy Clause does not bar retrial. Accordingly, the judgment of the Florida Supreme Court is affirmed.

Notes

1. As a matter of federal constitutional law, *Tibbs* held that a reversal based on the weight of the evidence does not, unlike a reversal based on insufficiency, require dismissal of the indictment. Various jurisdictions, state and federal, have taken different approaches to review of the weight of the evidence in criminal cases. As the opinion in *Tibbs* noted, Florida decided to do away with appellate inquiry into the weight of the evidence altogether. *Tibbs*, 457 U.S. at 38, n. 12.

New York, on the other hand, not only permits, but requires, its intermediate appellate courts to determine whether a verdict is against the weight of the evidence. *See* New York Criminal Procedure Law Section 470.15(5). In *People v. Bleakley,* 69 N.Y.2d 490, 508 N.E.2d 672, 515 N.Y.S.2d 761 (1987), the Court of Appeals explained:

Unlike this court which, with few exceptions, passes on only questions of law, intermediate appellate courts are empowered to review questions of law and questions of fact. They do so in both civil cases and criminal cases. Indeed, this unique factual review power is the linchpin of our constitutional and statutory design intended to afford each litigant at least one appellate review of the facts.

On the criminal side, however, the history of this unique review power had been the subject of some confusion. For years an appellate determination that the verdict was against the weight of the evidence warranted only the ordering of a new trial, while sufficiency and reasonable doubt deficiencies necessitated the corrective action of dismissal of the criminal charges. The Criminal Procedure Law revisors recommended and the Legislature enacted a significant clarifying change upgrading the corrective action to dismissal of criminal charges under either standard of review (see, CPL 470.20 [2], [5]). The change was justified because, in the words of the drafters, "[the] People, having had full opportunity to prove their case at trial and having failed to do so, should not be accorded another chance" (Staff Comment to Proposed CPL 240.40, at 328 [1967]).

Although the two standards of intermediate appellate review – legal sufficiency and weight of evidence – are related, each requires a discrete analysis. For a court to conclude, as the Appellate Division did in this case, that a jury verdict is supported by sufficient evidence, the court must determine whether there is any valid line of reasoning and permissible inferences which could lead a rational person to the conclusion reached by the jury on the basis of the evidence at trial and as a matter of law satisfy the proof and burden requirements for every element of the crime charged. If that is satisfied, then the verdict will be upheld by the intermediate appellate court on that review basis.

To determine whether a verdict is supported by the weight of the evidence, however, the appellate court's dispositive analysis is not limited to that legal test. Even if all the elements and necessary findings are supported by some credible evidence, the court must examine the evidence further. If based on all the credible evidence a different finding would not have been unreasonable, then the appellate court must, like the trier of fact below, "weigh the relative probative force of conflicting testimony and the relative strength of conflicting inferences that may be drawn from the testimony." If it appears that the trier of fact has failed to give the evidence the weight it should be accorded, then the appellate court may set aside the verdict (CPL 470.20 [2]).

Moreover, as the court notes, if the intermediate appellate court, upon its mandatory factual review power, finds the verdict to be against the weight of the evidence, the indictment must be dismissed. New York Criminal Procedure Law Section 470.20(5).

2. As the various appeals in *Tibbs* illustrate, the rules about what happens to a case after a reversal by an appellate court may well affect the way that the court approaches the case. The appellate attorney must evaluate, not only what the client is entitled to as a matter of law and precedent, but what relief the appellate court is most likely to be willing to grant, given the consequences of that decision. The court may be more receptive to an argument challenging the evidentiary basis for a verdict if the defendant, rather than going free, is subject to retrial upon reversal.

3. The four dissenting Justices in *Tibbs* observed:

> It must also be noted that judges having doubts about the sufficiency of the evidence under the *Jackson* standard may prefer to reverse on the weight of the evidence, since retrial would not be barred. If done recurringly, this would undermine *Jackson, Burks,* and *Greene.*

Tibbs, 457 U.S. at 51 (White, J. dissenting). Accordingly, the result of the rule announced in *Tibbs* may in fact be a dilution of the sufficiency requirement contained in *Jackson v. Virginia.*

Exercise

You have been assigned to perfect the appeal on behalf of William Costello. The trial record presents the following facts:

The People's Case

At about 12:00 a.m. on February 2, 1992, LEON ACOSTA, the manager of a Kentucky Fried Chicken restaurant located in the Flushing section of Queens, New York closed up the store. In so doing, he turned off all of the equipment, turned off the lights, locked all of the doors, and turned on the "silent system" alarm.

Later that morning, at about 6:05 a.m., Police Officers JAMES GALLAGHER and CHRISTOPHER LAMB received a radio communication, and as a result of that communication, responded to the Kentucky Fried Chicken. When they arrived, about two or three minutes later, Officer Gallagher drove the radio motor patrol car they were in into the rear parking lot, placing the car partly on the sidewalk and partly in the street. The location was well-lit even though it was closed for business.

As the officers started to get out of their car, Officer Gallagher observed that the rear door of the restaurant was open and saw defendant, WILLIAM COSTELLO, who was empty-handed, walk out of the restaurant in the direction of the car. Defendant was wearing a sports jacket, grey pants, and shoes (not sneakers).

Officer Lamb, who had been watching the front door of the restaurant, heard Officer Gallagher say "We got one," and then saw defendant in the parking lot. Defendant walked about ten feet towards the officers' patrol car and then broke into a very fast run, right past Officer Gallagher, just as Officer Gallagher called out "Police, don't move."

The officers got back into their automobile and started to chase defendant, who was still running very fast away from them up the street in a northwest direction. They caught defendant in a minute or so, and then placed him under arrest.

Examination of Kentucky Fried Chicken premises revealed that a side window near the front of the building was broken. Inside, there were several stray wires pulled out of a hole in the wall. A television, computer printer, and video cassette recorder were missing; and the restaurant's computer was moved and appeared to have been tampered with. Although the manager, Mr. Acosta, recognized defendant from the neighborhood and as a customer, defendant had no permission or authority to be inside the Kentucky Fried Chicken in the early morning hours of February 2, 1992.

Defendant's Case

Twenty-four year-old defendant WILLIAM COSTELLO is an apprentice electrician with no criminal record who had been unemployed for one or two months in February 1992. He had lived his whole life in his family's home about two blocks from the Kentucky Fried Chicken.

At about 8:00 or 9:00 p.m. on Saturday evening, February 1, 1992, defendant went with travel agent ANTHONY D'ANNOLFO, his long-time close friend, and Neil and Randy, neighborhood acquaintances, to a party in Woodhaven. Between 11:00 and 11:30 p.m., the trio left the party and went to a night club named Zachary's on Long Island, where they stayed until closing time, about 4:00 a.m. the next morning. The next stop was a trip across the street to the Colony diner for breakfast with several other people.

At about 6:00 or 6:10 a.m., D'Annolfo drove Randy, Neil, and defendant home. Instead of being dropped off directly at his home, defendant told D'Annolfo to drop him off about one and one-half blocks away at the deli, located right next to the Kentucky Fried Chicken, so that he could buy a pack of cigarettes. Defendant went to the all-night window of the deli and tried to obtain a pack of cigarettes on credit, because he had run out of money. This attempt proved to be unsuccessful, but the man at the window gave him two cigarettes.

Defendant started to walk towards his home, crossing through Kentucky Fried Chicken's parking lot, walking within about fifteen feet of the building. At no time did he enter the premises or break any of its windows.

Defendant testified that when a car "flew by me, screeched behind me, I began to run." Defendant heard someone call out "Stop." Defendant did not stop even though he realized by this time that he was being followed by two uniformed police officers. He thought that he would run back to his house and then see what happened. He was heading towards his own home when he was arrested.

ROBERT SUMMERS, Customer Service Manager of the Silent Watchman Division for the National Guard Security Services, testified that Kentucky Fried Chicken was a client and had a Silent Watchman type of alarm system. Despite its name, if triggered, the alarm has an audible component that sounds uninterrupted for about sixteen minutes unless it is turned off. At 5:17 a.m., February 2, 1992, the computer in the alarm at the Kentucky Fried Chicken transmitted a message to the computer in the alarm company's central station. The police were notified by the central station operator at 5:18 a.m.

* * *

William Costello was convicted of burglary in the third degree. Can he make a viable argument that the evidence was legally insufficient? That the verdict was against the weight of the evidence? Draft an argument asking the Appellate Division to reverse on *sufficiency* or, in the alternative, on *weight,* using only the information provided above.

B. Trials by the Court: Appellate Courts May Set Aside Only "Clearly Erroneous" Factual Findings

If the trial in a civil case was conducted without a jury, the trial court, in its role as fact-finder, is also afforded considerable deference. In federal court, by statute, factual findings of a trial judge may not be set aside on appeal unless they are "clearly erroneous." Fed. R. Civ. P. 52(a). Although this is a rule of civil procedure, it is applied in criminal cases as well. The following cases explore the circumstances under which a federal judge's factual determinations may be reversed by the court of appeals.

United States v. United States Gypsum Co.

333 U.S. 364 (1948)

Mr. Justice REED delivered the opinion of the Court.

... We turn now to a different phase of the case – the correctness of the findings. The trial court made findings of fact which if accurate would bar a reversal of its order. In Finding 118 the trial court found that the evidence "fails to establish that the defendants associated themselves in a plan to blanket the industry under patent licenses and stabilize prices." ... In examining the finding we follow *Interstate Cir-*

cuit v. United States, 306 U.S. 208, and *United States v. Masonite Corp.,* 316 U.S. 265, as to the quantum of proof required for the government to establish its claim that the defendants conspired to achieve certain ends. In those cases, as here, separate identical agreements were executed between one party and a number of other parties. This Court, in *Interstate Circuit,* concluded that proof of an express understanding that each party would sign the agreements was not a "prerequisite to an unlawful conspiracy." We held that it was sufficient if all the defendants had engaged in a concert of action within the meaning of the Sherman Act to enter into the agreements. In *Masonite* the trial court found that the defendants had not acted in concert and that finding was reversed by this Court. One of the things those two cases establish is the principle that when a group of competitors enters into a series of separate but similar agreements with competitors or others, a strong inference arises that such agreements are the result of concerted action. That inference is strengthened when contemporaneous declarations indicate that supposedly separate actions are part of a common plan.

In so far as Finding 118 and the subsidiary findings were based by the District Court on its belief that the General Electric rule justified the arrangements or because of a misapplication of *Masonite* or *Interstate Circuit,* errors of law occurred. These we can, of course, correct. In so far as this finding and others to which we shall refer are inferences drawn from documents or undisputed facts, heretofore described or set out, Rule 52(a) of the Rules of Civil Procedure is applicable. That rule prescribes that findings of fact in actions tried without a jury "shall not be set aside unless clearly erroneous, and due regard shall be given to the opportunity of the trial court to judge of the credibility of the witnesses." It was intended, in all actions tried upon the facts without a jury, to make applicable the then prevailing equity practice. Since judicial review of findings of

trial courts does not have the statutory or constitutional limitations on judicial review of findings by administrative agencies or by a jury, this Court may reverse findings of fact by a trial court where "clearly erroneous." The practice in equity prior to the present Rules of Civil Procedure was that the findings of the trial court, when dependent upon oral testimony where the candor and credibility of the witnesses would best be judged, had great weight with the appellate court. The findings were never conclusive, however. A finding is "clearly erroneous" when although there is evidence to support it, the reviewing court on the entire evidence is left with the definite and firm conviction that a mistake has been committed.

The government relied very largely on documentary exhibits, and called as witnesses many of the authors of the documents. Both on direct and cross-examination counsel were permitted to phrase their questions in extremely leading form, so that the import of the witnesses' testimony was conflicting. On cross-examination most of the witnesses denied that they had acted in concert in securing patent licenses or that they had agreed to do the things which in fact were done. Where such testimony is in conflict with contemporaneous documents we can give it little weight, particularly when the crucial issues involve mixed questions of law and fact. Despite the opportunity of the trial court to appraise the credibility of the witnesses, we cannot under the circumstances of this case rule otherwise than that Finding 118 is clearly erroneous. . . .

Notes

1. This leading case interpreting Rule 52(a) touches on several difficult questions often presented when appellate courts review determinations made by federal district courts. The Court emphasizes that the Rule applies to *factual* findings by the district court. At times what appear to be factual findings are based on misinterpretations of the law; such legal errors are subject to correction by appellate courts without reference to the clearly erroneous standard. At other times, as the Court notes, issues of fact are really "mixed questions of law and fact," to which apparently some less deferential standard of review may apply. (*See* discussion below on Review

of Mixed Questions.) Appellate courts, in applying Rule 52(a), must therefore grapple initially with the question of whether district court findings are factual, legal, or both.

2. The Court stresses the difference between factual findings based on documents as opposed to those based on live testimony. What argument might be made for a different standard of review when a finding is based on a written exhibit rather than on presentation of oral testimony by a witness? Note how the dissent deals with this issue in the following case.

Pullman-Standard v. Swint

456 U.S. 273 (1982)

Justice WHITE delivered the opinion of the Court.

Respondents were black employees at the Bessemer, Ala., plant of petitioner, Pullman-Standard (the Company), a manufacturer of railway freight cars and parts. They brought suit against the Company and the union petitioners – the United Steelworkers of America, AFL-CIO-CLC, and its Local 1466 (collectively USW) – alleging violations of Title VII of the Civil Rights Act of 1964. As they come here, these cases involve only the validity, under Title VII, of a seniority system maintained by the Company and USW. The District Court found "that the differences in terms, conditions or privileges of employment resulting [from the seniority system] are 'not the result of an intention to discriminate' because of race or color," and held, therefore, that the system satisfied the requirements of § 703(h) of the Act. The Court of Appeals for the Fifth Circuit reversed:

"Because we find that the difference in the terms, conditions and standards of employment for black workers and white workers at Pullman-Standard resulted from an intent to discriminate because of race, we hold that the system is not legally valid under section 703(h) of Title VII." 624 F.2d 525, 533-534 (1980).

We granted the petitions for certiorari

filed by USW and by the Company, limited to the first question presented in each petition: whether a court of appeals is bound by the "clearly erroneous" rule of Federal Rule of Civil Procedure 52(a) in reviewing a district court's findings of fact, arrived at after a lengthy trial, as to the motivation of the parties who negotiated a seniority system; and whether the court below applied wrong legal criteria in determining the bona fides of the seniority system. We conclude that the Court of Appeals erred in the course of its review and accordingly reverse its judgment and remand for further proceedings.

I

Title VII is a broad remedial measure, designed "to assure equality of employment opportunities." The Act was designed to bar not only overt employment discrimination, "but also practices that are fair in form, but discriminatory in operation." "Thus, the Court has repeatedly held that a prima facie Title VII violation may be established by policies or practices that are neutral on their face and in intent but that nonetheless discriminate in effect against a particular group." *Teamsters v. United States*, 431 U.S. 324, 349 (1977) (hereinafter *Teamsters*). The Act's treatment of seniority systems, however, establishes an exception to these general principles. Section 703(h) provides in pertinent part:

"Notwithstanding any other provision of this subchapter, it shall not be an unlawful employment practice for an employer to apply different standards of compensation, or different terms, conditions, or privileges of employment pursuant to a bona fide seniority ... system ... provided that such differences are not the result of an intention to discriminate because of race."

Under this section, a showing of disparate impact is insufficient to invalidate a seniority system, even though the result may be to perpetuate pre-Act discrimination. ... Thus, any challenge to a seniority system under Title VII will require a trial on the issue of discriminatory intent: Was the system adopted because of its racially discriminatory impact?

This is precisely what happened in these cases. Following our decision in *Teamsters,* the District Court held a new trial on the limited question of whether the seniority system was "instituted or maintained contrary to Section 703(h) of the new Civil Rights Act of 1964."[2] That court concluded, as we noted above and will discuss below, that the system was adopted and maintained for purposes wholly independent of any discriminatory intent. The Court of Appeals for the Fifth Circuit reversed.

II

Petitioners submit that the Court of Appeals failed to comply with the command of Rule 52(a) that the findings of fact of a district court may not be set aside unless clearly erroneous. We first describe the findings of the District Court and the Court of Appeals.

Certain facts are common ground for both the District Court and the Court of Appeals. The Company's Bessemer plant

was unionized in the early 1940's. Both before and after unionization, the plant was divided into a number of different operational departments. USW sought to represent all production and maintenance employees at the plant and was elected in 1941 as the bargaining representative of a bargaining unit consisting of most of these employees. At that same time, the International Association of Machinists and Aerospace Workers (IAM) became the bargaining representative of a unit consisting of five departments. Between 1941 and 1944, IAM ceded certain workers in its bargaining unit to USW. As a result of this transfer, the IAM bargaining unit became all white.

Throughout the period of representation by USW, the plant was approximately half black. Prior to 1965, the Company openly pursued a racially discriminatory policy of job assignments. Most departments contained more than one job category and as a result most departments were racially mixed. There were no lines of progression or promotion within departments.

The seniority system at issue here was adopted in 1954. Under that agreement, seniority was measured by length of continuous service in a particular department. Seniority was originally exercised only for purposes of layoffs and hirings within particular departments. In 1956 seniority was formally recognized for promotional purposes as well. Again, however, seniority, with limited exceptions, was only exercised within departments; employees transferring to new departments forfeited their seniority. This seniority system remained virtually unchanged until after this suit was brought in 1971.

The District Court approached the question of discriminatory intent in the manner suggested by the Fifth Circuit in *James v. Stockham Valves & Fittings Co.,* 559 F.2d 310 (1977). There, the Court of Appeals stated that under *Teamsters* "the totality of the circumstances in the development

---

[2] The procedural history of these cases is rather complex. The original complaint was filed in 1971. Since that time the case has been tried three times and has twice been reviewed by the Court of Appeals.

and maintenance of the system is relevant to examining that issue." There were, in its view, however, four particular factors that a court should focus on.[8]

First, a court must determine whether the system "operates to discourage all employees equally from transferring between seniority units." The District Court held that the system here "was facially neutral and . . . was applied equally to all races and ethnic groups." Although there were charges of racial discrimination in its application, the court held that these were "not substantiated by the evidence." It concluded that the system "applied equally and uniformly to all employees, black and white, and that, given the approximately equal number of employees of the two groups, it was quantitatively neutral as well."[9]

Second, a court must examine the rationality of the departmental structure, upon which the seniority system relies, in light of the general industry practice. The District Court found that linking seniority to "departmental age" was "the modal form of agreements generally, as well as with manufacturers of railroad equipment in particu-

lar." . . . Although unionization did produce an all-white IAM bargaining unit, it found that USW "cannot be charged with racial bias in its response to the IAM situation. [USW] sought to represent all workers, black and white, in the plant." Nor could the Company be charged with any racial discrimination that may have existed in IAM:

"The company properly took a 'hands-off' approach towards the establishment of the election units . . . It bargained with those unions which were afforded representational status by the NLRB and did so without any discriminatory animus."

Third, a court had to consider "whether the seniority system had its genesis in racial discrimination," by which it meant the relationship between the system and other racially discriminatory practices. Although finding ample discrimination by the Company in its employment practices and some discriminatory practices by the union,[11] the District Court concluded that the seniority system was in no way related to the discriminatory practices. . . .

Finally, a court must consider "whether the system was negotiated and has been maintained free from any illegal purpose." *James, supra,* at 352. Stating that it had "carefully considered the detailed record of negotiation sessions and contracts which span a period of some thirty-five years," the court found that the system was untainted by any discriminatory purpose. Thus, although the District Court focused

---

[8] The Fifth Circuit relied upon the following passage in *Teamsters,* 431 U.S., at 355-356: "The seniority system in this litigation is entirely bona fide. It applies equally to all races and ethnic groups. To the extent that it 'locks' employees into non-line-driver jobs, it does so for all. . . . The placing of line drivers in a separate bargaining unit from other employees is rational, in accord with the industry practice, and consistent with National Labor Relation Board precedents. It is conceded that the seniority system did not have its genesis in racial discrimination, and that it was negotiated and has been maintained free from any illegal purpose."
This passage was of course not meant to be an exhaustive list of all the factors that a district court might or should consider in making a finding of discriminatory intent.

[9] The court specifically declined to make any finding on whether the no-transfer provision of the seniority system had a greater relative effect on blacks than on whites, because of qualitative differences in the departments in which they were concentrated. It believed that such an inquiry would have been inconsistent with the earlier Fifth Circuit opinion in this case.

[11] With respect to USW, the District Court found that "[u]nion meetings were conducted with different sides of the hall for white and black members, and social functions of the union were also segregated." It also found, however, that "[w]hile possessing some of the trappings taken from an otherwise segregated society, the USW local was one of the few institutions in the area which did not function in fact to foster and maintain segregation; rather, it served a joint interest of white and black workers which had a higher priority than racial considerations."

on particular factors in carrying out the analysis required by § 703(h), it also looked to the entire record and to the "totality of the system under attack."

The Court of Appeals addressed each of the four factors of the *James* test and reached the opposite conclusion. First, it held that the District Court erred in putting aside qualitative differences between the departments in which blacks were concentrated and those dominated by whites, in considering whether the system applied "equally" to whites and blacks. This is a purported correction of a legal standard under which the evidence is to be evaluated.

Second, it rejected the District Court's conclusion that the structure of departments was rational, in line with industry practice, and did not reflect any discriminatory intent. Its discussion is brief but focuses on the role of IAM and certain characteristics unique to the Bessemer plant. The court concluded:

> "The record evidence, generally, indicates arbitrary creation of the departments by the company since unionization and an attendant adverse affect [sic] on black workers. The individual differences between the departmental structure at Pullman-Standard and that of other plants, and as compared with industry practice, are indicative of attempts to maintain one-race departments."

In reaching this conclusion, the Court of Appeals did not purport to be correcting a legal error, nor did it refer to or expressly apply the clearly-erroneous standard.

Third, in considering the "genesis" of the system, the Court of Appeals held that the District Court erred in holding that the motives of IAM were not relevant. This was the correction of a legal error on the part of the District Court in excluding relevant evidence. The court did not stop there, however. It went on to hold that IAM was acting out of discriminatory intent — an issue specifically not reached by the District Court — and that "considerations of race permeated the negotiation and the adoption of the seniority system in 1941 and subsequent negotiations thereafter."

Fourth, despite this conclusion under the third *James* factor, the Court of Appeals then recited, but did not expressly set aside or find clearly erroneous, the District Court's findings with respect to the negotiation and maintenance of the seniority system.

The court then announced that "[h]aving carefully reviewed the evidence offered to show whether the departmental seniority system in the present case is 'bona fide' within the meaning of § 703(h) of Title VII, we reject the district court's finding." Elaborating on its disagreement, the Court of Appeals stated:

> "An analysis of the totality of the facts and circumstances surrounding the creation and continuance of the departmental system at Pullman-Standard leaves us with the definite and firm conviction that a mistake has been made. There is no doubt, based upon the record in this case, about the existence of a discriminatory purpose. The obvious principal aim of the IAM in 1941 was to exclude black workers from its bargaining unit.
>
> That goal was ultimately reached when maneuvers by the IAM and USW resulted in an all-white IAM unit. The USW, in the interest of increased membership, acquiesced in the discrimination while succeeding in significantly segregating the departments within its own unit.
>
> "The district court might have reached a different conclusion had it given the IAM's role in the creation and establishment of the seniority system its due consideration."

Having rejected the District Court's finding, the court made its own findings as to whether the USW seniority system was protected by § 703(h):

"We consider significant in our decision the manner by which the two seniority units were set up, the creation of the various all-white and all-black departments within the USW unit at the time of certification and in the years thereafter, conditions of racial discrimination which affected the negotiation and renegotiation of the system, and the extent to which the system and the attendant no-transfer rule locked blacks into the least remunerative positions within the company. Because we find that the differences in the terms, conditions and standards of employment for black workers and white workers at Pullman-Standard resulted from an intent to discriminate because of race, we hold that the system is not legally valid under section 703(h) of Title VII."

In connection with its assertion that it was convinced that a mistake had been made, the Court of Appeals, in a footnote, referred to the clearly erroneous standard of Rule 52(a). *Id.*, at 533, n. 6.[14] It pointed out, however, that if findings "are made under an erroneous view of controlling legal principles, the clearly erroneous rule does not apply, and the findings may not stand." *Ibid.* Finally, quoting from *East v. Romine, Inc.*, 518 F.2d 332, 339 (CA5 1975), the Court of Appeals repeated the following view of its appellate function in Title VII cases where purposeful discrimination is at issue:

---

[14] In *United States v. United States Gypsum Co.*, 333 U.S. 364, 395 (1948), this Court characterized the clearly-erroneous standard as follows:

"A finding is 'clearly erroneous' when although there is evidence to support it, the reviewing court on the entire evidence is left with the definite and firm conviction that a mistake has been committed."

We note that the Court of Appeals quoted this passage at the conclusion of its analysis of the District Court opinion.

"'Although discrimination vel non is essentially a question of fact it is, at the same time, the ultimate issue for resolution in this case, being expressly proscribed by 42 USCA § 2000e-2(a). As such, a finding of discrimination or nondiscrimination is a finding of ultimate fact. [Cites omitted.] In reviewing the district court's findings, therefore, we will proceed to make an independent determination of appellant's allegations of discrimination, though bound by findings of subsidiary fact which are themselves not clearly erroneous.'" 624 F.2d, at 533, n. 6.

III

Pointing to the above statement of the Court of Appeals and to similar statements in other Title VII cases coming from that court, petitioners submit that the Court of Appeals made an independent determination of discriminatory purpose, the "ultimate fact" in this case, and that this was error under Rule 52(a). We agree with petitioners that if the Court of Appeals followed what seems to be the accepted rule in that Circuit, its judgment must be reversed.

Rule 52(a) broadly requires that findings of fact not be set aside unless clearly erroneous. It does not make exceptions or purport to exclude certain categories of factual findings from the obligation of a court of appeals to accept a district court's findings unless clearly erroneous. It does not divide facts into categories; in particular, it does not divide findings of fact into those that deal with "ultimate" and those that deal with "subsidiary" facts.

The Rule does not apply to conclusions of law. The Court of Appeals, therefore, was quite right in saying that if a district court's findings rest on an erroneous view of the law, they may be set aside on that basis. But here the District Court was not faulted for misunderstanding or applying an erroneous definition of intentional discrimination.[17] It was reversed for arriving at what the Court of Appeals thought was an erroneous finding as to whether the differential impact of the seniority system reflected an intent to discriminate on account of race. That question, as we see it, is a pure question of fact, subject to Rule 52(a)'s clearly-erroneous standard. It is not a question of law and not a mixed question of law and fact.

The Court has previously noted the vexing nature of the distinction between questions of fact and questions of law. *See Baumgartner v. United States,* 322 U.S. 665, 671, (1944). Rule 52(a) does not furnish particular guidance with respect to distinguishing law from fact. Nor do we yet know of any other rule or principle that will unerringly distinguish a factual finding from a legal conclusion. For the reasons that follow, however, we have little doubt about the factual nature of § 703(h)'s requirement that a seniority system be free of an intent to discriminate.

Treating issues of intent as factual matters for the trier of fact is commonplace. In *Dayton Board of Education v. Brinkman,* 443 U.S. 526, 534 (1979), the principal question was whether the defendants had intentionally maintained a racially segregated school system at a specified time in the past. We recognize that issue as essentially factual, subject to the clearly-erroneous rule. This is not to say that discriminatory impact is not part of the evidence to be considered by the trial court in reaching a finding on whether there was such a discriminatory intent as a factual matter. We do assert, however, that under § 703(h) discriminatory intent is a finding of fact to be made by the trial court; it is not a question of law and not a mixed ques-

tion of law and fact of the kind that in some cases may allow an appellate court to review the facts to see if they satisfy some legal concept of discriminatory intent. Discriminatory intent here means actual motive; it is not a legal presumption to be drawn from a factual showing of something less than actual motive. Thus, a court of appeals may only reverse a district court's finding on discriminatory intent if it concludes that the finding is clearly erroneous under Rule 52(a). Insofar as the Fifth Circuit assumed otherwise, it erred.

IV

Respondents do not directly defend the Fifth Circuit rule that a trial court's finding on discriminatory intent is not subject to the clearly-erroneous standard of Rule 52(a). Rather, among other things, they submit that the Court of Appeals recognized and, where appropriate, properly applied Rule 52(a) in setting aside the findings of the District Court. This position has force, but for two reasons it is not persuasive.

First, although the Court of Appeals acknowledged and correctly stated the controlling standard of Rule 52(a), the acknowledgment came late in the court's opinion. . . .

Second and more fundamentally, when the court stated that it was convinced that a mistake had been made, it then not only identified the mistake but also the source of that mistake. The mistake of the District Court was that on the record there could be no doubt about the existence of a discriminatory purpose. The source of the mistake was the District Court's failure to recognize the relevance of the racial purposes of IAM. Had the District Court "given the IAM's role in the creation and establishment of the seniority system its due consideration," it "might have reached a different conclusion."

When an appellate court discerns that a district court has failed to make a finding because of an erroneous view of the law,

---

[17] As we noted above, the Court of Appeals did at certain points purport to correct what it viewed as legal errors on the part of the District Court. The presence of such legal errors may justify a remand by the Court of Appeals to the District Court for additional factfinding under the correct legal standard.

the usual rule is that there should be a remand for further proceedings to permit the trial court to make the missing findings:

"[F]actfinding is the basic responsibility of district courts, rather than appellate courts, and . . . the Court of Appeals should not have resolved in the first instance this factual dispute which had not been considered by the District Court." *DeMarco v. United States*, 415 U.S. 449, 450, n. (1974).

Likewise, where findings are infirm because of an erroneous view of the law, a remand is the proper course unless the record permits only one resolution of the factual issue. . . . All of this is elementary. Yet the Court of Appeals, after holding that the District Court had failed to consider relevant evidence and indicating that the District Court might have come to a different conclusion had it considered that evidence, failed to remand for further proceedings as to the intent of IAM and the significance, if any, of such a finding with respect to the intent of USW itself. Instead, the Court of Appeals made its own determination as to the motives of IAM, found that USW had acquiesced in the IAM conduct, and apparently concluded that the foregoing was sufficient to remove the system from the protection of § 703(h).

Proceeding in this manner seems to us incredible unless the Court of Appeals construed its own well-established Circuit rule with respect to its authority to arrive at independent findings on ultimate facts free of the strictures of Rule 52(a) also to permit it to examine the record and make its own independent findings with respect to those issues on which the district court's findings are set aside for an error of law. As we have previously said, however, the premise for this conclusion is infirm: whether an ultimate fact or not, discriminatory intent under § 703(h) is a factual matter subject to the clearly-erroneous standard of Rule 52(a). It follows that when a district court's finding on such an ultimate fact is set aside

for an error of law, the court of appeals is not relieved of the usual requirement of remanding for further proceedings to the tribunal charged with the task of factfinding in the first instance.

Accordingly, the judgment of the Court of Appeals is reversed, and the cases are remanded to that court for further proceedings consistent with this opinion.

Justice MARSHALL, with whom Justice BLACKMUN joins except as to Part I, dissenting.

In 1971, a group of Negro employees at Pullman-Standard's Bessemer, Ala., plant brought this class action against Pullman-Standard, the United Steelworkers of America and its Local 1466 (USW), and the International Association of Machinists and its Local 372 (IAM). The plaintiffs alleged, *inter alia*, that the departmental seniority system negotiated by both unions discriminated against Negroes in violation of Title VII of the Civil Rights Act of 1964, and the Civil Rights Act of 1866. In 1974, the District Court for the Northern District of Alabama concluded that the seniority system did not operate to discriminate against Negroes. A unanimous panel of the Fifth Circuit reversed. The court ruled that the District Court had committed several errors of law, including failure to give proper weight to the role of the IAM, and had relied on patently inaccurate factual conclusions. *Swint v. Pullman-Standard*, 539 F.2d 77, 95-96 (1976). On remand, the District Court again ruled that the seniority system was immune from attack under Title VII, this time finding that respondents had failed to show discriminatory intent as required by this Court's decision in *Teamsters v. United States*, 431 U.S. 324 (1977). The Fifth Circuit again unanimously rejected the conclusion of the District Court. 624 F.2d 525 (1980). The majority now reverses the Fifth Circuit's second unanimous decision on the ground that the Court of Appeals did not pay sufficient homage to the "clearly erroneous" rule, Fed. R. Civ. Proc. 52(a), in concluding that the seniority system at Pullman-Standard was the product of intentional discrimination against Negroes. Because I cannot agree with the premise of the majority's decision to remand this case for yet another trial, or with its application of that premise to the facts of this case, I respectfully dissent.

I

The majority premises its holding on the assumption that " 'absent a discriminatory purpose, the operation of a seniority system cannot be an unlawful employment practice even if the system has some discriminatory consequences.' " As I have previously indicated, I do not find anything in the relevant statutory language or legislative history to support the proposition that § 703(h) of Title VII immunizes a seniority system that perpetuates past discrimination, as the system at issue here clearly does, simply because the plaintiffs are unable to demonstrate to this Court's satisfaction that the system was adopted or maintained for an invidious purpose. . . .

II

Even if I were to accept this Court's decision to impose this novel burden on Title VII plaintiffs, I would still be unable to concur in its conclusion that the Fifth Circuit's decision should be reversed for failing to abide by Rule 52(a). The majority asserts that the Court of Appeals in this case ignored the clearly-erroneous rule and made an independent determination of discriminatory purpose. I disagree. In my view, the court below followed well-established legal principles both in rejecting the District Court's finding of no discriminatory purpose and in concluding that a finding of such a purpose was compelled by all of the relevant evidence.

The majority concedes, as it must, that the "Court of Appeals acknowledged and correctly stated the controlling standard of Rule 52(a)." In a footnote to its opinion, the Court of Appeals plainly states that

findings of fact may be overturned only if they are either "clearly erroneous" or "made under an erroneous view of controlling legal principles." 624 F.2d, at 533, n. 6. Furthermore, as the majority notes, the Court of Appeals justified its decision to reject the District Court's finding that the seniority system was not the result of purposeful discrimination by stating: "An analysis of the totality of the facts and circumstances surrounding the creation and continuance of the departmental system at Pullman-Standard leaves us with the definite and firm conviction that a mistake has been made." I frankly am at a loss to understand how the Court of Appeals could have expressed its conclusion that the District Court's finding on the issue of intent was clearly erroneous with any more precision or clarity.

The majority rejects the Court of Appeals' clear articulation and implementation of the clearly-erroneous rule on the apparent ground that in the course of correctly setting forth the requirements of Rule 52(a), the court also included the following quotation from its prior decision in *East v. Romine, Inc.,* 518 F.2d 332, 339 (1975):

" ' 'Although discrimination vel non is essentially a question of fact it is, at the same time, the ultimate issue for resolution in this case, being expressly proscribed by 42 USCA § 2000e-2(a). As such, a finding of discrimination or nondiscrimination is a finding of ultimate fact. [Cites omitted]. In reviewing the district court's findings, therefore, we will proceed to make an independent determination of appellant's allegations of discrimination, though bound by findings of subsidiary fact which are themselves not clearly erroneous.' " 624 F.2d, at 533, n. 6.

The only question presented by this case, therefore, is whether this reference to *East v. Romine, Inc.,* should be read as negating the Court of Appeals' unambiguous acknowledgment of the "controlling standard of Rule 52." The majority bases its affirmative answer to that question on two factors. First, the majority contends that the Court of Appeals must not have properly respected the clearly-erroneous rule because its acknowledgment that Rule 52(a) supplied the controlling standard "came late in the court's opinion." Second, the Court of Appeals not only "identified the mistake" that it felt had been made, "but also the source of that mistake." If the Court of Appeals had really been applying the clearly-erroneous rule, it should have abided by the "usual requirement of remanding for further proceedings to the tribunal charged with the task of factfinding in the first instance."

Neither of these arguments justifies the majority's conclusion that this case must be remanded for a fourth trial on the merits. I am aware of no rule of decision embraced by this or any other court that places dispositive weight on whether an accurate statement of controlling principle appears "early" or late in a court's opinion. . . . The heart of the majority's argument, therefore, is that the failure to remand the action to the District Court after rejecting its conclusion that the seniority system was "bona fide" within the meaning of § 703(h) indicates that the Court of Appeals did not properly follow the clearly-erroneous rule.
. . .

However, as we have often noted, in some cases a remand is inappropriate where the facts on the record are susceptible to only one reasonable interpretation. . . . In such cases, "[e]ffective judicial administration" requires that the court of appeals draw the inescapable factual conclusion itself, rather than remand the case to the district court for further needless proceedings. . . . Such action is particularly appropriate where the court of appeals is in as good a position to evaluate the record evidence as the district court. The major premise behind the deference to trial courts expressed in Rule 52(a) is that find-ings of fact "depend peculiarly upon the credit given to witnesses by those who see and hear them." *United States v. Yellow Cab Co.,* 338 U.S. 338, 341 (1949). Indeed Rule 52(a) expressly acknowledges the importance of this factor by stating that "due regard shall be given to the opportunity of the trial court to judge of the credibility of the witnesses." Consequently, this Court has been especially reluctant to resolve factual issues which depend on the credibility of witnesses.

In the case before the Court today this usual deference is not required because the District Court's findings of fact were entirely based on documentary evidence. As we noted in *United States v. General Motors Corp.,* "the trial court's customary opportunity to evaluate the demeanor and thus the credibility of the witnesses, which is the rationale behind Rule 52(a) . . ., plays only a restricted role [in] a 'paper case.'"
. . .

I believe that the Court of Appeals correctly determined that a finding of discriminatory intent was compelled by the documentary record presented to the District Court. With respect to three of the four *James* factors, the Court of Appeals found overwhelming evidence of discriminatory intent. First, in ruling that the District Court erred by not acknowledging the legal significance of the fact that the seniority system locked Negroes into the least remunerative jobs in the company, the Court of Appeals determined that such disproportionate impact demonstrated that the system did not "'operat[e] to discourage all employees equally from transferring between seniority units.'" Second, noting that "[n]o credible explanation ha[d] been advanced to sufficiently justify" the existence of two separate Die & Tool Departments and two separate Maintenance Departments, a condition not found at any other Pullman-Standard plant, or the creation of all-white and all-Negro departments at the time of unionization and in subsequent years, the Court of Appeals concluded that the second *James* factor had not been satisfied. Finally, with respect to the third *James* factor the Court of Appeals found that once the role of the IAM was properly recognized, it was "crystal clear that considerations of race permeated the negotiation and the adoption of the seniority system in 1941 and subsequent negotiations thereafter."

After reviewing all of the relevant record evidence presented to the District Court, the Court of Appeals concluded: "There is no doubt, based upon the record in this case, about the existence of a discriminatory purpose." Because I fail to see how the Court of Appeals erred in carrying out its appellate function, I respectfully dissent from the majority's decision to prolong respondents' 11-year quest for the vindication of their rights by requiring yet another trial.

Notes

1. Justice Marshall referred to the fact that the district court's factual findings relied heavily on documentary evidence, rather than evidence presented through witnesses whose credibility must be assessed. Subsequently to the *Pullman-Standard* decision, the Federal Rules were amended to provide explicitly that the "clearly erroneous" standard applies to all factual findings, whether based on oral or documentary evidence. *See* Fed. R. Civ. P. 52(a) (amended, eff. August 1, 1985). Despite this amendment, might it be easier to convince a court of appeals that a trial judge's finding was indeed "clearly erroneous" in a case relying principally on documents that the appellate court could examine for itself?

2. The majority in *Pullman-Standard* criticized the Court of Appeals for the Fifth Circuit for distinguishing between subsidiary facts and "ultimate facts." The theoretical difference between the two types of factual findings may be illustrated by a more recent case involving a claim of discrimination based on gender. In *Price Waterhouse v. Hopkins,* 490 U.S. 228 (1989), Ann Hopkins asserted that she had been denied partnership in a major accounting firm because of sexual stereotyping. She had received excellent reports for her work, having played a key role in obtaining a multi-million dollar contract with the State Department. Her evaluations also contained, however, criticisms by some partners of her aggressive style: one man described her as "macho"; another thought she overcompensated for being a woman; and a third advised her to take a course at charm school. *Id.* at 1782. When her application for partnership was initially put on hold, the partner responsible for explaining why she had not been successful suggested that she should "walk more femininely, talk more femininely, dress more femininely, wear make-up, have her hair styled, and wear jewelry." *Id.*

The district court's findings that these comments were made, that they reflected sex stereotyping, and that they played a role in the partnership decision were subsidiary findings about the statements and actions of the participants. The court's conclusion that reliance on such comments constituted impermissible discrimination on the basis of sex might be regarded as a finding of "ultimate fact."

The Supreme Court had itself caused some of the confusion about the correct standard for review of so-called "ultimate facts" by its use of this term in *Baumgart-ner v. United States,* 322 U.S. 665 (1944). The Court there characterized as an "ultimate fact" subject to independent review the lower courts' finding that the government's proof in support of a denaturalization decree was clear and convincing. The Court explained in a footnote to *Pullman-Standard,* however, that the so-called "fact" at issue in *Baumgartner,* that is whether the clear-and-convincing standard of proof had been met, necessarily incorporated a legal standard, such as to take it out of the category of "pure fact." 256 U.S. at 286, n.16. Accordingly, *de novo* review of the question of whether the proof had indeed satisfied the legal standard was appropriate.

Rather than focusing on the incorporation of a legal standard as justifying more probing, independent review, the Fifth Circuit had apparently concluded that it could review independently any "ultimate fact," in the sense of any factual finding upon which the result in the case turns. The circuit court had, under this interpretation, reviewed *de novo* a finding of discrimination because, while "essentially a question of fact, it is, at the same time, the ultimate issue for resolution in this case." *Causey v. Ford Motor Co.,* 516 F.2d 416, 421 (5th Cir. 1975).

In *Pullman-Standard,* the Supreme Court firmly rejected any such gloss on Rule 52(a). Accordingly, in both *Pullman-Standard* and *Price Waterhouse,* the Court applied the clearly erroneous standard to the "ultimate" finding, which it found to be purely factual, of whether there had been intent to discriminate on impermissible grounds.

3. An exception to the clearly erroneous standard has been carved out for certain factual issues at the core of the freedom of expression protected by the First Amendment. In *Bose Corp. v. Consumers Union of U.S., Inc.,* 466 U.S. 485 (1984), the Supreme Court determined that the appellate court should review *de novo* a trial court's finding of actual malice on the part of a publisher of defamatory statements, rather than merely scrutinize it under the "clearly erroneous" standard, in order to ensure against unwarranted intrusions into protected speech.

4. A similar requirement of more extensive review of factfinding that implicates constitutional rights may also extend to judicial review of administrative agency determinations. *See generally,* Note, "*De Novo* Judicial Review of Administrative Agency Factual Determination Implicating Constitutional Rights," 88 Colum. L. Rev. 1483 (1988). Although the subject of appellate review of administrative decision-making is beyond the scope of this book, it should be noted that agency factfinding that does not touch on constitutional rights is subject to only limited judicial review, with deference granted to any findings that are based on substantial evidence.

5. The question of whether particular kinds of findings by district courts are findings of fact, reviewable under the clearly erroneous standard, or conclusions of law, reviewable *de novo,* continues to present problems, and different circuits at times arrive at different answers.

Exercise

A federal district court has entered judgment in favor of the plaintiff in a trademark infringement suit, finding that there was a likelihood of confusion between the two trademarks involved. Your firm has been approached by one of the parties to handle the case on appeal. Your supervising partner has asked you to find out whether such a finding of a likelihood of confusion is factual or legal. Upon researching the issue, you discover a split in the circuits. The partner now asks you to write an argument urging the Supreme Court to resolve the issue, in favor of either *de novo* review or the clearly erroneous standard.

Appellate Review of Mixed Questions of Law and Fact

One of the most difficult areas involving standards of appellate review concerns mixed questions of law and fact. Findings of historic facts, such as "the landlord changed the locks," are most firmly in the "fact" category. When the finding includes a legal component, however, such as "the landlord evicted the tenant," the issue is outside the "pure" fact category and may suggest a different standard of review.

Mixed questions generally involve both a legal standard to be interpreted, such as "what constitutes ineffective assistance of counsel?" and a factual component to be determined, such as "what did counsel do, or fail to do, during the course of trial?" The ultimate conclusion – counsel was, or was not, ineffective – incorporates both a legal ruling and factual findings. Courts have sent decidedly mixed signals about what is the appropriate standard of review for such hybrid questions, with some courts announcing that a *de novo* standard should apply, others deciding that mixed findings are essentially factual, and therefore entitled to great deference, and several courts swinging back and forth between the two positions.

In *United States v. McConney,* 728 F.2d 1195 (9th Cir. 1984), the court was called upon to review a trial court's determination that federal agents were faced with exigent circumstances when they executed a search warrant, thus allowing them to enter the premises without first announcing their purpose and being refused admittance. The court had agreed to hear the case *en banc* to reexamine the issue of the applicable standard of review. An earlier panel opinion had ruled that the "mixed fact-law question" of exigent circumstances was factual in nature, and thus subject to the clearly erroneous standard of review. Noting that "our jurisprudence concerning appellate review of mixed questions lacks clarity and coherence," the court proceeded to provide the following analysis of the issue:

> The Supreme Court has defined mixed questions as those in which "the historical facts are admitted or established, the rule of law is undisputed, and the issue is whether the facts satisfy the [relevant] statutory [or constitutional] standard, or to put it another way, whether the rule of law as applied

to the established facts is or is not violated." *Pullman-Standard v. Swint,* 456 U.S. 273, 289 n. 19 (1982). Thus, there are three distinct steps in deciding a mixed fact-law question. The first step is the establishment of the "basic, primary, or historical facts: facts 'in the sense of a recital of external events and the credibility of their narrators . . . .'" *Townsend v. Sain,* 372 U.S. 293, 309 n. 6 (1963) (quoting *Brown v. Allen,* 344 U.S. 443, 506 (1953) (opinion of Frankfurter, J.)). The second step is the selection of the applicable rule of law. The third step – and the most troublesome for standard of review purposes – is the application of law to fact or, in other words, the determination "whether the rule of law as applied to the established facts is or is not violated." *Pullman-Standard,* 456 U.S. at 289 n. 19.

The district court's resolution of each of these inquiries is, of course, subject to appellate review. The appropriate standard of review for the first two of the district court's determinations – its establishment of historical facts and its selection of the relevant legal principle – has long been settled. Questions of fact are reviewed under the deferential, clearly erroneous standard. *See* Fed. R. Civ. P. 52(a). Questions of law are reviewed under the non-deferential, *de novo* standard. . . . These established rules reflect the policy concerns that properly underlie standard of review jurisprudence generally.

Rule 52(a)'s mandate that appellate courts not disturb a trial court's findings of fact unless clearly erroneous serves two policy objectives. First, it minimizes the risk of judicial error by assigning primary responsibility for resolving factual disputes to the court in the "superior position" to evaluate and weigh the evidence – the trial court. Rule 52(a) emphasizes that the trial judge's opportunity to judge the accuracy of witnesses' recollections and make credibility determinations in cases in which live testimony is presented gives him a significant advantage over appellate judges in evaluating and weighing the evidence: "findings of fact shall not be set aside unless clearly erroneous, and due regard shall be given to the opportunity of the trial court to judge of the credibility of the witnesses." Fed. R. Civ. P. 52(a). Second, because under the clearly erroneous test, the reviewing court will affirm the trial court's determinations unless it "is left with the definite and firm conviction that a mistake has been committed," *Pullman-Standard v. Swint,* 456 U.S. 273, 284-85 n. 14 (1982), it is relieved of the burden of a full-scale independent review and evaluation of the evidence. Consequently, valuable appellate resources are conserved for those issues that appellate courts in turn are best situated to decide.

The converse rule – that conclusions of law are subject to plenary or *de novo* review – reflects similar concerns. Structurally, appellate courts have several advantages over trial courts in deciding questions of law. First, appellate judges are freer to concentrate on legal questions because they are not encumbered, as are trial judges, by the vital, but time-consuming, process of hearing evidence. Second, the judgment of at least three members of an appellate panel is brought to bear on every case. It stands to reason that the collaborative, deliberative process of appellate courts reduces the risk of judicial error on questions of law. Thus, *de novo* review of questions of law, like clearly erroneous review of questions of fact, serves to minimize judicial error by assigning to the court best positioned to decide the issue the primary responsibility for doing so.

De novo review of questions of law, however, is dictated by still another concern. Under the doctrine of *stare decisis*, appellate rulings of law become controlling precedent and, consequently, affect the rights of future litigants. Rulings on factual issues, on the other hand, are generally of concern only to the immediate litigants. From the standpoint of sound judicial administration, therefore, it makes sense to concentrate appellate resources on ensuring the correctness of determinations of law.

Thus, we have a well developed standard of review jurisprudence for issues of fact and issues of law. Yet, when we review the third of the district court's determinations – its application of law to fact – we confront "a much-mooted issue" with "substantial authority in the circuits on both sides of th[e] question." *Pullman-Standard,* 456 U.S. at 289-90 n.19. We believe, however, that the well developed jurisprudence relating to questions of pure law and pure fact offers guideposts for working our way out of this confusion.

The appropriate standard of review for a district judge's application of law to fact may be determined, in our view, by reference to the sound principles which underlie the settled rules of appellate review just discussed. If the concerns of judicial administration – efficiency, accuracy, and precedential weight – make it more appropriate for a district judge to determine whether the established facts fall within the relevant legal definition, we should subject his determination to deferential, clearly erroneous review. If, on the other hand, the concerns of judicial administration favor the appellate court, we should subject the district judge's finding to *de novo* review. Thus, in each case, the pivotal question is do the concerns of judicial administration favor the district court or do they favor the appellate court.

In our view, the key to the resolution of this question is the nature of the inquiry that is required to decide "whether the rule of law as applied to the established facts is or is not violated." *Id.* If application of the rule of law to the facts requires an inquiry that is "essentially factual," *id.* at 288, – one that is founded "on the application of the fact-finding tribunal's experience with the mainsprings of human conduct," *Commissioner v. Duberstein,* 363 U.S. 278, 289 (1960) – the concerns of judicial administration will favor the district court, and the district court's determination should be classified as one of fact reviewable under the clearly erroneous standard. If, on the other hand, the question requires us to consider legal concepts in the mix of fact and law and to exercise judgment about the values that animate legal principles, then the concerns of judicial administration will favor the appellate court, and the question should be classified as one of law and reviewed *de novo.*

Id. at 1200-02.

Applying this so-called "functional analysis," the court determined that the mixed question of whether exigent circumstances justify departure from the usual warrant procedures is subject to a *de novo* standard of review. The court found that "to decide if the facts satisfy the legal test of exigency," that is, whether, by an objective standard, the occupants were likely to escape, destroy evidence, or harm someone, "necessarily involves us in an inquiry that goes beyond the historical facts." *Id.* at 1204-05.

Another court used a similar approach in deciding the appropriate standard of review for an administrative agency's finding that a federal employee failed to come within the exemption for "independent candidates" of the Hatch Act's prohibition against active participation in political management or campaigns. *Campbell v. Merit Systems Protection Board,* 27 F.3d 1560 (Fed. Cir. 1994). The employee, Lynnwood Campbell, argued that the conclusion as to whether a person is indeed an "independent candidate" within the meaning of the regulations interpreting the Hatch Act is a question of law, subject to *de novo* review. The applicable state law regarded him as an independent candidate; accordingly, the decision of the Merit Systems Protection Board was in error and should be reversed. The Government, on the other hand, characterized the question of whether a candidate is independent for purposes of the Hatch Act exemption as turning on the particular facts of each case, facts as to which the agency should be granted considerable deference. Faced with the parties' different contentions regarding the proper standard of review, the Court of Appeals for the Federal Circuit first acknowledged that logical analysis could provide no clear answer:

It is often difficult to distinguish factual inferences from legal conclusions. See *Pullman-Standard v. Swint,* 456 U.S. 273, 288 (1982). Indeed, this case reveals the falseness of the fact-law dichotomy, since the determination at issue, involving as it does the application of a general legal standard to particular facts, is probably most realistically described as neither of fact nor law, but mixed. Mixed questions sometimes are impossible to categorize through sheer logic. Somewhere near the middle of the fact-law spectrum, a "finding of fact shades imperceptibly into a conclusion of law." The mixed questions in this zone of logical overlap fairly can be conceptualized as either essentially factual or essentially legal because they have a substantial normative element, yet are case-specific. . . .

In cases such as this, which fall within the zone of logical overlap, "there [can be] no fixed distinction . . . . The knife of policy alone effects an artificial cleavage at the point where the court chooses to draw the line . . . ." The court in *Mamiye Bros. v. Barber S.S. Lines,* 360 F.2d 774, 777 (2d Cir.) (Friendly, J.), *cert. denied,* 385 U.S. 835 (1966), for example, held that while a negligence determination must be characterized as a question of fact when tried to a jury, it is a question of law when tried to a judge, because in the latter case, there are no constitutional considerations to override concerns about uniformity of result. As these cases suggest, courts in such situations do not decide to defer because they have concluded *a priori* that something is a question of fact, but rather, decide something is a question of fact because they have concluded it is wise policy to defer.

The mixed question at issue here . . . is not sufficiently close to one end of the spectrum or another to permit an easy answer based on logic alone. Characterization therefore must follow from an *a priori* decision as to whether deferring to the Board's application of the "independent candidate" exception to the facts of cases before it is sound judicial policy. We would be less than candid to suggest otherwise. The question thus arises, exactly which policies properly inform the analysis and to what extent?

Courts in such situations typically have balanced considerations of judicial economy, comparative institutional advantage (e.g., the relative expertise of agencies and relative non-expertise of juries vis-a-vis judges), and constitutional concerns (e.g., the separation of powers in administrative appeals, and the right of trial by jury in actions at law) against the effect of appellate deference on consistency and uniformity in the law. We turn now to consider the nature of the determination at issue here in light of the policies underlying standards of review.

If the record before us is any indication, most of the Hatch Act cases will be *sui generis,* presenting unique combinations of numerous specific episodes that shed light on the question of political independence *vel non.* The ultimate conclusion is simply the net impression created by this totality of circumstances. Such case-specificity severely limits the scope of any one decision's precedential relevance. Few cases will be so factually indistinguishable that apparently divergent results would not be seen best as a function of the peculiarities of the case rather than some deeper normative conflict. This at once minimizes the adverse effect that a deferential standard of review might have on uniformity and maximizes judicial economy by avoiding a rule that would tend to encourage entirely fact-bound appeals.

As for considerations of comparative institutional advantage, the trier is in a better position to make an overall assessment than a court of appeals, because demeanor evidence – invisible to us – ordinarily will be an important ingredient in the mix. Moreover, while the Board is perhaps more akin to a lower court than the typical agency (since Congress assigned it an essentially adjudicatory function), its determinations nevertheless represent the actions of an independent branch of government for which Congress prescribed the same standards of review. This suggests the Board is entitled to the same deference typically accorded agencies resolving fact-intensive mixed questions – that is, questions involving the straight application of a rule in need of no further elaboration to highly particularized facts.

To be sure, the factor of relative expertise as between the Board and this court is not dispositive as to whether the standard of review should be deferential. Because we alone review the Board's decisions under the Hatch Act as they affect federal employees, we are as well versed in the applicable law as is the Board. The Board, however, hears and decides also those Hatch Act cases that are not appealed here, which involve employees of state agencies that receive federal funds. Consequently, the Board has broad exposure to the many varied fact settings in which Hatch Act cases may arise. To the extent that familiarity with factual underpinnings of Hatch Act cases may lead to expertise in deciding such cases, the Board's experience tilts in the direction of according a measure of deference to their conclusions.

Finally, there are no countervailing constitutional concerns that might outweigh the separation of powers and other considerations favoring deference to the agency here. *Cf. Bose,* 466 U.S. at 485 (the firstness of the First Amendment dictates *de novo* review of "actual malice" determination in libel suit despite the cost to judicial economy and the right to trial by jury). Congress unquestionably has the power to forbid federal employees absolutely from running for elective office, for while Mr. Campbell "may have a constitutional right to [run for elective office], . . . he has no constitutional right to be a [federal employee]." It follows that if Congress can forbid federal employees absolutely from running for elective office, *a fortiori* it can permit them to do so subject to non-arbitrary restrictions. The greater power subsumes the lesser. Applying the minimal scrutiny of rationality review to Board determinations under the "independent candidate" exception does not fairly implicate the First Amendment, much less raise a serious constitutional question.

For the foregoing reasons, we hold that the mixed question of "independent candidate" must be placed in the category of fact for purposes of judicial review. We now turn to the merits of this appeal and whether the record contains "such relevant evidence as a reasonable mind might accept as adequate to support [the Board's] conclusion" that candidate Campbell was not really independent of a political party.

Campbell, 27 F.3d at 1565-67. The court then proceeded to hold that the agency's conclusion that Campbell was not really independent of a political party had been supported by adequate relevant evidence.

As the *Campbell* case illustrates, parties on appeal are well advised to pay considerable attention to the threshold issue of what standard of review should apply to so-called mixed questions of law and fact. Just as appellate counsel must research the merits of a client's claims in the particular jurisdiction where the appeal will be heard, so also counsel should look into that jurisdiction's approach to such mixed questions, and try to formulate the issue raised to as to maximize the chance of victory for the client. If the particular appellate court tends towards *de novo* review of such issues, of course appellant should attempt to fit the claim into the "mixed," rather than purely factual category. Respondent, on the other hand, seeking to take advantage of the deference due factual findings, should stress the factual elements, in addition to providing support for the court's application of the legal standard to those facts. Given the current approach used by several appellate courts, exemplified by the *McConney* and *Campbell* excerpts, counsel would also do well to emphasize those policies underlying the different standards of review that might lead the court to adopt the standard most advantageous to the client.

Review of Matters Within Trial Court's Discretion

Trial judges make numerous decisions during the course of proceedings on a case, before, during and after trial, for which it would be virtually impossible to devise general rules to assess the "correctness" of the decisions. Such decisions are said to be committed to the discretion of trial courts, subject to reversal only for abuse or improvident exercise of that discretion, or upon finding that the trial court failed to exercise discretion at all.

Some decisions in this discretionary category are primarily administrative, such as those dealing with pre-trial conferences, continuances, and the mechanics of motion practice. These decisions, ancillary to the merits of a case, are considered appropriately left to the trial judge's discretion except in highly unusual circumstances. A judge's decision about whether to grant a continuance, for example, is firmly within the trial court's discretion. *See Ungar v. Sarafite*, 376 U.S. 575, 589 (1964). Denial of additional time has provided a basis for reversal, however, where, in a deportation proceeding, the judge granted little more than two workings days to a petitioner who was "in custody, spoke only Spanish, had limited education, was unfamiliar with this country and its legal procedures, and had been removed nearly 3,000 miles from his only friend in this country." *Rios-Berrios v. I.N.S.*, 776 F.2d 859, 862-63 (9th Cir. 1985).

Other kinds of discretionary decisions are so closely tied to the particular facts and circumstances of the case that it is simply inappropriate to second-guess the trial court's judgment in most situations. For example, many evidentiary rulings depend on an evaluation of whether the probative value of the proffered evidence outweighs its possible improper prejudicial effect. In general, the trial court's decision about that balance will be given great weight, since the judge is in the best position to gauge the probable effect of admission of the evidence in the context of the entire trial.

Different types of discretionary rulings may call for different standards of review. Some decisions said to be within the discretion of the trial court are actually circumscribed by fairly specific boundaries, so that reversal for abuse of discretion is relatively common. On the other hand, some types of decisions are so squarely within the control of the trial court that an appellate court will virtually never review them. In the federal system, for example, a trial court's refusal to submit a special verdict will be upheld, no matter how misguided the appellate court may have thought it was.[5] *See Skidmore v. Baltimore & Ohio R.R. Co.,* 167 F.2d 54 (2d Cir. 1948). Appellate courts are essentially saying that they do not want even to look at such questions; trial courts have the right to be wrong.

A. Abuse of Discretion

Even with regard to matters committed to the discretion of the trial court, that discretion is likely to be circumscribed by certain guidelines, either expressed in the pertinent statute or developed through case law, such that failure to adhere to those guidelines may result in reversal. Consistent reversal by appellate courts of a given category of decisions, once held to have been within the court's discretion, may move that particular category out of the realm of discretion and into the realm of law. The following sets of materials, the first involving control over discovery in a federal civil case, and the second concerning management of a criminal jury trial in a New York state court, illustrate that process.

1. The Scope of Discretion

National Hockey League v. Metropolitan Hockey Club
427 U.S. 639 (1976)

Per Curiam.

This case arises out of the dismissal, under Fed. R. Civ. P. 37, of respondents' antitrust action against petitioners for failure to timely answer written interrogatories as ordered by the District Court. The Court of Appeals for the Third Circuit reversed the judgment of dismissal, finding that the District Court had abused its discretion. The question presented is whether the Court of Appeals was correct in so concluding. Rule 37(b)(2) provides in pertinent part as follows:

"If a party . . . fails to obey an order to provide or permit discovery . . . the court in which the action is pending may make such orders in regard to the failure as are just, and among others the following:

"(C) An order striking out pleadings or parts thereof, or staying further proceedings until the order is obeyed, or dismissing the action or proceed-

---

[5] Professor Rosenberg has described such decisions as involving "Grade A discretion," which is "unreviewable and unreversible." Rosenberg, *Appellate Court Review of Trial Court Discretion,* 79 F.R.D. 173, 176 (1979).

ing or any part thereof, or rendering a judgment by default against the disobedient party."

This Court held in *Societe Internationale v. Rogers,* 357 U.S. 197, 212 (1958), that Rule 37

"should not be construed to authorize dismissal of [a] complaint because of petitioner's noncompliance with a pretrial production order when it has been established that failure to comply has been due to inability and not to willfulness, bad faith, or any fault of petitioner."

. . .

The District Court, in its memorandum opinion directing that respondents' complaint be dismissed, summarized the factual history of the discovery proceeding in these words:

"After seventeen months where crucial interrogatories remained substantially unanswered despite numerous extensions granted at the eleventh hour and, in many instances, beyond the eleventh hour, and notwithstanding several admonitions by the Court and promises and commitments by the plaintiffs, the Court must and does conclude that the conduct of the plaintiffs demonstrates the callous disregard of responsibilities counsel owe to the Court and to their opponents. The practices of the plaintiffs exemplify flagrant bad faith when after being expressly directed to perform an act by a date certain, viz., June 14, 1974, they failed to perform and compounded that noncompliance by waiting until five days afterwards before they filed any motions.

Moreover, this action was taken in the face of warnings that their failure to provide certain information could result in the imposition of sanctions under Fed. R. Civ. P. 37. If the sanction of dismissal is not warranted by the circumstances of this case, then the Court can envisage no set of facts whereby that sanction should ever be applied." 63 FRD 641, 656 (1974).

The Court of Appeals, in reversing the order of the District Court by a divided vote, stated:

"After carefully reviewing the record, we conclude that there is insufficient evidence to support a finding that M-GB's failure to file supplemental answers by June 14, 1974 was in flagrant bad faith, willful or intentional." 531 F.2d 1188, 1195 (1976).

The Court of Appeals did not question any of the findings of historical fact which had been made by the District Court, but simply concluded that there was in the record evidence of "extenuating factors." The Court of Appeals emphasized that none of the parties had really pressed discovery until after a consent decree was entered between petitioners and all of the other original plaintiffs except the respondents approximately one year after the commencement of the litigation. It also noted that respondents' counsel took over the litigation, which previously had been managed by another attorney, after the entry of the consent decree, and that respondents' counsel encountered difficulties in obtaining some of the requested information. The Court of Appeals also referred to a colloquy during the oral argument on petitioners' motion to dismiss in which respondents' lead counsel assured the District Court that he would not knowingly and willfully disregard the final deadline.

While the Court of Appeals stated that the District Court was required to consider the full record in determining whether to dismiss for failure to comply with discovery orders, we think that the comprehensive memorandum of the District Court supporting its order of dismissal indicates that the court did just that. That record shows that the District Court was extremely patient in its effort to allow the respondents ample time to comply with its discovery orders. Not only did respondents fail to file their responses on time, but the responses which they ultimately did file were found by the District Court to be grossly inadequate.

The question, of course, is not whether this Court, or whether the Court of Appeals, would as an original matter have dismissed the action; it is whether the District Court abused its discretion in so doing. Certainly the findings contained in the memorandum opinion of the District Court quoted earlier in this opinion are fully supported by the record. We think that the lenity evidence in the opinion of the Court of Appeals, while certainly a significant factor in considering the imposition of sanctions under Rule 37, cannot be allowed to wholly supplant other and equally necessary considerations embodied in that Rule.

There is a natural tendency on the part of reviewing courts, properly employing the benefit of hindsight, to be heavily influenced by the severity of outright dismissal as a sanction for failure to comply with a discovery order. It is quite reasonable to conclude that a party who has been subjected to such an order will feel duly chastened, so that even though he succeeds in having the order reversed on appeal he will nonetheless comply promptly with future discovery orders of the District Court.

But here, as in other areas of the law, the most severe in the spectrum of sanctions provided by statute or rule must be available to the District Court in appropriate cases, not merely to penalize those whose conduct may be deemed to warrant such a sanction, but to deter those who might be tempted to such conduct in the absence of such a deterrent. If the decision of the Court of Appeals remained undisturbed in this case, it might well be that *these* respondents would faithfully comply with all future discovery orders entered by the District Court in this case. But other parties to other lawsuits would feel freer than we think Rule 37 contemplates they should feel to flout other discovery orders of other District Courts. Under the circumstances of this case, we hold that the district judge did not abuse his discretion in finding bad faith on the part of these respondents, and concluding that the extreme sanction of dismissal was appropriate in this case by reason of respondents' "flagrant bad faith" and their counsel's "callous disregard" of their responsibilities. Therefore, the petition for a writ of certiorari is granted and the judgment of the Court of Appeals is reversed.

Notes

1. In the earlier *Societe Internationale v. Rogers* case, the Supreme Court had limited the dismissal remedy, which the language of the statute appears to make broadly available, to situations involving willful or blameworthy failure to comply with discovery orders. Within the area of willful conduct, however, a trial court's exercise of its discretion is likely to be upheld on appeal. What policy reasons did the Court rely on in approving the trial court's use of the drastic remedy of dismissal of the complaint? Even when faced with an area committed to the courts' discretion, appellate counsel on both sides would be well advised to examine the rationale behind the rule in question, rather than discussing the notion of discretion in the abstract.

2. The Court in *National Hockey League* was clearly impressed, not only with the district judge's patience, but with his detailed memorandum in support of dismissal, in which he reviewed the extensive history of the discovery proceedings in the case. Some circuits require, pursuant to their supervisory powers, articulation

of reasons for the exercise of discretion in particular situations. *See, e.g., Quality Prefabrication v. Daniel J. Keating Co.,* 675 F.2d 77, 81 (3d Cir. 1982). Failure to provide any reasons, or reliance on factors inappropriate to the situation at hand, may assist appellate counsel in obtaining reversal of discretionary decisions.

2. The Limits of Discretion

New York Criminal Procedure Law Section 270.35 states, in part:

If at any time after the trial jury has been sworn and before the rendition of its verdict, a juror is unable to continue serving by reason of illness or other incapacity, or for any other reason is unavailable for continued service . . ., the court must discharge such juror. If an alternate juror or jurors are available for service, the court must order that the discharged juror be replaced by the alternate juror whose name was first drawn and called . . .

By what standards, if any, does the language of this section circumscribe a trial court's decision to substitute an alternate juror for a sworn juror who does not appear at the time scheduled for trial?

People v. Page

72 N.Y.2d 69, 526 N.E.2d 783, 531 N.Y.S.2d 83 (1988)

BELLACOSA, J.

In each case, defendant appeals from an affirmance of his criminal conviction. Each contends he was deprived of his constitutional and statutory right to trial by a jury of his choice when the Trial Justices in the two different cases discharged a sworn juror on the ground that the juror was "unavailable for continued service" (CPL 270.35).

In Supreme Court, Criminal Term, New York County, on the first scheduled day of trial of *People v. Page,* the Trial Justice, outside the presence of the jury, explained to the defendant, his counsel and the Assistant District Attorney: "We got a call from juror No. 1 [the foreperson] and she said she just got up and she'll get here when she can." The Trial Justice indicated his desire, with the consent of all counsel, to start the trial by discharging the absent juror and substituting an alternate juror. Defense counsel asked, "Did she give an indication when she would be here?" and the court responded, "I can't hold up the whole judicial process for some lady who just got up." Defense counsel objected. The court again asked for cooperation and defense counsel, never having received an answer to her question, persisted in the objection. Shortly thereafter, when the jury was ready to be seated, the substitution was made and defense counsel asked that it be noted on the record that it was 10:17 a.m.; the late juror still had not arrived for the trial which had been scheduled to begin at 9:30 a.m.

In *People v. Washington,* also in Supreme Court, Criminal Term, New York County, the court discharged juror No. 5 on the second day of a continued trial, after waiting two hours for the absent juror to arrive, making particularized inquiries and placing them on the record. Prior to the discharge, court personnel made "repeated and numerous" but unsuccessful attempts to locate the juror. They did reach the juror's mother who explained that her son had gone to a hospital because he had a cold, but she refused to tell the court to which hospital he had gone. The court stated on the record that "we have no way of finding out where he [the juror] is," and that it was "already 11:30 a.m."

Defense counsel asked the court to explore alternatives, including a one-day adjournment to attempt to find the juror. The Trial Justice refused, noting on the record that she might have been willing to grant an adjournment if there were any reason to believe that the juror would be available "in the relatively near future." The court added that the mother's unconvincing story, failing to disclose specific details about her son's illness and specific whereabouts, led the court to believe the juror was "trying to avoid coming to court." The record also disclosed that four prosecution witnesses were scheduled to testify that day, one of whom had failed to appear previously and had to be subpoenaed.

There is no claim in these cases that our court's holding in *People v. Buford* (69 N.Y.2d 290) is directly controlling, since that case involved a different statutory clause which authorizes the discharge of jurors who, after the trial begins, are discovered to be unfit to serve because of bias or misconduct. That case is, however, pressed as being persuasive and analogous authority affecting the two instant cases. Like the provision in the same statute, CPL 270.35, pertaining to the discharge of a juror found to be grossly unqualified, the provision at issue in this case is intended also to secure the right to be tried by a jury in whose selection defendant has had a voice (see, *People v. Buford*, 69 N.Y.2d 290, 297-298, *supra*).

However, the statutory provision at issue in the two instant cases has an entirely different root purpose and requires the discharge of jurors who are found to be unavailable for continued service. It is intended to serve the orderly, fair and prompt progress of a trial so it is broader and more flexible in its terms than the provision in *Buford* (*id.*), which pertains to juror qualification, to the ability of a particular juror to be impartial in deciding a case, and to the avoidance of direct prejudice to the defendant from unlawful discharge of that juror. The statute here—in requiring the discharge of a juror who is unavailable for continued service "by reason of illness or other incapacity, or for any other reason" (CPL 270.35 [emphasis added])—invests a trial court with latitude to make a balanced determination affecting the administration of justice based on the facts required to be adduced, recognizing that criminal proceedings should not be unnecessarily or unfairly delayed against the interests of either the defense or the prosecution, especially when the trial is under way and so many other participants are involved.

No inflexible rule or catechism was contemplated or need be judicially crafted to determine the precise parameters of when a juror is unavailable under this statutory prescription. Rather, illustrative factors that may be considered in making such determinations include the stage of trial, the expected length of the absence of the juror if known, whether the juror's return is ascertainable and reasonably imminent and certain, whether reasonable attempts have been made to locate the absent juror, and other relevant circumstances such as the continued availability of key witnesses. A trial court's decision dismissing a juror must safeguard the important right of a defendant to be tried by jurors in whose selection the defendant has had a voice. It thus necessitates a reasonably thorough inquiry and recitation on the record of the facts and reasons for invoking the statutory authorization of discharging and replacing a juror based on continued unavailability. This requires a reasonable attempt to ascertain where the absent juror is, why the juror is absent, and when the juror will be present. Several benefits flow from this rule: a defendant's rights are protected; the statute can be properly employed; and appellate courts, in the exercise of their respective powers, will be able to review the determination based on an adequate record.

In *People v. Washington*, the trial court's particularized findings and action on the record in the effort to ascertain the circumstances of the juror's absence and of the likelihood of his continued availability to serve cannot be said to constitute error as a matter of law. Thus, the order affirming the conviction in that case must be affirmed.

The same cannot be said in *People v. Page* where the trial court failed to ascertain when the absent juror might arrive at the courthouse. Without some reasonable effort shown on the record, we cannot infer a sufficient legal basis upon which the court could invoke the "unavailable for continued service" provision. There must therefore be a reversal and a new trial.

Accordingly, the order of the Appellate Division in *People v. Page* should be reversed and a new trial ordered, and in *People v. Washington*, the order should be affirmed.

Notes

1. The New York Court of Appeals is a "law" court. It is empowered to review only questions of law raised in the lower courts. It has, in other cases, decided that "abuse of discretion" is a question of law, while "improvident exercise of discretion" is *not* a legal issue, and is therefore reviewable only in the interests of justice by the intermediate appellate courts, which have broader jurisdiction. *See People v. Washington,* 71 N.Y.2d 916, 523 N.E.2d 818, 528 N.Y.S.2d 531 (1988). What standard must the Court of Appeals have used to reverse the conviction and order a new trial in the *Page* case? What does this indicate about the limits of a trial court's discretion to replace an absent juror with an alternate?

2. It will, in most cases, be difficult to convince an appellate court that a trial judge abused the broad discretion provided by statute or case law. Meaningful review is more likely to be secured if the advocate seeking reversal can assert that the trial court's decision was based on consideration of improper factors, or failure to consider relevant factors, rather than simply characterizing the judge's decision itself as improper. For example, if a judge denied a motion for a new trial, despite declaring it otherwise meritorious, on the grounds that the case, which had already been tried three times, was now seven years old, an appellate court might find that the court abused its discretion by relying on extraneous factors beyond the parties' control. *Cf. Mallis v. Bankers Trust Co.,* 717 F.2d 683, 690-92 (2d Cir. 1983).

3. In areas in which no real guidelines can be discerned, the appellate lawyer may still try to obtain reversal of adverse discretionary decisions. For example, although states generally give broad discretion to trial courts on the matter of sentencing, in some states, such as New York, intermediate appellate courts are empowered to, and occasionally do, reduce a sentence as "unduly harsh or excessive," given the particular facts of the case.

B. The Failure to Exercise Discretion

When an area of decision-making has been characterized as within the trial judge's discretion, it is worth checking to be sure that the trial court realized the various options open to it. In other words, rather than arguing that a court abused its discretion, the appellate lawyer could try to persuade the reviewing court that the trial judge *failed to exercise* the discretion provided. Such an argument was successful, in *Dorszynski v. United States,* 418 U.S. 424 (1974), in convincing the United States Supreme Court to reverse a sentence imposed by a federal judge who may not have been aware of the possibility of committing a youthful offender for treatment, instead of sending him to prison. Federal sentencing, until the recent advent of the Federal Sentencing Guidelines, was totally off limits to the appellate courts. As long as a sentence was within statutory limits, and not unconstitutional, the courts of appeal had no control whatever over a sentence imposed by a trial court, no matter how harsh they might think it was. The Supreme Court's reversal of Dorszynski's sentence was therefore all the more surprising, and may well have been obtained through careful framing of the issue as one of determining whether discretion was exercised at all, rather than one of reviewing the exercise of discretion. *Id.* at 443.

On the other hand, when a court purports to exercise discretionary powers, it also pays to check into whether in fact, under the particular circumstances at issue, discretion was indeed available. For example, in *Noonan v. Cunard Steamship Co.,* 375 F.2d 69 (2d Cir. 1967), the district court permitted plaintiff's action to be dismissed without prejudice pursuant to Fed. R. Civ. P. 41 (a)(2), a dismissal normally within the court's broad discretionary powers. In this case, however, plaintiff's motion to dismiss without prejudice was made specifically so as to allow her to refile the complaint and make a timely demand for a jury trial, which counsel had inadvertently failed to make in the initial action. Another provision of the Federal Rules gives the court discretion to order a jury trial despite a party's failure to demand a jury, Fed. R. Civ. P. 39(b), but that discretion had been universally interpreted *not* to include the situation of mere inadvertence in filing a timely jury demand. In an opinion by Judge Friendly, the Court of Appeals for the Second Circuit reversed the decision as a matter of law, despite its apparent discretionary nature:

> If this were truly the type of case where an appellate court must respect the trial judge's exercise of discretion, we might indeed be troubled in saying, in Judge Magruder's oft-quoted phrase, that we had "a definite and firm conviction that the court below committed a clear error of judgment in the conclusion it reached upon a weighing of the relevant factors." *In re Josephson,* 218 F.2d 174, 182 (1 Cir. 1954). However, we doubt that to be the appropriate test here; the fact that dismissal under Rule 41(a) (2) usually rests on the judge's discretion does not mean that this is always so. Several of the most important reasons

for deferring to the trial judge's exercise of discretion – his observation of the witnesses, his superior opportunity to get "the feel of the case," and the impracticability of framing a rule of decision where many disparate factors must be weighed, are inapposite when a question arising in advance of trial can be stated in a form susceptible of a yes-or-no answer applicable to all cases. Whether dismissal without prejudice should be allowed simply to permit a plaintiff to overcome an inadvertent failure to make a timely jury demand without other excuse, is a question of that sort – as indeed a New York appellate court has held. See *Katz v. Austin*, 271 App. Div. 217, 62 N.Y.S.2d 912 (1st Dept.), *leave to appeal denied*, 271 App. Div. 773, 64 N.Y.S.2d 926 (1946). When the self-same issue has arisen before three other district judges in this circuit, all have decided against allowing dismissal without prejudice, and if "abuse of discretion" were the test, we would have no more basis for interfering with those decisions than with that here *sub judice*. The desirability of achieving consistency among district judges in the same circuit on such an issue and of avoiding judge-shopping outweighs that of appellate deference to a determination of the district judge on a preliminary procedural matter, as we think the judge here might well have decided if the application had come before him in a motion part with opportunity for fuller consideration.

Since we thus consider ourselves bound to choose one way or the other, we think the decisions denying leave to discontinue without prejudice for the sole purpose of overcoming inadvertent failure to make a timely jury demand accord better than an opposite view with the policies of Rule 38(a) insisting on promptness and of Rule 41(a)(2) limiting the former freedom of dismissal of plaintiffs in actions of law. Moreover, to allow leave to discontinue without prejudice solely for this purpose would work a discrimination, for which we see no sufficient justification, in favor of plaintiffs whose attorneys had been guilty of inadvertent neglect in demanding a jury trial as against defendants similarly situated.

Noonan, 375 F.2d at 71-72.

Note

Judge Friendly ended his opinion with the following comment:

> There is, of course, not the slightest reason to doubt that a judge is quite as able as a jury to make a fair determination whether a roll of the Queen Elizabeth was due to negligence by her crew or unseaworthiness of the vessel – questions of the sort admiralty judges have been deciding for centuries.

Id. at 72. Might the nature of the lawsuit, which was an action for damages as a result of a fall suffered by the plaintiff in her stateroom on the "great vessel" Queen Elizabeth, have had an effect on the court's assessment of the propriety of the trial court's order dismissing the case without prejudice to permit refiling, with a jury demand?

Exercise

Assume that you have been assigned to represent a defendant on his appeal from a judgment entered in the Supreme Court of the State of New York, Queens County, convicting him of burglary in the second degree and related crimes. The transcript contains the following colloquy, occurring on the second day of trial:

THE COURT: Gentlemen, in connection with indictment number 3177 of 1988, William Berry, one of the jurors called in this morning and said she was ill and unable to appear.

ASSISTANT DISTRICT ATTORNEY BINSER: Which juror?

THE COURT: Juror Number One, Miss Joyner.

MR. BINSER: Well, what can we do? I am ready to proceed with my witnesses.

MR. GIANNELLI (defense counsel): Do you intend to substitute an alternate?

THE COURT: I do.

MR. GIANNELLI: On behalf of the defendant, I would object to the substitution of this juror. I'd like to inquire of the court as to whether the court or someone from the court spoke to her to find out the nature of her illness, and how long she's going to be ill.

THE COURT: As I read §270.35, if for any reason any sworn juror is unavailable for service, the court is empowered, and since an alternate is available, to make the substitution. I intend to do so. It does not appear that this will be a very long trial. We waited for the witnesses to be here. I intend to proceed.

MR. GIANNELLI: I take exception to your ruling.

THE COURT: Certainly. Send for the jury.

(Whereupon the jury roll was called by the court clerk.)

THE COURT: Ladies and gentlemen of the jury, forgive the delay, but as you can see, we are missing one of the jurors. Miss Joyner unfortunately came down with a bug that may have been flying around the room – I hope you all avoid it – and is ill. Under the provisions of the Criminal Procedure Law, therefore, I am going to direct that Mr. Bloom take seat number 1, move down there, Mr. Bloom. And now you know, ladies and gentlemen, why alternate jurors are selected in a trial, and I trust that you will take good care of yourselves until this trial is completed. All right, Mr. Binser, call your next witness.

Write a point heading and argument in support of reversal of the conviction.

Chapter 5

The Harmless Error Doctrine

From Automatic Reversal to Harmless Error Analysis

Until well into the 20th century, American appellate courts operated under the assumption that any trial error, no matter how trivial or technical, was prejudicial and required the automatic reversal of the judgment. For example, the misspelling in an indictment of the word "larceny" in one case and the omission of the word "the" in another both resulted in reversal. Lawyers, of course, took advantage of the presumption of prejudice by inserting inconsequential errors into their trials which would not affect the jury's verdict but would nevertheless ensure reversal on appeal in the event of a loss.

The result of the automatic reversal rule was the intolerable clogging of the courts with frivolous appeals and retrials, often delaying the decisions in meritorious cases.[1] This state of affairs gave rise to a reform movement during the first quarter of the 20th century which resulted in the adoption of federal and state "harmless error" legislation aimed at preventing "matters concerned with the mere etiquette of trials and with the formalities and minutiae of procedure from touching the merits of a verdict." *Bruno v. United States,* 308 U.S. 287, 294 (1939).

Today, federal law provides that in both civil and criminal cases the court must disregard "any error or defect in the proceeding which does not affect the substantial rights" of the parties. 28 U.S.C. § 2111; Fed. R. Civ. P. 61; Fed. R. Cr. P. 52(a). Moreover, all fifty states now have harmless error statutes or rules.

When is an Error Harmless?

The initial question that the appellate attorney must answer when arguing that a particular error is or is not harmless is what standard the appellate court should apply when deciding the issue. That is, how certain must the court be that the error did not affect the "substantial rights" of a party? The degree of certainty that an appellate court requires for a determination that a trial error was harmless is influenced by several considerations. These include the nature of the case, whether civil or criminal; whether the error affected the defendant's constitutional rights or a right guaranteed only by statute or common law; and whether trial took place before a judge or a jury, because a judge is assumed to have disregarded improper evidence while no such assumption can be made about a jury.

A. Constitutional Harmless Error

When an error implicates an appellant's constitutional rights, the burden on the prosecution to demonstrate that it was harmless is considerably higher than when the error involves a simple statutory or common law right that falls short of a constitutional violation. Indeed, for several decades after the enactment of the federal harmless error statute, courts continued to reverse automatically in cases involving constitutional error, presuming that any constitutional violation would invariably affect the "substantial rights" of the parties. In 1967, however, the Supreme Court ruled that at least some constitutional errors could be harmless.

---

[1] For example, *Pressley v. Bloomington and Normal Ry. & Light Co.,* 271 Ill. 622, 111 N.E. 511 (1916) was retried four times without a substantial error, and in *Conn. Mutual Life Ins. v. Hillman,* 145 U.S. 285 (1892), 188 U.S. 208 (1903) a widow appeared before the Supreme Court a second time twenty-three years after filing suit for the proceeds of her husband's life insurance.

Chapman v. California

386 U.S. 18 (1967)

Mr. Justice BLACK delivered the opinion of the Court.

Petitioners, Ruth Elizabeth Chapman and Thomas LeRoy Teale, were convicted in a California state court upon a charge that they robbed, kidnapped, and murdered a bartender. She was sentenced to life imprisonment and he to death. At the time of the trial, Art. I, § 13 of the State's Constitution provided that "in any criminal case, whether the defendant testifies or not, his failure to explain or to deny by his testimony any evidence or facts in the case against him may be commented upon by the court and by counsel, and may be considered by the court or the jury." Both petitioners in this case chose not to testify at their trial, and the State's attorney prosecuting them took full advantage of his right under the State Constitution to comment upon their failure to testify, filling his argument to the jury from beginning to end with numerous references to their silence and inferences of their guilt resulting therefrom. The trial court also charged the jury that it could draw adverse inferences from petitioners' failure to testify. Shortly after the trial, but before petitioners' cases had been considered on appeal by the California Supreme Court, this Court decided *Griffin v. California*, 380 U.S. 609, in which we held California's constitutional provision and practice invalid on the ground that they put a penalty on the exercise of a person's right not to be compelled to be a witness against himself, guaranteed by the Fifth Amendment to the United States Constitution and made applicable to California and the other States by the Fourteenth Amendment. On appeal, the State Supreme Court, admitting that petitioners had been denied a federal constitutional right by the comments on their silence, nevertheless affirmed, applying the State Constitution's harmless-error provision, which forbids reversal unless "the court shall be of the opinion that the error complained of has resulted in a miscarriage of justice." We granted certiorari limited to these questions:

"Where there is a violation of the rule of *Griffin v. California*, (1) can the error be held to be harmless, and (2) if so, was the error harmless in this case?" . . .

We are urged by petitioners to hold that all federal constitutional errors, regardless of the facts and circumstances, must always be deemed harmful. Such a holding, as petitioners correctly point out, would require an automatic reversal of their convictions and make further discussion unnecessary. We decline to adopt any such rule. All 50 States have harmless-error statutes or rules, and the United States long ago through its Congress established for its courts the rule that judgments shall not be reversed for "errors or defects which do not affect the substantial rights of the parties." 28 USC § 2111. None of these rules on its face distinguishes between federal constitutional errors and errors of state law or federal statutes and rules. All of these rules, state or federal, serve a very useful purpose insofar as they block setting aside convictions for small errors or defects that have little, if any, likelihood of having changed the result of the trial. We conclude that there may be some constitutional errors which in the setting of a particular case are so unimportant and insignificant that they may, consistent with the Federal Constitution, be deemed harmless, not requiring the automatic reversal of the conviction.

In fashioning a harmless-constitutional-error rule, we must recognize that harmless-error rules can work very unfair and mischievous results when, for example, highly important and persuasive evidence, or argument, though legally forbidden, finds its way into a trial in which the question of guilt or innocence is a close one. What harmless-error rules all aim at is a rule that will save the good in harmless-error practices while avoiding the bad, so far as possible.

The federal rule emphasizes "substantial rights" as do most others. The California constitutional rule emphasizes "a miscarriage of justice," but the California courts have neutralized this to some extent by emphasis, and perhaps overemphasis, upon the court's view of "overwhelming evidence." We prefer the approach of this Court in deciding what was harmless error in our recent case of *Fahy v. Connecticut*, 375 U.S. 85. There we said: "The question is whether there is a reasonable possibility that the evidence complained of might have contributed to the conviction." *Id.* at 86-87. Although our prior cases have indicated that there are some constitutional rights so basic to a fair trial that their infraction can never be treated as harmless error,[8] this statement in *Fahy* itself belies any belief that all trial errors which violate the Constitution automatically call for reversal. At the same time, however, like the federal harmless-error statute, it emphasizes an intention not to treat as harmless those constitutional errors that "affect substantial rights" of a party. An error in admitting plainly relevant evidence which possibly influenced the jury adversely to a litigant cannot, under *Fahy*, be conceived of as harmless. Certainly error, constitutional error, in illegally admitting highly prejudicial evidence or comments, casts on someone other than the person prejudiced by it a burden to show that it was harmless. It is for that reason that the original common-

law harmless-error rule put the burden on the beneficiary of the error either to prove that there was no injury or to suffer a reversal of his erroneously obtained judgment. There is little, if any, difference between our statement in *Fahy v. Connecticut* about "whether there is a reasonable possibility that the evidence complained of might have contributed to the conviction" and requiring the beneficiary of a constitutional error to prove beyond a reasonable doubt that the error complained of did not contribute to the verdict obtained. We, therefore, do no more than adhere to the meaning of our *Fahy* case when we hold, as we now do, that before a federal constitutional error can be held harmless, the court must be able to declare a belief that it was harmless beyond a reasonable doubt. While appellate courts do not ordinarily have the original task of applying such a test, it is a familiar standard to all courts, and we believe its adoption will provide a more workable standard, although achieving the same result as that aimed at in our *Fahy* case.

Applying the foregoing standard, we have no doubt that the error in these cases was not harmless to petitioners. To reach this conclusion one need only glance at the prosecutorial comments compiled from the record by petitioners' counsel and (with minor omissions) set forth in the appendix. The California Supreme Court fairly summarized the extent of these comments as follows:

"Such comments went to the motives for the procurement and handling of guns purchased by Mrs. Chapman, funds or the lack thereof in Mr. Teale's possession immediately prior to the killing, the amount of intoxicating liquors consumed by defendants at the Spot Club and other taverns, the circumstances of the shooting in the automobile and the removal of the victim's body therefrom, who fired the fatal shots, why defendants used a false registration at a motel shortly after the killing, the

---

[8] *See, e.g., Payne v. Arkansas,* 356 U.S. 560 (coerced confession); *Gideon v. Wainwright,* 372 U.S. 335 (right to counsel); *Tumey v. Ohio,* 273 U.S. 510 (impartial judge).

meaning of a letter written by Mrs. Chapman several days after the killing, why Teale had a loaded weapon in his possession when apprehended, the meaning of statements made by Teale after his apprehension, why certain clothing and articles of personal property were shipped by defendants to Missouri, what clothing Mrs. Chapman wore at the time of the killing, conflicting statements as to Mrs. Chapman's whereabouts immediately preceding the killing and, generally, the overall commission of the crime." 63 Cal.2d at 196, 404 P.2d at 220.

Thus, the state prosecutor's argument and the trial judge's instruction to the jury continuously and repeatedly impressed the jury that from the failure of petitioners to testify, to all intents and purposes, the inferences from the facts in evidence had to be drawn in favor of the State – in short, that by their silence petitioners had served as irrefutable witnesses against themselves. And though the case in which this occurred presented a reasonably strong "circumstantial web of evidence" against petitioners, it was also a case in which, absent the constitutionally forbidden comments, honest, fair-minded jurors might very well have brought in not-guilty verdicts. Under these circumstances, it is completely impossible for us to say that the State has demonstrated, beyond a reasonable doubt, that the prosecutor's comments and the trial judge's instruction did not contribute to petitioners' convictions. Such a machine-gun repetition of a denial of constitutional rights, designed and calculated to make petitioners' version of the evidence worthless, can no more be considered harmless than the introduction against a defendant of a coerced confession. Petitioners are entitled to a trial free from the pressure of unconstitutional inferences.

Reversed and remanded.

Note

In *Chapman* the Supreme Court recognized that some constitutional errors, such as the denial of the right to counsel or trial before an impartial judge, continue to require automatic reversal. As the following case shows, however, the number of such rights is extremely small.

Arizona v. Fulminante

499 U.S. 279 (1991)

Justice WHITE delivered an opinion, Parts I, II, and IV of which are the opinion of the Court, and Part III of which is a dissenting opinion. The Chief Justice delivered the opinion of the Court in Part III.[2]

The Arizona Supreme Court ruled in this case that respondent Oreste Fulminante's confession, received in evidence at

---

[2] This case sharply divided the Court, resulting in no single opinion commanding a majority. For the sake of clarity, the order of the excerpted opinions has been rearranged.

his trial for murder, had been coerced and that its use against him was barred by the Fifth and Fourteenth Amendments to the United States Constitution. The court also held that the harmless-error rule could not be used to save the conviction. We affirm the judgment of the Arizona court, although for different reasons than those upon which that court relied.

I

Early in the morning of September 14, 1982, Fulminante called the Mesa, Arizona,

Police Department to report that his 11-year-old stepdaughter, Jeneane Michelle Hunt, was missing. He had been caring for Jeneane while his wife, Jeneane's mother, was in the hospital. Two days later, Jeneane's body was found in the desert east of Mesa. She had been shot twice in the head at close range with a large caliber weapon, and a ligature was around her neck. Because of the decomposed condition of the body, it was impossible to tell whether she had been sexually assaulted.

Fulminante's statements to police concerning Jeneane's disappearance and his relationship with her contained a number of inconsistencies, and he became a suspect in her killing. When no charges were filed against him, Fulminante left Arizona for New Jersey. Fulminante was later convicted in New Jersey on federal charges of possession of a firearm by a felon.

Fulminante was incarcerated in the Ray Brook Federal Correctional Institution in New York. There he became friends with another inmate, Anthony Sarivola, then serving a 60-day sentence for extortion. The two men came to spend several hours a day together. Sarivola, a former police officer, had been involved in loansharking for organized crime but then became a paid informant for the Federal Bureau of Investigation. While at Ray Brook, he masqueraded as an organized crime figure. After becoming friends with Fulminante, Sarivola heard a rumor that Fulminante was suspected of killing a child in Arizona. Sarivola then raised the subject with Fulminante in several conversations, but Fulminante repeatedly denied any involvement in Jeneane's death. During one conversation, he told Sarivola that Jeneane had been killed by bikers looking for drugs; on another occasion, he said he did not know what had happened. Sarivola passed this information on to an agent of the Federal Bureau of Investigation, who instructed Sarivola to find out more.

Sarivola learned more one evening in October 1983, as he and Fulminante walked together around the prison track. Sarivola said that he knew Fulminante was "starting to get some tough treatment and whatnot" from other inmates because of the rumor. Sarivola offered to protect Fulminante from his fellow inmates, but told him, "'You have to tell me about it,' you know. I mean, in other words, 'For me to give you any help.'" Fulminante then admitted to Sarivola that he had driven Jeneane to the desert on his motorcycle, where he choked her, sexually assaulted her, and made her beg for her life, before shooting her twice in the head.

Sarivola was released from prison in November 1983. Fulminante was released the following May, only to be arrested the next month for another weapons violation. On September 4, 1984, Fulminante was indicted in Arizona for the first-degree murder of Jeneane.

Prior to trial, Fulminante moved to suppress the statement he had given Sarivola in prison, as well as a second confession he had given to Donna Sarivola, then Anthony Sarivola's fiancee and later his wife, following his May 1984 release from prison. He asserted that the confession to Sarivola was coerced, and that the second confession was the "fruit" of the first. Following the hearing, the trial court denied the motion to suppress, specifically finding that, based on the stipulated facts, the confessions were voluntary. The State introduced both confessions as evidence at trial, and on December 19, 1985, Fulminante was convicted of Jeneane's murder. He was subsequently sentenced to death.

Fulminante appealed, arguing, among other things, that his confession to Sarivola was the product of coercion and that its admission at trial violated his rights to due process under the Fifth and Fourteenth Amendments to the United States Constitution. After considering the evidence at trial as well as the stipulated facts before the trial court on the motion to suppress, the Arizona Supreme Court held that the confession was coerced, but initially determined that the admission of the confession at trial was harmless error, because of the overwhelming nature of the evidence against Fulminante. Upon Fulminante's motion for reconsideration, however, the court ruled that this Court's precedent precluded the use of the harmless-error analysis in the case of a coerced confession. The court therefore reversed the conviction and ordered that Fulminante be retried without the use of the confession to Sarivola. Because of differing views in the state and federal courts over whether the admission at trial of a coerced confession is subject to a harmless-error analysis, we granted the State's petition for certiorari. . . .

II

* * *

Although the question is a close one, we agree with the Arizona Supreme Court's conclusion that Fulminante's confession was coerced. The Arizona Supreme Court found a credible threat of physical violence unless Fulminante confessed. Our cases have made clear that a finding of coercion need not depend upon actual violence by a government agent; a credible threat is sufficient. As we have said, "coercion can be mental as well as physical, and . . . the blood of the accused is not the only hallmark of an unconstitutional inquisition." . . . Accepting the Arizona court's finding, permissible on this record, that there was a credible threat of physical violence, we agree with its conclusion that Fulminante's will was overborne in such a way as to render his confession the product of coercion.

III

Chief Justice REHNQUIST delivered the majority opinion with respect to part III.

* * *

Since this Court's landmark decision in *Chapman v. California,* in which we adopted the general rule that a constitutional error does not automatically require reversal of a conviction, the Court has ap-

plied harmless-error analysis to a wide range of errors and has recognized that most constitutional errors can be harmless. See *Clemons v. Mississippi,* (unconstitutionally overbroad jury instructions at the sentencing stage of a capital case); *Satterwhite v. Texas,* (admission of evidence at the sentencing stage of a capital case in violation of the Sixth Amendment Counsel Clause); *Carella v. California,* (jury instruction containing an erroneous conclusive presumption); *Pope v. Illinois,* (jury instruction misstating an element of the offense); *Rose v. Clark,* (jury instruction containing an erroneous rebuttable presumption); *Crane v. Kentucky,* (erroneous exclusion of defendant's testimony regarding the circumstances of his confession); *Delaware v. Van Arsdall,* (restriction on a defendant's right to cross-examine a witness for bias in violation of the Sixth Amendment Confrontation Clause); *Rushen v. Spain,* (denial of a defendant's right to be present at trial); *United States v. Hasting,* (improper comment on defendant's silence at trial, in violation of the Fifth Amendment Self-Incrimination Clause); *Hopper v. Evans,* (statute improperly forbidding trial court's giving a jury instruction on a lesser included offense in a capital case in violation of the Due Process Clause); *Kentucky v. Whorton,* (failure to instruct the jury on the presumption of innocence); *Moore v. Illinois,* (admission of identification evidence in violation of the Sixth Amendment Confrontation Clause); *Brown v. United States,* (admission of the out-of-court statement of a nontestifying codefendant in violation of the Sixth Amendment Confrontation Clause); *Milton v. Wainwright,* (confession obtained in violation of *Massiah v. United States); Chambers v. Maroney,* (admission of evidence obtained in violation of the Fourth Amendment); *Coleman v. Alabama,* (denial of counsel at a preliminary hearing in violation of the Sixth Amendment Counsel Clause).

The common thread connecting these

cases is that each involved "trial error" – error which occurred during the presentation of the case to the jury, and which may therefore be quantitatively assessed in the context of other evidence presented in order to determine whether its admission was harmless beyond a reasonable doubt. In applying harmless-error analysis to these many different constitutional violations, the Court has been faithful to the belief that the harmless-error doctrine is essential to preserve the "principle that the central purpose of a criminal trial is to decide the factual question of the defendant's guilt or innocence, and promotes public respect for the criminal process by focusing on the underlying fairness of the trial rather than on the virtually inevitable presence of immaterial error."

In *Chapman v. California,* the Court stated:

"Although our prior cases have indicated that there are some constitutional rights so basic to a fair trial that their infraction can never be treated as harmless error, this statement . . . belies any belief that all trial errors which violate the Constitution automatically call for reversal."

It is on the basis of this language in *Chapman* that Justice WHITE in dissent concludes that the principle of *stare decisis* requires us to hold that an involuntary confession is not subject to harmless-error analysis. We believe that there are several reasons which lead to a contrary conclusion. In the first place, the quoted language from *Chapman* does not by its terms adopt any such rule in that case. The language that "although our prior cases have indicated," coupled with the relegation of the cases themselves to a footnote, is more appropriately regarded as a historical reference to the holdings of these cases. This view is buttressed by an examination of the opinion in *Payne v. Arkansas,* 356 U.S. 560, which is the case referred to for the proposition that an involuntary confession may not be subject to harmless-error analysis. There the Court said:

"Respondent suggests that, apart from the confession, there was adequate evidence before the jury to sustain the verdict. But where, as here, a coerced confession constitutes a part of the evidence before the jury and a general verdict is returned, no one can say what credit and weight the jury gave to the confession. And in these circumstances this Court has uniformly held that even though there may have been sufficient evidence, apart from the coerced confession, to support a judgment of conviction, the admission in evidence, over objection, of the coerced confession vitiates the judgment because it violates the Due Process Clause of the Fourteenth Amendment."

It is apparent that the State's argument which the Court rejected in *Payne* is not the harmless-error analysis later adopted in *Chapman,* but a much more lenient rule which would allow affirmance of a conviction if the evidence other than the involuntary confession was sufficient to sustain the verdict. This is confirmed by the dissent of Justice Clark in that case, which adopted the more lenient test. Such a test would, of course – unlike the harmless-error test – make the admission of an involuntary confession virtually risk free for the State.

The admission of an involuntary confession – a classic "trial error" – is markedly different from the other two constitutional violations referred to in the *Chapman* footnote as not being subject to harmless-error analysis. One of those violations, involved in *Gideon v. Wainwright,* 372 U.S. 335 (1963), was the total deprivation of the right to counsel at trial. The other violation, involved in *Tumey v. Ohio,* 273 U.S. 510 (1927), was a judge who was not impartial. These are structural defects in the constitution of the trial mechanism, which defy analysis by "harmless-error" standards. The entire conduct of the trial from beginning to end is obviously affected by the absence of counsel for a criminal defendant, just as it is by the presence on the bench of a judge who is not impartial. Since our decision in *Chapman,* other cases have added to the category of constitutional errors which are not subject to harmless error the following: unlawful exclusion of members of the defendant's race from a grand jury, *Vasquez v. Hillery;* the right to self-representation at trial, *McKaskle v. Wiggins;* and the right to public trial, *Waller v. Georgia.* Each of these constitutional deprivations is a similar structural defect affecting the framework within which the trial proceeds, rather than simply an error in the trial process itself. "Without these basic protections, a criminal trial cannot reliably serve its function as a vehicle for determination of guilt or innocence, and no criminal punishment may be regarded as fundamentally fair."

It is evident from a comparison of the constitutional violations which we have held subject to harmless error, and those which we have held not, that involuntary statements or confessions belong in the former category. The admission of an involuntary confession is a "trial error," similar in both degree and kind to the erroneous admission of other types of evidence. The evidentiary impact of an involuntary confession, and its effect upon the composition of the record, is indistinguishable from that of a confession obtained in violation of the Sixth Amendment – of evidence seized in violation of the Fourth Amendment – or of a prosecutor's improper comment on a defendant's silence at trial in violation of the Fifth Amendment. When reviewing the erroneous admission of an involuntary confession, the appellate court, as it does with the admission of other forms of improperly admitted evidence, simply reviews the remainder of the evidence against the defendant to determine whether the admission of the confession was harmless beyond a reasonable doubt.

Nor can it be said that the admission of an involuntary confession is the type of error which "transcends the criminal process." This Court has applied harmless-error analysis to the violation of other constitutional rights similar in magnitude and importance and involving the same level of police misconduct. For instance, we have previously held that the admission of a defendant's statements obtained in violation of the Sixth Amendment is subject to harmless-error analysis. In *Milton v. Wainwright,* the Court held the admission of a confession obtained in violation of *Massiah v. United States,* to be harmless beyond a reasonable doubt. We have also held that the admission of an out-of-court statement by a nontestifying codefendant is subject to harmless-error analysis. The inconsistent treatment of statements elicited in violation of the Sixth and Fourteenth Amendments, respectively, can be supported neither by evidentiary or deterrence concerns nor by a belief that there is something more "fundamental" about involuntary confessions. This is especially true in a case such as this one where there are no allegations of physical violence on behalf of the police. The impact of a confession obtained in violation of the Sixth Amendment has the same evidentiary impact as does a confession obtained in violation of a defendant's due process rights. Government misconduct that results in violations of the Fourth and Sixth Amendments may be at least as reprehensible as conduct that results in an involuntary confession. For instance, the prisoner's confession to an inmate-informer at issue in *Milton,* which the Court characterized as implicating the Sixth Amendment right to counsel, is similar on its facts to the one we face today. Indeed, experience shows that law enforcement violations of these constitutional guarantees can involve conduct as egregious as police conduct used to elicit statements in violation of the Fourteenth Amendment. It is thus impossible to create a meaningful distinction between confessions elicited in violation of the Sixth

Amendment and those in violation of the Fourteenth Amendment.

Of course an involuntary confession may have a more dramatic effect on the course of a trial than do other trial errors — in particular cases it may be devastating to a defendant — but this simply means that a reviewing court will conclude in such a case that its admission was not harmless error; it is not a reason for eschewing the harmless-error test entirely. The Supreme Court of Arizona, in its first opinion in the present case, concluded that the admission of Fulminante's confession was harmless error. That court concluded that a second and more explicit confession of the crime made by Fulminante after he was released from prison was not tainted by the first confession, and that the second confession, together with physical evidence from the wounds (the victim had been shot twice in the head with a large calibre weapon at close range and a ligature was found around her neck) and other evidence introduced at trial rendered the admission of the first confession harmless beyond a reasonable doubt.

[Ed. note:

Justice WHITE's opinion, which continues as follows, constitutes the dissenting opinion on the applicability of harmless error analysis to coerced confessions.]

Four of us, Justices MARSHALL, BLACKMUN, STEVENS, and myself, would affirm the judgment of the Arizona Supreme Court on the ground that the harmless-error rule is inapplicable to erroneously admitted coerced confessions. We thus disagree with the Justices who have a contrary view.

The majority today abandons what until now the Court has regarded as the "axiomatic [proposition] that a defendant in a criminal case is deprived of due process of law if his conviction is founded, in whole or in part, upon an involuntary confession, without regard for the truth or falsity of the confession, and even though there is ample evidence aside from the confession to support the conviction." The Court has repeatedly stressed that the view that the admission of a coerced confession can be harmless error because of the other evidence to support the verdict is "an impermissible doctrine," for "the admission in evidence, over objection, of the coerced confession vitiates the judgment because it violates the Due Process Clause of the Fourteenth Amendment." . . . Today, a majority of the Court, without any justification, overrules this vast body of precedent without a word and in so doing dislodges one of the fundamental tenets of our criminal justice system.

In extending to coerced confessions the harmless-error rule of *Chapman v. California*, the majority declares that because the Court has applied that analysis to numerous other "trial errors," there is no reason that it should not apply to an error of this nature as well. The four of us remain convinced, however, that we should abide by our cases that have refused to apply the harmless-error rule to coerced confessions, for a coerced confession is fundamentally different from other types of erroneously admitted evidence to which the rule has been applied. Indeed, as the majority concedes, *Chapman* itself recognized that prior cases "have indicated that there are some constitutional rights so basic to a fair trial that their infraction can never be treated as harmless error," and it placed in that category the constitutional rule against using a defendant's coerced confession against him at his criminal trial. Moreover, cases since *Chapman* have reiterated the rule that using a defendant's coerced confession against him is a denial of due process of law regardless of the other evidence in the record aside from the confession.

Chapman specifically noted three constitutional errors that could not be categorized as harmless error: using a coerced confession against a defendant in a criminal trial, depriving a defendant of counsel, and trying a defendant before a biased judge. The majority attempts to distinguish the use of a coerced confession from the other two errors listed in *Chapman*. . . by drawing a meaningless dichotomy between "trial errors" and "structural defects" in the trial process.

The majority . . . attempts to distinguish "trial errors" which occur "during the presentation of the case to the jury," and which it deems susceptible to harmless-error analysis, from "structural defects in the constitution of the trial mechanism," which the majority concedes cannot be so analyzed. This effort fails, for our jurisprudence on harmless error has not classified so neatly the errors at issue. For example, we have held susceptible to harmless-error analysis the failure to instruct the jury on the presumption of innocence, while finding it impossible to analyze in terms of harmless error the failure to instruct a jury on the reasonable doubt standard. *Jackson v. Virginia*, 443 U.S. 307 (1979). These cases cannot be reconciled by labeling the former "trial error" and the latter not, for both concern the exact same stage in the trial proceedings. Rather, these cases can be reconciled only by considering the nature of the right at issue and the effect of an error upon the trial. A jury instruction on the presumption of innocence is not constitutionally required in every case to satisfy due process, because such an instruction merely offers an additional safeguard beyond that provided by the constitutionally required instruction on reasonable doubt. While it may be possible to analyze as harmless the omission of a presumption of innocence instruction when the required reasonable-doubt instruction has been given, it is impossible to assess the effect on the jury of the omission of the more fundamental instruction on reasonable doubt. In addition, omission of a reasonable-doubt instruction, though a "trial error," distorts the very structure of the trial because it creates the risk that the jury will

convict the defendant even if the State has not met its required burden of proof.

These same concerns counsel against applying harmless-error analysis to the admission of a coerced confession. A defendant's confession is "probably the most probative and damaging evidence that can be admitted against him," so damaging that a jury should not be expected to ignore it even if told to do so, and because in any event it is impossible to know what credit and weight the jury gave to the confession. Concededly, this reason is insufficient to justify a *per se* bar to the use of any confession. Thus, *Milton v. Wainwright*, 407 U.S. 371 (1972), applied harmless-error analysis to a confession obtained and introduced in circumstances that violated the defendant's Sixth Amendment right to counsel. Similarly, the Courts of Appeals have held that the introduction of incriminating statements taken from defendants in violation of *Miranda v. Arizona* is subject to treatment as harmless error.

Nevertheless, in declaring that it is "impossible to create a meaningful distinction between confessions elicited in violation of the Sixth Amendment and those in violation of the Fourteenth Amendment," the majority overlooks the obvious. Neither *Milton v. Wainwright* nor any of the other cases upon which the majority relies involved a defendant's coerced confession, nor were there present in these cases the distinctive reasons underlying the exclusion of coerced incriminating statements of the defendant. First, some coerced confessions may be untrustworthy. Consequently, admission of coerced confessions may distort the truth-seeking function of the trial upon which the majority focuses. More importantly, however, the use of coerced confessions, "whether true or false," is forbidden "because the methods used to extract them offend an underlying principle in the enforcement of our criminal law: that ours is an accusatorial and not an inquisitorial system − a system in which the State must establish guilt by evidence independently and freely secured and may not by coercion prove its charge against an accused out of his own mouth." This reflects the "strongly felt attitude of our society that important human values are sacrificed where an agency of the government, in the course of securing a conviction, wrings a confession out of an accused against his will," as well as "the deep-rooted feeling that the police must obey the law while enforcing the law; that in the end life and liberty can be as much endangered from illegal methods used to convict those thought to be criminals as from the actual criminals themselves." Thus, permitting a coerced confession to be part of the evidence on which a jury is free to base its verdict of guilty is inconsistent with the thesis that ours is not an inquisitorial system of criminal justice.

As the majority concedes, there are other constitutional errors that invalidate a conviction even though there may be no reasonable doubt that the defendant is guilty and would be convicted absent the trial error. For example, a judge in a criminal trial "is prohibited from entering a judgment of conviction or directing the jury to come forward with such a verdict, regardless of how overwhelmingly the evidence may point in that direction." A defendant is entitled to counsel at trial, and as *Chapman* recognized, violating this right can never be harmless error. See also *White v. Maryland,* 473 U.S. 59 (1963) where a conviction was set aside because the defendant had not had counsel at a preliminary hearing without regard to the showing of prejudice. In *Vasquez v. Hillery,* 474 U.S. 254 (1986), a defendant was found guilty beyond reasonable doubt, but the conviction had been set aside because of the unlawful exclusion of members of the defendant's race from the grand jury that indicted him, despite overwhelming evidence of his guilt. The error at the grand jury stage struck at fundamental values of our society and "undermined the structural integrity of the criminal tribunal itself, and

[was] not amenable to harmless-error review." *Vasquez,* like *Chapman,* also noted that rule of automatic reversal when a defendant is tried before a judge with a financial interest in the outcome, *Tumey v. Ohio,* 273 U.S. 510, 535 (1927), despite a lack of any indication that bias influenced the decision. *Waller v. Georgia,* 467 U.S. 39, 49 (1984), recognized that violation of the guarantee of a public trial required reversal without any showing of prejudice and even though the values of a public trial may be intangible and unprovable in any particular case.

The search for truth is indeed central to our system of justice, but "certain constitutional rights are not, and should not be, subject to harmless-error analysis because those rights protect important values that are unrelated to the truth-seeking function of the trial." *Rose v. Clark,* 478 U.S., at 587 (Stevens, J., concurring in judgment). The right of a defendant not to have his coerced confession used against him is among those rights, for using a coerced confession "aborts the basic trial process" and "renders a trial fundamentally unfair." For the foregoing reasons the four of us would adhere to the consistent line of authority that has recognized as a basic tenet of our criminal justice system, before and after both *Miranda* and *Chapman,* the prohibition against using a defendant's coerced confession against him at his criminal trial. *Stare decisis* is "of fundamental importance to the rule of law"; the majority offers no convincing reason for overturning our long line of decisions requiring the exclusion of coerced confessions.

IV

Since five Justices have determined that harmless-error analysis applies to coerced confessions, it becomes necessary to evaluate under that ruling the admissibility of Fulminante's confession to Sarivola. *Chapman v. California* made clear that "before a federal constitutional error can be held harmless, the court must be able to declare a belief that it was harmless beyond a reasonable doubt." The Court has the power to review the record *de novo* in order to determine an error's harmlessness. In so doing, it must be determined whether the State has met its burden of demonstrating that the admission of the confession to Sarivola did not contribute to Fulminante's conviction. Five of us are of the view that the State has not carried its burden and accordingly affirm the judgment of the court below reversing petitioner's conviction.

A confession is like no other evidence. Indeed, "the defendant's own confession is probably the most probative and damaging evidence that can be admitted against him. . . . The admissions of a defendant come from the actor himself, the most knowledgeable and unimpeachable source of information about his past conduct. Certainly, confessions have profound impact on the jury, so much so that we may justifiably doubt its ability to put them out of mind even if told to do so." . . . While some statements by a defendant may concern isolated aspects of the crime or may be incriminating only when linked to other evidence, a full confession in which the defendant discloses the motive for and means of the crime may tempt the jury to rely upon that evidence alone in reaching its decision. In the case of a coerced confession such as that given by Fulminante to Sarivola, the risk that the confession is unreliable, coupled with the profound impact that the confession has upon the jury, requires a reviewing court to exercise extreme caution before determining that the admission of the confession at trial was harmless.

In the Arizona Supreme Court's initial opinion, in which it determined that harmless-error analysis could be applied to the confession, the court found that the admissible second confession to Donna Sarivola rendered the first confession to Anthony Sarivola cumulative. The court also noted that circumstantial physical evidence concerning the wounds, the ligature around Jeneane's neck, the location of the body, and the presence of motorcycle tracks at the scene corroborated the second confession. The court concluded that "due to the overwhelming evidence adduced from the second confession, if there had not been a first confession, the jury would still have had the same basic evidence to convict."

We have a quite different evaluation of the evidence. Our review of the record leads us to conclude that the State has failed to meet its burden of establishing, beyond a reasonable doubt, that the admission of Fulminante's confession to Anthony Sarivola was harmless error. Three considerations compel this result.

First, the transcript discloses that both the trial court and the State recognized that a successful prosecution depended on the jury believing the two confessions. Absent the confessions, it is unlikely that Fulminante would have been prosecuted at all, because the physical evidence from the scene and other circumstantial evidence would have been insufficient to convict. Indeed, no indictment was filed until nearly two years after the murder. Although the police had suspected Fulminante from the beginning, as the prosecutor acknowledged in his opening statement to the jury, "What brings us to Court, what makes this case fileable, and prosecutable and triable is that later, Mr. Fulminante confesses this crime to Anthony Sarivola and later, to Donna Sarivola, his wife." After trial began, during a renewed hearing on Fulminante's motion to suppress, the trial court opined, "You know, I think from what little I know about this trial, the character of this man [Sarivola] for truthfulness or untruthfulness and his credibility is the centerpiece of this case, is it not?" The prosecutor responded, "It's very important, there's no doubt." Finally, in his closing argument, the prosecutor prefaced his discussion of the two confessions by conceding: "We have a lot of [circumstantial] evidence that indicates that this is our suspect, this is the fellow that did it, but it's a little short as far as saying that it's proof that he actually put the gun to the girl's head and killed her. So it's a little short of that. We recognize that."

Second, the jury's assessment of the confession to Donna Sarivola could easily have depended in large part on the presence of the confession to Anthony Sarivola. Absent the admission at trial of the first confession, the jurors might have found Donna Sarivola's story unbelievable. Fulminante's confession to Donna Sarivola allegedly occurred in May 1984, on the day he was released from Ray Brook, as she and Anthony Sarivola drove Fulminante from New York to Pennsylvania. Donna Sarivola testified that Fulminante, whom she had never before met, confessed in detail about Jeneane's brutal murder in response to her casual question concerning why he was going to visit friends in Pennsylvania instead of returning to his family in Arizona. Although she testified that she was "disgusted" by Fulminante's disclosures, she stated that she took no steps to notify authorities of what she had learned. In fact, she claimed that she barely discussed the matter with Anthony Sarivola, who was in the car and overheard Fulminante's entire conversation with Donna. Despite her disgust for Fulminante, Donna Sarivola later went on a second trip with him. Although Sarivola informed authorities that he had driven Fulminante to Pennsylvania, he did not mention Donna's presence in the car or her conversation with Fulminante. Only when questioned by authorities in June 1985 did Anthony Sarivola belatedly recall the confession to Donna more than a year before, and only then did he ask if she would be willing to discuss the matter with authorities.

Although some of the details in the confession to Donna Sarivola were corroborated by circumstantial evidence, many, including details that Jeneane was choked and sexually assaulted, were not. As to other aspects of the second confession, including Fulminante's motive and state of mind, the only corroborating evidence was the first confession to Anthony Sarivola. Thus, contrary to what the Arizona Supreme Court found, it is clear that the jury might have believed that the two confessions reinforced and corroborated each other. For this reason, one confession was not merely cumulative of the other. While in some cases two confessions, delivered on different occasions to different listeners, might be viewed as being independent of each other, it strains credulity to think that the jury so viewed the two confessions in this case, especially given the close relationship between Donna and Anthony Sarivola.

The jurors could also have believed that Donna Sarivola had a motive to lie about the confession in order to assist her husband. Anthony Sarivola received significant benefits from federal authorities, including payment for information, immunity from prosecution, and eventual placement in the federal Witness Protection Program. In addition, the jury might have found Donna motivated by her own desire for favorable treatment, for she, too, was ultimately placed in the Witness Protection Program.

Third, the admission of the first confession led to the admission of other evidence prejudicial to Fulminante. For example, the State introduced evidence that Fulminante knew of Sarivola's connections with organized crime in an attempt to explain why Fulminante would have been motivated to confess to Sarivola in seeking protection. Absent the confession, this evidence would have had no relevance and would have been inadmissible at trial. The Arizona Supreme Court found that the evidence of Sarivola's connections with organized crime reflected on Sarivola's character, not Fulminante's, and noted that the evidence could have been used to impeach Sarivola. This analysis overlooks the fact that had the confession not been admitted, there would have been no reason for Sarivola to testify and thus no need to impeach his testimony. Moreover, we cannot agree that the evidence did not reflect on Fulminante's character as well, for it depicted him as someone who willingly sought out the company of criminals. It is quite possible that this evidence led the jury to view Fulminante as capable of murder.

Finally, although our concern here is with the effect of the erroneous admission of the confession on Fulminante's conviction, it is clear that the presence of the confession also influenced the sentencing phase of the trial. Under Arizona law, the trial judge is the sentencer. At the sentencing hearing, the admissibility of information regarding aggravating circumstances is governed by the rules of evidence applicable to criminal trials. In this case, "based upon admissible evidence produced at the trial," the judge found that only one aggravating circumstance existed beyond a reasonable doubt, i.e., that the murder was committed in "an especially heinous, cruel, and depraved manner." In reaching this conclusion, the judge relied heavily on evidence concerning the manner of the killing and Fulminante's motives and state of mind which could only be found in the two confessions. For example, in labeling the murder "cruel," the judge focused in part on Fulminante's alleged statements that he choked Jeneane and made her get on her knees and beg before killing her. Although the circumstantial evidence was not inconsistent with this determination, neither was it sufficient to make such a finding beyond a reasonable doubt. Indeed, the sentencing judge acknowledged that the confessions were only partly corroborated by other evidence.

In declaring that Fulminante "acted with an especially heinous and depraved state of mind," the sentencing judge relied solely on the two confessions. While the judge found that the statements in the confessions regarding the alleged sexual assault on Jeneane should not be considered on the issue of cruelty because they were not corroborated by other evidence, the judge determined that they were worthy of belief on the issue of Fulminante's state of mind. The judge then focused on Anthony Sarivola's statement that Fulminante had made vulgar references to Jeneane during the first confession, and on Donna Sarivola's statement that Fulminante had made similar comments to her. Finally, the judge stressed that Fulminante's alleged comments to the Sarivolas concerning torture, choking, and sexual assault, "whether they all occurred or not," depicted "a man who was bragging and relishing the crime he committed."

Although the sentencing judge might have reached the same conclusions even without the confession to Anthony Sarivola, it is impossible to say so beyond a reasonable doubt. Furthermore, the judge's assessment of Donna Sarivola's credibility, and hence the reliability of the second confession, might well have been influenced by the corroborative effect of the erroneously admitted first confession. Indeed, the fact that the sentencing judge focused on the similarities between the two confessions in determining that they were reliable suggests that either of the confessions alone, even when considered with all the other evidence, would have been insufficient to permit the judge to find an aggravating circumstance beyond a reasonable doubt as a requisite prelude to imposing the death penalty.

Because a majority of the Court has determined that Fulminante's confession to Anthony Sarivola was coerced and because a majority has determined that admitting this confession was not harmless beyond a reasonable doubt, we agree with the Arizona Supreme Court's conclusion that Fulminante is entitled to a new trial at which the confession is not admitted. Accordingly the judgment of the Arizona Supreme Court is
AFFIRMED.

B. Federal Non-Constitutional Error

1. Criminal Cases

The Supreme Court has never clearly decided the precise standard for determining whether federal non-constitutional errors in criminal cases are harmless, and federal courts are split on the issue. The leading discussion of non-constitutional errors affecting "substantial rights" appears in the following criminal case.

Kotteakos v. United States

328 U.S. 748 (1945)

Mr. Justice RUTLEDGE delivered the opinion of the Court.

The only question is whether petitioners have suffered substantial prejudice from being convicted of a single general conspiracy by evidence which the Government admits proved not one conspiracy but some eight or more different ones of the same sort executed through a common key figure, Simon Brown. Petitioners were convicted under the general conspiracy section of the Criminal Code of conspiring to violate the provisions of the National Housing Act. The judgments were affirmed by the Circuit Court of Appeals. We granted certiorari because of the importance of the question for the administration of criminal justice in the federal courts.

The indictment named thirty-two defendants, including the petitioners. The gist of the conspiracy, as alleged, was that the defendants had sought to induce various financial institutions to grant credit, with the intent that the loans or advances would then be offered to the Federal Housing Administration for insurance upon applications containing false and fraudulent information.

Of the thirty-two persons named in the indictment nineteen were brought to trial and the names of thirteen were submitted to the jury. Two were acquitted; the jury disagreed as to four; and the remaining seven, including petitioners, were found guilty.

The Government's evidence may be summarized briefly, for the petitioners have not contended that it was insufficient, if considered apart from the alleged errors relating to the proof and the instructions at the trial.

Simon Brown, who pleaded guilty, was the common and key figure in all of the transactions proven. He was president of the Brownie Lumber Company. Having had experience in obtaining loans under the National Housing Act, he undertook to act as broker in placing for other loans for modernization and renovation, charging a five percent commission for his services. Brown knew, when he obtained the loans, that the proceeds were not to be used for the purposes stated in the applications.

In May, 1939, petitioner Lekacos told Brown that he wished to secure a loan in order to finance opening a law office, to say the least a hardly auspicious professional launching. Brown made out the application, as directed by Lekacos, to state that the purpose of the loan was to modernize a house belonging to the estate of Lekacos' father. Lekacos obtained the money. Later in the same year Lekacos secured another loan through Brown, the application being in the name of his brother and sister-in-law. Lekacos also received part of the proceeds of a loan for which one Gerakeris, a defendant who pleaded guilty, had applied.

In June, 1939, Lekacos sent Brown an application for a loan signed by petitioner

Kotteakos. It contained false statements. Brown placed the loan, and Kotteakos thereafter sent Brown applications on behalf of other persons. Two were made out in the names of fictitious persons. The proceeds were received by Kotteakos and petitioner Regenbogen, his partner in the cigarette and pinball machine business. Regenbogen, together with Kotteakos, had indorsed one of the applications. Kotteakos also sent to Brown an application for a loan in Regenbogen's name. This was for modernization of property not owned by Rogenbogen. The latter, however repaid the money in about three months after he received it.

The evidence against the other defendants whose cases were submitted to the jury was similar in character. They too had transacted business with Brown relating to National Housing Act loans. But no connection was shown between them and petitioners, other than that Brown had been the instrument in each instance for obtaining the loans. In many cases the other defendants did not have any relationship with one another, other than Brown's connection with each transaction. As the Circuit Court of Appeals said, there were "at least eight, and perhaps more, separate and independent groups, none of which had any connection with any other, though all dealt independently with Brown as their agent." As the Government puts it, the pattern was "that of separate spokes meeting at a common center," though we may add without the rim of the wheel to enclose the spokes.

The proof therefore admittedly made out a case, not of a single conspiracy, but of several, notwithstanding only one was charged in the indictment. The Court of Appeals aptly drew analogy in the comment, "Thieves who dispose of their loot to a single receiver—a single 'fence'—do not by that fact alone become confederates: they may, but it takes more than knowledge that he is a 'fence' to make them such." It stated that the trial judge "was

plainly wrong in supposing that upon the evidence there could be a single conspiracy; and in the view which he took of the law, he should have dismissed the indictment." Nevertheless the appellate court held the error not prejudicial, saying among other things that "especially since guilt was so manifest, it was 'proper' to join the conspiracies," and "to reverse the conviction would be a miscarriage of justice." It is indeed the Government's entire position. It does not now contend that there was no variance in proof from the single conspiracy charged in the indictment. Admitting that separate and distinct conspiracies were shown, it urges that the variance was not prejudicial to the petitioners.

In *Berger v. United States*, 295 U.S. 78, this Court held that in the circumstances presented the variance was not fatal where one conspiracy was charged and two were proved, relating to contemporaneous transactions involving counterfeit money. One of the conspiracies had two participants; the other had three; and one defendant Katz, was common to each. "The true inquiry," said the Court, "is not whether there has been a variance in proof, but whether there has been such a variance as to 'affect the substantial rights' of the accused."

The Court held the variance not fatal, resting its ruling on what has become known as the "harmless error statute," which is controlling in this case and provides:

> "On the hearing of any appeal, certiorari, writ of error, or motion for a new trial, in any case, civil or criminal, the court shall give judgment after an examination of the entire record before the court, without regard to technical errors, defects, or exceptions which do not affect the substantial rights of the parties."

Applying that section, the Court likened the situation to one where the four persons implicated in the two conspiracies had been charged as conspirators in separate counts, but with a failure in the proof to connect one of them (Berger) with one of the conspiracies, and a resulting conviction under one count and acquittal under the other. In that event, the Court said, "Plainly enough, his substantial rights would not have been affected." The situation supposed and the one actually presented, the opinion stated, though differing greatly in form, were not different in substance. The proof relating to the conspiracy with which Berger had not been connected could be regarded as incompetent as to him. But nothing in the facts, it was concluded, could reasonably be said to show that prejudice or surprise resulted; and the court went on to say, "Certainly the fact that the proof disclosed two conspiracies instead of one, each within the words of the indictment, cannot prejudice his defense of former acquittal of the one or former conviction of the other, if he should again be prosecuted."

The question we have to determine is whether the same ruling may be extended to a situation in which one conspiracy only is charged and at least eight having separate, though similar objects, are made out by the evidence, if believed; and in which the more numerous participants in the different schemes were, on the whole, except for one, different persons who did not know or have anything to do with one another.

The salutary policy embodied in § 269 [the harmless error statute] was adopted by the Congress in 1919 after long agitation under distinguished professional sponsorship, and after thorough consideration of various proposals designed to enact the policy in successive Congresses from the Sixtieth to the Sixty-fifth. It is not necessary to review in detail the history of the abuses which led to the agitation or of the progress of the legislation through the various sessions to final enactment without debate. But anyone familiar with it knows that § 269 and similar state legislation grew out of widespread and deep conviction over the general course of appellate review in American criminal causes. This was shortly, as one trial judge put it after § 269 had become law, that courts of review "tower above the trials of criminal cases as impregnable citadels of technicality." So great was the threat of reversal, in many jurisdictions, that criminal trials became a game for sowing reversible error in the record, only to have repeated the same matching of wits when a new trial had been thus obtained.

In the broad attack on this system great legal names were mobilized, among them Taft, Wigmore, Pound and Hadley, to mention only four. The general object was simple, to substitute judgment for automatic application of rules; to preserve review as a check upon arbitrary action and essential unfairness in trials, but at the same time to make the process perform that function without giving men fairly convicted the multiplicity of loopholes which any highly rigid and minutely detailed scheme of errors, especially in relation to procedure, will engender and reflect in a printed record.

The task was too big, too various in detail, for particularized treatment. The effort at revision therefore took the form of the essentially simple command of § 269. It comes down on its face to a very plain admonition: "Do not be technical, where technicality does not really hurt the party whose rights in the trial and in its outcome the technicality affects." It is also important to note that the purpose of the bill in its final form was stated authoritatively to be "to cast upon the party seeking a new trial the burden of showing that any technical errors that he may complain of have affected his substantial rights, otherwise they are to be disregarded." But that this burden does not extend to all errors appears from the statement which follows immediately. "The proposed legislation affects only technical errors. If the error is of such a character that its natural effect is to prejudice a litigant's substantial rights, the burden of sustaining a verdict will, notwithstanding this legislation, rest upon the one who claims under it."

Easier was the command to make than it has been always to observe. This, in part because it is general; but in part also because the discrimination it requires is one of judgment transcending confinement by formula or precise rule. That faculty cannot ever be wholly imprisoned in words, much less upon such a criterion as what are only technical, what substantial rights; and what really affects the latter hurtfully. Judgment, the play of impression and conviction along with intelligence, varies with judges and also with circumstance. What may be technical for one is substantial for another; what minor and unimportant in one setting crucial in another.

Moreover, lawyers know, if others do not, that what may seem technical may embody a great tradition of justice, or a necessity for drawing lines somewhere between great areas of law; that, in other words, one cannot always segregate the technique from the substance or the form from the reality. It is of course highly technical to confer full legal status upon one who has just attained his majority, but deny it to another a day, a week or a month younger. Yet that narrow line, and many others like it, must be drawn. The "hearsay" rule is often grossly artificial. Again in a different context it may be the very essence of justice, keeping out gossip, rumor, unfounded report, second-, third-, or further-hand stories. . . .

In the final analysis judgment in each case must be influenced by conviction resulting from examination of the proceedings in their entirety, tempered but not governed in any rigid sense of *stare decisis* by what has been done in similar situations. Necessarily the character of the proceeding, what is at stake upon its outcome, and the relation of the error asserted to casting the balance for decision on the case as a whole, are material factors in judgment.

The statute in terms makes no distinc-tion between civil and criminal causes. But this does not mean that the same criteria shall always be applied regardless of this difference. Indeed the legislative history shows that the proposed legislation went through many revisions, largely at the instance of the Senate, because there was fear of too easy relaxation of historic securities thrown around the citizen charged with crime. Although the final form of the legislation was designed, and frequently has been effective, to avoid some of the absurdities by which skillful manipulation of procedural rules had enabled the guilty to escape just punishment, § 269 did not make irrelevant the fact that a person is on trial for his life or his liberty. It did not require the same judgment in such a case as in one involving only some question of civil liability. There was no purpose, for instance, to abolish the historic difference between civil and criminal causes relating to the burden of proof placed in the one upon the plaintiff and in the other on the prosecution. Nor does § 269 mean that an error in receiving or excluding evidence has identical effects, for purposes of applying its policy, regardless of whether the evidence in other respects is evenly balanced or one-sided. Errors of this sort in criminal causes conceivably may be altogether harmless in the face of other clear evidence, although the same error might turn scales otherwise level, as constantly appears in the application of the policy of § 269 to questions of the admission of cumulative evidence. So it is with errors in instructions to the jury.

Some aids to right judgment may be stated more safely in negative than in affirmative form. Thus, it is not the appellate court's function to determine guilt or innocence. Nor is it to speculate upon probable reconviction and decide according to how the speculation comes out. Appellate judges cannot escape such impressions. But they may not make them sole criteria for reversal or affirmance. Those judgments are exclusively for the jury, given always the necessary minimum evidence legally sufficient to sustain the conviction unaffected by the error.

But this does not mean that the appellate court can escape altogether taking account of the outcome. To weigh the error's effect against the entire setting of the record without relation to the verdict or judgment would be almost to work in a vacuum. In criminal causes that outcome is conviction. This is different, or may be, from guilt in fact. It is guilt in law, established by the judgment of laymen. And the question is, not were they right in their judgment, regardless of the error or its effect upon the verdict. It is rather what effect the error had or reasonably may be taken to have had upon the jury's decision. The crucial thing is the impact of the thing done wrong on the minds of other men, not on one's own, in the total setting.

This must take account of what the error meant to them, not singled out and standing alone, but in relation to all else that happened. And one must judge others' reactions not by his own, but with allowance for how others might react and not be regarded generally as acting without reason. This is the important difference, but one easy to ignore when the sense of guilt comes strongly from the record.

If, when all is said and done, the conviction is sure that the error did not influence the jury, or had but very slight effect, the verdict and the judgment should stand, except perhaps where the departure is from a constitutional norm or a specific command of Congress. But if one cannot say, with fair assurance, after pondering all that happened without stripping the erroneous action from the whole, that the judgment was not substantially swayed by the error, it is impossible to conclude that substantial rights were not affected. The inquiry cannot be merely whether there was enough to support the result, apart from the phase affected by the error. It is rather, even so, whether the error itself had substantial influence. If so, or if one is left in

grave doubt, the conviction cannot stand.

. . .

It follows that the *Berger* case is not controlling of this one, notwithstanding that, abstractly considered, the errors in variance and instructions were identical in character. The *Berger* opinion indeed expressly declared: "We do not mean to say that a variance such as that here dealt with might not be material in a different case. We simply hold, following the view of the court below, that applying § 269 of the Judicial Code, as amended, to the circumstances of this case the variance was not prejudicial and hence not fatal."

On the face of things it is one thing to hold harmless the admission of evidence which took place in the *Berger* case, where only two conspiracies involving four persons all told were proved, and an entirely different thing to apply the same rule where, as here, only one conspiracy was charged, but eight separate ones were proved, involving at the outset thirty-two defendants. The essential difference is not overcome by the fact that the thirty-two were reduced, by severance, dismissal or pleas of guilty, to nineteen when the trial began and to thirteen by the time the cases went to the jury. The sheer difference in numbers, both of defendants and of conspiracies proven, distinguishes the situation. Obviously the burden of defense to a defendant, connected with one or a few of so many distinct transactions, is vastly different not only in preparation for trial, but also in looking out for and securing safeguard against evidence affecting other defendants, to prevent its transference as "harmless error" or by psychological effect in spite of instructions for keeping separate transactions separate.

The Government's theory seems to be, in ultimate logical reach, that the error presented by the variance is insubstantial and harmless, if the evidence offered specifically and properly to convict each defendant would be sufficient to sustain his conviction, if submitted in a separate trial. For reasons we have stated and in view of the authorities cited, this is not and cannot be the test under § 269. . . .

[T]he error permeated the entire charge, indeed the entire trial. Not only did it permit the jury to find each defendant guilty of conspiring with thirty-five other potential coconspirators, or any less number as the proof might turn out for acquittal of some, when none of the evidence would support such a conviction, as the proof did turn out in fact. It had other effects. One was to prevent the court from giving a precautionary instruction such as would be appropriate, perhaps required, in cases where related but separate conspiracies are tried together. . . .

Moreover, the effect of the court's misconception extended also to the proof of overt acts. . . . On [the court's] instructions it was competent not only for the jury to find that all of the defendants were parties to a single common plan, design and scheme, where none was shown by the proof, but also for them to impute to each defendant the acts and statements of the others without reference to whether they related to one of the schemes proven or another, and to find an overt act affecting all in conduct which admittedly could only have affected some. . . .

All this the Government seeks to justify as harmless error. . . . All this, it is said also, the *Berger* case sustains.

We do not agree. It is true, as we have said, that taken in abstraction from the particular facts the cases are alike. . . .

These are the abstract similarities. They are only abstract. To strip them from the separate and distinct total contexts of the two cases, and disregard the vast difference in those contexts, is to violate the whole spirit, and we think the letter also, of § 269. Numbers are vitally important in trial, especially in criminal matters. Guilt with us remains individual and personal, even as respects conspiracies. It is not a matter of mass application. . . .

Accordingly the judgments are reversed and the causes are remanded for further proceedings in conformity with this opinion.

Note

Kotteakos leaves open the question of exactly how probable it must be that a non-constitutional error affected the substantial rights of the parties in a criminal case. In his book *The Riddle of Harmless Error,* Roger Traynor, former Chief Justice of the California Supreme Court, wrote:

> [A]n appellate court realistically has three options in choosing a standard for reviewing trial error. The reviewing court might affirm if it believes: (a) that it is *more probable than not* that the error did not affect the judgment, (b) that it is *highly probable* that the error did not contribute to the judgment, or (c) that it is *almost certain* that the error did not taint the judgment.''

Justice Traynor chose the middle ground, arguing that ''unless the appellate court believes it highly probable that the error did not affect the judgment, it should reverse.'' This was the standard adopted by the Third Circuit in *Government of the Virgin Islands v. Tato,* 529 F.2d 278 (3d Cir. 1976). The Ninth Circuit, on the other hand, adopted the less stringent ''more probable than not'' standard. *United States v. Valle-Valdez,* 554 F.2d 911 (9th Cir. 1977).

2. Civil Cases

A split also exists among the federal courts as to the precise standard for judging harmless error that should be applied in civil cases. For example, the Third Circuit has adopted the "highly probable" standard (*McQueeney v. Wilmington Trust Co.*, 779 F.2d 916 (3d Cir. 1985)) while the Eleventh Circuit has held that in civil cases the court will apply the same standard as that set forth in *Kotteakos* for criminal cases. *Aetna Casualty and Sur. Co. v. Gosdin*, 803 F.2d 1153 (11th Cir. 1986). In the following case, the Court of Appeals for the Ninth Circuit explains the reasoning behind its adoption of the intermediate "more probable than not" standard for evaluating whether an error has affected the substantial rights of parties in a civil case.

Haddad v. Lockheed California Corporation

720 F.2d 1454 (9th Cir. 1983)

NELSON, Circuit Judge.

Appellant Robert Haddad appeals from the district court's judgment on his national origin discrimination claim, 42 U.S.C. §§ 2000e et seq. (1976 & Supp. V 1981), and from the jury's verdict on his age discrimination in employment claim, 29 U.S.C. §§ 621 et seq. (1976 & Supp. V 1981). Both claims arise from the same allegedly improper acts by appellee Lockheed. Despite the admission of improper evidence at trial, we affirm both the court's judgment and the jury's verdict.

FACTUAL AND PROCEDURAL BACKGROUND

Appellant Robert Haddad worked for appellee Lockheed California Corporation from early 1969 until his resignation in July 1979. Appellant claims that while in Lockheed's employ he was subject to a variety of forms of disparate treatment. This treatment, appellant alleged below, was the product of discrimination on the basis of national origin and age.

After filing a timely charge with the Equal Employment Opportunity Commission and receiving statutory notice of final action from the Commission, appellant initiated the present lawsuit in the Central District of California. Pursuant to 42

U.S.C. § 2000e-5(f)(4) (1976), appellant's claim of discrimination based on national origin was tried by the district court judge. Appellant's age discrimination claim was submitted to a jury. Both claims were decided in favor of appellee Lockheed. Appellant brought this timely appeal.

DISCUSSION

Appellant bases his appeal on purported errors in the district court's jury instructions and evidentiary rulings. Two of appellant's claims on appeal merit only brief discussion. Appellant's third claim, involving the admission of testimony in violation of appellant's marital privilege, merits fuller consideration as it calls into question the proper standard for determining harmless error in a civil trial.

* * *

Haddad attacks the admission of certain testimony of his ex-wife, claiming that such evidence was protected by the confidential marital communication privilege. The privilege properly protects the marital communication about which the witness testified. Therefore, the district court should have excluded this testimony.

Since this evidence is cumulative of other evidence in the record and the record contains no evidence to the contrary, we presume that the improper admission of this testimony had no effect on the court's decision rejecting Haddad's national origin discrimination claim. Thus, we affirm the court's decision on this claim.

The improper admission of Haddad's ex-wife's testimony poses a more serious problem for the jury verdict on Haddad's age discrimination claim. A jury, unlike a judge, cannot be presumed to have based its verdict only on properly admitted evidence. Our task, then, is to determine whether the evidentiary error committed below affected a "substantial right" of appellant and so requires reversal of the age discrimination verdict.

As an initial inquiry, we must determine what standard to use to determine whether the error in this case was sufficient to require reversal. Some errors involve "constitutional rights so basic to a fair trial that their infraction can never be treated as harmless error." A second type of constitutional error does not involve the fundamental integrity of the judicial process but does implicate the constitutional rights of the criminally accused. These errors must be shown by an appellate court to be harmless beyond a reasonable doubt. See, e.g., *Chapman v. California*, (drawing inferences in violation of the right against self-incrimination); *Schneble v. Florida*, (admitting testimony in violation of the confrontation clause).

It would be possible to end our inquiry here merely by distinguishing the error in the case at bar from the constitutional errors discussed in *Chapman*. This court first stressed the importance of such a distinction in dicta, *United States v. Valle-Valdez*, 554 F.2d 911, 915-19 (9th Cir. 1977), and suggested that the harmlessness of trial error might be gauged under two standards: harmless beyond a reasonable doubt for constitutional errors and more probably than not harmless for non-constitutional errors. The *Valle-Valdez* opinion, however, noted that ruling Ninth Circuit authority

could be interpreted to require non-constitutional errors in criminal cases to be measured by the more rigorous "harmless beyond a reasonable doubt" standard. Subsequent cases have relied upon the *Valle-Valdez* distinction between constitutional and non-constitutional errors as dispositive, and measured non-constitutional errors in criminal cases using a standard requiring reversal unless the error was more probably than not harmless.

Despite its convenience, we will not rely on the reasoning in *Valle-Valdez* to resolve the open question of what standard of harmlessness should prevail in a civil appeal. Neither the distinction between constitutional and non-constitutional error nor the strictly bifurcated standard of harmlessness it creates has been uniformly accepted.[5] Courts frequently avoid relying on the distinction by finding harmlessness under all standards. Commentators have cautioned against making the standard for harmless error turn entirely on a distinction between constitutional and non-constitutional error.[6] Finally, we are not

---

[5] See, e.g., *United States v. Herbert*, 698 F.2d 981, 986 (9th Cir. 1983) (applying higher standard to jury instruction error concerning elements of charge); *United States v. Cusino*, 694 F.2d 185, 187 (9th Cir.), ("there may be room for argument about the appropriate standard for measuring instructional errors"), *cert. denied*, 461 U.S. 932, 103 S. Ct. 2096, 77 L. Ed. 2d 305 (1983); *U.S. v. Indian Boy X*, 565 F.2d 585, 592-93 (9th Cir. 1977) (dicta that low standard is used to gauge harm caused by purported violation of *Miranda* rights), *cert. denied*, 439 U.S. 841 (1978); *United States v. Rea*, 532 F.2d 147, 149 (9th Cir.) (higher standard used to evaluate erroneous jury instruction), *cert. denied*, 429 U.S. 837 (1976); *United States v. Duhart*, 496 F.2d 941, 944-45 (9th Cir.) (same), *cert. denied*, 419 U.S. 967 (1974); cf. *United States v. Goldberg*, 582 F.2d 483, 489 (9th Cir. 1978) (using a middle standard of probable harm in creating an analogy between harmless error rule and prosecutorial failure to respond to a general request for evidence), *cert. denied*, 440 U.S. 973 (1979).

[6] *E.g.*, 1 J. Weinstein & M. Berger, Weinstein's Evidence P103[06], at 103-59 to -60. (no other circuit explicitly supports claim that more probable than not standard is "general rule"); R. Traynor, supra, (arguing for a highly probable standard of harmlessness in all ap-

certain that application of the more lenient standard to errors involving the improper admission of evidence in a criminal trial can be reconciled with the Supreme Court's language in *Chapman:* "An error in admitting plainly relevant evidence which possibly influenced the jury adversely to a litigant cannot, under *Fahy v. Connecticut,* be conceived of as harmless." Because of our concern that courts' adoption of this bifurcated standard of harmlessness may have occurred through misinterpretation of *Chapman* and *Valle-Valdez,* we decline to perpetuate the mistake by extending the analysis to civil cases. We therefore put this distinction to one side, and address directly the question before us: How probable must the harm from an error in a civil trial be before it affects substantial rights and thus requires reversal?[7]

The purpose of a harmless error standard is to enable an appellate court to gauge the probability that the trier of fact was affected by the error. Perhaps the most important factor to consider in fashioning such a standard is the nature of the particular fact-finding process to which the standard is to be applied. Accordingly, a crucial first step in determining how we should gauge the probability that an error was harmless is recognizing the distinction between civil and criminal trials. See *Kotteakos v. United States,* 328 U.S. 750, 763 (1946); *Valle-Valdez,* 544 F.2d at 914-15.

This distinction has two facets, each of which reflects the differing burdens of proof in civil and criminal cases. First, the lower burden of proof in civil cases implies a larger margin of error. The danger of the harmless error doctrine is that an appellate court may usurp the jury's function, by merely deleting improper evidence from the record and assessing the sufficiency of the evidence to support the verdict below. This danger has less practical importance where, as in most civil cases, the jury verdict merely rests on a more probable than not standard of proof.

The second facet of the distinction between errors in civil and criminal trials involves the differing degrees of certainty owed to civil and criminal litigants. Whereas a criminal defendant must be found guilty beyond a reasonable doubt, a civil litigant merely has a right to a jury verdict that more probably than not corresponds to the truth.

The civil litigant's lessened entitlement to veracity continues when the litigant becomes an appellant. We conclude that a proper harmless error standard for civil cases should reflect the burden of proof. Just as the verdict in a civil case need only be more probably than not true, so an error in a civil trial need only be more probably than not harmless. See Saltzburg, The Harm of Harmless Error, 59 Va.L.Rev. 988, 1018-21 (1973). In other words, when an appellate court ponders the probable effect of an error on a civil trial, it need only find that the jury's verdict is more probably than not untainted by the error.

In the case at bar, appellant had a "substantial right" to a jury determination as to whether the treatment accorded him by Lockheed was more probably than not the product of age discrimination. Our task on appeal is to determine whether the evidentiary error of which appellant complains has deprived appellant of the degree of certainty to which he is entitled. Although not

---

peals). Saltzburg, "The Harm of Harmless Error," 59 Va. L. Rev. 988 (1973) (arguing for a harmless beyond a reasonable doubt standard in all criminal appeals); Note, "The Harmless Error Rule Reviewed," 47 Colum. L. Rev. 450, 462 (1947) (suggesting reversal in all cases where it is "within the range of appreciable probability" that an error affected the verdict).

[7] Where an error could have been and was the subject of an objection at trial, then appellate courts have three possible standards of review: harmless beyond a reasonable doubt; high probability of harmlessness; and more probably than not harmless. See generally R. Traynor, The Riddle of Harmless Error (1972). Our present task is to determine which of these standards properly applies to review of an evidentiary error in a civil case.

beyond a reasonable doubt harmless,[8] the error in this case more probably than not had no effect on the jury's rejection of Haddad's age discrimination claim. We therefore hold the admission of privileged testimony in this case to have been harmless and we affirm the jury's verdict below.

Our assessment of the probable harmlessness of Mrs. Haddad's testimony rests partially on the relation between that testimony and the factual issues underlying Haddad's age discrimination claim. Mrs. Haddad improperly testified to the effect that in 1977 Haddad told her that he intended to resign from Lockheed and go into a real estate and consulting business with his brother. This testimony might have harmed Haddad by tending to undercut his claim that he was constructively discharged in 1979 and by casting suspicion on his work attitudes during his last two years at Lockheed. However, constructive discharge was just a small part of appellant's disparate treatment claim. Moreover, although Haddad's "abrasive" personality was frequently discussed, Haddad's commitment to his work was not a point of contention. The eight-day trial focused primarily on the specific Lockheed employment practices described in Haddad's complaint.

Haddad's age discrimination claim recited a catalogue of grievances: no promotion in salary grade in ten-and-one-half years; improper distribution of merit

raises to those within his salary grade; the imposition of travel restrictions and record-keeping requirements; the imposition of telephone use restrictions; the rejection of appellant's suggestions for company improvements; the referral of appellant to the company doctor. To each of these specific complaints of disparate treatment, Lockheed responded with non-discriminatory explanations. For example, a very large portion of the trial, perhaps 20 to 30 percent, dealt with appellant's salary grade. Appellant stressed this topic; it was the grievance that appellant's counsel chose to describe first in his closing remarks. Lockheed's response on this issue was to show that appellant's salary grade was dictated by the position he filled and the constraints of Lockheed's contracts with the United States Navy. Lockheed also produced testimony of specific instances wherein appellant was advised that a higher salary grade would be available to him if he agreed to apply to another division within the corporation.

Mrs. Haddad's testimony was not only largely tangential to an evaluation of Lockheed's employment practices, it was also partially cumulative of other competent testimony regarding Haddad's attitudes towards Lockheed. Even without Mrs. Haddad's testimony, the jury was probably aware that Haddad was considering alternative careers in 1977. Many witnesses testified to Haddad's dissatisfaction with his salary during and prior to 1977. Haddad himself testified that he obtained a real estate license in 1977. Haddad also testified that he engaged in consulting and in the practice of real estate in 1979, immediately after leaving Lockheed. Mrs. Haddad's testimony may have reinforced the suspicion that Haddad was planning to leave Lockheed in 1977, but it probably did not create that suspicion.

The minimal extent to which counsel emphasized Mrs. Haddad's testimony to

---

[8] We cannot say that Mrs. Haddad's testimony was harmless beyond a reasonable doubt. It is reasonably possible that the jury could have discredited Haddad's description of his work conditions if it suspected that Haddad had been planning to leave Lockheed two years before his actual departure. Still, we conclude that the testimony was more probably than not harmless. Although the credibility of a plaintiff undoubtedly has great impact on a jury verdict, in this case it was the credibility of Lockheed's witnesses that was crucial. Haddad had apparently made a prima facie case of age discrimination and the task of the jury was to determine whether or not Lockheed's non-discriminatory explanations were mere pretext.

the jury supports our conclusion that the error in this case was more probably than not harmless. Counsel for Haddad and counsel for Lockheed had numerous discussions before the judge as to whether Mrs. Haddad was to testify at all. Nevertheless, these confrontations, although perhaps showing the value Lockheed placed on Mrs. Haddad's testimony, were out of the jury's hearing. Lockheed's counsel examined Mrs. Haddad for a very short period. The purpose of this examination seems to have been to show that Haddad was under substantial personal pressure during his last two years at Lockheed. In his closing argument, Lockheed's counsel mentioned Mrs. Haddad's testimony only briefly, suggesting that it showed Haddad's emotional strain in 1977. The overwhelming thrust of Lockheed's closing argument, like the overwhelming bulk of the trial, dealt with a point by point analysis of Lockheed's employment practices.

AFFIRMED.

C. State Non-Constitutional Error

1. Harmless Error Analysis

In state courts the formulation of the harmless error doctrine with regard to non-constitutional errors varies considerably. The appellate lawyer simply must learn what standard is applied in the court hearing the appeal. The leading case in New York, *People v. Crimmins,* 36 N.Y.2d 230 (1975), discusses the difference between the standards to be applied to constitutional and non-constitutional errors in the New York state courts.

People v. Crimmins

36 N.Y.2d 230, 326 N.E.2d 787, 367 N.Y.S.2d 213 (1975)

JONES, J.

On this appeal we are called on principally to consider the doctrine of harmless error as applied to errors which occurred on defendant's second trial. In this case a mother was charged with criminal responsibility in connection with the deaths of her son and her daughter. On her first trial defendant was charged only with the death of the daughter and was convicted of manslaughter. On appeal this conviction was reversed and a new trial was ordered. On her second trial the jury convicted defendant of murder of her son and manslaughter of her daughter. The Appellate Division then reversed the conviction of murder of the son and dismissed the charge against defendant with respect to his death. As to the manslaughter conviction, the Appellate Division also reversed defendant's conviction but ordered a new trial with respect to her responsibility for the death of her daughter. The case is now before us on appeal by the People.

The procedural aspects of this appeal and of our dispositions of its several branches call for exposition. The ultimate issues turn on the procedural significance and consequences properly to be attached to errors of law which occurred during the second trial. We conclude that these errors fall into separate categories calling for different legal results.

I. As to defendant's conviction of murder of her infant son:

The Appellate Division's reversal of this conviction (as distinguished from that court's attendant dismissal of this count in the indictment) was explicitly recited to be "on the law and facts." An appeal may be taken to our court only where the reversal is expressly stated to be on the law alone; accordingly an appeal from this reversal may not be taken to our court.

By contrast, the corrective action directed by the Appellate Division in consequence of its reversal of the murder conviction, i.e., the dismissal of the murder count, is subject to an appeal to and review by our court. We find that corrective action to have been what was required by the Criminal Procedure Law. The reversal of the conviction was based on the conclusion of the Appellate Division that, as a matter of law, the People did not prove that the son's death resulted from a criminal act and, in the alternative, that any finding that it did would be contrary to the weight of the evidence. CPL 470.20 (subd. 2) mandates dismissal of the accusatory instrument in the event of reversal of a judgment after trial for legal insufficiency of trial evidence; subdivision 5 of the same section mandates the same corrective action where the reversal is on the ground that the verdict is against the weight of the trial evidence. Accordingly the Appellate Division's dismissal of the murder count with respect to the death of the son must be affirmed.

II. As to defendant's conviction of manslaughter in the homicide of her infant daughter:

The Appellate Division determined that because of errors committed on the second trial this conviction should be reversed. Because such determination was expressly stated to be on the law alone, that aspect of the present appeal, as well as the associated corrective action directed by the Appellate Division, is properly before us (CPL 450.90, subd. 2, pars. [a], [b]). For reasons discussed below, a majority of our court is of the view that this determination of the Appellate Division should itself be reversed. In that circumstance, since the order of the Appellate Division reversing the manslaughter conviction was based on the law alone, the provisions of CPL 470.40 (subd. 2, par. [b]) dictate that the manslaughter conviction be remitted to the Appellate Division for determination of the facts. Presumably consideration will then be revived, too, as to defendant's separate and distinct appeal from the order of Supreme Court denying her motion for a new trial on the grounds of newly-discovered evidence and of improper conduct by the prosecutor in withholding from defendant information potentially helpful to her defense. In view of the other determinations made at the Appellate Division in the order from which appeal is now being taken it was not then necessary formally to reach or dispose of defendant's contentions with respect to denial of her motion for a new trial. Defendant now becomes entitled to consideration and disposition of such contentions by that court.

We turn then to a discussion of our reasons for concluding that the reversal of the manslaughter conviction should be overturned.

A. As to the constitutional error:

The People concede that the comment of the prosecutor in summation with respect to defendant's failure to testify on her own behalf was improper and constituted constitutional error under the provisions of both the Federal and our State Constitutions (U.S. Const., 5th Amdt.; N.Y. Const., art. I, § 6). All of the members of the court agree that such error calls for reversal and a new trial unless it was harmless under the test for harmless constitutional error laid down by the Supreme Court of the United States, namely, that there is no reasonable possibility that the error might have contributed to defendant's conviction and that it was thus harmless beyond a reasonable doubt.

We of the majority are satisfied that this test is met here in view of the circumstances in which the constitutional error occurred – *inter alia*, the unsworn outbursts by defendant herself which both preceded and followed the prosecutor's error, the comments of defense counsel and the reactions in the courtroom at the time, and the explicitly clear instructions of the trial court – coupled with what, as indicated below, we think was the overwhelming proof of defendant's guilt.

Although in our view this case presents no appropriate instance for its application, our discussion of the effect to be given constitutional error should not overlook a parallel, and in some instances an overlapping doctrine, also of constitutional proportion, namely, the right to a fair trial. Not only the individual defendant but the public at large is entitled to assurance that there shall be full observance and enforcement of the cardinal right of a defendant to a fair trial. The appellate courts have an overriding responsibility, never to be eschewed or lightly to be laid aside, to give that assurance. So, if in any instance, an appellate court concludes that there has been such error of a trial court, such misconduct of a prosecutor, such inadequacy of defense counsel, or such other wrong as to have operated to deny any individual defendant his fundamental right to a fair trial, the reviewing court must reverse the conviction and grant a new trial, quite without regard to any evaluation as to whether the errors contributed to the defendant's conviction. The right to a fair trial is self-standing, and proof of guilt, however overwhelming, can never be permitted to negate this right. There is no predicate here, however, for any claim that this defendant on her second trial was deprived of any such basic right.

B. As to the non-constitutional errors:

For the purpose of our disposition of this appeal we assume, although each of the Judges in the majority would not necessarily so decide, that the Appellate Division was correct in concluding that in the circumstances of this trial: (1) it was error to permit introduction of testimony with respect to the witness Rorech's having been given a sodium pentothal (truth serum) test (although nothing was said as to any results thereof); (2) it was error to permit the prosecutor to elicit testimony in cross-examination of defendant's witness Colabella that the latter had refused to sign a waiver of immunity when questioned by the prosecutor during the pretrial investigation of the case; and (3) it was error, after the prosecutor had put before the jury an apparently damaging admission by Colabella to one Sullivan but had thereafter failed to call Sullivan or to explain the failure to do so, for the trial court to deny defendant's request for a charge that the jury could draw an unfavorable inference from the People's failure to call Sullivan as a witness. None of these errors, however, was of constitutional dimension.

We turn then to the question whether any one of such errors, or all taken in combination, calls for a reversal of the jury verdict here.

The definition and elaboration of the doctrine of harmless error as applied to non-constitutional error involve peculiarly questions of the law of the State of New York to be determined by our State courts. The doctrine has received expression in our court over the last 20 years in various forms, accompanied usually explicitly, always at least implicitly, by a recognition that "[e]rrors are almost inevitable in any trial, improprieties almost unavoidable, [and that] the presence of one or the other furnishes no automatic signal for reversal and retrial." (*People v. Kingston*, 8 N.Y.2d 384, 387).

Examination of the language chosen to describe the doctrine and its application in individual cases, as well as analysis of the authorities selected for citation, discloses that we have not always been either consistent in our classification or uniform in our expression. Forms of our verbalization of the doctrine cannot be nicely harmonized.

Often there has been no explicit recognition that there is a distinction between constitutional and non-constitutional error; citations and verbiage have frequently been indiscriminately interchanged. On the other hand, we have never expressly held, as the dissent now urges, that there is no difference in the application of the doctrine of harmless error between constitutional and non-constitutional error. When we have reached the conclusion that the error was harmless we have stated the rule loosely, in terms relatively easily satisfied. On the other hand when we have concluded that the error was not harmless our statement has been of a tight, demanding rule. The ultimate result in the individual case has been more significant than the particular formulation of the rule.

The presently applicable legislative statement of our State's rule, like its predecessor, has not been helpful. "An appellate court must determine an appeal without regard to technical errors or defects which do not affect the substantial rights of the parties" (CPL 470.05, subd. 1). The choice of the adjective "technical" in referring to errors may be said to connote those of a formalistic or minor character. On the other hand, to refer to errors which may affect "substantial" rights suggests errors of a somewhat more serious nature. Notably there has never been incorporated in the statutory language any concept of "harmlessness beyond a reasonable doubt." In any event, our decisions have not turned on or even been significantly affected by the legislative diction of present CPL 470.05 (subd. 1) or of section 542 of the former Code of Criminal Procedure.

It is appropriate therefore to recognize and to delineate the difference between the Federal harmless error rule with respect to constitutional error and our State's harmless error rule with respect to non-constitutional error.

Two discrete considerations are relevant and have combined in varying proportions to produce specific results in particular cases. The first of such factors is the quantum and nature of proof of the defendant's guilt if the error in question were to be wholly excised. The second is the causal effect which it is judged that the particular error may nonetheless have had on the actual verdict. It appears that it is the latter consideration which is critical in the application of the Supreme Court test as to harmlessness of constitutional error. Thus, however overwhelming may be the quantum and nature of other proof, the error is not harmless under the Federal test if "there is a reasonable possibility that the . . . [error] might have contributed to the conviction" – perhaps the most demanding test yet formulated. *Fahy v. Connecticut,* 375 U.S. 85, 86; *Chapman v. California,* 86 U.S. 18.

Our State rule to determine harmlessness of non-constitutional error is not the same as the Federal rule.

The ultimate objective, grounded in sound policy considerations, is the wise balancing, in the context of the individual case, of the competing interests of the defendant and those of the People. "While we are ever intent on safeguarding the rights of a defendant . . . we recognize at the same time that the State has its rights too." Thus, it does not follow that an otherwise guilty defendant is entitled to a reversal whenever error has crept into his trial. On the other hand, we recognize that a finding that an error has not been harmless does not result in fatal consequences to the People; they are put to a new trial, but the defendant does not go free.

Our State test with respect to non-constitutional error is not so exacting as the Supreme Court test for constitutional error. We observe that in either instance, of course, unless the proof of the defendant's guilt, without reference to the error, is overwhelming, there is no occasion for consideration of any doctrine of harmless error. That is, every error of law (save, perhaps, one of sheerest technicality) is, *ipso facto,* deemed to be prejudicial and to require a reversal, unless that error can be found to have been rendered harmless by the weight and the nature of the other proof. That "overwhelming proof of guilt" cannot be defined with mathematical precision does not, of course, mean that the concept cannot be understood and applied in individual cases, although not always without some difficulty. It surely does not invite merely a numerical comparison of witnesses or of pages of testimony; the nature and the inherent probative worth of the evidence must be appraised. As with the standard, "beyond a reasonable doubt," recourse must ultimately be to a level of convincement. What is meant here, of course, is that the quantum and nature of proof, excising the error, are so logically compelling and therefore forceful in the particular case as to lead the appellate court to the conclusion that "a jury composed of honest, well-intentioned, and reasonable men and women" on consideration of such evidence would almost certainly have convicted the defendant.

If, however, an appellate court has satisfied itself that there was overwhelming proof of the defendant's guilt, its inquiry does not end there. Under our system of justice a jury is not commanded to return a verdict of guilty even in the face of apparently conclusive proof of the defendant's guilt. Similarly it may and often does exercise a positive sense of moderating mercy. Further inquiry must accordingly be made by the appellate court as to whether, notwithstanding the overwhelming proof of the defendant's guilt, the error infected or tainted the verdict. An evaluation must therefore be made as to the potential of the particular error for prejudice to the defendant. We hold that an error is prejudicial in this context if the appellate court concludes that there is a significant probability, rather than only a rational possibility, in the particular case that the jury would have acquitted the defendant had it not been for the error or errors which occurred.

Turning then to the record now before us, we of the majority conclude that, excising both the evidence erroneously admitted (with respect to Rorech's taking a truth test and as to Colabella's refusal to sign a waiver of immunity) and the prosecutor's interrogation of Colabella (as to the latter's damaging admission to Sullivan), there was overwhelming proof that this defendant was guilty of manslaughter in the death of her daughter. In addition to other compelling circumstantial evidence, there was eyewitness testimony (unavailable to support the conviction on the first trial because it had been infected by the wholly improper visit of jurors to the scene) that on the night before the daughter's body was found, defendant, carrying what was described as a "bundle" and accompanied by an unidentified man, was seen leading her son from the Crimmins home; that as the man threw the "bundle" into a parked car defendant cried out, "Please don't do this to her," to which the man responded, "Does she know the difference now? . . . Now you're sorry." Additionally defendant herself later confessed her guilt to her paramour — "Joseph, forgive me, I killed her." On the other hand the description which defendant offered of the events of the evening preceding the children's disappearance was completely discredited and the prosecution conclusively exploded defendant's theory of an outside kidnapper. We read this record as leading only to a single, inexorable conclusion, as two juries have indeed found: defendant was criminally responsible for the death of her daughter.

Proceeding further, then, as we must, we also conclude that in the circumstances of this case there is no significant probability in the light of the overwhelming proof that, had it not been for the errors which occurred, this jury would have acquitted the defendant or that a third jury might do so. Our ultimate conclusion, therefore, is that under our State rule the non-constitutional errors which occurred on this defendant's second trial were harmless.

The order of the Appellate Division with respect to the manslaughter conviction should accordingly be reversed, and the case remitted to the Appellate Division for determination of the facts in conformity with CPL 470.40 (subd. 2, par. [b]]).

Notes

1. Whether a court applies the constitutional "no reasonable possibility that the error might have contributed to the defendant's conviction" or the non-constitutional "significant probability that the jury would have acquitted the defendant had it not been for the error" test can unquestionably determine the outcome of an appeal. In *Crimmins*, for example, one of the non-constitutional errors complained of on appeal was the improper bolstering of the testimony of the prosecution's most important witness by the persistent mentioning of the fact that he had been given a sodium pentothal "truth serum" test. While there may not have been a significant probability that Crimmins would have been acquitted in the absence of the error, there surely is a "reasonable possibility" that the information that the key prosecution witness's credibility had been put to a scientific test "might have contributed to her conviction."

2. Like many other states, New York has made it easier for courts to disregard an error as harmless in civil than in criminal cases. In *Walker v. State of New York*, 111 A.D.2d 164, 488 N.Y.S.2d 793 (N.Y. App. Div. 1985), the court affirmed the lower court's dismissal of a suit to recover damages for injuries allegedly sustained as a result of medical malpractice. The appellate court found that the lower court had clearly erred in refusing to admit into evidence a medical report in which a physician stated that the plaintiff's behavioral abnormalities several months after the operation might have been attributable to the surgery. The court held that this error did not require a reversal, stating that the erroneous exclusion of evidence warrants a reversal only if it can be said that such evidence, had it been admitted, "probably would have had a substantial influence upon the result of the trial." *Id.* at 165.

3. The California state constitution provides that "no judgment shall be set aside ...unless, after an examination of the entire cause, including the evidence, the court shall be of the opinion that the error complained of has resulted in a miscarriage of justice." Although this language regarding when error should call for reversal is quite different from the New York statute, the California harmless error test has evolved in much the same way as New York's has. The California Supreme Court has held that a "miscarriage of justice" should be declared only when the court "after our examination of the entire cause including the evidence is of the opinion that it is reasonably probable that a result more favorable to the appealing party would have been reached in the absence of error." *People v. Watson,* 16 Cal.2d 818, 299 P.2d 243, 254 (1956). The court stressed that "the test ... must necessarily be

based upon reasonable probabilities rather than upon mere possibilities; otherwise the entire purpose of the constitutional provision would be defeated." *Id.*

2. Errors Requiring Automatic Reversal Under State Law

The courts of each state also have the power to determine whether, under their own state constitutions or statutes, particular errors are subject to harmless error analysis. In New York, for example, a prosecutor's failure to turn over prior statements by witnesses as required by a case called *People v. Rosario,* 9 N.Y.2d 286, 173 N.E.2d 881, 213 N.Y.S.2d 448 (1961), and later by statute, has been declared, as a matter of state law, to call for automatic reversal.

> When the People delay in producing *Rosario* material, the reviewing court must ascertain whether the defense was substantially prejudiced by the delay. When, however, the prosecution fails completely in its obligation to deliver such material to defense counsel, the courts will not attempt to determine whether any prejudice accrued to the defense. The failure constitutes *per se* error requiring that the conviction be reversed and a new trial ordered.

People v. Ranghelle, 69 N.Y.2d 56, 63, 503 N.E.2d 1011, 511 N.Y.S.2d 280 (1986).

Submission of written instructions to the jury incorporating portions of the oral charge also calls for a *per se* reversal under New York law. *People v. Owens,* 69 N.Y.2d 585, 509 N.E.2d 314, 516 N.Y.S.2d 619 (1987). Similarly, in Florida, a court's refusal to sequester a jury during deliberations has been held not subject to harmless error analysis. *Taylor v. State,* 498 So.2d 943 (Fla. 1982). It is therefore important for the appellate advocate to research state law on the issue of harmless error, since it may provide a stronger argument than the federal Constitution that a particular error requires a reversal *per se.*

Appellate Strategy: The Harmless Error Argument

The harmless error doctrine significantly changed the practice of litigation in general and appellate advocacy in particular. Because almost no errors presumptively call for reversal, an appellant's lawyer can no longer rest after making a convincing argument that an error indeed occurred at trial. Counsel has the additional job of demonstrating that the error prejudiced the client. Counsel for respondent, on the other hand, must now take advantage of the fall-back argument that any error that did occur at trial had, in any event, no prejudicial effect. Such harmless error analysis is a crucial section of almost every point in every appellate brief. The lawyer who omits it has done only half the job.

The first task facing the appellant's lawyer when writing a harmless error argument is to determine the appropriate harmless error test to be applied by the court in deciding whether a particular error is harmless or prejudicial. This, of course, involves identifying the nature of the case, whether civil or criminal, and the nature of the error, whether constitutional or non-constitutional. Because it is more difficult to demonstrate that a constitutional error was harmless, wherever it is fairly possible to do so, the lawyer for appellant will want to characterize an error as one that has denied the client a constitutional right. Respondent's lawyer will naturally want to argue that no such significant right was affected at all.

Upon determining that the error was constitutional, appellant's lawyer in a criminal case will argue that under the *Chapman* standard a reasonable possibility exists that the error might have contributed to the defendant's conviction and that it therefore cannot be said to be harmless beyond a reasonable doubt. If the error is non-constitutional, the lawyer must, in federal, civil, and criminal cases determine the degree of assurance required in the particular jurisdiction that the judgment was not substantially swayed by the error test and argue accordingly. Likewise, the lawyer in state court must research and argue the correct state harmless error test.

The next step is to convince the court that under the applicable standard, the error was prejudicial (or was harmless, in the case of respondent). This requires the lawyer to make a showing that the evidence was not (or was) overwhelming, and that the error complained of may well have (or was unlikely to have) affected the verdict.

A good harmless error argument must in most cases make a connection between a weakness in the evidence and the particular error. For example, if the error complained of involves the court's charge on intent, it will certainly be found harmless if the defendant's only defense at trial was misidentification. Often pointing to another event at trial can indicate that the jury was, in fact, influenced by the error. For example, if the error complained of is the admission of unfairly prejudicial evidence, it would be important to point to the fact that the opposing attorney dwelled on that evidence on summation or that the judge referred to it specifically when instructing the jury. All such connected facts should be laid out clearly in the statement of facts so that the harm of the error is immediately apparent.

Exercise

The transcript of the trial of People of the State of New York against Barry Lister and James Taylor reveals the following:

> The complainant was robbed in a park by two men. The complainant stopped a police car in the area, and canvassed the neighborhood to search for his assailants. A few blocks away, the complainant pointed out to the officers a group of ten to fifteen people standing on a stoop, saying that two of the men were the ones who robbed him. As the patrol car pulled up, the codefendant, James Taylor, ran down the street, while the defendant, Barry Lister, ran into a nearby building. The officers pursued the defendant into the building and arrested him on the first floor landing. The complainant

followed the officers inside and identified the defendant, the knife used during the commission of the robbery and the radio which he claimed that the defendant had taken from him. The knife and radio were recovered from the first floor.

During the evening following the robbery, the codefendant, who had not been apprehended, approached Carol Amado, the sister of the complainant's girlfriend, and told her that he would not have robbed the complainant if he had known he was her sister's friend. He also told her that the complainant's property would be returned to him if he did not press charges against "his man Barry." The complainant and Amado both testified that a week later, they were riding together in a car when they saw the codefendant walking along the street. The codefendant approached their car and told the complainant that he would give him $250 if he did not press charges against Barry.

Defense counsel objected to admission of the nontestifying codefendant's statements as testified to by the complainant and Amado, arguing that they violated his rights under the Confrontation Clause (*Cruz v. New York*, 481 U.S. 186, on remand, 70 N.Y.2d 733; *Bruton v. United States*, 391 U.S. 123). The trial court allowed the statements into evidence.

The jury deliberated for two and a half days. Just before returning with a verdict finding both the defendant and Taylor guilty of robbery, the jury asked to have the codefendant's statements read back.

Assume that the appellate court agrees that the statements were improperly admitted. Write an argument either on behalf of Barry Lister asserting that the error in admitting the codefendant's statements was unfairly prejudicial, or on behalf of the prosecution arguing that the error was harmless.

Chapter 6

The Role of Appellate Counsel

Introduction

The attorney's task in representing clients on appeal, as at other stages of litigation, may be complicated by the different obligations to the client, the adversary, and the court. Counsel's duty to represent a client competently and zealously may come into conflict with counsel's ethical obligation to refrain from pressing frivolous claims and to be candid with opposing counsel and the court.

The A.B.A. Code of Professional Responsibility provides:[1]

EC 6-1 Because of his vital role in the legal process, a lawyer should act with competence and proper care in representing clients. He should strive to become and remain proficient in his practice and should accept employment only in matters which he is or intends to become competent to handle.

EC 7-1 The duty of a lawyer, both to his client and to the legal system, is to represent his client zealously within the bounds of the law, which includes Disciplinary Rules and enforceable professional regulations.

DR 7-102 Representing a Client Within the Bounds of the Law

A. In his representation of a client, a lawyer shall not:

2. Knowingly advance a claim or defense that is unwarranted under existing law, except that he may advance such claim or defense if it can be supported by good faith argument for an extension, modification, or reversal of existing law.

DR 7-106 Trial Conduct

B. In presenting a matter to a tribunal, a lawyer shall disclose:

1. Legal authority in the controlling jurisdiction known to him to be directly adverse to the position of his client and which is not disclosed by opposing counsel.

Counsel's relationship with an adversary whom counsel must face frequently may interfere with the kind of forceful, uncompromising representation to which the client is entitled. For example, an attorney with several cases presenting similar claims may be placed in a position of comparing the relative strength of those claims, to the detriment of some clients. In addition, counsel working for an institution such as a prosecutor's office may need to consider the implications of a position taken in one case for other cases. For example, if a prosecutor concedes on appeal that the trial assistant made improper statements during summation in a particular case, defense counsel will doubtless argue in subsequent cases in which similar remarks were made that "even the prosecution concedes that such statements are improper."

When the appellate court has assigned counsel to represent an indigent client, counsel's role as an officer of the court may come into conflict with undivided loyalty to the client's desires. When a client is entitled to an appeal as of right, but the case presents no meritorious claims, counsel will be unable to satisfy both the court and the client. Counsel's task is made even more complicated in

---

[1] Similar provisions are contained in the A.B.A. Model Rules of Professional Conduct. See 1.1 and 3.1.

light of the difficulty of classifying claims as frivolous, weak, or strong. The law is not a science, so that reasonably competent attorneys may well differ regarding an assessment of a claim as frivolous, as opposed to merely weak. And it is not hard to imagine that counsel's judgment about whether an issue might be meritorious could be affected, consciously or not, by whether the client is in a position to pay the costs of framing and developing that issue.

Effective Assistance of Appellate Counsel

The appellate attorney's task consists primarily of trying to convince an appellate court that the client, whether appellant or respondent, should prevail on the claims presented to the court. In order to perform that role, the attorney should, of course, follow all applicable rules in the court in which the case is pending. Failure to follow required procedures can have disastrous consequences for the client, as the following case demonstrates.

Evitts v. Lucey

469 U.S. 387 (1985)

Justice BRENNAN delivered the opinion of the Court.

Douglas v. California, 372 U.S. 353 (1963), held that the Fourteenth Amendment guarantees a criminal defendant the right to counsel on his first appeal as of right. In this case, we must decide whether the Due Process Clause of the Fourteenth Amendment guarantees the criminal defendant the effective assistance of counsel on such an appeal.

I

On March 21, 1976, a Kentucky jury found respondent guilty of trafficking in controlled substances. His retained counsel filed a timely notice of appeal to the Court of Appeals of Kentucky, the state intermediate appellate court. Kentucky Rule of Appellate Procedure 1.095(a)(1) required appellants to serve on the appellate court the record on appeal and a "statement of appeal" that was to contain the names of appellants and appellees, counsel, and the trial judge, the date of judgment, the date of notice of appeal, and additional information. . . . Respondent's counsel failed to file

a statement of appeal when he filed his brief and the record on appeal on September 12, 1977.

When the Commonwealth filed its brief, it included a motion to dismiss the appeal for failure to file a statement of appeal. The Court of Appeals granted this motion because "appellant has failed to supply the information required by RAP 1.095(a)(1)." Respondent moved for reconsideration, arguing that all of the information necessary for a statement of appeal was in fact included in his brief, albeit in a somewhat different format. At the same time, respondent tendered a statement of appeal that formally complied with the Commonwealth Rules. The Court of Appeals summarily denied the motion for reconsideration. Petitioner sought discretionary review in the Supreme Court of Kentucky, but the judgment of the Court of Appeals was affirmed in a one-sentence order. In a final effort to gain state appellate review of his conviction, respondent moved the trial court to vacate the judgment or to grant a belated appeal. The trial court denied the motion. Respondent then sought federal habeas corpus relief in the United States District Court for the Eastern District of Kentucky. He challenged the constitutionality of the Commonwealth's dismissal of his appeal because of his lawyer's failure to file the statement of appeal, on the ground that the dismissal deprived him of his right to effective assistance of counsel on appeal guaranteed by the Fourteenth Amendment. The District Court granted respondent a conditional writ of habeas corpus ordering his release unless the Commonwealth either reinstated his appeal or retried him.[3] Petitioner appealed to the Court of Appeals for the Sixth Circuit, which reached no decision on the merits but instead remanded the case to the District Court for determination whether respondent had a claim under the Equal Protection Clause.

On remand, counsel for both parties stipulated that there was no equal protection issue in the case, the only issue being whether the Commonwealth's action in dismissing respondent's appeal violated the Due Process Clause. The District Court thereupon reissued the conditional writ of habeas corpus. On January 12, 1984, the Court of Appeals for the Sixth Circuit affirmed the judgment of the District Court. . . . We granted the petition for certiorari. . . . We affirm.

II

Respondent has for the past seven years unsuccessfully pursued every avenue open to him in an effort to obtain a decision on the merits of his appeal and to prove that his conviction was unlawful. The Kentucky appellate courts' refusal to hear him on the merits of his claim does not stem from any view of those merits, and respondent does not argue in this Court that the Common-

wealth was constitutionally required to render judgment on the appeal in his favor. Rather the issue we must decide is whether the Commonwealth's dismissal of the appeal, despite the ineffective assistance of respondent's counsel on appeal, violates the Due Process Clause of the Fourteenth Amendment.

Before analyzing the merits of respondent's contention, it is appropriate to emphasize two limits on the scope of the question presented. First, there is no challenge to the District Court's finding that respondent indeed received ineffective assistance of counsel on appeal. Respondent alleges – and petitioners do not deny in this Court – that his counsel's failure to obey a simple court rule that could have such drastic consequences required this finding. We therefore need not decide the content of appropriate standards for judging claims of ineffective assistance of appellate counsel. *Cf. Strickland v. Washington,* 466 U.S. 668 (1984); *United States v. Cronic,* 466 U.S. 648 (1984). Second, the stipulation in the District Court on remand limits our inquiry solely to the validity of the State's action under the Due Process Clause of the Fourteenth Amendment.[5]

Respondent's claim arises at the intersection of two lines of cases. In one line, we have held that the Fourteenth Amendment guarantees a criminal appellant pursuing a first appeal as of right certain minimum safeguards necessary to make that appeal "adequate and effective," *see Griffin v. Illinois,* 351 U.S. 12, 20 (1956); among those safeguards is the right to counsel, *see Douglas v. California,* 372 U.S. 353 (1963). In the second line, we have held that the trial-level right to counsel, created by the Sixth Amendment and applied to the States through the Fourteenth Amendment, *see Gideon v. Wainwright,* 372 U.S. 335, 344 (1963), comprehends the right to effective

---

[3] The District Court also referred respondent's counsel to the Board of Governors of the Kentucky State Bar Association for disciplinary proceedings for "attacking his own work product." Respondent is not represented by the same counsel before this Court.

[5] Seemingly, respondent entered the stipulation because his attorney on appeal had been retained, not appointed.

assistance of counsel. . . . The question presented in this case is whether the appellate-level right to counsel also comprehends the right to effective assistance of counsel.

A

Almost a century ago, the Court held that the Constitution does not require States to grant appeals as of right to criminal defendants seeking to review alleged trial court errors. *McKane v. Durston,* 153 U.S. 684 (1894). Nonetheless, if a State has created appellate courts as "an integral part of the . . . system for finally adjudicating the guilt or innocence of a defendant," *Griffin v. Illinois,* 351 U.S. at 18, the procedures used in deciding appeals must comport with the demands of the Due Process and Equal Protection Clauses of the Constitution. In *Griffin* itself, a transcript of the trial court proceedings was a prerequisite to a decision on the merits of an appeal. *See id.,* at 13-14. We held that the State must provide such a transcript to indigent criminal appellants who could not afford to buy one if that was the only way to assure an "adequate and effective" appeal. *Id.,* at 20. . . .

Just as a transcript may by rule or custom be a prerequisite to appellate review, the services of a lawyer will for virtually every layman be necessary to present an appeal in a form suitable for appellate consideration on the merits. *See Griffin, supra,* at 20. Therefore, *Douglas v. California, supra,* recognized that the principles of *Griffin* required a State that afforded a right of appeal to make that appeal more than a "meaningless ritual" by supplying an indigent appellant in a criminal case with an attorney. . . .

B

Gideon v. Wainwright, supra, held that the Sixth Amendment right to counsel was "'so fundamental and essential to a fair trial, and so, to due process of law, that it is made obligatory upon the States by the Fourteenth Amendment.'" *Id.,* at 340. . . . *Gideon* rested on the "obvious truth"

that lawyers are "necessities, not luxuries" in our adversarial system of criminal justice. 372 U.S., at 344. "The very premise of our adversary system of criminal justice is that partisan advocacy on both sides of a case will best promote the ultimate objective that the guilty be convicted and the innocent go free." *Herring v. New York,* 422 U.S. 853, 862 (1975). The defendant's liberty depends on his ability to present his case in the face of "the intricacies of the law and the advocacy of the public prosecutor," *United States v. Ash,* 413 U.S. 300, 309 (1973); a criminal trial is thus not conducted in accord with due process of law unless the defendant has counsel to represent him.[6]

As we have made clear, the guarantee of counsel "cannot be satisfied by mere formal appointment,' *Avery v. Alabama,* 308 U.S. 444, 446 (1940). "That a person who happens to be a lawyer is present at trial alongside the accused, however, is not enough to satisfy the constitutional command . . . An accused is entitled to be assisted by an attorney, whether retained or appointed, who plays the role necessary to ensure that the trial is fair." *Strickland v. Washington,* 466 U.S., at 685. . . . Because

_____

[6] Our cases dealing with the right to counsel – whether at trial or on appeal – have often focused on the defendant's need for an attorney to meet the adversary presentation of the prosecutor. *See, e.g., Douglas v. California,* 372 U.S. 353, 358 (1963) (noting the benefit of "counsel's examination into the record, research of the law, and marshalling of arguments on [client's] behalf"). Such cases emphasize the defendant's need for counsel in order to obtain a *favorable* decision. The facts of this case emphasize a different, albeit related, aspect of counsel's role, that of expert professional whose assistance is necessary in a legal system governed by complex rules and procedures for the defendant to obtain a decision at all – much less a favorable decision – on the merits of the case. In a situation like that here, counsel's failure was particularly egregious in that it essentially waived respondent's opportunity to make a case on the merits; in this sense, it is difficult to distinguish respondent's situation from that of someone who had no counsel at all. *Cf. Anders v. California,* 386 U.S. 738 (1967).

the right to counsel is so fundamental to a fair trial, the Constitution cannot tolerate trials in which counsel, though present in name, is unable to assist the defendant to obtain a fair decision on the merits.

As the quotation from *Strickland, supra,* makes clear, the constitutional guarantee of effective assistance of counsel at trial applies to every criminal prosecution, without regard to whether counsel is retained or appointed. . . . The constitutional mandate is addressed to the action of the State in obtaining a criminal conviction through a procedure that fails to meet the standards of due process of law. "Unless a defendant charged with a serious offense has counsel able to invoke the procedural and substantive safeguards that distinguish our system of justice, a serious risk of injustice infects the trial itself. When a State obtains a criminal conviction through such a trial, it is the State that unconstitutionally deprives the defendant of his liberty." *Cuyler v. Sullivan, supra,* at 343 (citations omitted).

C

The two lines of cases mentioned – the cases recognizing the right to counsel on a first appeal as of right and the cases recognizing that the right to counsel at trial includes a right to effective assistance of counsel – are dispositive of respondent's claim. In bringing an appeal as of right from his conviction, a criminal defendant is attempting to demonstrate that the conviction, and the consequent drastic loss of liberty, is unlawful. To prosecute the appeal, a criminal appellant must face an adversary proceeding that – like a trial – is governed by intricate rules that to a layperson would be hopelessly forbidding. An unrepresented appellant – like an unrepresented defendant at trial – is unable to protect the vital interests at stake. To be sure, respondent did have nominal representation when he brought this appeal. But nominal representation on an appeal as of right – like nominal representation at

trial – does not suffice to render the proceedings constitutionally adequate; a party whose counsel is unable to provide effective representation is in no better position than one who has no counsel at all.

A first appeal as of right therefore is not adjudicated in accord with due process of law if the appellant does not have the effective assistance of an attorney. . . .

Recognition of the right to effective assistance of counsel on appeal requires that we affirm the Sixth Circuit's decision in this case. Petitioners object that this holding will disable state courts from enforcing a wide range of vital procedural rules governing appeals. Counsel may, according to petitioners, disobey such rules with impunity if the state courts are precluded from enforcing them by dismissing the appeal.

Petitioners' concerns are exaggerated. The lower federal courts – and many state courts – overwhelmingly have recognized a right to effective assistance of counsel on appeal. These decisions do not seem to have had dire consequences for the States' ability to conduct appeals in accordance with reasonable procedural rules. . . .

To the extent that a State believes its procedural rules are in jeopardy, numerous courses remain open. For example, a State may certainly enforce a vital procedural rule by imposing sanctions against the attorney, rather than against the client. Such a course may well be more effective than the alternative of refusing to decide the merits of an appeal and will reduce the possibility that a defendant who was powerless to obey the rules will serve a term of years in jail on an unlawful conviction. If instead a State chooses to dismiss an appeal when an incompetent attorney has violated local rules, it may do so if such action does not intrude upon the client's due process rights. For instance the Commonwealth of Kentucky itself in other contexts has permitted a postconviction attack on the trial judgment as "the appropriate remedy for a frustrated right of appeal," *Hammershoy v. Commonwealth,* 398 S.W.2d 883 (Ky

1966); this is but one of several solutions that state and federal courts have permitted in similar cases. A system of appeal as of right is established precisely to assure that only those who are validly convicted have their freedom drastically curtailed. A State may not extinguish this right because another right of the appellant – the right to effective assistance of counsel – has been violated. . . .

Notes

1. The Court's recognition of a right to the effective assistance of counsel in the first appeal as of right in a criminal case is premised on the due process clause. Other rights of appellants in criminal cases, such as the right to a free transcript, had been based on the equal protection clause. The equal protection clause would not have provided a remedy for Mr. Lucey, however, since the attorney handling his appeal had been retained, rather than appointed.

2. No similar right to the effective assistance of counsel exists in civil cases. A party aggrieved by incompetent representation in a civil suit is limited to seeking relief through a malpractice action against the attorney.

3. The parties in *Evitts* agreed that the attorney failed to provide effective assistance of counsel when he omitted a critical step in the appellate process. The appellate attorney who neglects to inform a client of the right to appeal, or who fails to comply with the procedural requirements to have the case heard by the appellate court, has not provided effective assistance of counsel. For example, in *Clay v. Director, Juvenile Division, Department of Corrections,* 749 F.2d 427 (7th Cir. 1984), the federal court found that a state practitioner had provided ineffective assistance of counsel when he let lapse the time to appeal the denial of a motion to vacate the judgment, while unsuccessfully pursuing an amended motion to vacate. Since Illinois case law was clear in holding that successive motions to vacate do not toll the running of the appeal period, appeal from the denial of the *original* motion was the only route to relief. *Id.* at 431. *See also Miller v. McCarthy,* 607 F.2d 854 (9th Cir. 1979) (hearing ordered to determine whether counsel had in fact been retained, and then failed to prosecute appeal). Such instances of failure to perfect an appeal constitute incompetent representation because they have no conceivable strategic purpose and are clearly damaging to the client, in that the appellate court declines to hear the merits of the case at all.

4. The attorney who meets all the necessary deadlines and files a brief in the appellate court is much less likely to be deemed ineffective than one who fails to get the court's attention altogether. If the brief consists of one sentence, however, or if, in three sentences, it merely invites the court to review the transcript to determine whether appellant's guilt was established beyond a reasonable doubt, counsel's representation may be found inadequate. *See e.g. Passmore v. Estelle,* 607 F.2d 662 (5th Cir. 1979); *High v. Ray,* 519 F.2d 109 (9th Cir. 1975).

5. Aside from missed deadlines and totally superficial briefs, the other main reason for a finding of ineffective assistance of appellate counsel is failure to argue a

meritorious issue that might well have secured reversal of the conviction or sentence. Courts faced with claims of ineffective assistance of appellate counsel generally rely on the definition of ineffectiveness of trial counsel set forth by the Supreme Court in *Strickland v. Washington,* 466 U.S. 668 (1984). The Court, recognizing the temptation, in looking at trial strategies that proved unsuccessful, to see specific acts or omissions as unreasonable, announced a presumption of competent representation. *Id.* at 689. In order to overcome this presumption, a defendant must show both that counsel's conduct fell below the standard of reasonably competent representation, and second, demonstrate a reasonable probability that, but for counsel's unprofessional error, the result of the proceeding would have been different. *Id.* at 694. It is thus not sufficient that an arguable issue was not raised; appellant must be able to show a likelihood that the judgment would have been reversed, or at least modified, if the issue had been presented.[2] *See e.g. People v. De La Hoz,* 131 A.D.2d 154, 158, 520 N.Y.S.2d 386 (N.Y.App.Div. 1987).

6. Courts are in the process of further defining the meaning of ineffective assistance of counsel in the context of particular types of appeals. A threshold question, considered by the Seventh Circuit in *Gray v. Greer,* is what an appellate court must examine before deciding a claim of ineffective assistance of counsel. The series of cases that follows illustrates the kinds of omissions that have caused courts to grant relief based on ineffective assistance of appellate counsel.

Gray v. Greer

800 F.2d 644 (7th Cir. 1986)

FLAUM, Circuit Judge.

In 1978, petitioner David Gray was convicted of rape, attempted murder and armed robbery and sentenced to sixty years in prison. Petitioner appeals from the dismissal of his habeas corpus petition. For the reasons stated below, we reverse the magistrate's order of dismissal and remand to the district court for proceedings consistent with this opinion.

David Gray was first tried for the rape of Ann Brewer on March 28, 1978. His defense was mistaken identity. The government's case was weakened by the inability of one eyewitness to identify Gray and the lack of corroborating physical evidence to support the in-court identification of Gray

by the complaining witness. The trial resulted in a hung jury. The state retried Gray, presenting an additional witness, a former cellmate of Gray's who testified that he had heard Gray admit to the crimes. This time, the jury convicted Gray. The Illinois State Appellate Defender's office represented Gray on appeal of his conviction. The appellate brief raised the following issues: 1) insufficiency of the evidence; 2) improper use of the testimony of Gray's former cellmate; 3) misleading remarks by the prosecutor regarding reasonable doubt; and 4) improper sentencing. The Illinois Appellate Court upheld Gray's conviction and the Illinois Supreme Court denied leave to appeal.

---

[2] Failure to raise a nonfrivolous issue has, in fact, specifically been held *not* to deny an indigent appellant the right to effective assistance of counsel. *See Jones v. Barnes, infra.*

Gray filed a habeas corpus petition in federal court . . . The petition alleged ineffective assistance of appellate counsel and improper jury selection procedures. The parties agreed to proceed before a magistrate pursuant to 28 U.S.C. § 636(c). The magistrate . . . reviewed Gray's brief on direct appeal and concluded that appellate counsel was not ineffective but rather "did a good job in citing applicable case law. . . . The four issues raised are wide-ranging and forcefully argued." The magistrate then found that "Gray's legal representation by the appellate public defender was, in fact, well above the average in the profession." The magistrate dismissed Gray's claim of improper jury selection procedures, finding that absent constitutionally defective counsel, petitioner could not show cause for the failure to raise this issue on direct appeal. This appeal followed.

I.

Petitioner contends that the district court erred in dismissing his claim of ineffective assistance of counsel without reviewing the record or conducting an evidentiary hearing. In dismissing petitioner's claim of ineffective assistance of appellate counsel, the magistrate did not review the trial court record. Instead, the magistrate relied solely on his examination of the appellate brief, and, finding the brief to be "a thorough discussion of the four issues raised," determined that appellate counsel was not ineffective. The basis for the district court's failure to examine the record was a reluctance to "second guess" appellate counsel regarding the choice of appropriate issues for appeal.

The right to appellate counsel is now firmly established. *Evitts v. Lucey,* 469 U.S. 387 (1985). *Strickland v. Washington,* 466 U.S. 668 (1984), established the standard for ineffective assistance of counsel, and though it is phrased in terms of ineffective assistance of trial counsel, it can be used as a basis for establishing a standard for effective assistance of appellate coun-

sel. Under *Strickland,* ineffective assistance of counsel will be found when "counsel's conduct so undermined the proper functioning of the adversarial process that the trial cannot be relied on as having produced a just result." *Strickland* at 2064. The *Strickland* standard envisions a two-prong analysis. First, counsel's performance must have been deficient, and second, the deficiency must have prejudiced the defense. *Id.* Had appellate counsel failed to raise a significant and obvious issue, the failure could be viewed as deficient performance. If an issue which was not raised may have resulted in a reversal of the conviction, or an order for a new trial, the failure was prejudicial. Were it legitimate to dismiss a claim of ineffective assistance of counsel on appeal solely because we found it improper to review appellate counsel's choice of issues, the right to effective assistance of counsel on appeal would be worthless. When a claim of ineffective assistance of counsel is based on failure to raise viable issues, the district court must examine the trial court record to determine whether appellate counsel failed to present significant and obvious issues on appeal. Significant issues which could have been raised should then be compared to those which were raised. Generally, only when ignored issues are clearly stronger than those presented, will the presumption of effective assistance of counsel be overcome.

The district court supported its decision by analogy to cases in which we have declined to "second guess" trial counsel's strategic decisions. These cases, however, are inapposite. They involved decisions of counsel which were arguably appropriate at the time, but, with the benefit of "hindsight," appeared less than brilliant. A reviewing court can evaluate appellate counsel's choice of issues on appeal by examining the trial record and the appellate brief. While it is true that decisions which were arguably correct at the time will not be "second-guessed," a reviewing court must initially determine whether such decisions were, in fact, strategic.

Respondent may well be correct in its assertion that appellate counsel strategically chose not to raise certain issues on appeal. We hold only that the determination of whether the decision was strategic requires an examination of the trial record. In conducting such an examination, the district court should be guided by defendant's careful presentation of those issues which allegedly should have been raised on appeal, with accompanying citations to the trial record.

. . . .

In holding that a reviewing court must review the trial record, we emphasize that the right to effective assistance of appellate counsel does not require an attorney to advance every conceivable argument on appeal which the trial record supports. *Evitts v. Lucey,* 469 U.S. 387 (1985); *Jones v. Barnes,* 463 U.S. 745 (1983). We require only that appellate counsel's choice of issues for appeal did not fall below "an objective standard of reasonableness." *Strickland v. Washington,* 466 U.S. 668 (1984).

We therefore remand to the district court with instructions to review the trial court record and determine whether the issues which petitioner claims appellate counsel failed to raise, would have been clearly more likely to result in reversal or an order for a new trial, and were so obvious from the trial record that the failure to present such issues amounted to ineffective assistance of appellate counsel.

Petitioner further seeks an evidentiary hearing to resolve his claim of ineffective assistance of counsel. An evidentiary hearing is required only if a review of the record is not sufficient to resolve factual disputes regarding the choice of issues. Given the nature of petitioner's claims, it is difficult to envision the evidence or testimony which petitioner would present at such a hearing. When a claim of ineffective assistance of counsel is based on failure to raise issues on appeal, we note it is the exceptional case that could not be resolved on an examination of the record alone. We leave the determination of whether an evidentiary hearing is required to the discretion of the district court after review of the trial court record.

. . . .

Tyler v. State

507 So.2d 660 (Fla. Dist. Ct. App. 1987)

PER CURIAM.

The *pro se* petition for a writ of habeas corpus, alleging ineffectiveness of appellate counsel, is granted. Petitioner's conviction for first degree murder and armed robbery was affirmed by this court, *per curiam,* in 1980. The petition raises three grounds for relief, one of which has merit.

Petitioner's counsel on appeal committed fundamental error in failing to argue that the trial court erred in refusing to sequester the jury during deliberation in the capital trial. It is undisputed that the trial court denied defense counsel's timely motion for sequestration during the jury delib-

eration. The issue was properly preserved for appeal. In *Taylor v. State,* 498 So.2d 943 (Fla. 1986), the supreme court held that it is reversible error *per se* for a trial court to refuse to sequester a jury during deliberations. The court found that such reasoning in *Livingston v. State,* 458 So.2d 235 (Fla. 1984), a capital case, was equally applicable to non-capital cases. The court, in *Taylor,* cited *Raines v. State,* 65 So.2d 558 (Fla. 1953).

In *Johnson v. Wainwright,* 498 So.2d 938 (Fla. 1986), the supreme court held that the petitioner's appellate counsel was ineffective for failing to raise the jury separation issue on direct appeal, even though *Livingston* had not yet been decided, because in *Raines* it was determined that reversible error occurred where a jury was allowed to separate for fifteen hours during deliberations. In *Johnson,* it was recognized that a new appeal was unnecessary because undisputed reversible error had occurred and appellate counsel proved ineffective in failing to raise it. The court, therefore, granted the petition, vacated the sentences, and directed that he be retried.

We recognize that a new trial ten years after petitioner's initial arrest will pose serious difficulties for the state, which has committed no error causing this decision. However, *Johnson* requires that this petition be granted.

We therefore reverse the judgment and sentence in this cause and remand for a new trial.

People v. Reyes

542 N.Y.S.2d 178 (N.Y. App. Div. 1989)

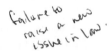

MEMORANDUM DECISION.

Application by defendant, *pro se,* for a writ of error *coram nobis* pursuant to *People v. Bachert,* 69 N.Y.2d 593, 516 N.Y.S.2d 623, 509 N.E.2d 318, on grounds of ineffective assistance of assigned appellate counsel, unanimously granted, to the extent of permitting defendant to file a brief on the issue of whether the prosecution's exercise of peremptory challenges to remove all Hispanic veniremen comports with the constitutional standards set forth in *Batson v. Kentucky,* 476 U.S. 79, and made retroactively applicable hereto under *Griffith v. Kentucky,* 479 U.S. 314, said filing to occur no later than the October 1989 Term, and the order of this Court affirming the judgment of conviction [*People v. Reyes,* 131 A.D.2d 982, 516 N.Y.S.2d 1002] is vacated, and determination of defendant's entire appeal held in abeyance pending further review and order of this Court.

On June 9, 1987, this Court heard defendant's appeal from a judgment of the Supreme Court, New York County rendered March 21, 1985, which, after a jury trial, convicted defendant of criminal sale of a controlled substance in the first degree (P.L. §220.43), and criminal possession of a controlled substance in the first degree (P.L.§220.21), and sentenced him to two concurrent indeterminate terms of impris-

onment of from 15 years to life. The judgment was unanimously affirmed by this Court on June 23, 1987, and leave to appeal to the Court of Appeals was denied on October 1, 1987.

On April 30, 1986, a date subsequent to the trial but prior to both the November 25, 1986 filing of appellant's brief and the June 9, 1987 appellate argument, the United States Supreme Court issued its decision in *Batson v. Kentucky, supra,* which held that the Equal Protection Clause of the Fourteenth Amendment forbids prosecutorial exercise of peremptory challenges to exclude potential jurors solely on the basis of race or on the assumption that they could not impartially determine the State's case against a defendant of the same race. It is appellate counsel's failure to raise a *Batson* claim on appeal which forms the basis of the within *pro se* writ of error *coram nobis* by defendant.

In the transcripts of the trial proceedings is contained the following application by trial counsel:

My second motion is for a mistrial on the grounds that [the prosecutor] deliberately and knowingly excluded Hispanics from the jury panel and as a matter of fact during the challenges there was one individual with an Italian name [and the prosecutor] left him on and then became very, very concerned about the fact because he thought he might be Hispanic but it was too late to knock him off.

Inasmuch as this assertion of prosecutorial exercise of racially-motivated peremptory challenges appears on the record and, indeed, was not challenged or otherwise answered by the prosecutor, defendant argues, and we agree, that the record was sufficient to alert appellate counsel of the existence of a *Batson* issue and to, at minimum, warrant further investigation on that question. Had counsel, for example, ordered the minutes of the colloquy among trial counsel and the court during *voir dire*, which was the only portion of the *voir dire* proceedings recorded, he would have obtained the following additional information on this issue:

> [Defense Counsel]: [The prosecutor] challenged the only Hispanic on the panel.
> [Prosecutor]: I would indicate that the

People have a right to exercise peremptory challenges as they desire.

* * *

> [Defense Counsel]: Let the record reflect [the prosecutor] again excluded all the Hispanics who were on the next panel.

In light of the fact that the use of peremptory challenges by the prosecutor to systematically exclude Hispanics from the jury for discriminatory purposes would, if established, warrant a reversal and a new trial, *Batson v. Kentucky, supra* . . . we find appellate counsel's omission of argument in this regard sufficient ground to constitute ineffective assistance with respect thereto. . . .

Accordingly, the writ of error *coram nobis* is granted, the order of this Court affirming the judgment of conviction vacated, and defendant is permitted to develop and argue his claim that the prosecutor improperly exercised peremptory challenges to exclude Hispanic persons from the jury.

Notes

1. As these cases show, the mechanism for raising a claim of ineffective assistance of appellate counsel varies among the jurisdictions. In Florida, a writ of habeas corpus is appropriate; in New York, a common law writ of error *coram nobis* must be filed in the appellate court.

2. The *Reyes* case illustrates the importance of incorporating any favorable developments in the law subsequent to the trial in the appellate brief. Almost universally, defendants are entitled to the benefits of such expanded rights, as long as their direct appeal is still pending when the new case is announced. Given modern communications and technology, counsel can be held to a stringent standard of knowledge regarding recent developments in the law. In a district court decision granting relief based on ineffective assistance of trial counsel, the key omission concerned counsel's failure to be aware of the fact that the United States Supreme Court had granted certiorari in a case from another circuit on a question of the proper interpretation of the statute being applied to the defendant. *McNamara v. United States,* 867 F.Supp. 369 (E.D. Va. 1994).

3. The relief secured by a claim of ineffective assistance of appellate counsel is usually the granting of another appeal, often with new counsel assigned. If, however, as was the case in *Tyler,* the error is fully reflected in the record and requires *per*

se reversal, the appellate court may vacate the conviction as part of the proceeding in which appellant demonstrated that counsel was ineffective.

Special Concerns of Assigned Appellate Counsel

A. The No-Merit Appeal

The question of what an appellate attorney must do to represent a client effectively on an appeal can become complicated when the attorney is assigned to provide representation to an indigent defendant on an appeal as of right. The case that follows, *Anders v. California,* involves the situation where the assigned attorney decides that the case is not worth the court's attention, in that no nonfrivolous issues would be raised by the appeal.

Anders v. California

386 U.S. 738 (1967)

Mr. Justice CLARK delivered the opinion of the Court.

We are here concerned with the extent of the duty of a court-appointed appellate counsel to prosecute a first appeal from a criminal conviction, after that attorney has conscientiously determined that there is no merit to the indigent's appeal.

After he was convicted of the felony of possession of marijuana, petitioner sought to appeal and moved that the California District Court of Appeal appoint counsel for him. Such motion was granted; however, after a study of the record and consultation with petitioner, the appointed counsel concluded that there was no merit to the appeal. He so advised the court by letter and, at the same time, informed the court that petitioner wished to file a brief in his own behalf. At this juncture, petitioner requested the appointment of another attorney. This request was denied and petitioner proceeded to file his own brief *pro se.* The State responded and petitioner filed a reply brief. On January 9, 1959, the District Court of Appeal unanimously affirmed the conviction, *People v. Anders,* 167 Cal.App.2d 65, 333 P.2d 854.

On January 21, 1965, petitioner filed an application for a writ of habeas corpus in the District Court of Appeal in which he sought to have his case reopened. In that application he raised the issue of deprivation of the right to counsel in his original appeal because of the court's refusal to appoint counsel at the appellate stage of the proceedings. The court denied the application on the same day, in a brief unreported memorandum opinion. The court stated that it "ha[d] again reviewed the record and [had] determined the appeal [to be] without merit." . . . On June 25, 1965, petitioner submitted a petition for a writ of habeas corpus to the Supreme Court of California, and the petition was denied without opinion by that court on July 14, 1965. Among other trial errors, petitioner claimed that both the judge and the prosecutor had commented on his failure to testify contrary to the holding of this Court in *Griffin v. California,* 380 U.S. 609 (1965). We have concluded that California's action does not comport with fair procedure and lacks that equality that is required by the Fourteenth Amendment.

I.

For a decade or more, a continuing line of cases had reached this Court concerning discrimination against the indigent defendant on his first appeal. Beginning with *Griffin v. Illinois,* 351 U.S. 12 (1956), where it was held that equal justice was not afforded an indigent appellant where the nature of the review "depends on the amount of money he has," at 19, and continuing through *Douglas v. California,* 372 U.S. 353 (1963), this Court has consistently held invalid those procedures "where the rich man, who appeals as of right, enjoys the benefit of counsel's examination into the record, research of the law, and marshalling of arguments on his behalf, while the indigent, already burdened by a preliminary determination that his case is without merit, is forced to shift for himself." At 358. . . .

II.

In petitioner's case, his appointed counsel wrote the District Court of Appeal, stating:

> "I will not file a brief on appeal as I am of the opinion that there is no merit to the appeal. I have visited and communicated with Mr. Anders and have explained my views and opinions to him. . . . [H]e wishes to file a brief in this matter on his own behalf."

The District Court of Appeal, after having examined the record, affirmed the conviction. We believe that counsel's bare conclusion, as evidenced by his letter, was not enough. . . . Here the court appointed-counsel had the transcript but refused to proceed with the appeal because he found no merit in it. He filed a no-merit letter with the District Court of Appeal whereupon the court examined the record itself and affirmed the judgment. On a petition for a writ of habeas corpus some six years later it found the appeal had no merit. It failed, however, to say whether it was frivolous or not, but, after consideration, simply found the petition to be "without merit." The Supreme Court, in dismissing this habeas corpus application, gave no rea-

son at all for its decision and so we do not know the basis for its action. We cannot say that there was a finding of frivolity by either of the California courts or that counsel acted in any greater capacity than merely as *amicus curiae.* . . . Hence California's procedure did not furnish petitioner with counsel acting in the role of an advocate nor did it provide that full consideration and resolution of the matter as is obtained when counsel is acting in that capacity. The necessity for counsel so acting is highlighted by the possible disadvantage the petitioner suffered here. In his *pro se* brief, which was filed in 1959, he urged several trial errors but failed to raise the point that both the judge and the prosecutor had commented to the jury regarding petitioner's failure to testify. In 1965, this Court in *Griffin v. California, supra,* outlawed California's comment rule, as embodied in Art. I, § 13, of the California Constitution.

III.

The constitutional requirement of substantial equality and fair process can only be attained where counsel acts in the role of an active advocate in behalf of his client, as opposed to that of *amicus curiae.* The no-merit letter and the procedure it triggers do not reach that dignity. Counsel should, and can with honor and without conflict, be of more assistance to his client and to the court. His role as advocate requires that he support his client's appeal to the best of his ability. Of course, if counsel finds his case to be wholly frivolous, after a conscientious examination of it, he should so advise the court and request permission to withdraw. That request must, however, be accompanied by a brief referring to anything in the record that might arguably support the appeal. A copy of counsel's brief should be furnished the indigent and time allowed him to raise any points that he chooses; the court – not counsel – then proceeds, after a full examination of all the proceedings, to decide whether the case is wholly frivolous. If it so finds it may grant counsel's request to withdraw and dismiss the appeal insofar as federal requirements are concerned, or proceed to a decision on the merits, if state law so requires. On the other hand, if it finds any of the legal points arguable on their merits (and therefore not frivolous) it must, prior to decision, afford the indigent the assistance of counsel to argue the appeal.

This requirement would not force appointed counsel to brief his case against his client but would merely afford the latter that advocacy which a nonindigent defendant is able to obtain. It would also induce the court to pursue all the more vigorously its own review because of the ready references not only to the record, but also to the legal authorities as furnished it by counsel. The no-merit letter, on the other hand, affords neither the client nor the court any aid. The former must shift entirely for himself while the court has only the cold record which it must review without the help of an advocate. Moreover, such handling would tend to protect counsel from the constantly increasing charge that he was ineffective and had not handled the case with that diligence to which an indigent defendant is entitled. This procedure will assure penniless defendants the same rights and opportunities on appeal – as nearly as is practicable – as are enjoyed by those persons who are in a similar situation but who are able to afford the retention of private counsel.

The judgment is reversed and the case is remanded for further proceedings not inconsistent with this opinion.

Note

Pursuant to the decision in *Anders,* most states set up procedures to be followed by assigned counsel who decide their client's appeal presents no meritorious issues. Wisconsin's rules included a requirement that counsel provide the court with reasons for the conclusion that the appeal would be frivolous. In the following case, *McCoy v. Court of Appeals of Wisconsin,* the Supreme Court rejected a public defender's challenge to this provision on the grounds that it required him to "brief his case against his client."

McCoy v. Court of Appeals of Wisconsin, District 1
486 U.S. 429 (1988)

Justice STEVENS delivered the opinion of the Court.

Like *Anders v. California,* 386 U.S. 738 (1967), this case concerns the scope of court-appointed appellate counsel's duty to an indigent client after counsel has conscientiously determined that the indigent's appeal is wholly frivolous. In *Anders,* we held that counsel could not withdraw by simply advising the court of his or her conclusion, but must include with the request to withdraw "a brief referring to anything in the record that might arguably support the appeal." *Id.* at 744. The Wisconsin Supreme Court has adopted a rule that requires such a brief also to include "a discussion of why the issue lacks merit." Appellant challenged the constitutionality of the rule in the Wisconsin Supreme Court. Over the dissent of three of its justices, the court upheld the rule, rejecting appellant's contentions that the rule is inconsistent with *Anders* and that it forces counsel to violate his or her client's Sixth Amendment rights. We noted probable jurisdiction, and now affirm.

I

Appellant is indigent. A Wisconsin trial

judge found him guilty of abduction and sexual assault and sentenced him to prison for 12 years. He has filed an appeal from that conviction and an attorney has been appointed to represent him. After studying the case, the attorney advised him that further appellate proceedings would be completely useless and that he had three options: He could voluntarily dismiss the appeal; he could go forward without a lawyer; or he could authorize the attorney to file a brief that would present the strongest arguments the lawyer could make in support of the appeal but would also advise the court of the lawyer's conclusion that the appeal is frivolous. Appellant selected the third option.

Appellant's counsel then prepared a brief that can fairly be characterized as schizophrenic. In his role as an advocate for appellant, counsel stated the facts, advanced four arguments for reversal, and prayed that the conviction be set aside. In his role as an officer of the court, counsel stated that further appellate proceedings on behalf of his client "would be frivolous and without any arguable merit," and prayed that he be permitted to withdraw. Thus, in the same document, the lawyer purported to maintain that there were arguments warranting a reversal and also that those arguments were wholly without merit. The brief did not contain an explanation of the reasons for counsel's conclusion. Instead, counsel explained why he believed that it would be both unethical and contrary to Anders to discuss the reasons why the appeal lacked merit. Because the brief did not comply with the discussion requirement in Rule 809.32(1), the court ordered it stricken and directed counsel to submit a conforming brief within 15 days.

Appellant's counsel did not comply with that order. Instead, after unsuccessfully attempting to obtain a ruling on the constitutionality of the rule in the appellate court, he filed an original action in the Wisconsin Supreme Court seeking to have the discussion requirement in Rule 809.32(1) declared unconstitutional. The supreme court agreed with portions of the appellant's argument, but rejected his ultimate conclusion. The court reaffirmed its acceptance of the principle that appointed counsel have the same obligations as paid counsel to provide their clients with adequate representation, and it agreed that the Anders opinion had not sanctioned a discussion requirement. Moreover, the court also agreed that it is ultimately the responsibility of the court – and not of counsel – to decide whether an appeal is wholly frivolous. It is explained, however, that the discussion requirement in the Wisconsin rule assists the court in making that determination:

> "When the court has before it a reasoned summary of the law militating against further appellate proceedings, it can be assured that the attorney has made an inquiry into the relative merits of the appeal and that the attorney's withdrawal request is valid and grounded in fact and in the law."

The court noted that because its procedures for handling frivolous appeals were far removed from the simple statement of counsel's conclusion that this Court condemned in Anders, they did not raise the "quality and equality of attorney representation" concerns that underlay our decision in Anders. The court also pointed out that the rule does not require an attorney to argue against his or her client; rather it merely requires the attorney to fulfill his or her duty to the courts. Accordingly, the court upheld the rule.

The dissenting justices expressed the view that the discussion requirement was not necessary and that it improperly required defense counsel to assume the role of either an amicus curiae or even an adversary, instead of acting exclusively as an advocate for the client.

In this Court appellant makes two basic attacks on the rule. He argues that it discriminates against the indigent appellant and that it violates his right to effective representation by an advocate. Both arguments rest largely on the assumption that retained counsel will seldom, if ever, advise an appellate court that he or she has concluded that a client's appeal is meritless, or provide the court with a discussion of the reasons supporting such a conclusion. In determining whether Wisconsin's rule requiring appointed counsel to provide an appellate court with such advice is constitutional, it is appropriate to begin by restating certain propositions established by our previous decisions concerning the right to counsel and the obligations of both paid and appointed counsel.

II

A State's enforcement of its criminal laws must comply with the principles of substantial equality and fair procedure that are embodied in the Fourteenth Amendment. The Sixth Amendment's requirement that "the accused shall enjoy the right to have the Assistance of Counsel for his defense" is therefore binding on the States. *Gideon v. Wainwright,* 372 U.S. 335 (1963). As we explained in *Gideon,* "in our adversary system of criminal justice, any person haled into court, who is too poor to hire a lawyer, cannot be assured a fair trial unless counsel is provided for him." *Id.,* at 344. It is therefore settled law that an indigent defendant has the same right to effective representation by an active advocate as a defendant who can afford to retain counsel of his or her choice. The "guiding hand of counsel," see *Powell v. Alabama,* 287 U.S. 45, 68-69 (1932), is essential for the evaluation of the prosecution's case, the determination of trial strategy, the possible negotiation of a plea bargain and, if the case goes to trial, making sure that the prosecution can prove the State's case with evidence that was lawfully obtained and may lawfully be considered by the trier of fact.

At the trial level, defense counsel's view of the merits of his or her client's case never gives rise to a duty to withdraw.

That a defense lawyer may be convinced before trial that any defense is wholly frivolous does not qualify his or her duty to the client or to the court. Ethical considerations and rules of court prevent counsel from making dilatory motions, adducing inadmissible or perjured evidence, or advancing frivolous or improper arguments, but those constraints do not qualify the lawyer's obligation to maintain that the stigma of guilt may not attach to the client until the presumption of innocence has been overcome by proof beyond a reasonable doubt.

After a judgment of conviction has been entered, however, the defendant is no longer protected by the presumption of innocence. If a convicted defendant elects to appeal, he retains the Sixth Amendment right to representation by competent counsel, but he must assume the burden of convincing an appellate tribunal that reversible error occurred at trial. Although trial counsel may remain silent and force the prosecutor to prove every element of the offense, counsel for an appellant cannot serve the client's interest without asserting specific grounds for reversal. In so doing, however, the lawyer may not ignore his or her professional obligations. Neither paid nor appointed counsel may deliberately mislead the court with respect to either the facts or the law, or consume the time and the energies of the court or the opposing party by advancing frivolous arguments. An attorney, whether appointed or paid, is therefore under an ethical obligation to refuse to prosecute a frivolous appeal.

When retained counsel concludes that an appeal would be frivolous, he or she has a duty to advise the client that it would be a waste of money to prosecute the appeal and that it would be unethical for the lawyer to go forward with it. When appointed counsel come to the same conclusion, the same duty to withdraw arises. Appointed counsel, however, is presented with a dilemma because withdrawal is not possible without leave of court, and advising the court of counsel's opinion that the appeal is frivolous would appear to conflict with the advocate's duty to the client. It is well settled, however, that this dilemma must be resolved by informing the court of counsel's conclusion. . . .

We reaffirmed this basic proposition in *Anders.* Moreover, the fact that an appointed appellate lawyer may find it necessary to file a motion to withdraw because he or she has concluded that an appeal is frivolous does not indicate that the indigent defendant has received less effective representation than the affluent. . . . In *Anders* we squarely held that the principle of substantial equality is not compromised when appointed counsel files a "no merit" brief even though such briefs are seldom, if ever, filed by retained counsel. As we stated in *Douglas v. California,* "[a]bsolute equality is not required." 372 U.S., at 357.

The principle of substantial equality does, however, require that appointed counsel make the same diligent and thorough evaluation of the case as a retained lawyer before concluding that an appeal is frivolous. Every advocate has essentially the same professional responsibility whether he or she accepted a retainer from a paying client or an appointment from a court. The appellate lawyer must master the trial record, thoroughly research the law, and exercise judgment in identifying the arguments that may be advanced on appeal. In preparing and evaluating the case, and in advising the client as to the prospects for success, counsel must consistently serve the client's interest to the best of his or her ability. Only after such an evaluation has led counsel to the conclusion that the appeal is "wholly frivolous" is counsel justified in making a motion to withdraw. This is the central teaching of *Anders.*

In *Anders* we held that a motion to withdraw must be accompanied by "a brief referring to anything in the record that might arguably support the appeal." 386

U.S., at 744. That requirement was designed to provide the appellate courts with a basis for determining whether appointed counsel have fully performed their duty to support their clients' appeals to the best of their ability. The *Anders* requirement assures that indigent defendants have the benefit of what wealthy defendants are able to acquire by purchase – a diligent and thorough review of the record and an identification of any arguable issues revealed by that review. Thus, the *Anders* brief assists the court in making the critical determination whether the appeal is indeed so frivolous that counsel should be permitted to withdraw.

III

The question whether the Wisconsin rule is consistent with our holding in *Anders* must be answered in light of the Wisconsin Supreme Court's explanation of the rule's requirements:

> "We interpret the discussion rule to require a statement of reasons why the appeal lacks merits which might include, for example, a brief summary of any case or statutory authority which appears to support the attorney's conclusions, or a synopsis of those facts in the record which might compel reaching that same result. We do not contemplate the discussion rule to require an attorney to engage in a protracted argument in favor of the conclusion reached; rather, we view the rule as an attempt to provide the court with 'notice' that there are facts on record or cases or statutes on point which would seem to compel a conclusion of no merit." 137 Wis.2d, at 100, 403 N.W.2d, at 454.

As so construed, the rule appears to require that the attorney cite the principal cases and statutes and the facts in the record that support the conclusion that the appeal is meritless. The rule also requires a brief statement of why these citations lead the attorney to believe the appeal lacks merit. The former requirement is, as far as the federal constitution is concerned, entirely unobjectionable. Attorneys are obligated to act with candor in presenting claims for judicial resolution. The rules of ethics already prescribe circumstances in which an attorney must disclose facts and law contrary to his or her client's interests.[14] That the Wisconsin rule requires counsel also to do so when seeking to withdraw on the ground that the appeal is frivolous does not deny the client effective assistance of counsel any more than the rules of ethics do.

The aspect of the rule that has provoked the concern of counsel for petitioner and other members of the defense bar is that which calls for the attorney to reveal the basis for his or her judgment. Although neither appellant nor *amici* supporting appellant debate the propriety of allowing defense counsel to satisfy his or her ethical obligations to the court by asserting his or her belief that the appeal is frivolous and seeking to withdraw, they do contend that requiring the attorney to assert the basis for this conclusion violates the client's Sixth and Fourteenth Amendment rights and is contrary to *Anders*. We disagree.

The Wisconsin rule is fully consistent with the objectives that are served by requiring that a motion to withdraw be ac-

companied by a brief referring to all claims that might arguably support the appeal. Unlike the typical advocate's brief in a criminal appeal, which has as its sole purpose the persuasion of the court to grant relief to the defendant, the *Anders* brief is designed to assure the court that the indigent defendant's constitutional rights have not been violated. To satisfy federal constitutional concerns, an appellate court faces two interrelated tasks as it rules on counsel's motion to withdraw. First, it must satisfy itself that the attorney has provided the client with a diligent and thorough search of the record for any arguable claim that might support the client's appeal. Second, it must determine whether counsel has correctly concluded that the appeal is frivolous. Because the mere statement of such a conclusion by counsel in *Anders* was insufficient to allow the court to make the required determinations, we held that the attorney was required to submit for the court's consideration references to anything in the record that might arguably support the appeal. Wisconsin's rule merely requires that the attorney go one step further. Instead of relying on an unexplained assumption that the attorney has discovered law or facts that completely refute the arguments identified in the brief, the Wisconsin court requires additional evidence of counsel's diligence. This requirement furthers the same interests that are served by the minimum requirements of *Anders*. Because counsel may discover previously unrecognized aspects of the law in the process of preparing a written explanation for his or her conclusion, the discussion requirement provides an additional safeguard against mistaken conclusions by counsel that the strongest arguments he or she can find are frivolous. Just like the references to favorable aspects of the record required by *Anders*, the discussion requirement may forestall some motions to withdraw and will assist the court in passing on the soundness of the lawyer's conclusion that the appeal is frivolous.

---

[14] Rule 3.3 of the ABA Model Rules of Professional Conduct (1984) provides in part:

"CANDOR TOWARD THE TRIBUNAL

"(a) A lawyer shall not knowingly:

"(1) make a false statement of material fact or law to a tribunal;

"(2) fail to disclose a material fact to a tribunal when disclosure is necessary to avoid assisting a criminal or fraudulent act by the client;

"(3) fail to disclose to the tribunal legal authority in the controlling jurisdiction known to the lawyer to be directly adverse to the position of the client and not disclosed by opposing counsel; or

"(4) offer evidence that the lawyer knows to be false.

The commentary to the rule explains, "[t]here are circumstances where failure to make a disclosure is the equivalent of an affirmative misrepresentation."

The rule does not place counsel in the role of *amicus curiae*. In *Anders,* petitioner argued that California's rule allowing counsel to withdraw on the basis of a conclusory statement that the appeal was meritless posed the danger that some counsel might seek to withdraw not because they thought the appeal frivolous but because, seeing themselves as friends of the court, they thought after weighing the probability of success against the time burdens on the court and the attorney if full arguments were presented that it would be best not to pursue the appeal. Brief for Petitioner in *Anders v. California,* O.T. 1966, No. 98. p. 13. We agreed that the California rule might improperly encourage counsel to consider the burden on the court in determining whether to prosecute an appeal. Wisconsin's rule requiring the attorney to outline why the appeal is frivolous obviously does not pose this danger.

We also do not find that the Wisconsin rule burdens an indigent defendant's right to effective representation on appeal or to due process on appeal. We have already rejected the contention that by filing a motion to withdraw on the ground that the appeal is frivolous counsel to an indigent defendant denies his or her client effective assistance of counsel or provides a lesser quality of representation than an affluent defendant could obtain. If an attorney can advise the court of his or her conclusion that an appeal is frivolous without impairment of the client's fundamental rights, it must follow that no constitutional deprivation occurs when the attorney explains the basis for that conclusion. A supported conclusion that the appeal is frivolous does not implicate Sixth or Fourteenth Amendment concerns to any greater extent than does a bald conclusion. . . .

It bears emphasis that the attorney's obligations as an advocate are not diminished by the additional requirement imposed by the Wisconsin rule. The attorney must still provide his or her client precisely the services that an affluent defendant could obtain from paid counsel – a thorough review of the record and a discussion of the strongest arguments revealed by that review. In searching for the strongest arguments available, the attorney must be zealous and must resolve all doubts and ambiguous legal questions in favor of his or her client. Once that obligation is fulfilled, however, and counsel has determined that the appeal is frivolous – and therefore that the client's interests would not be served by proceeding with the appeal – the advocate does not violate his or her duty to the client by supporting a motion to withdraw with a brief that complies with both *Anders* and the Wisconsin rule.

The judgment of the Wisconsin Supreme Court is affirmed.

Justice KENNEDY took no part in the consideration or decision of this case.

Justice BRENNAN, with whom Justice MARSHALL and Justice BLACKMUN join, dissenting.

Indigent and incarcerated, appellant Ellis T. McCoy fights an uphill battle to overturn his conviction. Standing alone, he is hardly a match against the formidable resources the State has committed to keeping him behind bars. Appellant's most crucial ally in this fight is the court-appointed appellate counsel that the State is constitutionally obligated to furnish him. Because the very State that is resolved to deprive appellant of liberty pays his defense counsel, he might understandably suspect his defender's allegiance. Sensitive to that natural distrust, we have always assured indigent defendants such as appellant that our Constitution's guarantee that "the accused shall enjoy the right . . . to have the Assistance of Counsel for his defense," U.S. Const., Amdt. 6, "contemplates the services of an attorney devoted solely to the interests of his client." *Von Moltke v. Gillies,* 332 U.S. 708, 725 (1948) (plurality opinion) (citation omitted). We have counseled them not to fear that they will receive no more justice than they can afford, because the "constitutional requirement of substantial equality and fair process" means that the rich and poor alike deserve "the same rights and opportunities on appeal. . . ." *Anders v. California,* 386 U.S. 738, 744, 745 (1967). The Court today reneges on these longstanding assurances by permitting a State to force its appointed defender of the indigent to advocate against his client upon unilaterally concluding that the client's appeal lacks merit. I dissent.

I

"The very premise of our adversary system of criminal justice is that partisan advocacy on both sides of a case will best promote the ultimate objective that the guilty be convicted and the innocent go free." *Herring v. New York,* 422 U.S. 853, 862 (1975). Accordingly, our Constitution imposes on defense counsel an "overarching duty," *Strickland v. Washington,* 466 U.S. 668, 688 (1984), to "advanc[e] 'the undivided interests of his client,'" *Polk County v. Dodson,* 454 U.S. 312, 318-319 (1981) (quoting *Ferri v. Ackerman,* 444 U.S. 193, 204 (1979)), and on the State a concomitant "constitutional obligation . . . to respect the professional independence of the public defenders whom it engages," 454 U.S., at 321-322 (footnote omitted). Once "the process loses its character as a confrontation between adversaries, the constitutional guarantee is violated." *United States v. Cronic,* 466 U.S. 648, 656-657 (1984) (footnote omitted). Our commitment to the adversarial process, we have repeatedly recognized, is every bit as crucial on appeal of a criminal conviction as it is at trial. *See, e.g., Douglas v. California,* 372 U.S. 353 (1963); *Entsminger v. Iowa,* 386 U.S. 748, 751 (1967); *Evitts v. Lucey,* 469 U.S. 387 (1985). On appeal, as at trial, our Constitution guarantees the accused "an active advocate, rather than a mere friend of the court assisting in a detached evaluation of the appellant's claim." *Evitts, supra,* at 394 (citations omitted).

Naturally, the defense counsel's duty to advocate, whether on appeal or at trial, is tempered by ethical rules. For example, counsel may not in her zeal to advocate her client's case fabricate law or facts or suborn perjury, and must at times disclose law contrary to her client's position. Similarly, defense counsel have an ethical duty not to press appeals they believe to be frivolous, even though other lawyers might see an issue of arguable merit. For retained counsel, who may decline to represent a paying client in what counsel believes to be a frivolous appeal, the latter duty does not interfere with the duty of unwavering allegiance to the client. Since, however, court-appointed counsel may withdraw only with court approval, the indigent client who insists on pursuing an appeal his counsel finds frivolous presents a unique dilemma: Appointed counsel, cast ostensibly in the role of defender, must announce to the court that will rule on her client's appeal that she believes her client has no case.

We have struck a delicate balance permitting an appointed counsel to satisfy his ethical duty to the court in the manner that least compromises the constitutional duty to advocate his client's case and that thereby minimizes the disadvantage to the indigent. Our cases make abundantly clear that an appointed counsel's constitutional duty to advocate zealously on his client's behalf does not end abruptly upon his conclusion that the client has no case. We have, for example, flatly disapproved of a regime that permits appointed defense counsel – or anyone other than the appellate tribunal itself – to adjudge finally the worthiness of an indigent defendant's appeal.

Similarly, our Constitution strictly limits the appointed counsel's latitude to depart from the role of defender – either by declining to advocate at all or, worse yet, by opposing the client – when that counsel believes his client's appeal lacks merit. In *Anders, supra,* we held that a court may not permit appointed counsel to withdraw from a criminal appeal on the basis of the bald assertion that "'there is no merit to the appeal.'" Instead, appointed counsel's "role as advocate requires that he support his client's appeal to the best of his ability" and that any request to withdraw on the ground that the appeal is frivolous "must . . . be accompanied by a brief referring to anything in the record that might arguably support the appeal." Central to our analysis was the constitutional imperative to "assure penniless defendants the same rights and opportunities on appeal – as nearly as is practicable – as are enjoyed by those persons who are in a similar situation but who are able to afford the retention of private counsel." This "constitutional requirement of substantial equality and fair process," we held, "can only be attained where counsel acts in the role of an active advocate in behalf of his client, as opposed to that of *amicus curiae.*" We took pains to emphasize that the *Anders*-brief requirement "would not force appointed counsel to brief his case against his client but would merely afford the latter that advocacy which a nonindigent defendant is able to obtain." . . .

Appointed counsel must advocate anything in the record arguably supporting the client's position. When counsel has nothing further to say in his client's defense, he should say no more. At that point, an unadorned statement that counsel believes the appeal to be frivolous satisfies the appointed counsel's constitutional duty to his client and ethical duty to the court, and any further discussion of the merits impermissibly casts defense counsel in the role of *amicus.*

II

Wisconsin's Rule 809.32(1) forces appointed counsel to do exactly what we denounced in . . . *Anders.* The rule begins with the requirement, consistent with *Anders,* that appointed counsel "shall file with the court of appeals . . . a brief in which is stated anything in the record

that might arguably support the appeal," but in the next breath it departs from *Anders'* prescription by requiring also "a discussion of why the issue lacks merit." Wis. Rule App. Proc. 809.32(1). The Wisconsin Supreme Court . . . extolled the discussion requirement "as a significant administrative aid to the reviewing court [which] serves an informational function and, equally important, enables the court to operate in a more efficient, expeditious and cost-saving manner." . . . Far from providing the accused "Assistance of Counsel for his defense," as the Sixth Amendment mandates, the rule explicitly "force[s] appointed counsel to brief his case against his client."

The Court's curious conclusion that counsel nevertheless does not act as an *amicus curiae* when she files the requisite no-merit discussion is rooted in a single observation: that the requirement poses little danger that counsel, in deciding whether "to pursue the appeal," will improperly "weig[h] the probability of success against the time burdens on the court and the attorney." But declining to burden the court with another case or another brief is not the only, nor even the most common, sense in which counsel act as *amici.* . . . The most common definition of *"amicus curiae"* is "[a] person with a strong interest in or views on the subject matter of an action [who] petition[s] the court for permission to file a brief. . .to suggest a rationale consistent with its own views." Black's Law Dictionary 75 (5th ed., 1979). . . . Thus, the Wisconsin rule falls squarely within our flat prohibition against casting defense counsel in the role of *amici.*

Not only does Wisconsin's rule impinge upon the right to counsel, but – contrary to our admonition that "there can be no equal justice where the kind of appeal a man enjoys 'depends on the amount of money he has,'" *Douglas,* 372 U.S., at 355 (quoting *Griffin v. Illinois,* 351 U.S. 12, 19 (1956) (plurality opinion)) – it does so in manner that ensures the poor will not have "the same rights and opportunities on appeal" as the rich. *Anders, supra,* at 745. Central to the Court's contrary position is its repeated observation that neither rich nor poor are entitled to pursue a frivolous appeal. At issue here, however, is not the indigent's right "'to pester a court with frivolous arguments that cannot conceivably persuade the court,'" nor the right to a state-funded "unscrupulous attorney" to do so, but the indigent's right to the usual adversary appellate process to test the validity of a conviction even though a single attorney unilaterally concludes that the appeal lacks merit. Legal issues do not come prepackaged with the labels "frivolous" or "arguably meritorious." If such characterizations were typically unanimous or uncontroversial, we could freely permit defense counsel to decide finally whether an appeal should proceed, or to advise the court without any advocacy on their clients' behalf that an appeal is frivolous. It by no means impugns the legal profession's integrity to acknowledge that reasonable attorneys can differ as to whether a particular issue is arguably meritorious.

Therein lies the Wisconsin rule's inequity. When retained counsel in Wisconsin declines to appeal a case on the ground that he believes the appeal to be frivolous, the wealthy client can always seek a second opinion and might well find a lawyer who in good conscience believes it to have arguable merit. In no event, however, will any lawyer file in the wealthy client's name a brief that undercuts his position. In contrast, when appointed counsel harbors the same belief, the indigent client has no recourse to a second opinion, and (unless he withdraws his appeal) must respond in court to the arguments of his own defender. . . .

The Court is left, then, to justify the inequality on the basis of an imagined distinction between the "typical advocate's brief in a criminal appeal" and the *Anders* brief. It is true that the question presented to the court in an *Anders* brief (whether the appeal has arguable merit) differs from that presented in a brief on the merits (whether the accused should prevail). Any substantive difference between the two questions, however, does not in itself suggest, as the Court maintains, that counsel's advocacy on behalf of his client should be any less forceful in the one context than in the other. *Anders* itself makes clear that the role of counsel writing an *Anders* brief, like her role in a "typical advocate's brief," is to advocate. The no-merit letter filed by Anders' lawyer was flawed because it "did not furnish [Anders] with counsel acting *in the role of an advocate* nor did it provide that full consideration and resolution of the matter as is obtained when counsel is acting in that capacity," *Anders,* 386 U.S., at 743 (emphasis added). The *Anders* brief is supposed to aid the reviewing court, but not in the sense that an *amicus* does. Rather the *Anders* brief was designed to spare the reviewing court from having to sift through "only the cold record . . . *without the help of an advocate,*" *id.,* at 745 (emphasis added).

To be sure, the *Anders* brief, unlike the typical brief on the merits, concludes with an assertion – "This appeal is frivolous" – that is contrary to the client's interest. It does not, however, follow that "no constitutional deprivation occurs when the attorney explains the basis for that conclusion." Such a conclusion, the Court seems to agree, is no different in type from other statements that defense attorneys are obligated to make against their clients' best interests, such as an admission that the weight of authority is against the client's position or that certain facts belie the client's case. No one would suppose that the limited obligation to cite contrary law and facts translates into a general obligation to expose all the weaknesses in a client's case, or even to explain why the particular law or facts cited disfavor the defense. Merely because counsel constitutionally may take slight deviations from the role of advancing the client's undivided interests does not mean that counsel constitutionally may entirely abandon that role, nor even that counsel may depart from that role any more than is absolutely necessary to satisfy the ethical obligation.

Neither the Court nor the State identifies any interest that demands so drastic a departure from defense counsel's "overarching duty," *Strickland,* 466 U.S., at 688, to advocate "the undivided interests of his client," *Ferri v. Ackerman,* 444 U.S., at 204. No doubt, a counsel's refutation of the argument that he deems frivolous lightens the court's load, and in some circumstances might even expose an analytical flaw that is not apparent from counsel's bare conclusion. But an issue that is so clearly without merit as to be frivolous should reveal itself to the court as such with minimal research and no guidance. One might perhaps hypothesize an issue whose frivolity is so elusive as to require refutation. In such an event, as in every other stage of a criminal prosecution, the Wisconsin Supreme Court was surely correct that "[t]he court will be better equipped to make the correct decision about the potential merits of the appeal if it has before it not only the authori-

ties which might favor an appeal, but also the authorities which might militate against it." Never before, however, have we permitted a court to further the interest in having "powerful statements on both sides of [a] question" by compelling a single advocate to take both sides. *Cronic,* 466 U.S., at 655 (footnotes and internal quotations omitted). There is no more reason to command defense counsel to refute defense arguments they deem frivolous than there is to force them to refute their own arguments on the merits of nonfrivolous appeals. In either situation, the State has a corps of lawyers ready and able to perform that task.

III

The Court purports to leave unscathed the constitutional axiom that appellate counsel "must play the role of an active advocate, rather than a mere friend of the court," *Evitts,* 469 U.S., at 394. Our disagreement boils down to whether defense counsel who details for a court why he believes his client's appeal is frivolous befriends the client or the court. The Court looks at Wisconsin's regime and sees a friend of the client who "assur[es] that the constitutional rights of indigent defendants are scrupulously honored." I look at the same regime and see a friend of the court whose advocacy is so damning that the prosecutor never responds. Either way, with friends like that, the indigent criminal appellant is truly alone.

Notes

1. Is the Court correct in its conclusion that the indigent defendant is not denied equal protection by assigned counsel's motion to withdraw on the ground that an appeal would be frivolous? Consider the following comment by Chief Justice Jack G. Day of the Ohio Court of Appeals:

I can never remember a case, really never, in a long life at the Bar . . . where if the money was there the appeal was so frivolous that the lawyer couldn't make it. I'm not suggesting nobody ever stood up and said grandly, "Take away that $10,000; there's nothing to this case; I will not appeal it." Maybe that happened, but maybe there are angels in the balcony, too. . . . Moreover, there is always the probability that unless there's an excellent reason, beyond being busy, the lawyer at least ought to be told that he might try to present what the client wanted. He doesn't have to argue as his own points matters that are stupid or ridiculous, but at least there ought to be some effort made to present the point the client believes important.

Proceedings at the National Judicial Conference on Standards for the Administration of Criminal Justice (1972), 57 F.R.D. 229, 309 (1973).

2. As the dissenters in *McCoy* pointed out, not all lawyers would agree on when an appeal is frivolous. In fact, the very notion of 'frivolousness' in the context of an appeal eludes precise and ready definition.[3] The ethical rules do not even attempt to define it, and the Supreme Court has not offered a definition, either. 'Frivolous' is a word that both litigants and judges tend to toss about with rather reckless abandon; while the word has become a free-lance pejorative in courthouses, it remains one with no settled definition. Generally, appellate courts use the word to rid themselves of the burden of writing an opinion on that issue. Courts seldom intend the term to describe as unethical appellate counsel's conduct in including a losing issue. By and large, though, 'frivolous' encompasses a sort of undebatable futility, an argument which "on its face requires no argument" to refute it. *See Bachrach v. Manhattan R.R. Co.,* 154 N.Y. 178, 47 N.E. 1087 (1897).

One authority has described the frivolous appeal as "a loser, not just a probable loser but a clearly hopeless loser." Hermann, *Frivolous Criminal Appeals,* 47 N.Y.U. L. Rev. 701, 707 (1972). He set forth the following attributes of such a case:

A frivolous criminal appeal can be concretely described even if it cannot be satisfactorily defined. It is an appeal with all or most of the following attributes: It is a loser, not just a probable loser, but a clearly hopeless loser, in the judgment of counsel who has read the record and researched the law. The record contains few, if any, motions or objections by defense counsel. No novel matter of constitutional law or statutory interpretation was raised below or is presented by the facts. The evidence of guilt is so overwhelming that most errors, even if clearly shown to be such, would have to be regarded as harmless ones. There is no evidence on or outside the record of official misconduct or overreaching tactics by the police or prosecution. Nothing which might strike a sympathetic chord in a reasonable person, either with regard to the defendant's character or his involve-

---

[3] The 25 pages of annotations in U.S.C.A. following Fed.R.App.P. 38, which provides – "If a court of appeals shall determine that an appeal is frivolous, it may award just damages and single or double costs to the appellee" – give some indication of the disagreement generated by the question of whether an appeal might be frivolous.

ment in the crime, is presented by the facts of the case. The only matters even tenuously assignable as error are evidentiary rulings which pertain to matters of small consequence, were not objected to in the trial court or can be faulted only by an abstruse exegesis of the law. During the trial, the judge did not conduct himself unseemingly or as an advocate for the prosecution; later, he delivered without objection a bland, technical charge to the jury, not attempting to marshal the evidence on either side. [footnotes omitted.]

Id. at 707.

3. Definitional problems aside, other factors make it hazardous even for conscientious appellate counsel to determine whether an appeal is frivolous. First, many appellate courts, both state and federal, affirm a large portion of appeals without writing any opinion; this practice makes it hard to discern which issues (and on which facts) were deemed to be so devoid of merit as to not even be worth the effort. Second, all intermediate federal (and most state) courts of appeal hear appeals in panels. The three or more appellate judges assigned to hear a particular day's calendar of cases are drawn from a much larger roster of judges who sit in that appellate court. It is much harder to predict an outcome with certainty in that appellate setting than it is in appellate courts where *all* judges hear and decide *all* appeals.

4. The rules of several of the federal courts of appeals impose an obligation on counsel assigned pursuant to the Criminal Justice Act to file a petition for writ of certiorari in the United States Supreme Court on behalf of any indigent defendant who requests that such a petition be filed. Must the attorney file a petition even when the case presents no meritorious claims? Faced with an attorney's application to withdraw as assigned counsel, the Supreme Court answered that question as follows:

> . . . nothing in the Criminal Justice Act compels counsel to file papers in contravention of this Court's Rules against frivolous filings. And though indigent defendants pursuing appeals as of right have a constitutional right to a brief filed on their behalf by an attorney, *Anders v. California,* 386 U.S. 738 (1967), that right does not extend to forums for discretionary review. *Ross v. Moffitt,* 417 U.S. 600, 616-617 (1974). Our Rules dealing with the grounds for granting certiorari, and penalizing frivolous filings, apply equally to petitioners using appointed or retained counsel.

Austin v. United States, 115 S. Ct. 380 (1994).

5. What should an appellate court do if it receives what it suspects to be an inadequate submission pursuant to *Anders v. California*? May the court independently (through its staff of law clerks) determine whether any meritorious issues are available for the appeal?

United States v. Zuluaga

981 F.2d 74 (2d Cir. 1992)

PER CURIAM.

Alba Denis Zuluaga helped her boyfriend, Herson Hoyos, distribute cocaine. She pled guilty to one count of conspiracy to distribute and possess with intent to distribute between 400 and 500 grams of cocaine, in violation of 21 U.S.C. §§ 846, 841(a)(1) and 841(b)(1)(C) (1988). Chief Judge Brieant sentenced her to fifty-one months imprisonment, three years of supervised release, a drug testing and treatment program, and a mandatory special assessment of fifty dollars. She appealed from this sentence.

Her appeal was first dismissed as untimely but was subsequently reinstated. Thereafter, her counsel, appointed pursuant to the Criminal Justice Act, filed a brief pursuant to *Anders v. California,* 386 U.S. 738 (1967), stating that there were no non-frivolous grounds for reversal. Based on his brief, counsel has moved to be relieved, and the government has moved for summary affirmance. We grant the motion to be relieved, deny the motion for summary affirmance, and order the appointment of new counsel.

The entire argument section of the *Anders* brief reads as follows:

> An examination of the record herein reveals no rulings by the Court regarding evidentiary or other matters which might be pursued on appeal. The sentence received by the defendant was within the applicable guideline level and the level fixed was the one most favorable to the defendant. Such a sentence is unappealable.

This brief conclusory statement does not fulfill counsel's obligations under *Anders,* which requires that counsel conduct a "conscientious examination" of possible grounds for appeal and submit a "brief referring to anything in the record that might arguably support the appeal," including references both to the record and to potentially applicable legal authorities. *Anders,* 386 U.S. at 744. Counsel's conclusory statement is inadequate under this standard.

Counsel's failure to submit a proper *Anders* brief works two harms. First, it fails "to assist an appellate court . . . in its review of a motion to affirm summarily a district court order or judgment." *Id.* Second, and more importantly, it amounts to a constructive denial of counsel to appellants. "The *Anders* requirement assures that indigent defendants have the benefit of what wealthy defendants are able to acquire by purchase – a diligent and thorough review of the record and an identification of any arguable issues revealed by that review." *McCoy v. Court of Appeals of Wisconsin,* 486 U.S. 429, 439 (1988); *see also Penson v. Ohio,* 488 U.S. 75, 82 n.4 (1988) (*Anders* briefs important element of right to counsel).

We thus come to the question of remedy. There are two options. The first option is for us to examine the record and determine on our own whether there are non-frivolous grounds to be argued. Should we determine that such grounds exist, we would then appoint new counsel. Should we determine that such grounds do not exist, we would grant the motions to be relieved as counsel and for summary affirmance. The second option is to appoint new counsel to pursue the appeal without our first determining whether there are non-frivolous arguments for reversal. We believe that only the second course affords appellant her right to counsel. In *Penson,* it was argued that new counsel was not necessary when an appellate court, after an inadequate *An-*

ders brief had been filed, had itself searched the record, found error (on less than all counts of conviction), and redressed it. *Id.* at 79. The Court held that judicial scrutiny is no substitute for adversary representation. *Id.* at 86-87. We believe that, similarly, a procedure in which appellate courts, after an inadequate *Anders* brief, review the record and appoint counsel only if they find nonfrivolous arguments is constitutionally inadequate. Indeed, in *Penson,* the requirement of counsel clearly concerned the counts of conviction that had been found not to give rise to a non-frivolous argument for reversal, precisely the *Anders* situation.

Accordingly, rather than inquire into the merits of Zuluaga's appeal, we order new counsel to be appointed to pursue the appeal. We do not of course preclude the filing of a proper *Anders* brief. The motion to be relieved is granted. The motion for summary affirmance is denied. We order the appointment of new counsel.

Note

Essentially, the courts refuse to consider whether the filing of an inadequate *Anders* brief might be harmless in a particular case. The defendant is entitled to actual appellate advocacy, and appellate courts will not speculate about whether such advocacy would have affected the outcome, particularly when the courts' speculation about possible prejudice would itself be conducted without the benefit of advocacy on behalf of the defendant. *See United States v. Burnett,* 989 F.2d 100 (2d Cir. 1993).

B. Whose Case is it Anyway?

Fortunately for conscientious appellate attorneys, Justice Day is right in believing that most trial records are not so error-free that the attorney has no choice but to file a no-merit brief. (*See Note 1.* at p. 236 above.) Even if a claim is a long shot, not likely to prevail in the particular court to which an appeal may be had, appellate counsel's duty of zealous representation requires that counsel, whether retained or appointed, present such a claim as effectively as possible. The case involving one or two relatively weak, but arguable claims thus does not usually present a problem for the diligent appellate attorney.

Much more difficult is the case with one or two very strong issues along with several weaker ones. The cases which follow, *Jones v. Barnes* and *People v. Vasquez,* explore the dilemma that may face an attorney when the client has a different view of how to proceed with the appeal.

Jones v. Barnes

463 U.S. 745 (1983)

Chief Justice BURGER delivered the opinion of the Court.

We granted certiorari to consider whether defense counsel assigned to prosecute an appeal from a criminal conviction has a constitutional duty to raise every nonfrivolous issue requested by the defendant.

I

In 1976, Richard Butts was robbed at knifepoint by four men in the lobby of an apartment building; he was badly beaten and his watch and money were taken. Butts informed a Housing Authority Detective that he recognized one of his assailants as a person known to him as "Froggy," and gave a physical description of the person to the detective. The following day the detective arrested respondent David Barnes, who is known as "Froggy."

Respondent was charged with first and second degree robbery, second degree assault, and third degree larceny. The prosecution rested primarily upon Butts' testimony and his identification of respondent. During cross-examination, defense counsel asked Butts whether he had ever undergone psychiatric treatment; however, no offer of proof was made on the substance or relevance of the question after the trial judge *sua sponte* instructed Butts not to answer. At the close of trial, the trial judge declined to give an instruction on accessorial liability requested by the defense. The jury convicted respondent of first and second degree robbery and second degree assault.

The Appellate Division of the Supreme Court of New York, Second Department, assigned Michael Melinger to represent respondent on appeal. Respondent sent Melinger a letter listing several claims

that he felt should be raised.[2] Included were claims that Butts' identification testimony should have been suppressed, that the trial judge improperly excluded psychiatric evidence, and that respondent's trial counsel was ineffective. Respondent also enclosed a copy of a *pro se* brief he had written.

In a return letter, Melinger accepted some but rejected most of the suggested claims, stating that they would not aid respondent in obtaining a new trial and that they could not be raised on appeal because they were not based on evidence in the record. Melinger then listed seven potential claims of error that he was considering including in his brief, and invited respondent's "reflections and suggestions" with regard to those seven issues. The record does not reveal any response to this letter.

Melinger's brief to the Appellate Division concentrated on three of the seven points he had raised in his letter to respondent: improper exclusion of psychiatric evidence, failure to suppress Butts' identification testimony, and improper cross-examination of respondent by the trial judge. In addition, Melinger submitted respondent's own *pro se* brief. Thereafter, respondent filed two more *pro se* briefs, raising three more of the seven issues Melinger had identified.

At oral argument, Melinger argued the three points presented in his own brief, but not the arguments raised in the *pro se* briefs. On May 22, 1978, the Appellate Division affirmed by summary order. The New York Court of Appeals denied leave to appeal.

On August 8, 1978, respondent filed a

---

[2] Respondent's letter is not in the record. Its contents may be inferred from Melinger's letter in response.

pro se petition for a writ of habeas corpus in the United States District Court for the Eastern District of New York. Respondent raised five claims of error, including ineffective assistance of trial counsel. The District Court held the claims to be without merit and dismissed the petition. The Court of Appeals for the Second Circuit affirmed, and we denied a petition for a writ of certiorari.

In 1980, respondent filed two more challenges in state court. On March 4, 1980, he filed a motion in the trial court for collateral review of his sentence. That motion was denied on April 28, and leave to appeal was denied on October 3. Meanwhile, on March 31, 1980, he filed a petition in the New York Court of Appeals for reconsideration of that court's denial of leave to appeal. In that petition, respondent for the first time claimed that his appellate counsel, Melinger, had provided ineffective assistance. The New York Court of Appeals denied the application on April 16, 1980.

Respondent then returned to United States District Court for the second time, with a petition for habeas corpus based on the claim of ineffective assistance by appellate counsel. The District Court concluded that respondent had exhausted his state remedies, but dismissed the petition, holding that the record gave no support to the claim of ineffective assistance of appellate counsel on "any . . . standard which could reasonably be applied." The District Court concluded:

> "It is not required that an attorney argue every conceivable issue on appeal, especially when some may be without merit. Indeed, it is his professional duty to choose among potential issues, according to his judgment as to their merit and his tactical approach."

A divided panel of the Court of Appeals reversed, 665 F.2d 427 (CA2 1981).[3] Lay-

ing down a new standard, the majority held that when "the appellant requests that [his attorney] raise additional colorable points [on appeal], counsel *must argue the additional points to the full extent of his professional ability." Id.* at 433 (emphasis added). In the view of the majority, this conclusion followed from *Anders v. California,* 386 U.S. 738 (1967). In *Anders,* this Court held that an appointed attorney must advocate his client's cause vigorously and may not withdraw from a nonfrivolous appeal. The Court of Appeals majority held that, since *Anders* bars counsel from abandoning a nonfrivolous appeal, it also bars counsel from abandoning a nonfrivolous issue on appeal.

> "[A]ppointed counsel's unwillingness to present particular arguments at appellant's request functions not only to abridge defendant's right to counsel on appeal, but also to limit the defendant's constitutional right of equal access to the appellate process. . . ." *Ibid.*

The Court of Appeals went on to hold that, "[h]aving demonstrated that appointed counsel failed to argue colorable claims at his request, an appellant need not also demonstrate a likelihood of success on the merits of those claims." *Id.,* at 434.

The court concluded that Melinger had not met the above standard in that he had failed to press at least two nonfrivolous claims: the trial judge's failure to instruct on accessory liability and ineffective assistance of trial counsel. The fact that these issues had been raised in respondent's own *pro se* briefs did not cure the error, since "[a] *pro se* brief is no substitute for the advocacy of experienced counsel." *Ibid.* The court reversed and remanded with instructions to grant the writ of habeas corpus unless the State assigned new counsel and granted a new appeal.

Circuit Judge Meskill dissented, stating

---

[3] By this time, at least 26 state and federal judges had considered respondent's claims that he was unjustly convicted for a crime committed five years earlier; and many of the judges had reviewed the case more than once. Until the latest foray, all courts had rejected his claims.

that the majority had overextended *Anders*. In his view, *Anders* concerned only whether an attorney must pursue nonfrivolous *appeals;* it did not imply that attorneys must advance all nonfrivolous *issues.*

We granted certiorari, and we reverse.

II

In announcing a new *per se* rule that appellate counsel must raise every nonfrivolous issue requested by the client,[4] the Court of Appeals relied primarily upon *Anders v. California, supra.* There is, of course, no constitutional right to an appeal, but in *Griffin v. Illinois*, 351 U.S. 12, 18 (1955), and *Douglas v. California*, 372 U.S. 353 (1963), the Court held that if an appeal is open to those who can pay for it, an appeal must be provided for an indigent. It is also recognized that the accused has the ultimate authority to make certain fundamental decisions regarding the case, as to whether to plead guilty, waive a jury, testify in his or her own behalf, or take an appeal, *see Wainwright v. Sykes*, 433 U.S. 72, 93 n. 1 (1977) (BURGER, C.J., concurring); ABA Standards for Criminal Justice 4-5.2, 21-22 (2d ed. 1980). In addition, we have held that, with some limitations, a defendant may elect to act as his or her own advocate, *Faretta v. California*, 422 U.S. 806 (1975). Neither *Anders* nor any other decision of this Court suggests, however, that the indigent defendant has a constitutional right to compel appointed counsel to press nonfrivolous points requested by the client, if counsel, as a matter of professional judgment, decides not to present those points.

This Court, in holding that a State must provide counsel for an indigent appellant on his first appeal as of right, recognized

the superior ability of trained counsel in the "examination into the record, research of the law, and marshalling of arguments on [the appellant's] behalf," *Douglas v. California*, 372 U.S., at 358. Yet by promulgating a *per se* rule that the client, not the professional advocate, must be allowed to decide what issues are to be pressed, the Court of Appeals seriously undermines the ability of counsel to present the client's case in accord with counsel's professional evaluation.

Experienced advocates since time beyond memory have emphasized the importance of winnowing out weaker arguments on appeal and focusing on one central issue if possible, or at most on a few key issues. Justice Jackson, after observing appellate advocates for many years, stated:

> "One of the first tests of a discriminating advocate is to select the question, or questions, that he will present orally. Legal contentions, like the currency, depreciate through over-issue. The mind of an appellate judge is habitually receptive to the suggestion that a lower court committed an error. But receptiveness declines as the number of assigned errors increases. Multiplicity hints at lack of confidence in any one. . . . [E]xperience on the bench convinces me that multiplying assignments of error will dilute and weaken a good case and will not save a bad one." Jackson, *Advocacy Before the Supreme Court*, 25 Temple L.Q. 115, 119 (1951).

Justice Jackson's observation echoes the advice of countless advocates before him and since. An authoritative work on appellate practice observes:

> "Most cases present only one, two, or three significant questions. . . . Usually, . . . if you cannot win on a few major points, the others are not likely to help, and to attempt to deal with a great many in the limited number of pages allowed for briefs will mean that none

---

[4] The record is not without ambiguity as to what respondent requested. We assume, for purposes of our review, that the Court of Appeals majority correctly concluded that respondent insisted that Melinger raise the issues identified, and did not simply accept Melinger's decision not to press those issues.

may receive adequate attention. The effect of adding weak arguments will be to dilute the force of the stronger ones." R. Stern, *Appellate Practice in the United States* 266 (1981).

There can hardly be any question about the importance of having the appellate advocate examine the record with a view to selecting the most promising issues for review. This has assumed a greater importance in an era when oral argument is strictly limited in most courts – often to as little as 15 minutes – and when page limits on briefs are widely imposed. Even in a court that imposes no time or page limits, however, the new *per se* rule laid down by the Court of Appeals is contrary to all experience and logic. A brief that raises every colorable issue runs the risk of burying good arguments – those that, in the words of the great advocate John W. Davis, "go for the jugular," Davis, *The Argument of an Appeal,* 26 A.B.A.J. 895, 897 (1940) – in a verbal mound made up of strong and weak contentions. *See generally, e.g.,* Godbold, *Twenty Pages and Twenty Minutes – Effective Advocacy on Appeal,* 30 Sw.L.J. 801 (1976).[6]

---

[6] The ABA Model Rules of Professional Conduct provide:

"A lawyer shall abide by a client's decisions concerning the objectives of representation . . . and shall consult with the client as to the means by which they are to be pursued . . . In a criminal case, the lawyer shall abide by the client's decision . . . as to plea to be entered, whether to waive jury trial and whether the client will testify." Model Rules of Professional Conduct, Proposed Rule 1.2(a) (Final Draft 1982) (emphasis added).

With the exception of these specified fundamental decisions, an attorney's duty is to take professional responsibility for the conduct of the case, after consulting with his client.

Respondent points to the ABA Standards for Criminal Appeals, which appear to indicate that counsel should accede to a client's insistence on pressing a particular contention on appeal, *see* ABA Standards for Criminal Justice 21-3.2, at 21-42 (2d ed. 1980). The ABA Defense Function Standards provide, however, that, with the exceptions specified above, strategic and tactical decisions are the exclusive province of the defense counsel, after consultation with the client.

This Court's decision in *Anders,* far from giving support to the new *per se* rule announced by the Court of Appeals, is to the contrary. *Anders* recognized that the role of the advocate "requires that he support his client's appeal to the best of his ability." 386 U.S., at 744. Here the appointed counsel did just that. For judges to second-guess reasonable professional judgments and impose on appointed counsel a duty to raise every "colorable" claim suggested by a client would disserve the very goal of vigor and effective advocacy that underlies *Anders.* Nothing in the Constitution or our interpretation of that document requires such a standard.[7] The judgment of the Court of Appeals is accordingly

Reversed.

Justice BLACKMUN, concurring in the judgment.

I do not join the Court's opinion, because I need not decide in this case whether there is or is not a constitutional right to a first appeal of a criminal conviction, and because I agree with Justice Brennan, and the American Bar Association, ABA Standards for Criminal Justice, Criminal Appeals, Standard 21-3.2, Comment, p. 21-42 (2d ed., 1980), that, as an ethical matter, an attorney should argue on appeal all nonfrivolous claims upon which his client insists. Whether or not one agrees with the Court's view of legal strategy, it seems to me that the lawyer, after giving his client

---

See ABA Standards for Criminal Justice 4-5.2 (2d ed. 1980). . . . In any event, the fact that the ABA may have chosen to recognize a given practice as desirable or appropriate does not mean that that practice is required by the Constitution.

[7] The only question presented by this case is whether a criminal defendant has a constitutional right to have appellate counsel raise every nonfrivolous issue that the defendant requests. The availability of federal habeas corpus to review claims that counsel declined to raise is not before us, and we have no occasion to decide whether counsel's refusal to raise requested claims would constitute "cause" for a petitioner's default within the meaning of *Wainwright v. Sykes,* 433 U.S. 72 (1977). See also *Engle v. Isaac,* 456 U.S. 107, 128 (1982).

his best opinion as to the course most likely to succeed, should acquiesce in the client's choice of which nonfrivolous claims to pursue.

Certainly, *Anders v. California*, 386 U.S. 738 (1967), and *Faretta v. California*, 422 U.S. 806 (1975), indicate that the attorney's usurpation of certain fundamental decisions can violate the Constitution. I agree with the Court, however, that neither my view, nor the ABA's view, of the ideal allocation of decisionmaking authority between client and lawyer necessarily assumes constitutional status where counsel's performance is "within the range of competence demanded of attorneys in criminal cases," *McCann v. Richardson*, 397 U.S. 759, 771 (1970), and "assure[s] the indigent defendant an adequate opportunity to present his claims fairly in the context of the State's appellate process," *Ross v. Moffitt*, 417 U.S. 600, 616 (1974). I agree that both these requirements were met here.

But the attorney, by refusing to carry out his client's express wishes, cannot forever foreclose review of nonfrivolous constitutional claims. As I noted in *Faretta v. California*, 422 U.S. 806, 848 (1975) (dissenting opinion), "[f]or such overbearing conduct by counsel, there is a remedy." . . . The remedy, of course, is a writ of habeas corpus. Thus, while the Court does not reach the question, I state my view that counsel's failure to raise on appeal nonfrivolous constitutional claims upon which his client has insisted must constitute "cause and prejudice" for any resulting procedural default under state law. *See Wainwright v. Sykes*, 433 U.S. 72 (1977).

Justice BRENNAN, with whom Justice MARSHALL joins, dissenting.

The Sixth Amendment provides that "[i]n all criminal prosecutions, the accused shall enjoy the right . . . to have the *Assistance* of counsel for his defence" (emphasis added). I find myself in fundamental disagreement with the Court over what a right to "the assistance of counsel" means.

The import of words like "assistance" and "counsel" seems inconsistent with a regime under which counsel appointed by the State to represent a criminal defendant can refuse to raise issues with arguable merit on appeal when his client, after hearing his assessment of the case and his advice, has directed him to raise them. I would remand for a determination whether respondent did in fact insist that his lawyer brief the issues that the Court of Appeals found were not frivolous.

It is clear that respondent had a right to the assistance of counsel in connection with his appeal. "As we have held again and again, an indigent defendant is entitled to the appointment of counsel to assist him on his first appeal. . . ." *Entsminger v. Iowa*, 386 U.S. 748, 751 (1967). In recognizing the right to counsel on appeal, we have expressly relied not only on the Fourteenth Amendment's Equal Protection Clause, which in this context prohibits disadvantaging indigent defendants in comparison to those who can afford to hire counsel themselves, but also on its Due Process Clause and its incorporation of Sixth Amendment standards. The two theories converge in this case also. A State may not incarcerate a person, whether he is indigent or not, if he has not had (or waived) the assistance of counsel at all stages of the criminal process at which his substantial rights may be affected. *Argersinger v. Hamlin*, 407 U.S. 25 (1972). In my view, that right to counsel extends to one appeal, provided the defendant decides to take an appeal and the appeal is not frivolous.[2]

The Constitution does not on its face define the phrase "assistance of counsel,"

---

[2] Both indigents and those who can afford lawyers have this right. However, with regard to issues involving the allocation of authority between lawyer and client, courts may well take account of paying clients' ability to specify at the outset of their relationship with their attorneys what degree of control they wish to exercise, and to avoid attorneys unwilling to accept client direction.

but surely those words are not empty of content. No one would doubt that counsel must be qualified to practice law in the courts of the State in question,[3] or that the representation afforded must meet minimum standards of effectiveness. *See Powell v. Alabama,* 287 U.S. 45, 71 (1932). To satisfy the Constitution, counsel must function as an advocate for the defendant, as opposed to a friend of the court. *Anders v. California,* 386 U.S., at 744. Admittedly, the question in this case requires us to look beyond those clear guarantees. What is at issue here is the relationship between lawyer and client — who has ultimate authority to decide which nonfrivolous issues should be presented on appeal? I believe the right to "the assistance of counsel" carries with it a right, personal to the defendant, to make that decision, against the advice of counsel if he chooses.

If all the Sixth Amendment protected was the State's interest in substantial justice, it would not include such a right. However, in *Faretta v. California,* 422 U.S. 806 (1975), we decisively rejected that view of the Constitution, ably advanced by Justice Blackmun in dissent. Holding that the Sixth Amendment requires that defendants be allowed to represent themselves, we observed:

"It is undeniable that in most criminal prosecutions defendants could better defend with counsel's guidance than by their own unskilled efforts. But where the defendant will not voluntarily accept representations by counsel, the potential advantage of a lawyer's training can be realized, if at all, only imperfectly. To force a lawyer on a defendant can only lead him to believe that the law contrives against him. . . . Personal liberties are not rooted in the law of averages. The right to defend is personal.

The defendant, and not his lawyer or the State, will bear the personal consequences of a conviction. It is the defendant, therefore, who must be free personally to decide whether in his particular case counsel is to his advantage." . . . 422 U.S., at 834.

Faretta establishes that the right to counsel is more than a right to have one's case presented competently and effectively. It is predicated on the view that the function of counsel under the Sixth Amendment is to protect the dignity and autonomy of a person on trial by assisting him in making choices that are his to make, not to make choices for him, although counsel may be better able to decide which tactics will be most effective for the defendant. *Anders v. California* also reflects that view. Even when appointed counsel believes an appeal has no merit, he must furnish his client a brief covering all arguable grounds for appeal so that the client may "raise any points that he chooses." 386 U.S., at 744.

The right to counsel as *Faretta* and *Anders* conceive it is not an all-or-nothing right, under which a defendant must choose between forgoing the assistance of counsel altogether or relinquishing control over every aspect of his case beyond its most basic structure (*i.e.,* how to plead, whether to present a defense, whether to appeal). A defendant's interest in his case clearly extends to other matters. Absent exceptional circumstances, he is bound by the tactics used by his counsel at trial and on appeal. *Henry v. Mississippi,* 379 U.S. 443, 451 (1963). He may want to press the argument that he is innocent, even if other stratagems are more likely to result in the dismissal of charges or in a reduction of punishment. He may want to insist on certain arguments for political reasons. He may want to protect third parties. This is just as true on appeal as at trial, and the proper role of counsel is to assist him in these efforts, insofar as that is possible consistent with the lawyer's conscience, the law, and his duties to the court.

---

[3] Of course, a State may also allow properly supervised law students to represent indigent defendants. *Argersinger v. Hamlin,* 407 U.S. 25, 40-41 (1972) (Brennan, J., concurring).

I find further support for my position in the legal profession's own conception of its proper role. The American Bar Association has taken the position that

"[W]hen, in the estimate of counsel, the decision of the client to take an appeal, *or the client's decision to press a particular contention on appeal,* is incorrect, [c]ounsel has the professional duty to give to the client fully and forcefully an opinion concerning the case and its probable outcome. *Counsel's role, however, is to advise. The decision is made by the client."* ABA Standards for Criminal Justice, Criminal Appeals, Standard 21-3.2, Comment, at 21-42 (1980) (emphasis added).

The Court disregards this clear statement of how the profession defines the "assistance of counsel" at the appellate stage of a criminal defense by referring to standards governing the allocation of authority between attorney and client at trial. In the course of a trial, however, decisions must often be made in a matter of hours, if not minutes or seconds. From the standpoint of effective administration of justice, the need to confer decisive authority on the attorney is paramount with regard to the hundreds of decisions that must be made quickly in the course of a trial. Decisions regarding which issues to press on appeal, in contrast, can and should be made more deliberately, in the course of deciding whether to appeal at all.

The Court's opinion seems to rest entirely on two propositions. First, the Court observes that we have not yet decided this case. This is true in the sense that there is no square holding on point, but as I explain above, *Anders* and *Faretta* describe the right to counsel in terms inconsistent with today's holding. Moreover, the mere fact that a constitutional question is open is no argument for deciding it one way or the other. Second, the Court argues that good appellate advocacy demands selectivity among arguments. That is certainly true –

the Court's advice is good. It ought to be taken to heart by every lawyer called upon to argue an appeal in this or any other court, and by his client. It should take little or no persuasion to get a wise client to understand that, if staying out of prison is what he values most, he should encourage his lawyer to raise only his two or three best arguments on appeal, and he should defer to his lawyer's advice as to which are the best arguments. The Constitution, however, does not require clients to be wise, and other policies should be weighed in the balance as well.

It is no secret that indigent clients often mistrust the lawyers appointed to represent them. . . . There are many reasons for this, some perhaps unavoidable even under perfect conditions – differences in education, disposition, and socio-economic class – and some that should (but may not always) be zealously avoided. A lawyer and his client do not always have the same interests. Even with paying clients, a lawyer may have a strong interest in having judges and prosecutors think well of him, and, if he is working for a flat fee – a common arrangement for criminal defense attorneys – or if his fees for court appointments are lower than he would receive for other work, he has an obvious financial incentive to conclude cases on his criminal docket swiftly. Good lawyers undoubtedly recognize these temptations and resist them, and they endeavor to convince their clients that they will. It would be naive, however, to suggest that they always succeed in either task. A constitutional rule that encourages lawyers to disregard their clients' wishes without compelling need can only exacerbate the clients' suspicion of their lawyers. As in *Faretta,* to force a lawyer's *decisions* on a defendant "can only lead him to believe that the law conspires against him." *See* 422 U.S., at 834. In the end, what the Court hopes to gain in effectiveness of appellate representation by the rule it imposes today may well be lost to decreased effectiveness in other areas of representation.

The Court's opinion also seems to overstate somewhat the lawyer's role in an appeal. While excellent presentation of issues, especially at the briefing stage, certainly serves the client's best interests, I do not share the Court's implicit pessimism about appellate judges' ability to recognize a meritorious argument, even if it is made less elegantly or in fewer pages than the lawyer would have liked, and even if less meritorious arguments accompany it. If the quality of justice in this country really depended on nice gradations in lawyers' rhetorical skills, we could not longer call it "justice." Especially at the appellate level, I believe that for the most part good claims will be vindicated and bad claims rejected, with truly skillful advocacy making a difference only in a handful of cases.[6] In most of such cases – in most cases generally – clients ultimately will do the wise thing and take their lawyers' advice. I am not willing to risk deepening the mistrust between clients and lawyers in all cases to ensure optimal presentation for that fraction-of-a-handful in which presentation might really affect the result reached by the Court of Appeals.

Finally, today's ruling denigrates the values of individual autonomy and dignity central to many constitutional rights, especially those Fifth and Sixth Amendment rights that come into play in the criminal process. Certainly a person's life changes when he is charged with a crime and brought to trial. He must, if he harbors any

hope of success, defend himself on terms – often technical and hard to understand – that are the State's, not his own. As a practical matter, the assistance of counsel is necessary to that defense. Yet, until his conviction becomes final and he has had an opportunity to appeal, any restrictions on individual autonomy and dignity should be limited to the minimum necessary to vindicate the State's interest in a speedy, effective prosecution. The role of the defense lawyer should be above all to function as the instrument and defender of the client's autonomy and dignity in all phases of the criminal process.

As Justice Black wrote in *Von Moltke v. Gillies*, 332 U.S. 708, 725-726 (1948):

> "The right of counsel guaranteed by the Constitution contemplates the services of an attorney devoted solely to the interests of his client. *Glasser v. United States*, 315 U.S. 60, 70. . . . Undivided allegiance and faithful, devoted service to a client are prized traditions of the American lawyer. It is this kind of service for which the Sixth Amendment makes provision. And nowhere is this service deemed more honorable than in case of appointment to represent an accused too poor to hire a lawyer, even though the accused may be a member of an unpopular or hated group, or may be charged with an offense which is peculiarly abhorrent." (footnote omitted).

The Court subtly but unmistakably adopts a different conception of the defense lawyer's role – he need do nothing beyond what the State, not his client, considers most important. In many ways, having a lawyer becomes one of the many indignities visited upon someone who has the ill fortune to run afoul of the criminal justice system.

I cannot accept the notion that lawyers are one of the punishments a person receives merely for being accused of a crime. Clients, if they wish, are capable of making informed judgments about which issues to

---

[6] I do not mean to suggest that this "handful" of cases is not important – it may well include many cases that shape the law. Furthermore, the relative skill of lawyers certainly makes a difference at the trial and pre-trial stages, when a lawyer's strategy and ability to persuade may do his client a great deal of good in almost every case, and when his failure to investigate facts or to present them properly may result in their being excluded altogether from the legal system's official conception of what the "case" actually involves.

appeal, and when they exercise that prerogative their choices should be respected unless they would require lawyers to violate their consciences, the law, or their duties to the court. On the other hand, I would not presume lightly that, in a particular case, a defendant has disregarded his lawyer's obviously sound advice. The Court of Appeals, in reversing the District Court, did not address the factual question whether respondent, having been advised by his lawyer that it would not be wise to appeal on all the issues respondent has suggested, actually insisted in a timely fashion that his lawyer brief the nonfrivolous issues identified by the Court of Appeals. If he did not, or if he was content with filing his *pro se* brief, then there would be no deprivation of the right to the assistance of counsel. I would remand for a hearing on this question.

Notes

1. The Justices clearly have very different views about the appropriate relationship between the assigned appellate attorney and the indigent client. What is the primary basis for Justice Blackmun's concurring opinion?

2. As with the assessment of when an appeal is frivolous (*See* Note 2 at p. 237 following *McCoy*), different attorneys may well have diverging views about which issues are "strong" and which ones should be omitted as "weak." Similarly, a particular panel of an appellate court may regard as reversible error what a different panel of the same court might dismiss as "without merit."

3. What could a lawyer do who is contacted by a defendant whose previous counsel failed to brief or argue an issue that seems meritorious?

People v. Vasquez

70 N.Y.2d 1, 509 N.E.2d 934, 516 N.Y.S.2d 921 (1987)

Per Curiam.

Defendant was granted leave to appeal by a Judge of this court so that we could determine whether he was denied effective assistance of counsel in his appeal to the Appellate Division.

After entry of the judgment against him, defendant appealed to the Appellate Division and, at his request, the court assigned appellate counsel to represent him. Counsel prepared his brief, stating in it that defendant had evaluated the record, and prefaced his discussion of the legal merits with this statement: "As shall be indicated this is the fifth point out of a total of ten points the defendant-appellant wishes his appellate counsel to address. It has substantial merit in light of two recent decisions of the United States Supreme Court in appellate counsel's opinion; *whereas the other points the defendant-appellant seeks to raise do not.*" (Emphasis added.) Counsel then developed and argued the one point he considered meritorious, ineffectiveness of trial counsel. He set forth defendant's remaining contentions in point II of the appellate brief as follows:

POINT II

"*THE REMAINING NINE POINTS THE DEFENDANT-APPELLANT REQUESTED HIS COUNSEL TO REVIEW HAVE BEEN CAREFULLY REVIEWED*

BY HIS COUNSEL, AND IN LIGHT OF THE RECORD, THE APPLICABLE STATUTORY AND CASE LAW, THEY HAVE BEEN FOUND TO BE WITHOUT MERIT."

"These points (issues), *which appellate counsel has reviewed and found to be lacking in merit,* as submitted by the defendant-appellant to his counsel, are as follows:" (emphasis added).

Counsel thus dismissed out of hand nine arguments that defendant wished to assert. In our view, the procedure he followed denied defendant effective assistance of counsel and requires reversal of the order appealed.

The rule in *Anders v. California* (386 U.S. 738, 744) permits appellate counsel to withdraw from representing a defendant if his appeal is "wholly frivolous." This was not a frivolous appeal, however; counsel determined that one of the issues advanced by defendant had substantial merit. That being so, counsel was duty bound to advance it and to serve as an "active advocate in behalf of his client" (*Anders v. California, supra,* at 744). He was not obliged to discuss the nine allegedly meritless claims his client wanted addressed (*see,*

Jones v. Barnes, 463 U.S. 745), and he should not have identified them and then disparaged them before the court. By doing so, counsel affirmatively undermined arguments his client wished the court to review and, for all practical purposes, precluded his client from presenting them effectively in a *pro se* brief.

The procedure to be followed by appellate counsel when a client requires that several points be presented to the court, some with merit and some with none, is to argue the claim found meritorious and make no comment about claims considered frivolous. As to them, counsel should instruct his client why he believes the points frivolous and advise him that if he still thinks they should be addressed, defendant may file a *pro se* brief with the court. If the client chooses to do so, counsel should protect his client's opportunity to submit written argument on the points by notifying the court of his intentions.

Inasmuch as the required procedure was not followed in this case, the order should be reversed and the matter remitted to the Appellate Division, which should assign new counsel and consider the appeal *de novo.* . . .

Note

Assume that counsel has followed the procedure set forth in *Vasquez* to deal with the situation where the client insists on presenting claims that, in the best professional judgment of the attorney about the most effective way to present the case, were omitted from the brief. The court allowed the client to file a *pro se* supplementary brief, which addresses issues that counsel knows to be very weak. How should the attorney respond, during oral argument, to questions from the court regarding those issues?

Pro Se Representation on Appeal

A defendant in a state criminal trial has a constitutional right to proceed without the assistance of counsel, assuming that the defendant possesses a minimal level of competence. *Faretta v. California,* 422 U.S. 806 (1975). As the following excerpt demonstrates, the right to self-representation on appeal is less clear.

Chamberlain v. Ericksen

744 F.2d 628 (8th Cir. 1984)

. . . Contrary to Chamberlain's argument, it is not settled whether the right of self-representation under *Faretta* extends to a defendant's appeal from a conviction. In *Price v. Johnston,* 334 U.S. 266 (1948), the Supreme Court recognized the discretionary power in an appellate court to allow a defendant to appear before it and participate in oral argument. The Court stated:

The discretionary nature of the power in question grows out of the fact that a prisoner has no absolute right to argue his own appeal or even to be present at the proceedings in an appellate court. . . . The absence of that right is in sharp contrast to his constitutional prerogative of being present in person at each significant stage of a felony prosecution. . . . Oral argument on appeal is not an essential ingredient of due process and it may be circumscribed as to prisoners where reasonable necessity so dictates.

Id. at 285-86.

The Court in *Faretta* quoted with approval the *Price* distinction between trial and appellate self-representation rights. This court and other courts have also expressly or implicitly recognized a difference between the right at trial and on appeal. In *Baker v. Arkansas,* 505 F.2d 750 (8th Cir. 1974) (*per curiam*), this court upheld an Arkansas Supreme Court rule requiring *pro se* briefs in criminal appeals to be accompanied by an affidavit stating that the prisoner prepared his or her brief without the assistance of another prison inmate. This court held that neither a person's right of access to the court nor the right to petition the court was impaired by the Arkansas court rule. In *In Re Walker,*

56 Cal. App. 3d 225, 128 Cal. Rptr. 291 (Cal. Ct. App. 1976), the California court cited the language quoted from *Faretta* and *Price* to support its holding that a criminal defendant has no constitutional right of self-representation on appeal.

A defendant's right to file a *pro se* brief or motion is distinguishable from a defendant's right to make oral argument before the court. We have no doubt that a defendant is not required to have counsel forced upon him or her. *See Price,* 334 U.S. at 280. This rule is true not only at trial but on appeal. Recognition of this principle lends itself to the recognition that all defendants have a basic right to address the court with a *pro se* brief.

In the present case, the Minnesota court entered an order allowing Chamberlain to file a *pro se* supplemental brief. The court also had the brief of the Public Defender. Chamberlain's problem was that the Public Defender denied Chamberlain access to his transcript.[2] Because the transcript is now available, this problem has been obviated. Under these circumstances, we feel we need not address Chamberlain's constitutional claims.

---

[2] The Court in *United States v. MacCollom,* 26 U.S. 317, 326 (1976) stated: "[t]he basic question is one of adequacy of respondent's access to procedures for review of his conviction. . . . *See also Britt v. North Carolina,* 404 U.S. 226 (1971) (stating that a state must provide an indigent defendant with a transcript of prior proceedings when that transcript is necessary to mounting an effective defense or appeal); *cf.* Note, *The Jailed Pro Se Defendant and the Right to Prepare a Defense,* 86 Yale L.J. 292 (1976) (arguing that an adequate opportunity to prepare one's own defense is a fundamental component of due process).

Notes

1. The Court of Appeals for the Fifth Circuit has recently expressed agreement with the Eighth Circuit, finding that a defendant is not required to accept unwanted counsel on appeal. *Myers v. Collins,* 8 F.3d 249, 252 (5th Cir. 1993). The court's decision did not appear to differentiate between *pro se* briefs filed by a client who chooses self-representation and those filed by a client represented by counsel: ". . . we hold that a state criminal defendant has a constitutional right to present *pro se* briefs and motions on appeal." *Id.*

2. Some courts do differentiate between appellants who are represented by counsel and those who wish to proceed entirely *pro se*. Courts addressing the issue of so-called "hybrid" representation on appeal generally regard the opportunity of the client to submit a *pro se* supplemental brief to be a matter within the courts' discretion, rather than a matter of entitlement: "Although there is no Sixth Amendment right to file a *pro se* brief when the appellant is represented by counsel, nothing precludes an appellate court from accepting the *pro se* brief and considering the arguments contained therein for whatever they may be worth." *Hayes v. Hawes,* 921 F.2d 100, 102 (7th Cir. 1990). *See also People v. White,* 73 N.Y.2d 468, 539 N.E.2d 577 (1989); *Whitfield v. State,* 517 So.2d 23 (Fla. Dist. Ct. App. 1987); *Callahan v. State,* 30 Md. App. 628, 354 A.2d 191 (1976). Some courts have expressed a policy against consideration of *pro se* briefs when appellant is represented by assigned counsel. *See e.g. Commonwealth v. Kibler,* 294 Pa. Super. 30, 439 A.2d 734 (1982). In such courts, the solution to disagreements between counsel and client suggested by the opinion of the New York Court of Appeals in *Vasquez* would obviously not be available.

3. Some courts, without declaring that clients generally have a right to present *pro se* briefs, have found such a right when counsel has filed an *Anders* brief. Would failure to allow a client to file a brief in light of counsel's motion to withdraw pursuant to *Anders* present constitutional problems?

4. As is suggested by the *Chamberlain* excerpt, defendants seeking to represent themselves are likely to have additional requests in connection with their attempts to persuade appellate courts of the merits of their claims. One court refused to give the defendant a free copy of his trial transcript, on the grounds that he effectively had access to the transcript through the attorney who had filed an *Anders* brief. *Perry v. Texas,* 456 F.2d 879 (5th Cir.), *cert. denied sub nom. Von Perry v. Texas,* 409 U.S. 916 (1972). The Eleventh Circuit, on the other hand, insisted that the state provide a defendant with a copy of his transcript in order to enable him to seek further discretionary review *pro se. Byrd v. Wainwright,* 722 F.2d 716 (11th Cir. 1984).

Chapter 7

The Appellate Brief

Introduction

The purpose of an appellate brief is to marshal the facts in a case and to present legal arguments on behalf of one party. It is the modern appellate advocate's most important means of persuading a court to rule in the client's favor. In more leisurely eras than our own, appellate practice was largely oral. Lawyers argued for hours and even days before the Supreme Court, and briefs were mere summaries of the points made at oral argument. Times have changed, however, and today the appellate brief is not only the most important, but often the only means of presenting a client's case as an increasing number of courts strictly limit oral argument.

The format of a brief is controlled by court rules. Rule 28 of the Federal Rules of Appellate Procedure governs the formal aspects of briefs submitted in the federal courts of appeals, but in addition, each circuit has its own rules concerning the format of briefs. Moreover, each state court has its own parallel rules. Court rules change frequently, and it is counsel's responsibility to keep abreast of them or risk the rejection of the brief for failure to conform. Certainly, a brief is more likely to persuade the court if it complies with the rules that the court has adopted governing how briefs should be written.

Many law offices, including prosecutors' offices and legal defenders' offices (as well as moot court honor societies), have their own style of brief-writing. If you work in such an office or are participating in a moot court competition, you will, of course, follow the preferred format. Unfortunately, however, experienced appellate practitioners, whether real or moot, frequently do not make clear to their new associates (sometimes because they themselves do not know) which of their rules of brief-writing are simply a matter of style and a desire for uniformity within the office, and which are basic rules of good appellate practice. The fact is that once a court's requirements have been satisfied, the appellate advocate has considerable freedom in matters of brief-writing style; there are only a few generally-accepted, hard and fast rules. Indeed, placement of one's own personal stamp on a brief can be desirable.

On the other hand, there are certain conventions of brief-writing, just as there are rules of etiquette, that one might as well follow unless there is a good reason for doing otherwise. For example, although generally we place the fork to the left of the plate when setting a table, if we are having soup for lunch we might decide to put a soup spoon there instead. In the absence of such a reason for straying from convention, however, we stick to the fork-on-left rule simply because it is convenient not to have to search for the silverware each time we dine. Likewise, in a particular case, there may be an excellent reason for summarizing the defense testimony before the prosecution testimony. Generally, however, one sets out the prosecution testimony first and this is the position in which judges expect to find it. There is nothing to be gained by surprising them unnecessarily with a variation from standard practice for, just as guests, faced for no apparent reason with a fork on the right, may conclude that we do not know any better, so a court faced with a needlessly unconventional brief may conclude that we have not bothered to learn standard appellate practice and hold it against us, however unfairly. The materials in this chapter are therefore designed first to help you understand the purpose behind many of the rules and conventions of appellate brief-writing so that you can judge them for yourself and second to provide guidance in writing an effective appellate brief.

Know Your Audience

The most important rule of writing generally is to keep in mind your audience. When writing an appellate brief, your audience is, of course, an appellate court. This fact gives you an enormous advantage over, say, a newspaper reporter, who must write to a large, general audience, the members of which vary considerably in knowledge, education, intelligence and interests. You, in contrast, have a small, specialized audience about which you have a large quantity of information.

You know, for example, not simply that your readers will be literate and intelligent, but also that they are judges who are generally familiar with the law. This tells you that you need not spend time in your brief explaining basic concepts – that the United States Constitution has a Bill of Rights contained in ten amendments the first of which guarantees freedom of speech – but can get right to your point that a law prohibiting burning the American flag violates the First Amendment.

You also may know that your audience has particular ideas on the subjects about which you are writing because they have expressed them in prior cases. Thus, you know which arguments in your case will be a waste of time and which have a chance of succeeding. For example, however strong your conviction that the identification of your client was unreliable, you will not argue that the police behaved improperly in displaying him to the complainant in a prompt, on-the-scene show-up to a court that has said many times that such show-ups are permissible.

Equally important as understanding what your audience already knows is keeping in mind what they do *not* know. What a court does not know is the facts in your case. Although at some point some or all of the judges may read the record in the case, in the first instance, and perhaps for always, the court will learn the facts of the case from the parties' briefs. This should indicate to you the importance of writing a clear, complete statement of facts. Likewise, although you can assume that the court is generally knowledgeable about the law, you should be aware that it may very well be unfamiliar with particular cases and statutes. Thus, you know to avoid unexplained string cites and to give the full text of the relevant parts of statutes.

A final and extremely important piece of information you have about the audience for an appellate brief is the circumstances under which the judges will be reading what you write. That is, they will not be settling down to read your brief for pleasure but rather because they have to. Moreover, you are aware of the realities of modern appellate adjudication; the volume of appeals has increased so many times during the past few decades that your brief will be one of perhaps hundreds that the judges have to read that month. Put yourself in the judges' position and imagine the relief they must feel upon finding in the midst of the ceiling-high pile of their required reading an accurate, concise, self-contained, well-reasoned, thoroughly-supported, elegantly-written, carefully-produced brief. Obviously, such a brief will make your client's case stand out from the many as one worthy of the court's careful review and will provide the judges with a useful tool to help them in making their decision. Such consideration for the judge-reader can surely help to persuade him or her in your favor. And this, of course, is the Golden Rule of the appellate brief-writer: Be Persuasive.

Preparing to Write Appellant's Brief

A. Identifying Issues for Appeal

1. Assembling the Record

It is, of course, the job of the party seeking to overturn a judgment to come forward and explain in a brief what errors occurred in the proceedings below that require the appellate court to reverse the judgment. Therefore, the first step in writing the appellant's brief is to assemble the entire record of the proceedings in the lower court so that errors, if any, can be located. The record includes the pleadings (or the indictment and bill of particulars in a criminal case); any pre-trial motions and decisions; the transcript of hearings, trial and (in a criminal case) sentencing; written requests to charge the jury; interrogatories and answers (in a civil case); exhibits; post-trial motions and decisions; and any other documents that might provide an issue for appeal.

2. Annotating the Transcript

After the entire record has been assembled, the next step is to read it through once quickly to get an idea of the nature of the case. Many appellate lawyers find it useful after reading the pleadings to turn first to the opening statements and summations of trial lawyers to get an idea of their view of the evidence and the issues in the case and to hear their arguments on behalf of their clients. Appellate counsel is not required to adopt these arguments (except to the extent necessary to comply with preservation requirements, *See* Chapter 3), but it is helpful to know what another lawyer intimately familiar with the case thinks about its merits. A telephone call to trial counsel to discuss the case may also provide some information to put the record in context.

After the first, quick reading to familiarize oneself generally with the case and to get a gut feeling about the basic unfairness or fairness of the proceedings below, the transcript of hearings and trial should be carefully read and annotated. This means simply noting at what page important facts and legal arguments appear for easy reference later on. Record annotations are for an attorney's own use; you should develop whatever note-taking method works for you. The only purpose of the annotations is to enable you to write your brief without having to sift through the entire record all over again to look for the page at which a particular witness made a particular statement or a lawyer made a motion or an objection. Thus, you want your annotations to contain all of the important information while being as concise as possible; after all, if your annotations are as long as the transcript they will not be much of a time-saver when you are writing your brief.

Traditionally, lawyers used yellow legal pads with wide left-hand margins for annotating records. These are handy because objections to rulings can be specifically noted in the margin provided. Obviously, these days lap-top computers may be the preferred method, but do be sure to include notes of objections to make writing a preservation argument easier. A useful transcript annotation of one witness's testimony might look like this:

P.O. Michael Jones

	25	10 years NYPD; undercover narcotics May 5, 1994 2-10 p.m. shift
	26	Drove from pct. to Grand and Bedford Aves. for buy and bust 2:30.
id D in court		At So. 2nd and Bedford D approached; asked what MJ looking for; MJ told D had $50 for 6 tins; D took MJ to schoolyard.
	27	D asked around for Ricky and Paddy Boy; not there; kept looking; finally found in park; D took money, told MJ to look out for cops.
	28	MJ watched D and Ricky exchange money/drugs; D told MJ "Check it out, it's good stuff."

           29   MJ said wanted 6; D said keeping one for his trouble.

objection   30   D.A. asked did D sell drugs; obj. legal conclusion overruled.

3. Listing Possible Issues

Once the transcript is fully annotated, a list should be made of every issue that might possibly be raised on appeal. Most of these will ultimately be discarded, but the first list should contain all nonfrivolous issues. Appealable issues generally fall into three basic categories. The first category is procedural, that is, whether the case is properly before the court. The second category contains those issues involving the sufficiency or weight of evidence. The third category contains those issues arising out of the conduct of the proceedings below.

The first place to look for issues is therefore in the procedural history of the case. For example, did the plaintiff in a civil case exhaust all administrative remedies before filing suit in court? Did the defendant in a criminal case receive a speedy trial?

The second place to look for issues is in the indictment or pleadings to determine whether these were supported by the evidence at trial. Did the prosecution produce evidence of each element of the crime? Did the plaintiff produce sufficient evidence on each element of the statute or regulation or common law rule? Is the verdict supported by the evidence under the correct standard of review? Decisions on pretrial motions and hearings should also be examined to determine if factual findings are supported by the record.

When you are satisfied that the underlying offense or claim has been made out, and that any additional factual findings are supported by the record, you should look for issues in the third category. The court's evidentiary rulings at all stages must be examined. Has the court exercised its discretion appropriately? Were its rulings on dispositive legal issues correctly decided? Did its procedural rulings comport with the applicable rules of civil or criminal procedure? Trial counsel's objections should alert you to possible issues, but the appellate advocate must also be on the look-out for unobjected-to errors. In particular, those rulings which interfere with a defendant's ability to defend him or herself should be noted, such as, for example, rulings excluding evidence or limiting cross-examination. Opening statements and summations should be considered for impropriety. Most important, the court's charge should be scrutinized with great care for errors of law or fact, omissions of necessary instructions and unfair marshalling of evidence.

Counsel should also note carefully the length of jury deliberations, any questions the jury has asked while deliberating, and the answers given by the court. These can be crucial to an argument that the jury was in fact confused or misled or prejudiced by improper instructions or rulings on issues. Any interference with the jury either during trial or deliberations, such as the substitution of a juror or improper communication with the jury, may provide an issue for appeal.

Obviously, issue identification requires considerable familiarity with the substantive law governing the case, as well as a thorough command of the facts in the record. This familiarity comes with the regular practice of law in the appellate courts. At the beginning of your career you will simply have to research many issues that will not pan out. If you are not in an office where you are receiving careful supervision on your first cases, you should attempt to find an experienced mentor to read your records to make sure that you are not overlooking any issues – the greatest fear of any appellate practitioner. Even if your first briefs are imperfectly argued, you still may win as long as you have presented the court with the issue. If the issue simply isn't there, however, there is no way the court can decide it. Therefore, if limited help is available to you, ask for it at the issue-spotting rather than the editing stage.

Even experienced practitioners must be conscientious about keeping up with the latest issues in appellate practice. Certain issues become "hot" while the courts lose interest in others. For example, recently many appellate courts have been particularly receptive to a variety of issues involving the composition of juries. It is therefore crucial for the appellate advocate to read advance sheets for help in spotting issues and trends. Appellate attorneys who stay abreast of opinions in the courts where they have active practices can often get a good sense of the issues to which those courts are especially sensitive, as well as those that are unlikely, despite objective strengths, to persuade the court to grant relief.

B. Selecting Issues for Appeal

Once a comprehensive list of possible issues has been made, the next step is to cross most of them off. A useful rule of thumb for the good appellate brief writer is that less is often more. This maxim refers not only to the desirability of concise legal arguments but equally to the selection of the issues to be raised on the appeal. A brief should never be cluttered up with harmless errors and make-weight arguments. Many experienced appellate lawyers believe that the key to an effective appeal is knowing which issues to omit. Of course, it is important not to omit issues about which a respectable argument can be made, and a lawyer may choose to include an issue simply because the client particularly wishes to raise it. It is possible, however, to damage a client's cause by diluting the strong points in a brief with a collection of weak ones.[1]

Unless a trial was unusually long, it is unlikely that more than two or three strong issues will present themselves, and there is nothing disreputable about a one-point brief. It is extremely difficult to imagine a good brief containing more than six good points. Indeed, if such a situation should arise, it would probably be a good idea to combine two or more arguments into a single point. A good question

---

[1] The Supreme Court acknowledged this point in *Jones v. Barnes*, 463 U.S. 745 (1983). See Chapter 6.

to ask yourself when debating whether to include another issue in your brief is whether a court that has already rejected your stronger points is likely to be convinced by this one.

1. Identifying The Strongest Issues

The relative strength of an issue can be measured in different ways. A clear, preserved legal error is strong in the sense that it may be likely to result in reversal. On the other hand, if in a criminal case, for example, it would result simply in the dismissal of a lesser count on which a shorter concurrent sentence was imposed, the issue is not so strong in terms of the relief it can provide for the client. In contrast, a less clear or unpreserved legal issue could nevertheless be viewed as strong if it could result in the dismissal of all charges or the entire complaint.

Of course, no matter how clear a legal error is, it cannot be considered "strong" if it is ultimately harmless. It is crucial that the advocate consider whether a clear error was mooted by events occurring later at trial, whether the court's ruling was supported by correct as well as erroneous reasoning, and whether there is any causal connection between an erroneous ruling or other impropriety and the outcome of the case. And, of course, preservation will affect issue selection. A serious but unpreserved error may have to be abandoned while a weaker issue may be included if trial counsel did a good job of preserving it.

2. Cumulative Error

Sometimes, a single error standing alone is weak in itself, but combined with another error creates a strong issue. For example, at the trial of defendant charged with murdering his wife, the erroneous admission of evidence that years before he had assaulted her may be harmless error. Similarly, the defendant might not have been prejudiced by the refusal of the court to admit into evidence the wife's diary in which she described her happy marriage. Together, however, these two errors can add up to a strong argument that the defendant's right to present a defense and to a fair trial was impaired. Similarly, while a single improper remark by a court or lawyer would not be worth raising, a pattern of impropriety could very well support a persuasive point.

A shot-gun approach to issue selection is to be avoided. It is not always possible, but it is desirable, to organize even strong issues around a theme. For example, if a defendant's claim is that the jury awarded excessive damages to the plaintiff because it was aware that the defendant was well insured, it would be effective to make Point I the improper conduct of plaintiff's lawyer who mentioned insurance in opening; Point II, the failure of the trial judge to take corrective action when a witness blurted out that the defendant had lots of insurance; and Point III, the omission of a charge instructing the jury to disregard any collateral source of funds the defendant might have to pay damages, *i.e.* insurance. Less effective would be three points on entirely separate issues. In short, the way in which issues interrelate can be an important factor in determining their relative strength.

C. Ordering the Issues

Once the issues for appeal have been determined, counsel must next decide in which order they should be presented. As a general rule, the most persuasive point should go first. In other types of writing there may be something to be said for leading up to a forceful climax, but the brief writer who follows this pattern runs the risk of losing readers before they get to the crucial argument. Appellate judges do not want to be forced to read any more than is absolutely necessary. If your first point is convincing, the judge may not have to go on to consider your second point at all. At the very least, the reader who is persuaded by the powerful Point I is more likely to be well disposed to a somewhat weaker Point II.

At times, however, there is good reason for deviating from the strongest-point-first rule. As discussed above, it may be a good idea to group related issues together, either as separate points or as sub-sections of a single point if they are not quite strong enough to stand on their own. In this way the ideas in the brief will flow smoothly.

Sometimes, one issue can pave the way for another. For example, if a strong argument can be made that the evidence failed to prove the defendant's guilt beyond a reasonable doubt, it should be Point I. Even if the court is not entirely convinced by this argument, it may view the trial errors raised in a subsequent point or points more sympathetically. In other briefs logic will dictate placing an issue first even if it is not the strongest; for example, an argument questioning the jurisdiction of the court should always be Point I because if there is a possibility that the court has no jurisdiction to hear the case it makes no sense to make the judges review the other issues. Occasionally, an advocate who is familiar with the court in which the brief is being filed might place an issue first, even if it is not especially persuasive, if the court hearing the case has been particularly receptive to that argument in other cases.

The correct order for points in a brief is therefore simply the one that makes the most sense in a particular case. Any order that can be justified rationally is acceptable. The appellate lawyer must think about the question, however, and not simply order the points either randomly or according to a rigid formula.

Preparing to Write Respondent's Brief

Respondent's preparation for writing a brief is, of course, somewhat different from appellant's, although some of the steps are the same. The first thing respondent must do is to read the appellant's brief very carefully and make a list of the arguments made under each point in it.

Many arguments are similar to one another so it is important to pin down precisely what appellant claims went wrong in the court below to avoid answering the wrong argument and leaving the real argument unanswered. For example, a criminal defendant's claim that his confession was improperly admitted at trial may have any number of bases. Did he receive his *Miranda* warnings? Was the confession psychologically or physically coerced? Was it the fruit of the poisonous tree?

Once respondent has pinned down appellant's claims, it is time to read and annotate the record. Respondent will, of course, pay special attention to the portions of the record on which appellant relies to support any claims of unfairness, but it is also important to read with the goal of putting those instances in the context of the whole record. Has a claimed error been cured elsewhere in the record? Did the court's charge as a whole set out the correct legal standards? Was the prosecutor's intemperate remark on summation a response to provoking conduct by defense counsel?

And, of course, respondent will be always on the look-out for what is missing from the record – objections to the court's rulings of which the appellant now complains – and changes in theory on appeal for objections which were made.

Writing the Brief

Once the issues have been selected, the next step is to start writing the brief. Every appellate attorney has a favorite way of writing a brief. Some start from the beginning and end at the end, while others prefer to write the argument first and the statement of facts last. Some select the order of issues first; others wait until the brief is written to order the issues. It is probably wise, however, to frame the Questions Presented first to narrow the issues and guide the writing of the arguments. It is difficult to answer a question that has not yet been asked and framing a question is a crucial step in clarifying one's own thoughts.

A. Statement of the Issues

Under the rules of most appellate courts, including the United States Supreme Court, every brief must contain a statement of the issues presented for review. The statement of the issues is often referred to as the Questions Presented. The importance of this section of the brief cannot be overstated, for it is the court's first introduction to the case. Indeed, the Rules of the Supreme Court of the United States require that Questions Presented appear on the very first page of certiorari petitions and briefs submitted to that Court, even before the table of contents. *See* Supreme Court Rules 14.1(a) and 24.1(a). This prominent placement of the questions will generally ensure that, if nothing else is read, the Justices can at least get an overview of the issues addressed in the papers. Not infrequently, the Court's reaction to the questions presented will determine, not only whether to read on, but, at least in a preliminary way, how to vote in disposing of the case.

The Supreme Court Rules provide a useful set of guidelines for framing the issues on appeal.

Rule 14

1. The petition for a writ of certiorari shall contain . . .: (a) The questions presented by the appeal, [1] expressed in the terms and circumstances of the case [2] but without unnecessary detail. [3] The statement of the questions should be short and concise and [4] should not be argumentative or repetitious. They must be set forth on the first page following the cover with no other information appearing on that page. [5] The statement of any question presented will be deemed to comprise every subsidiary question fairly included therein. [6] Only the questions set forth in the petition, or fairly included therein, will be considered by the Court.

The bracketed numbers identify the various aspects of a formulation of questions presented which the advocate should have in mind when drafting the questions presented for a brief in any appellate court.

1. Terms and Circumstances of the Case

The requirement that [1] the questions presented be expressed in the terms and circumstances of the case means that the question should contain facts sufficient to allow the court to come to a preliminary conclusion as to the correct answer. A question that asks "Whether the plaintiff was contributorily negligent" or "Whether the conduct of the defendant fell within the statutory prohibitions" is meaningless. Without more factual information the reader can glean little idea of what the case is about, let alone begin to guess at an answer. Better formulations might be "Whether plaintiff's failure to fasten his seat belt prior to the accident rendered him contributorily negligent" and "Whether defendant's conduct, consisting merely of calling the complainant on an intercom to ask her out, fails to satisfy the requirements of the harassment statute." Similarly, instead of saying, "Did the officers have probable cause to search the defendant?" one might ask, "Was the search based on probable cause when the officers had received specific information accurately identifying the defendant as being in possession of a gun?" In other words, it is generally necessary to give the court the legally significant facts around which the issue revolves.

An exception to this rule is where you are intending to argue a broad, purely legal proposition. For example, "Whether a corporation is a person within the meaning of the act" is a good Question Presented. Frequently, appellate attorneys raise the same issue both broadly and narrowly: broadly, for example on constitutional grounds to attract interest in the case, and narrowly on the specific facts so as not to sacrifice the willingness of more cautious judges to rule in the client's favor. The ability to raise the issue broadly will often make a narrower but still favorable resolution more likely. An example of a broad and narrow formulation of the same issue might be:

Broad: Whether a government-licensed adoption agency can ever con-
          stitutionally consider a prospective parent's sexual orientation
          in determining whether to allow that person to adopt a child.

Narrow: Whether the refusal of defendants, directors of a government-
          licensed adoption agency, to permit plaintiffs, a homosexual cou-
          ple, to adopt a child solely because of their sexual orientation
          violated their constitutional right to privacy and due process.

Obviously, the narrower proposition requires more facts in the Question Presented.

2. No Unnecessary Detail

The admonition to include facts is qualified by the phrase [2] without unnecessary
detail. This proviso means that the Question Presented should not be so lengthy
and fact-specific that it obscures the rule of law. Only significant facts should be
included in the question and these should be put into a category that would be
applicable to other situations. Thus, instead of asking "Whether a ten-year-old girl
who has played doubles squash only twice before and does not know that a warning is
required when crossing the court can be found negligent for striking her 37-year-old
partner and knocking out his two front teeth in an attempt to hit a ball on his side
of the court without warning," a preferable question is "Whether an inexperienced
child squash player who injures her adult partner as a result of her ignorance of
the safety rules of the game can be found negligent."

Proper names, places, dates, amounts and other minor details should generally
be omitted from the issues statement. Since the statement is the first section of a
brief, the question "Whether the trial court erred in refusing to admit Jane Taylor's
psychiatric record into evidence" is meaningless to a reader who is as yet unfamiliar
with the case and has no idea whether Jane Taylor is the crime victim or a police
officer or an eye-witness or the defendant's mother. Far clearer is the question
"Whether evidence of the alleged rape victim's psychiatric record was improperly
excluded."

3. Short and Concise

The third rule that questions should be [3] short and concise often runs into
conflict with the rule that questions should be presented in terms and circumstances
of the case. The challenge is to write a short, concise question that at the same
time conveys a lot of information. This is why it often takes a long time to write a
good Question Presented. Just keep in mind that the point of an issue statement is
to make the question raised in the appeal immediately comprehensible to the reader.
A judge should not have to puzzle out the meaning of a Question Presented and if
asked to do so probably will not.

There are a few tricks for writing a concise Question Presented. First, put facts at the beginning of the question and the legal claim at the end. Thus, instead of asking "Whether the defendant was denied his constitutional rights to the adequate assistance of counsel and due process by the lower court's refusal to grant him an adjournment to seek a new attorney on the eve of trial" it is preferable to turn the question around: "Whether the trial court's refusal to grant defendant's request for an adjournment to seek a new attorney, made on the eve of trial, denied him his constitutional rights to due process and the adequate assistance of counsel." This saves the reader from having to wade through familiar material – a Sixth Amendment/due process claim – before getting to the unfamiliar fact that the lower court denied defendant's untimely request to substitute counsel, which is the information that you really want to impart. Second, keep sentence structure as simple as possible. One way to shorten and simplify a question is to avoid all double negative forms of expression such as "Whether the court improperly refused to enjoin. . . ." A better formulation is "Whether the injunction should have been issued. . . ."

Another way to be concise is to omit any lengthy reference to the actions of the courts below, particularly when more than one court has already dealt with the matter. It is preferable to say simply what the proper course of action would have been. For example, it is far more complicated to parse "Whether the circuit court of appeals erred in overruling petitioner's motion to dismiss the indictment in the absence of a finding by the military tribunal that the soldier had been guilty of desertion," than "Whether the indictment must be dismissed in the absence of a finding by the military tribunal that the soldier had been guilty of desertion." In short, by eliminating words and simplifying structure the question becomes comprehensible to a judge or law clerk on first reading.

4. Avoid Argumentation and Repetition (but don't be neutral)

The rule next cautions advocates to frame questions that are [4] not argumentative or repetitive. The advice to avoid repetition requires no discussion. The meaning of the warning against argumentation is not so obvious. It is certainly true that an issue statement should not be strident. More important, however, it should not present disputed facts as givens. For example, it is useless for appellant's attorney to state the issue as "Whether appellant's suspension from school for his refusal to cut his hair violated his constitutional right to privacy where the short hair rule served no legitimate state purpose," when respondents' entire defense is that the short-hair rule is crucial to their ability to provide students with a good education. While appellant's Question Presented might certainly elicit an affirmative answer, which is desirable in a Question Presented, it does not accurately state the issue in the case.

Similarly, being nonargumentative means not overstating the applicable law. For example, "Whether appellant's suspension from school for his refusal to cut his hair violated his absolute right under the First and Fourteenth Amendments to govern his own personal appearance" might be an excellent question if such an absolute right had ever been held to exist. Since it has not, the question fails to focus on the real issue.

On the other hand, the question should not be framed with complete objectivity. Respondent's counsel should almost never accept appellant's characterization of the issues and *vice versa*. A good advocate is careful to frame the issues from the client's viewpoint. It is entirely possible to frame a question in a factually and legally accurate way while still leading the reader to the conclusion the advocate is urging. For this reason it is generally preferable to have the question call for an affirmative answer. The effective Question Presented should cause the reader to respond, "Well, yes, of course!" An example of opposing ways to frame the same issue would be:

Appellant: Whether by precluding cross-examination of the prosecution's principal witness on his commission of tax fraud the court's rulings deprived appellant of a fair trial and his right to confrontation?

Respondent: Whether the court properly exercised its substantial discretion over the conduct of cross-examination when it precluded the defense from cross-examining a prosecution witness about the failure to file a single tax return?

Both of these questions are good because neither attorney could quarrel that the other's characterization of either the facts or the law was inaccurate or misleading; both agree to the facts that tax fraud was the charge and that cross-examination was precluded. Likewise, neither could fairly dispute that the defendant does have the right to a fair trial and confrontation or that a court has substantial discretion over the conduct of cross-examination. On the other hand, neither attorney would choose to adopt the other's Question Presented.

5. Match Question to Argument

The fifth and sixth aspects of questions presented deal with the problem of what particular arguments will be considered "fairly included in the formulation selected." The Supreme Court has said that its "power to decide is not limited by the precise terms of the question presented," *Procunier v. Navarette*, 434 U.S. 555, 559 n.6 (1978), but its willingness to reach a claim that presents a somewhat different argument from that suggested by the Question Presented may depend on the importance of the question and any possible prejudice to the adversary. *See, e.g., United States v. Arnold Schwinn & Co.*, 388 U.S. 368, 371 n.4 (1967).

If various theories could support the same result, the safest course is to include a question presenting each possible approach. The careful appellate attorney will not risk being stranded outside the "fairly included" boundary. *See Arkansas Elec.*

Co-op v. Arkansas Public Service Comm., 461 U.S. 375, 382 n.6 (1983) (relationship between legislative and judicial enforcement of commerce clause found close enough for preemption issue to come, "if by the barest of margins, within those 'subsidiary question[s] fairly included' in the principal question on appeal.") A well-known advocate lost the opportunity to have the Supreme Court review a particular argument by failing to frame a question that included it:

> Petitioners devote a substantial portion of their brief on the merits to arguing that Arizona has given an unconstitutionally broad construction to the aggravating factors in its capital sentencing statute. This Court granted certiorari on the following question:
>
> > "Is the December 4, 1984 decision of the Arizona Supreme Court to execute petitioners in conflict with the holding of *Enmund v. Florida,* 458 U.S. 782 (1982), where—in words of the Arizona Supreme Court—petitioners 'did not specifically intend that the [victims] die, . . . did not plot in advance that these homicides would take place, or—did not actually pull the triggers on the guns which inflicted the fatal wounds . . .'"
>
> Pet. for Cert. 2. In our view, the question presented does not fairly encompass an attack on Arizona's construction of its aggravating factors and we express no view on that subject. See this Court's Rule 21.1(a).

Tison v. Arizona, 481 U.S. 137, 146 n.2 (1987).

B. The Statement of Facts

1. Function

Most appellate practitioners agree that the statement of facts is the most important part of the brief because, as discussed above, while appellate courts are generally familiar with most legal issues, they do not know the facts of your case. Your first goal in writing a statement of facts is therefore simply to provide the court with the information it needs to decide the case in as clear and simple a form as possible. This means that all of the facts necessary for the determination of the issues you intend to raise must be included and all extraneous facts should be excised so that the important facts stand out.

While brevity and conciseness are laudable aims when writing a statement of facts, as they are when writing a Question Presented, it is preferable to err on the side of inclusiveness. An appellate court is capable of weeding out a few extraneous facts that you have included unnecessarily, but it cannot add facts that you have omitted. This is why it is not unusual to find a brief in which the statement of facts is considerably longer than the argument.

The next goal of the statement of facts is to alert the court to the legal arguments that will follow. You have failed to write an effective statement of facts if the judge's response to reading it is, "Well, that was interesting. So what?" Rather, a good statement of facts is one from which the legal arguments are apparent and flow naturally. A judge should understand upon reading the facts what legal arguments a party will be making.

The final goal of a statement of facts is to predispose the court to rule in your client's favor. This does not mean that you should be argumentative. Indeed, a statement of facts that the court views as argument and not fact has failed in its basic purpose. On the other hand, a statement of facts need not be entirely neutral. Rather, you should present the facts in the light most favorable to your client. If, after reading your statement of facts, the judges have the impression that your client is a fiend, they will be less receptive to your legal arguments on his or her behalf. If, on the other hand, they see a human being who has been treated unfairly in the court below, you are well on your way to winning your case. And *vice versa*, if you are respondent. At that point, the legal arguments in your brief will simply give the court the authority it needs to follow its own inclination.

Finally, it should be apparent that none of your goals can be achieved if your statement of facts is not scrupulously accurate. Remember, your aim is not to win a hypothetical case in which the facts are all favorable to you but rather to win your client's case. Misrepresenting the facts either by omitting bad ones, misstating them or taking testimony out of context is not only dishonest, but it ultimately does no service to the client. Any competent appellate attorney will, of course, be vigilant when reading an adversary's brief and will be quick to point out to the court any factual misstatements in it. Once the court perceives that it cannot rely on one attorney's brief for the facts, it has no alternative but to rely on the other's. The attorney who has played fast and loose with the facts will then have lost the precious opportunity to persuade the court to view the case in the light most favorable to his or her client.

Keep in mind that every case has bad facts. If all of the facts were in your favor there would be no case. If you attempt to deny the existence of bad facts you will be unable to deal with them straightforwardly. On the same principle that a trial attorney brings out a witness's criminal record on direct examination rather than waiting for opposing counsel to do it on cross-examination, an appellate attorney who candidly states the unfavorable evidence in fact downplays it.

2. Fact Selection and Organization

One of the most important tasks the appellate attorney must perform is the selection of facts to include in the statement of facts. The facts in a case fall into two different categories. The first category consists of the narrative of the underlying event or situation that caused the parties to end up in court – the crime, car accident, breach of contract, civil rights violation or whatever. The second category consists of the description of the errors that are claimed to have occurred during the course of the litigation that appellant wants the appellate court to correct. Both types of facts should appear in the statement of facts.

Your guide to which specific facts should be included in your statement of facts is your argument. This is why appellate attorneys frequently write the statement of facts last. For example, if you find yourself arguing that a particular issue has not been preserved, then you know that you must include a description of the trial attorney's objections. This may be as simple as saying "Over defense objection the witness testified that . . ." or it may require a more extended discussion.

Likewise, if your point is that the trial court abused its discretion in ruling that the prosecution might introduce evidence of the defendant's entire lengthy record of drug convictions should he testify at trial, you will surely want to mention that at the time of making the ruling the judge opined that all drug dealers should be imprisoned for life. Conversely, if your client's defense at trial is that he shot the victim by accident, it is unnecessary to include a description of the pre-trial identification procedure. Similarly, if a party's sole argument on appeal is that the lower court lacked the jurisdiction to hear the case, then the facts of the underlying case may be summarized quickly. If, on the other hand, the argument is that a verdict in a criminal case was not supported by the weight of the evidence, a description of that evidence will necessarily be lengthy and detailed.

Respondents, in particular, may find it necessary to include facts which at first appear irrelevant to appellant's argument but which are, in fact, necessary to put the error in a context that reveals it to be harmless. For example, in cases in which an appellant in a criminal case argues that the prosecutor made improper remarks on summation, the prosecution on appeal frequently responds that the remarks were fair response to defense counsel's summation and that, in any event, the summation as a whole was not inflammatory. In such a case the statement of facts on appeal will contain excerpts from defense counsel's summation and additional portions of the prosecutor's summation. Similarly, a complaint of an erroneous jury instruction may require inclusion of lengthy portions of the court's charge which make clear that the charge as a whole conveyed the correct legal standard to the jury.

After the facts have been selected for inclusion in the brief, the attorney's next task is to combine the two types of facts into a single coherent statement. This presents a challenge to the appellate lawyer, particularly when the error claimed is one that pervades the entire proceedings – excessive judicial interference with the questioning of witnesses or persistent improper remarks by a prosecutor, for example.

A decision to be made in many briefs is whether the description of the trial errors should be combined with the narrative of the incident so that the error is noted at the point when it occurred during testimony, or, alternatively, whether the errors should be set forth in a separate sub-section of the statement of facts. The answer is: It depends. Just understand that this is a stylistic, not a legal question and the answer is dictated solely by considerations of clarity and persuasiveness. If the error is discrete and easily described, it may be preferable to mention it where it occurred, for example the improper admission of documentary evidence on a collateral issue.

On the other hand, where you are complaining of several cumulative small errors, the facts may be easier to understand if they are grouped under a heading such as "Comments and Rulings Concerning Defendant's Failure to Testify."

Some lawyers choose to mention facts for the first time in the argument section of the brief in situations in which this adds to clarity. For example, where an appellant complains of prosecutorial misconduct on summation, it may be easier for readers to see the offensive remarks at the beginning of the argument on that point rather than to have to return to the statement of facts to refresh their recollection.

Usually, but not necessarily or invariably, both the narrative of the underlying incident and the description of the proceedings are organized chronologically because this order tends to be the clearest for the reader in most cases. Thus, a typical statement of facts in a criminal case begins with a description of any pre-trial proceedings that present appealable issues. If there has been a pre-trial hearing, a summary of the testimony will be set forth, divided into the prosecution and defense testimony. The hearing court's decision will follow.

Next comes the account of the trial, again divided into prosecution and defense cases. If the prosecutor's summation is problematic, the improper remarks will be excerpted in a separate section. Likewise, if jury charge errors are claimed, these will be repeated in a section entitled "The Court's Charge." If the jury has taken a long time to deliberate and has asked questions indicating that they are troubled by certain evidence or cannot understand an instruction, these facts should be included in a section on jury deliberations and verdict.

Finally, defendant's sentence should be set out. If an argument is being made that the sentence is illegal or excessive, facts from the sentencing including remarks by the judge and any information such as a pre-sentence report or letters from victims should appear in the brief. Following is an outline of a Statement of Facts in a criminal case.

STATEMENT OF FACTS

Introduction
The Pre-Trial Hearing
    The People's Case
    The Defense Case
    The Hearing Court's Decision
The Trial
    The People's Case
    The Mistrial Motion
    The Defense Case
    The Prosecutor's Summation
    Requests to Charge and Charge
    The Jury Deliberations
    The Verdict and Sentence

Many appellate lawyers like to begin their statements of facts with an introduction that puts the evidence about to be described in a favorable light. For example, in an appeal from a criminal conviction of a defendant for assaulting a police officer who was trying to arrest him, defense counsel on appeal began the statement of facts with an introduction highlighting the fact that the defendant had been acquitted of the underlying crime that was the basis for the arrest.

An introduction may also be useful simply to explain something that might puzzle the court about the case that does not comfortably fit in another part of the statement of facts. For example, in another criminal case, the appellate attorney upon reading a 7,000 page record discovered that her client had been tried for murder under two different theories, felony murder and intentional murder. 6500 pages of the transcript had been devoted to proving the intentional murder and the remaining 500 pages dealt with the felony murder. Defendant was convicted only of felony murder, making 6500 pages of the transcript irrelevant to the single strong issue raised on appeal in a twenty-page brief. The attorney anticipated that the court might understandably wonder how such a vast record could have resulted in such a short brief. She therefore explained in an introduction what had occurred.

In any case a well-crafted introductory paragraph will give the reader some helpful background as well as stir up the reader's interest in the story which is about to follow. If court rules permit it (and most do), the procedural history of the case should be placed in a separate preliminary statement so as not to begin the statement of facts with dull technicalities.

The summary of the trial testimony should generally follow the chronology of the underlying event that precipitated the litigation. The summary need not, and usually should not, follow the order in which the evidence was presented at trial. This is because the order of trial testimony is often governed by such factors as the police officer's tour of duty or the expert witness's vacation rather than by the logic of the case. Moreover, the trial testimony may well not have been presented in an order that favors a client's position.

Thus, the easiest way to organize a factual summary of trial—first X testified; then Y testified—is usually the least effective. Even if it is neither confusing nor positively harmful to present the facts in this manner, a good statement of facts is more than just an accurate synopsis of the testimony. Rather, the brief-writer's goal is to tell a compelling story that the court will want to keep reading.

While it is neither necessary nor desirable to preface every sentence with the words "the witness testified that . . .," it is important to make clear whose testimony is being reported and for which party the witness is testifying. In most cases this can be done by placing the testimony of the witnesses for the opposing parties, on both direct and cross-examination, in separate sections designated as "The Plaintiff's (or The Prosecution's) Case" and "The Defendant's Case." The name of the testifying witness should be stated at least once. It is customary to put the name of a testifying witness in capital letters or to underline it the first time it is mentioned.

Parenthetical page references containing the name of the testifying witness where necessary for clarity should indicate the place in the record where the particular testimony can be found. Page references need not follow every sentence, but they should be sufficiently frequent to enable the reader to turn to the precise page where testimony occurs. A judge should never be forced to leaf through a transcript in search of particular testimony. If a witness has said the same thing in more than one place, all of those page references should be included. Likewise, if two witnesses have testified similarly, the substance of their testimony can be set out and both names can be included in parentheses with appropriate page references.

a. Fact Emphasis

Keep in mind that advocacy of your client's position begins in the statement of facts. Although the primary purpose of a statement of facts is to set forth accurately the evidence on which the appeal turns, its goal is also to make the court want to rule in the client's favor. As discussed above, this does not mean being argumentative or omitting legally significant unfavorable evidence. It does mean, however, condensing unfavorable facts and expanding favorable ones.

Which facts to emphasize depends, of course, on the particular case. Generally, where possible, appellant will emphasize facts that indicate that the wrong party has prevailed the case. Respondent, on the other hand, will expand on the facts indicating that defendant received a full, fair hearing in the lower court. It is important, however, to be realistic. While appellate counsel in a criminal case may hope to portray a client as innocent or at least as having acted excusably, if the defendant is clearly guilty of an unspeakable crime, it will be wiser to take another tack. In such a case, appellate counsel should probably state the facts of the incident as briefly and matter-of-factly as possible and emphasize instead facts that show that the proceedings below simply did not comport with our American notions of justice. On the other hand, if a clear error did take place at trial, respondent will probably do well to emphasize the strong evidence of defendant's guilt to pave the way for a subsequent harmless error argument.

In short, before writing the statement of facts, appellate counsel should candidly assess the strengths and weaknesses of the evidence and decide what view of the case would best set up the legal arguments to be made in the next section of the brief. Facts that support that view are the ones to emphasize.

An example of a highly readable statement of facts in the appellate brief of an unsympathetic criminal defendant convicted of having mugged an elderly Russian immigrant in a New York subway station appears in the Appendix to this chapter. What impression was the attorney trying to convey?

Often facts are emphasized or deemphasized in a brief on the basis of their emotional impact. A good illustration of the different ways opposing attorneys can treat such facts might arise in a negligence action in which the issue on appeal is simply whether the defendant was, in fact, negligent. In this situation, the extent of the plaintiff's injuries is not strictly relevant. If, however, the trial record contains detailed testimony concerning the plaintiff's gaping wounds, dangerous surgery, lengthy hospital stay and incomplete recovery, plaintiff's attorney will, of course, include it verbatim. The respondent's attorney, on the other hand, will satisfy the obligation to state the facts accurately by saying that the plaintiff was seriously injured, was hospitalized for whatever period of time and had, at the time of trial, recovered to whatever extent, and by then providing page references to the place in the transcript where the gruesome evidence appears.

One word of advice is to go easy on facts that have purely emotional impact and no legal significance. For example, while a prosecutor at trial may very well bring out before jury the fact that the victim was murdered while on his way to deliver Christmas presents to the children in the orphanage, an appellate court may be offended by the suggestion that it can be swayed by sympathy for the victim rather than by legal argument.

b. Techniques For Presenting Facts Favorably

Sentence and Paragraph Structure

It will serve to highlight favorable facts if they are placed in prominent positions, particularly at the beginning of paragraphs. On the other hand, unfavorable facts can be deemphasized by placing them in the middle of paragraphs, and, if possible, juxtaposing them with facts that soften their negative impact. Thus, for example, if a witness has given damaging testimony, but was impeached to some extent, either on cross-examination or by the testimony of another witness, the damage can be reduced by placing the impeaching evidence right next to the damaging evidence. This should be done without comment; any characterization of the contradictions should be saved for the argument section. Letting the facts speak for themselves has the advantage of letting the reader draw his or her own conclusion, as well as keeping an objective tone for the statement of the facts.

Sub-headings

Another organizational technique that allows the facts to begin to persuade the reader is the use of sub-headings to draw attention to favorable facts relevant to the points being raised on the appeal. For example, consider a case raising the argument that the jury in a capital case was prevented from considering the massive amount of mitigating material that had been introduced into evidence, because the material was presented to them by simply placing 4000 pages of medical records in bags for them to do with what they wished. The fact statement could be divided into what the jury actually heard, through testimony; then, in a separate section, perhaps called "The untold story of petitioner's life," counsel could summarize the medical history contained in the 4000 pages of undigested material.

Word Choice

Facts in a statement of facts should not be characterized with adverbs and adjectives except those that come from the mouths of the witnesses. The language chosen to set out the facts can, however, affect the reader's reaction to the events being recounted. Words with basically synonymous meanings often have different connotations and the persuasive writer will choose the word that better suits the argument to follow. For example, in a brief on an issue revolving around the search of a dwelling, the defendant might refer to it as his home to emphasize the personal nature of the intrusion while the prosecutor would call it a house or an apartment to minimize it. Similarly, while the use of an adjective might be overly argumentative – "the outrageous invasion of his home" – the substitution of a single strong verb might be acceptable. Thus, appellant might say that the police "burst into his home," while the prosecution would merely say that they entered it.

Using witnesses' own words can often be effective. Thus, while appellate counsel would not describe a witness as a "crazy lady" or a "sleaze," quoting a witness who uses the words might serve to get the point across in an acceptable manner. Similarly, in a case involving a car accident, the defendant's lawyer may refer to his client as Mr. Jones, but if a witness refers to him by his nickname "Speed Demon" plaintiff's counsel would be acting within the bounds of propriety to use that name instead.

One method prosecutors often use to present the facts in their favor is to relate the testimony of prosecution witnesses as fact – after all the jury found it to be so beyond a reasonable doubt – while presenting the defense case as simply the witness's testimony. For example, the prosecutor might write, "Police Officer JOHN O'TOOLE was on routine patrol at 2:00 a.m. in the area of Times Square, a high crime neighborhood, when he saw defendant run past him and discard an object underneath a parked car. The officer retrieved the object and found it to be a gun. He radioed to fellow officers who pursued defendant and captured him." When summarizing the defense case, however, the prosecutor might say, "Defendant FRANK JAMES, a convicted drug dealer, claimed that he was out for an evening stroll when Officer O'Toole grabbed him, reached into his pocket and seized his gun."

Defense counsel cannot, of course, do the reverse and report as fact defendant's testimony, since his defense has been rejected by the jury. The lawyer can however, at least indicate that the facts were disputed by describing the prosecution's case simply as testimony: "Officer O'Toole stated that he saw defendant throw the gun."

In sum, the line between being argumentative and persuasive is a fine one, and the inexperienced briefwriter is probably well advised to err on the side of caution. Too often, however, attorneys neglect the statement of facts in favor of the legal arguments and thus fail to make use of one of the strongest tools of persuasion in appellate advocacy.

C. Summary of Argument

Some courts require that appellate lawyers briefly summarize their arguments in a separate section of the brief immediately following the statement of facts and before the argument. Even in courts that do not have this requirement, many experienced appellate practitioners nevertheless include one in the well-founded belief that busy judges find them useful. The summary of argument should succinctly set forth each of counsel's arguments, ideally in one page. It can be organized in any logical manner, but generally it should follow the organization of the brief. Writing a summary of argument can, incidentally, clarify one's own thoughts about the case and thus may be useful even if it is not included in the brief.

Following is a sample summary of argument:

SUMMARY OF ARGUMENT

Where a person claims a *de facto* parent/child relationship as a result of co-parenting a child from birth with a legal/biological parent, a rule of law which would allow the legally-defined parent to terminate all contact between the child and the co-parent without allowing a court to consider whether continuing contact would be in the child's best interest is unconstitutional. The interests of children and adults in *de facto* parent/child relationships are protected by the Constitution. In a line of decisions dating from at least 1944, the United States Supreme Court has held that relationships between children and their non-biological parents are worthy of constitutional protection. The Supreme Court has also held – as did this court in its (non-constitutionally based) ruling in *Braschi v. Stahl Associates Co.,* 74 N.Y.2d 201, 544 N.Y.S.2d 784 (1989) – that the strength of those rights is a function not of biological or legal status, but of the substance and quality of the relationship between the child and the adult. Thus, the facts of the relationship itself must establish what process is due in this sort of claim.

Yet the courts below selected a rule of law which affords no process whatsoever. By denying standing to the co-parent, the lower courts in essence established an irrebuttable presumption that joint custody in or visitation with a co-parent can *never* be in the child's best interest. When a fundamental right is involved, such as the right to intimate relationships implicated in this case, the use of an irrebuttable presumption is improper. Such irrebuttable presumptions are violative of the Due Process Clause, particularly in the family law context. In circumstances such as these, the interest of children and adults in being able to show that maintaining their relationships is in the best interests of the child outweighs any state interest in preventing a court from considering that question.

D. The Argument

One reason that inexperienced appellate practitioners find argumentative writing difficult is that generally they have not read many briefs. Rather, their legal reading has been limited, for the most part, to judicial opinions and law review articles and perhaps a few office memoranda. All of these documents have very different purposes from an argumentative brief, however, and therefore they are not good models for the appellate advocate to follow. Law review articles, for example, are designed to give a broad overview of the law in a particular area and perhaps to express the writer's own opinions and policy considerations. It is the job of a court writing a judicial opinion to weigh both sides of the issue presented to it in a neutral manner and to explain the reason for its conclusion in a way that will be meaningful to the public as well as to the parties in the case. An office memorandum's purpose is to take a cold, hard look at the law affecting a client and perhaps to conclude that the client has no chance of success. Obviously an appellate brief that resembles any of these models is unlikely to be effective.

The single idea for the appellate advocate to keep in mind is that, regardless of the legal or factual issues in the case, every appellate brief has the same purpose. That purpose is to persuade the court either to overturn (in the case of appellant) or to uphold (in the case of respondent) the judgment of the lower court. This invariable rule should give you a point of reference that will guide you to write an effective appellate argument.

After reading this book you know that in deciding whether to reverse or affirm the judgment below, an appellate court is influenced by many considerations having little to do with the substantive law governing the issues raised on appeal. For example, whether or not an issue was preserved for appellate review may determine if the court agrees even to consider it. The perception that a particular issue is a question of law rather than one of fact within the province of the jury will lead the appellate court to apply a standard of review that may result in a decision for appellant rather than respondent. And, of course, a finding that an error, however egregious, was entirely harmless will require an affirmance instead of a reversal. Therefore, it follows logically that some of these issues or other similar ones will require a prominent position in your brief, a fact that inexperienced practitioners often ignore to their client's peril.

Again, keeping in mind that your goal is either the reversal or the affirmance of the judgment in your case, you can see that in writing the substantive arguments it is crucial you link your legal discussion to your facts. An appellate court rarely wishes to read a dispassionate lecture on the steam-valve theory of the First Amendment. What it wants to hear from you is why the court below did or did not err in upholding a ban on picketing in the public library. The most fascinating legal discussion is of little help to a court trying to decide a case as long as it remains abstract.

1. Types of Arguments

Legal arguments are generally of two types: those that rely entirely on the application of a particular legal doctrine, and those based almost exclusively on the analysis of facts. The doctrinal argument tells the appellate court that the law, whether embodied in a statute or binding precedent, requires a certain result. Accordingly, the argument section of the brief should clearly and forcefully set forth the applicable law, demonstrate that it was (or was not) applied correctly by the court below, and call for appropriate relief.

The fact-centered argument, on the other hand, analyzes the facts in light of the applicable legal standard, draws such inferences as naturally flow from the evidence, and tries to persuade the court that the result below was improper (or proper) given the facts adduced at trial. The entire argument may well be made without a single citation to authority. The focus, rather, is on the specific evidence adduced with an evaluation of the reliability and persuasiveness of that evidence.

Doctrinal arguments may also incorporate policy arguments. Policy arguments are generally made by advocates who seek to convince a court to overturn existing law or to extend it into a new area. Such arguments rely on a broader range of authority than pure doctrinal arguments and may include law review articles by prominent commentators, psychological and sociological studies and other sorts of empirical evidence. Policy arguments have been relied on in such landmark cases as *Brown v. Board of Education* and in other cases involving important social issues such as the legality of the Vietnam War, abortion, euthanasia, the death penalty, affirmative action, and the implications of computers and other technology on the First Amendment.

a. Structure of a Doctrinal Argument

The Thesis Paragraph

Although the different character of the different types of arguments will have a decided impact on how they are framed, every argument should begin with a forceful thesis paragraph that sums up persuasively the argument being made in the particular point and captures the court's interest. Subsequent paragraphs in the point simply support the argument made in the thesis paragraph. In the doctrinal argument, the clear applicability of the settled law to the facts of the case should be stressed in the thesis paragraph. Following is an example of a persuasive thesis paragraph of a doctrinal argument:

ARGUMENT

POINT I

BY EXITING THE COURTROOM AND DELEGATING JUDICIAL DUTIES TO NONJUDICIAL PERSONNEL DURING A READBACK OF THE COMPLAINANT'S TESTIMONY, THE TRIAL COURT DEPRIVED THE APPELLANT OF HIS CONSTITUTIONAL RIGHT TO A TRIAL BY A JURY.

The trial court denied the appellant his constitutional right to a trial by jury when the judge exited the courtroom and relinquished control of the proceedings to nonjudicial personnel – the court reporter and the attorneys – during a readback of the complainant's testimony. *See People v. Ahmed,* 66 N.Y.2d 307 (1985). During its deliberations, the jury requested that a portion of the complainant's testimony be read back. The court granted the request, but was not present during the read-back. Rather, upon consent of counsel, the judge informed counsel and the jury that he would be in the back room, and that should any problems arise, he should be notified immediately. When the judge exited the courtroom, leaving the attorneys and court reporter to supervise the readback, he delegated judicial authority to nonjudicial personnel, thereby depriving the appellant of his constitutional right to a trial by jury.

The Legal Discussion

The second paragraph of argument begins the discussion of the law or the facts or the policies that provide support for the thesis stated in the first paragraph. One of the most common mistakes that inexperienced briefwriters make is to begin their paragraphs with a discussion of various precedents (in a doctrinal argument) or facts (in a fact-centered argument) and end with a statement of a principle gleaned from those cases (or worse, leave the readers to glean the principle for themselves). It is far easier for a reader to follow an argument that is structured the other way around, that is, one that begins with a legal conclusion and uses precedent to support that conclusion.

Therefore, in a doctrinal argument, the paragraph should begin with a topic sentence that makes a legal point. This topic sentence is often a direct quote or a paraphrase of statutory language or a common law rule. For example, an argument on behalf of a near-sighted baby sitter who brought the wrong child home from the park might begin with the sentence "The defendant's 'intent to deceive a parent' is an element of the crime of substitution of children that must be proven beyond a reasonable doubt. P.L. Sec.135.55." Or, an argument that "right-to-life" protestors must be permitted to demonstrate in the parking lot outside an abortion clinic might begin, "In places which by long tradition or by government fiat have been devoted to assembly and debate, the rights of the state to limit expressive activity are sharply circumscribed." *Perry Ed. Assn. v. Perry Local Educators Assn.,* 460 U.S. 37 (1983). Some topic sentences can and should have an argumentative tone: "Even though it is beyond cavil that a defendant has a basic and fundamental right to be informed of the charges against him so that he will be able to prepare a defense, the People here changed the theory of the case during summations."

The important thing is that the topic sentence should make a point. If you see that you have begun a paragraph by saying, "In *Smith v. Jones* the plaintiff claimed that the defendant caused him to slip on a banana peel," you know you are missing a topic sentence. Go back and ask yourself what principle *Smith v. Jones* illustrates and make that principle your topic sentence (e.g. "In an unbroken line of cases the courts of this state have held that it is negligent to leave a banana peel on the sidewalk"). Since most legal arguments require more than one paragraph of discussion, some paragraphs will be devoted to discussion of precedents that support the point made in the preceding paragraph. These paragraphs should begin with a transitional sentence indicating the connection with the preceding paragraph: "*Smith v. Jones* is an example of a case in which the court found negligence by a defendant who left a banana peel on his sidewalk." As you can see, a transitional sentence also makes a point.

Following the topic sentence is the discussion of the precedents that support the point made in it, for example, cases in which the prosecution did or did not adduce sufficient evidence to prove a child-substituter's intent to deceive a parent or which upheld or struck down bans on picketing in particular locations or in which a prosecutor did nor did not change the theory of an indictment. Remember that the purpose of the discussion of the cases is to illustrate or amplify a point that you have already made.

Applying the Law to the Facts

When, and only when, you have made the reader fully familiar with the relevant law, you must apply that law to the facts in your case. A second common flaw in the briefs of inexperienced writers is the failure to keep the law and the facts separate. To be avoided is alternating discussion of law and facts in a single paragraph. Just remember, law first, facts second. The application of the law to the facts is the most important part of the argument. The legal discussion that precedes it is essentially background for your point that the existing law applied in your case requires a particular result.

After you have made your affirmative legal argument as to why your client should prevail, you can answer anticipated counter-arguments. Treatment of contrary authority should be kept short, to the point and a defensive tone should be avoided. If at all possible, present your counter-argument affirmatively, thus addressing the other side's argument implicitly without setting it forth in a neutral way or, even worse, as a terrible obstacle to be overcome. While counter-arguments must be anticipated and answered, the brief that sets out all of the opposing arguments and then answers them in the manner of a judicial opinion simply results in the court's hearing the adversary's argument twice.

The following examples illustrate the difference between advocacy and a judicial opinion:

Judge: While it is true that counsel's failure to object to the improper jury charge should, in most cases, result in an affirmance, there are exceptions to this general rule.

Advocate: Counsel's failure to object to the improper charge by no means

> mandates an affirmance.
>
> Judge: It is conceded that the court's charge on identification adhered to the pattern jury instructions. Nevertheless, in this particular case, the charge was unfair.
>
> Advocate: Adherence to the pattern jury instructions does not guarantee the fairness or appropriateness of the identification charge on the facts of this case.

In other words, the goal for the advocate is to answer the opposing argument without actually setting it out.

Finally, after answering counter-arguments and distinguishing contrary authority, you should come to a brief conclusion: "The injunction banning all picketing by abortion opponents, but not by pro-choice advocates, is overbroad and content based and therefore violates the First Amendment."

b. Structure of a Fact-Centered Argument

A fact-centered argument also begins with a thesis paragraph that sets out your argument in a nutshell. It differs from the thesis paragraph of a doctrinal argument in that it focuses on the key facts of the case in some detail. Following is an example:

> In this one-witness identification case, the elderly complainant was robbed at gun-point by someone who approached him from behind as he opened his apartment door and followed him inside. There the intruder tied the complainant to a chair, threatened to kill him if he moved, and ransacked the apartment, finally fleeing with various items that he found in his search. The understandably hysterical complainant subsequently described his assailant as a very tall, white man wearing sneakers and a baseball hat. On the basis of this description, the police detained the 5' 9" defendant who was in a near-by park and displayed him in handcuffs to the complainant. Unsurprisingly, the complainant identified defendant as the robber. Given the terrifying circumstances under which the complainant viewed the robber at the time of the crime and his inability to provide a detailed description of him to the police, the only reasonable conclusion is that his identification of defendant as the robber was the product of the highly suggestive identification procedure.

The subsequent paragraphs of a fact-centered argument also must begin with forceful topic sentences that make legal points. For example, you might begin your argument by saying, "The eyewitness identification in this case is so unreliable that it is impossible to conclude beyond a reasonable doubt that the defendant is in fact the man who committed the robbery." After having made this point, you next want to support it. Rather than supporting your point with law, however, as you do in a doctrinal argument, you support it with facts. While precedent can occasionally be helpful in a fact-centered argument, the case must generally be virtually identical to yours to be helpful. Because each case turns on its own facts, slight variations in the facts of a precedent can render it entirely unpersuasive in your case.

When discussing supporting facts, similar types of facts should be grouped together in paragraphs starting with topic sentences. For example, one paragraph might discuss the circumstances under which the victim observed his assailant at the time of the crime, including the lighting, distance and length of time the incident took. This paragraph would begin with a topic sentence making the point that the opportunity of the witness to view the robber was minimal.

Another paragraph might be devoted to the witness's state of mind and body at the time of making the identification. This paragraph would contain such facts as the witness's eyesight or degree of fear or preoccupation. (Did he, for example, testify that he kept his eyes at all times on the gun?) The topic sentence would point out that the witness was physically and mentally incapable of seeing the robber clearly at the time of the incident.

A final paragraph would discuss the circumstances surrounding the identification. Was it a prompt, on-the-scene show-up? A line-up in which the defendant was the only person of his race? Was he displayed alone, handcuffed to a radiator in the police precinct? The topic sentence might make the point that the circumstances surrounding the subsequent identification were highly suggestive.

When discussing the facts in a fact-centered argument it is preferable *not* to let them speak for themselves because you can never be sure what they will say to a particular reader. It is important explicitly to draw the conclusions from the facts that you want the reader to draw.

As in a doctrinal argument, answers to counter-arguments follow the affirmative arguments. As with legal counter-arguments, factual counter-arguments should be set forth as affirmatively as possible rather than conceding at the outset that a fact is devastating to a client and then attempting to explain it away. Again, the judicial opinion and advocate's brief would approach the task differently:

Judge: It is true that the eyewitness was in the presence of the robber for a half hour while the robber ransacked his apartment. This fact is of less significance than it might be in other cases, however, because the witness had poor eyesight.

Advocate: The fact that the robbery took half an hour does not guarantee that the identification was reliable when throughout that time the near-sighted witness was without his glasses.

Judge: While it is true that appellant fled from the abandoned building upon seeing the police, this fact is only slight evidence of consciousness of guilt.

Advocate: Any number of innocent reasons exist to explain appellant's departure from the building at the time the police arrived.

As in the doctrinal argument, after counter-arguments have been refuted and contrary authority distinguished, the argument ends with a brief conclusion: "All of these factors lead directly to the conclusion that the defendant's identity as the robber was not proven beyond a reasonable doubt. Accordingly, his conviction should be reversed and the indictment dismissed."

c. Respondent's Arguments

For the most part, the same rules apply to both appellants' and respondents' arguments. There are, however, some differences arising from the different goals of the two sides and the fact that the appellant has the burden of coming forward first with reasons for overturning the judgment below. Respondents should not, however, see their job only as answering specific points tit for tat. Rather, as discussed earlier, respondent's goal is to convince the court that the proceedings below were fundamentally fair. Thus, respondent should not feel bound by appellant's framing of the issues.

Often, an effective thesis paragraph in a respondent's brief restates the defendant's claim in a manner more favorable to respondent's position. For example, in a case in which a defendant convicted of arson has argued that the evidence that he intended to damage a building was missing, the prosecutor's argument might begin with the following thesis paragraph:

> Defendant contends that the evidence that he set five separate fires in a sofa in his former girlfriend's apartment and then fled was insufficient to prove that he intended to damage the building. Defendant's claim is meritless. The Fire Marshal testified that the fire consumed all of the furnishings in the apartment; created an opaque wall of thick, black smoke from floor to ceiling inside the apartment; and generated heat intense enough to deteriorate the bedroom door. This evidence was ample to permit the jury to conclude beyond a reasonable doubt that defendant intended to damage the building and not simply to destroy his girlfriend's possessions.

The argument will then continue in a manner similar to appellant's brief.

2. Scope of Review, Preservation, Standard of Review, and Harmless Error Arguments

As you know from reading this book, an important part of most appellate briefs consists of the arguments concerning scope of review, preservation, standard of review and harmless error. Of course, not every point will necessarily deal with all four issues, but almost every brief will have to deal with at least one of them.

If there is a serious scope of review issue in a case—that is, whether the case is properly before the court – it will require a point of its own. This point will doubtless be the first point in the brief since if the case is not properly before the court, the court can stop reading the brief.

Preservation (in a court that has the jurisdiction to consider unpreserved errors), standard of review and harmless error arguments, on the other hand, are included within the substantive law arguments to which they are connected. If there is a question about whether a particular issue is preserved, the appellant may choose to discuss it at the end of the point, on the theory that if the substantive law argument is sufficiently persuasive, the court may overlook the fact that the error was unpreserved. Respondent, on the other hand, will probably begin the point with a discussion of preservation in the hope that the court will agree that the error was not preserved and will read no further.

Similarly, an argument that a particular standard of review favorable to a party should be applied to an issue will generally precede discussion of that issue. As with preservation, if the standard of review is clear, the disfavored party may omit discussions of standard of review, or at least downplay it, while the party it favors will put it at the beginning of the argument.

Finally, harmless error arguments follow the substantive discussion. Both appellant and respondent may give equal space to a harmless error argument.

Sample arguments about these issues appear at the end of this chapter.

E. Reply Briefs

A good appellant's brief should anticipate all of the obvious arguments that respondent will raise. Therefore, a reply brief should generally be unnecessary. On the other hand, an appellant will occasionally think of a possible argument that respondent might not raise, and it will be unwise to bring up the subject unless it is in fact argued by the adversary. If there is a possible argument that may be raised by respondent but is unimportant or easily answered, appellant may also rightly choose not to clutter up the brief answering it. In either situation, the issue, if raised, may be answered in a reply brief.

In any event, reply briefs should be used only to correct or address new matters of fact or law raised in respondent's brief and not adequately addressed in appellant's principal brief. Reply briefs may include any new cases that have been decided since the initial briefs were filed. Arguments raised for the first time in a reply brief run the risk of inviting a motion to strike the offending matters.

F. Supplemental Briefs

The general rule is that the parties to a lawsuit get the benefit of any new law decided during the time that the appeal in the case was pending. Occasionally, a new decision affecting the merits of an appeal may come down after a party's briefs have been filed. In this situation it is usually permissible to submit a supplemental brief addressing only the new matter. A new and unforeseeable factual matter that has legal consequences, for example the death of a party during the pendency of the appeal, can also be raised in a supplemental brief.

G. Principles of Good Briefwriting

1. Clarity: Paragraphing and Transitions

The greatest aids to clarity in brief writing, as in other expository writing, are unified, coherent paragraphs that begin with strong topic sentences. "Unified" means that a paragraph should express a single idea – the one in the topic sentence. "Coherent" means that every other sentence in the paragraph should support the main idea.

If you keep these rules in mind they will help you to edit your own work. First, look at your paragraph. Does it have a topic sentence? If not, think about the point you are trying to make and put it in a topic sentence. Next, check your paragraph for length. Does it take up a full page? Probably the paragraph lacks unity. Check to see where you may have added a new idea and begin a separate paragraph.

Finally, check for coherence. Does every sentence in the paragraph support the point made in the topic sentence? If not, rethink what you are trying to say.

The second important aid to clarity is transitional words. These are words that make an explicit, logical connection between each sentence and the next. Some writers appear to use these words and phrases randomly, which is very confusing to the reader. For example, look at the difference in meaning in the following sentences that results from adding a different transitional word to "Jones went to the movies. Smith went shopping."

> Jones went to the movies, but Smith went shopping.
> Jones went to the movies; therefore, Smith went shopping.
> Jones went to the movies despite the fact that Smith went shopping.
> First, Jones went to the movies. Then, Smith went shopping.
> Jones went to the movies because Smith went shopping.
> Jones went to the movies while Smith went shopping.
> Jones went to the movies. Furthermore, Smith went shopping.

Again, think of exactly the point you want to make. Do you want to express a cause and effect relationship between two events? A chronological sequence? Does the second sentence give an example of a point made in the previous one or is it making an additional point? In short, transitional words tell your reader the logical connection between ideas so that the reader can follow your argument more readily.

Two final admonitions are, first, paraphrase rather than quote. Long quotations are difficult to read simply because they are single spaced. More important, they break the flow of an argument and are rarely precisely on point. They require the reader to stop thinking about your case, begin thinking about the case from which the quote has been taken and apply the reasoning in that case to your case. This is a lot of work for a reader and most refuse to do it. They simply skip over long quotes and you have lost your opportunity to make your point. If you want to quote, excerpt a sentence or phrase and weave it into your sentence. The rule of thumb is that if a quote is so long that it must be single-spaced (more than 50 words), cut it and paraphrase.

The second admonition is to avoid footnotes in briefs for the same reason you avoid long quotes: They seldom are read. Footnotes can be useful to provide supplementary information such as the full text of a statute for the court's convenience, but do not put in a footnote anything you really want the court to know about or that the court needs to know about. It is often tempting to bury a bad fact in a footnote, but do not do it; the technique is transparent and may lead the court to think you are being dishonest. Indeed in one recent case, the Court of Appeals for the Second Circuit held that a point made in a footnote in a brief in state court was insufficient to exhaust state remedies for the purposes of bringing a federal habeas corpus petition.

2. Diction and Tone

Your choice of words is, of course, as important in a legal argument as it is in the statement of facts. While the advocate has more leeway when characterizing facts in argument than in the statement of facts, intensifying adverbs and adjectives should be used sparingly and precisely. If a party's conduct was "outrageous," that idea will emerge if the conduct is described accurately in detail. Similarly, describing a lower court's decision as a "travesty of justice" is unconvincing even if in your case it happens to be an accurate description of what went on. Showing the precise evil consequences that flowed from the decision will be far more persuasive than editorial comment. Prosecutors, in particular, are advised to maintain a judicious tone in keeping with the notion that their role is to see that justice is done, not to win at any cost.

Also important, weed out of your writing the legal jargon that seeps insidiously into every lawyer's brain. Phrases such as "the instant case," "the case at bar," "said witness," "sweeps within its ambit," "pass constitutional muster" all serve to make legal writing stilted and wordy. If a word or phrase appears only in legal writing (with the exception of a few terms of art), it is a clue that it is jargon and that you should find an English substitute. And remember, just because a court said it does not mean that it is good writing.

Finally, avoid humor in briefs. You never know what an anonymous reader will find amusing and if you do not take your own case seriously, why should the court?

Examples

1. Statement of Facts

Following is an excerpt from a statement of facts in a case in which the appellant argued that his criminal conviction should be reversed because of the conceded incompetence of the Russian interpreter provided for the complaining witness at trial. In it the writer deemphasizes the distasteful facts of the underlying incident out of which the prosecution arose, while emphasizing the facts indicating that the defendant did not receive a fair trial.

Statement of Facts

Appellant, Terry Lane, was indicted by a New York County grand jury on charges of first degree robbery and related offenses.

A. The Prosecution Case

It is fair to say that this case loses something in translation. The People's case rested entirely upon the testimony of the complainant, a Russian doctor named Boris Zelkov who spoke little English. Consequently, his testimony had to be relayed through an interpreter. Unfortunately, the interpreter, Sophia Mirkowski, also spoke little English. Her incompetence was so gross, in fact, that she had to be replaced in the midst of trial. It is difficult, therefore, to be entirely sure just what the facts in the case were. The basic story, culled from Zelkov's testimony, however, is as follows:

Around 1:00 on the afternoon of November 12, 1975, BORIS ZELKOV cashed his paycheck at a check-cashing establishment near 104th Street and Broadway in Manhattan and proceeded into a near-by subway (17-19).[1] When he reached the bottom of the stairs, he realized that he had entered a one-way-only exit and that the gate to the station was locked from the inside (20-21). At some point before he could return to the street, a man whom Zelkov identified as appellant, came down the stairs behind him, struck him and demanded his money, which Zelkov refused to hand over (21-22). The two men engaged in a struggle during which appellant menaced Zelkov with a screwdriver (23-24). Zelkov forced appellant to drop the screwdriver and shouted for help (25-26). His cries were heard by a police officer inside the subway station who came to his rescue (27).

The police officer, Ptl. THOMAS WEST, corroborated Zelkov's testimony concerning the arrest. He testified further, however, that Zelkov had stated to him at the time of the arrest that he had first seen appellant coming down the subway stairs and that the struggle had begun when Zelkov grabbed appellant's arm (129). Zelkov denied having made such statements (52, 97). He also denied ever having struck appellant, although the minutes of his testimony before the grand jury con-

---

[1] Numbers in parentheses refer to pagination in the trial transcript.

tained the statement that he had hit appellant in the neck. At trial, Zelkov claimed that the interpreter at the grand jury had misunderstood his testimony (85-86).

B. The Interpreter

No sooner had the trial started than it became clear that the interpreter, Ms. Mirkowski, was incapable of performing her job. Defense counsel first objected to her incompetence only three pages into the People's case (18-19):

> Q. [Prosecutor]: After you cashed your check, where did you go?
>
> THE INTERPRETER: Answer the question, please.
>
> DEFENSE COUNSEL: Objection, your Honor. The witness has been testifying, and we haven't heard any interpretation.
>
> THE COURT: Madam Interpreter, please, you have to explain to him that he has to use you as the Interpreter, and when the A.D.A. gives you the question, give it to him in Russian, and the answer, and that's all.
>
> THE INTERPRETER: Would you please repeat it.

The witness then began to answer questions in English himself, but soon gave up, whereupon the prosecutor had to remind Ms. Mirkowski that she must translate everything that was being said (19):

> A [Zelkov] (English) I'm sorry. You ask where – where you go after when you cash a check, yes.
>
> Q [Prosecutor] Yes.
>
> A (English) After I go to subway down 104th Street, I vant (phonetic) to go to 72 Street, pay my telephone bill.
>
> Q Would you prefer that we – would you prefer that we do the testimony in English or in Russian?
>
> A (English) Russian.
>
> THE INTERPRETER: What I answer – what I understand, and I answer, but I don't understand, and I will not answer.
>
> PROSECUTOR: If you do not – if you do not understand the question, please ask for a clarification. Agreed?
>
> THE WITNESS: Yes.
>
> THE INTERPRETER: Yes.
>
> PROSECUTOR: You have to translate my comment. Agreed? Okay?

Two pages later defense counsel again had to object as Ms. Mirkowski cut the witness off before he could finish his testimony (T. 20). As the witness continued, Ms. Mirkowski asked to have questions repeated and the court permitted the prosecutor to ask leading questions simply to help her out (23):

> Q [Prosecutor] What did the defendant do during the time that you and he were struggling?

THE INTERPRETER: Would you please repeat this question.

PROSECUTOR: All right. Let me ask another question.

THE INTERPRETER: Yes, another question.

Q Did there come a time when you saw a screwdriver?

DEFENSE COUNSEL: Objection.

THE COURT: Overruled. I know it's leading, but we're having a problem with the interpretation, and I'll allow it.

When cross-examination began, Ms. Mirkowski had even more trouble and defense counsel had to ask his questions phrase-by-phrase because she found his examination "very complicated" (40-41):

Q [Defense Counsel] Now, Mr. Zelkov, most of the questions I ask you, all you have to say is yes or no.

Now, when you entered into that subway stairway, you expected to find a token booth and a place to enter the subway when the – when you reached the bottom. Is that correct?

A I have to go to enter to open the door and go, but the door was closed.

Q I'll ask you once again, and I think you can answer this with a yes or no answer. When you enter that subway stairway –

THE COURT: Stop right there and let her translate.

(Segment) of question translated by Interpreter.

THE COURT: Go ahead.

Q (cont'g) you expected to find a token booth and a place to enter the subway platform at the bottom. Is that correct?

A I should go.

THE COURT: Strike it out. Ask it again.

DEFENSE COUNSEL: I would prefer it be read back.

(Question read by Court Reporter.)

A No, no, no.

PROSECUTOR: Well, could we have what he said. Perhaps it would clarify, help clarify.

THE COURT: What did he say?

THE INTERPRETER: No, no, no, nyet, nyet, nyet.

PROSECUTOR: But then he said something else. Could we have –

THE COURT: Why don't you rephrase the question. I think you're getting too complicated. I think if you asked simple questions, you could get further.

THE INTERPRETER: Very complicated questions.

When defense counsel again tried to ask his questions in sentence form the court and the prosecutor reminded him that he would have to slow down for Ms. Mirkowski's sake (42):

Q [Defense Counsel] Now, when you realized that there was nowhere else to go except back up those stairs, didn't you also realize that you had made a mistake and that it would never be appropriate for a person to go down those stairs?

THE COURT: She's never going to be able to translate that.

Q At that point did you realize that persons are not supposed to go down that stairway?

PROSECUTOR: Just remind him seven or eight words at a time.

A How can I explain, how can I explain?

PROSECUTOR: Seven or eight words at a time.

Apparently defense counsel was unable to make his questions sufficiently simple for Ms. Mirkowski, for at last she, herself, admitted that she could not understand him (58-59):

Q Now do you remember telling this police officer that the first physical contact between yourself and Mr. Lane was yourself grabbing Mr. Lane's wrist?

THE COURT: Do you understand that question?

THE INTERPRETER: Not quite, your Honor. I don't understand.

Finally the court called a bench conference to discuss the problem of Ms. Mirkowski's incompetence with counsel and the complaining witness (60):

THE COURT: Now, we're having some problems getting the translation. You [Zelkov] have got to give her a chance to translate. Now, this is your representative. Let him [the prosecutor] worry about straightening out any questions. He's on your side. He's on your side. He will straighten the thing out.

Now, if you can answer the question with a yes, answer it yes. If you can answer it with a no, answer it with a no. Keep your answers short and give her a chance to translate.

INTERPRETER[sic]: Silly question.

THE COURT: And don't use the word silly questions.

THE INTERPRETER: I'm sorry, your Honor.

THE COURT: *You have got to translate everything.*

THE INTERPRETER: *Sometimes I don't know. Shall I translate or not?* (emphasis added)

THE COURT: Let's go again.

The complaining witness paid no heed to the court's instructions and continued to interrupt the interpreter's attempts to translate his testimony. A hand signal was therefore devised in an attempt to facilitate the translation (61-62):

PROSECUTOR: If we had a hand signal to let him know and then let the Interpreter know when the question is not over. Perhaps have Defense Counsel hold his hand up until he has completed answering or asking for an answer, because some of these questions, understandably –

THE COURT: All right. Fine. Tell him that Defense Counsel will drop his hand when the question is over. Would you tell him that. Tell him that Defense Counsel will drop his hand down when the question is over, and then he can answer it.

The hand signal failed. The jury then asked if it might make some suggestions as to how to aid the translator. The court gratefully accepted their offer (67-68):

JUROR TWO: Your Honor, could I make a layman's suggestion?

THE COURT: I wish you would.

JUROR TWO: If she would only answer yes or no, maybe we would get a better concept. *If she would stop repeating his translation* –

THE COURT: She can't. She's got to give it word to word.

PROSECUTOR: It has to be as if he's talking.

JUROR TWO: I thought it was supposed to be an answer yes or no to most of the questions, because she keeps repeating everything, every other thing he says. *It's hard to comprehend.*

THE COURT: I know.

JUROR SEVEN: Can I say something?

THE COURT: We can't get in a free-for-all here. We have to go on with it. (emphasis added).

At the end of the first day of trial, the court gave up the struggle with Ms. Mirkowski (71):

(At the Bench the following occurred:)

THE COURT: *You are going to have to get yourself a new interpreter because we're not getting anything at all. You have to get a new one.*

PROSECUTOR: Well, if that's what your direction is –

THE COURT: Because I think you have got to explain to her. You have got to sit down with him and you have to tell him to just answer the question.

You can't go on like this. *You can't possibly run a trial like this.*

PROSECUTOR: All right.

THE COURT: You have to get a new interpreter.
        (emphasis added).

The court then recessed until the following morning at which time Ms. Mirkowski was replaced with another interpreter. Before the second day's testimony began, defense counsel moved for a mistrial based on Ms. Mirkowski's incompetence on the preceding day of trial. The motion was denied (76-77) and the new interpreter proceeded to translate the few remaining questions of defense counsel's cross-examination, re-direct examination, and re-cross (79-109).

2. Standard of Review Argument

The following paragraph presents an argument about the appropriate standard of review for findings made in a state court proceeding that is now the subject of a federal habeas corpus action. The state court judge had determined that trial counsel in a prison stabbing case was not ineffective, in part because, although counsel failed to introduce evidence of the victim's prior murder conviction, counsel did, by reference to the victim's nickname of "yard dog," effectively inform the jury of the victim's violent nature. The federal district judge refused to disturb this finding, treating it as a finding of fact entitled to a presumption of correctness under the federal habeas statute. Appellate counsel is now seeking to persuade the court of appeals to reverse, first by securing a less deferential standard of review.

ARGUMENT

The district court was incorrect in characterizing as a "factual finding" Judge Green's conclusion that Field [petitioner's trial attorney] adequately communicated the violent propensities of Smith [the victim] to the jury. A "factual issue" entitled to a presumption of correctness under 28 U.S.C. § 2254(d) is one that concerns "basic, primary, or historical facts: facts 'in the sense of a recital of external events and the credibility of their narrators. . . .'" *Townsend v. Sain*, 372 U.S. 293, 309 n.6 (1963) (citation omitted); *see also Strickland v. Washington*, 466 U.S. 698; *Oliver v. Wainwright*, 782 F.2d 1521, 1524 (11th Cir. 1986) (only "purely factual findings" entitled to presumption). Judge Green's determination that Field adequately communicated Smith's violent proclivities to the jury is not a finding of historical fact, a "purely factual finding," but a conclusion the judge has drawn from the purported facts. Whether Field rendered ineffective assistance of counsel by failing to adequately present that evidence to the jury is a mixed question of fact and law which required the district court to review the record *de novo*. *Oliver v. Wainwright*, 782 F.2d at 1524.

Note that the advocate has set forth in the thesis sentence the key argument to be made about why the district judge's conclusion, which affirmed the state court, rested on an improperly deferential standard of review. Counsel immediately questions the characterization of the issue as a "factual finding," and phrases the finding in such a way as to make it appear to include more than simple historical facts: whether trial counsel had "adequately communicated Hall's violent propensities to the jury."

The briefwriter then goes on to define, in very detailed terms, what *would* constitute a factual issue, using a quote from a United States Supreme Court case, as well as citations to other cases standing for the proposition that only purely factual findings are entitled to a presumption of correctness. Applying this definition to the finding at hand, the writer argues that the determination that trial counsel "adequately communicated" something to the jury involves a conclusion drawn from historical facts, rather than simple recitation of those facts. Accordingly, the district court was obligated to review the question *de novo*, as it presented a mixed question of law and fact subject to *de novo* review in that particular circuit.

3. Argument Regarding Failure to Exercise and Abuse of Discretion

Following is a point in a brief in an appeal of a criminal conviction. Prior to trial, the defendant moved pursuant to a New York case called *People v. Sandoval* to limit cross-examination concerning his criminal record should he take the witness stand. Instead of exercising its discretion to prohibit the prosecutor from questioning the defendant on all but a few of his prior convictions, the court refused to place any limits on cross-examination whatsoever.

Recognizing that a court's discretion is very broad in this area, and that an argument that the judge abused his discretion would therefore be difficult to make, the appellate attorney framed the issue first as the court's complete failure to exercise any discretion and argued abuse of discretion as a fall-back position.

ARGUMENT

POINT I

THE TRIAL COURT'S SUMMARY DENIAL *IN TOTO* OF APPEL-LANT'S MOTION TO LIMIT CROSS-EXAMINATION CONCERNING HIS CRIMINAL RECORD CONSTITUTED A FAILURE TO EXERCISE REQUIRED DISCRETION AND DEPRIVED APPELLANT OF HIS DUE PROCESS RIGHT TO A FAIR TRIAL (U.S. CONST., AMEND. XIV; N.Y. CONST. ART. 1, § 6).

When appellant moved prior to trial to limit cross-examination concerning his criminal record should he testify, the court, apparently concerned only that he not appear to the jury as a "paragon of virtue," summarily ruled that the prosecutor might inquire into all of his prior convictions. This ruling unquestionably influenced appellant's decision not to take the stand and effectively prevented him from putting on a defense. The court's abdication of its responsibility to balance the probative value of inquiry into appellant's past transgressions against its prejudicial effect thus denied appellant his due process right to a fair trial (U.S. Const., Amend. XIV; N.Y. Const., Art. I, § 6).

Evidence of a defendant's prior convictions or specific criminal, vicious or immoral acts is admissible only if it is more probative of the defendant's credibility, veracity or honesty as a witness than it is prejudicial. *People v. Sandoval*, 34 N.Y.2d 371, 376-377 (1974). The difficult task of balancing the prosecution's interest in exploring the veracity of a witness against the risk that a jury may unreasonably believe that a defendant who has committed crimes in the past must be guilty as charged requires "the exercise of a sound discretion on the part of the Trial Judge." *People v. Davis*, 44 N.Y.2d 269, 274 (1978). Where, as here, the trial judge, without explanation, permits inquiry into a defendant's entire past record, making no effort to distinguish among incidents or to limit the number into which inquiry may be made, it cannot be said that such "sound discretion" has been exercised. Accordingly, in numerous cases, the wholesale indiscriminate denial of a *Sandoval* motion has been held to constitute reversible error. [Citations omitted].

Even if the court's ruling had reflected an effort to exercise discretion in balancing the relevant factors, it would still be clear that there had been an abuse of discretion. Inevitably, the denial in its entirety of the *Sandoval* motion made it likely that the jury would have been improperly influenced by considerations of the defendant's propensity to commit the crime with which he was charged. Moreover, as even the prosecutor herself seemed to concede, the court's indiscriminate ruling was wholly unnecessary to protect the prosecution's right to elicit information appropriately bearing on the defendant's credibility which could have been adequately accomplished by permitting cross-examination with regard to fewer than all of the previous convictions.

4. Harmless Error Arguments

Following are the appellant's and respondent's harmless error arguments in a robbery case.

Facts

Around 1:30 a.m. on January 19, 1991, Bradford Chin was walking home from a grocery store when the defendant approached him, displayed what appeared to be a gun, and took Chin's money and groceries. Defendant was arrested and charged with robbery. At trial, evidence that at the time of his arrest defendant was driving a stolen car was erroneously admitted.

Argument for Appellant

The admission of the uncharged crime evidence was not harmless. *People v. Crimmins,* 34 N.Y.2d 230 (1974). The evidence at trial suggested that there was a substantial likelihood that appellant was mistakenly identified by the complainant as the robber. First, the complainant's description of his assailant varied substantially from appellant's appearance. While the complainant described his assailant as being between 6' 1" and 6' 2" tall and weighing 190 pounds, appellant was 6' 7", a half a foot taller than the complainant thought, and weighed over 200 pounds. In addition, while the complainant stated that the perpetrator had no mustache and beard but only a "scruff," the photograph of appellant taken after his arrest showed that he indeed had a mustache and a beard.

Second, the complainant did not have a substantial opportunity to observe the robber. Even though the complainant saw him three times while he was shopping, on each occasion he had only a few seconds to observe him. In fact, the complainant conceded that on the first and second occasions he mostly saw the man's clothing. The third occasion was when the man asked for the money and brandished the gun at Chin's face. Even then, as the complainant admitted, he concentrated on the hand brandishing the gun and not the robber's face. Thus, the complainant did not adequately observe the robber on any of these three occasions to be able to identify the robber at a later date.

Third, the complainant's ability to observe and mentally record the appearance of the perpetrator was also seriously hampered by the complainant's state of mind at the time of arrest. The event happened after midnight and the complainant had been working for hours on a school paper. Moreover, as the complainant conceded, during the robbery he was afraid when the man menacingly brandished the gun at him and threatened to kill him. He was, therefore, hardly in the state of mind conducive to careful observation of his assailant's features. Indeed, the trauma of such an unexpected and extraordinary experience undoubtedly greatly affected the complainant's perception and attention. Significantly, upon his arrest appellant's behavior was that of an innocent man, since he voluntarily approached the officer's car.

Under these circumstances, it is very likely that appellant was an unfortunate victim of mistaken identification. Significantly, the jury clearly had difficulty with the People's proof as suggested by their request for a read-back of the complainant's entire trial testimony. After hearing testimony that appellant had committed another theft-related crime, the jurors were both more likely to punish appellant, despite the shortfalls of the People's case, and less likely to give appellant the benefit of any doubt that may have arisen from the shaky identification testimony.

In sum, in this case, where there was a strong likelihood of mistaken identification, it was very likely that the jury was improperly influenced into rendering a guilty verdict because of the aforementioned errors.

Argument for Respondent

The evidence against defendant was so overwhelming that any error in admitting the testimony of Officer Keating that the jeep was stolen was harmless. *People v. Crimmins,* 36 N.Y.2d 230 (1975). Defendant, who had a distinctive appearance, was convicted on the strength of the identification testimony of the complainant, who had seen him twice immediately prior to the robbery. Chin's account of the crime and his description of defendant's appearance was detailed and entirely credible, and Chin saw defendant often enough and clearly enough to be able to identify him beyond a reasonable doubt as his robber. *See People v. Cook,* 42 N.Y.2d 204 (1977) (error in admitting testimony concerning uncharged sexual assault committed on victim of robbery harmless in light of overwhelming proof of guilt).

Moreover, contrary to defendant's contention (Defendant's Brief at 18), the complainant's description of the man who had robbed him matched defendant's appearance closely. Bradford Chin described defendant as "a rather tall man." (Chin: 71) He subsequently reiterated that his attention had initially been drawn to defendant because of defendant's height. Chin, who gave his own height as 5' 6", stated that, at the time of the crime, he thought defendant to be 6' 1" or 6' 2", rather than his actual 6' 7", but explained that he generally was unable to tell the exact height of anyone over six feet tall (Chin: 85). What was clear from Chin's testimony, however, was that he had taken note of defendant's above-average height.

Moreover, Chin also noted defendant's clothing and defendant's facial hair, which he described to the police as "scruff." The photograph of defendant, which was admitted into evidence as People's Exhibit 2 and which Chin confirmed depicted defendant accurately as he appeared on the night of the robbery (Chin: 79), indeed shows that defendant was unshaven and had a scruffy beard.

In sum, the trial court's admission of testimony that the police arrested defendant because they believed the car he was in to be stolen was proper and did not deprive defendant of a fair trial. In any event, the complainant's identification of defendant as the man who robbed him was based on his ample opportunity to observe him before and during the crime and was supported by his prior accurate description of him. In light of the court's limiting instructions and the overwhelming evidence of defendant's guilt, any error in admitting the testimony was harmless.

Chapter 8

Oral Argument

Oral argument provides a valuable opportunity for the appellate advocate to use personal persuasive powers on behalf of a client. Direct communication with the judges who are to decide the case also presents a unique opportunity to answer any of their questions about the case that remain after they have read the briefs. Although there is considerable debate among appellate lawyers and judges concerning the value of oral argument, with some judges even declaring it a waste of time, the effective appellate practitioner must develop the skill of good oral advocacy for those cases, whether they be few or many, in which the oral argument may make the difference. In addition, in most moot court competitions, the oral component of a team's performance can be decisive.

Many beginning appellate attorneys make the mistake of viewing oral argument as an actor regards opening night. The courtroom becomes a theater, the judges are the audience, the lawyers are actors, the brief is the script, and the argument is the end result of weeks of rehearsal. This notion is all but guaranteed to produce an ineffective oral argument. An argument is not a performance and judges do not behave like a polite audience. They do not sit quietly and attentively while the lawyers deliver carefully rehearsed lines. On the contrary, they interrupt the play with questions and demand to change the script mid-scene. This is disconcerting to the lawyer whose goal is to get on with an eloquent soliloquy. The only solution is to revise one's notion of oral argument.

It is not difficult to deliver a good oral argument if one understands clearly its purposes and limitations. Oral argument has four principal purposes. First, it is an opportunity to put a human face on the case. While it is unlikely that argument alone will convince the court of a party's position, a clear, forceful presentation can certainly make a case more memorable and may help to convince a judge who is wavering. Moreover, the failure to argue may leave the impression that the attorney does not think much of a client's cause.

The second purpose of oral argument is to focus the court's attention on the one or two crucial issues in the case. The brief has provided the court with the careful analysis of the law on which the arguments rest. The goal of the oral argument is to distill the essence of the case and to present it to the court in its simplest and clearest form.

Third, oral argument is an opportunity for the judges to ask questions about the issues they still find troublesome after reading the briefs. Questions from the bench should not be viewed as annoying interruptions, but should be welcomed as opportunities to put judges' doubts to rest.

Finally, oral argument is a time to update the brief with any new legal developments that have occurred since it was filed with the court, to correct any factual errors that may have been contained in the briefs, and to answer any new arguments raised by the adversary that were not worth addressing in a reply brief. Of course, if you intend to raise new law at oral argument, you must supply your adversary in advance with a copy of the case.

Understanding the limitations of oral argument is as important as grasping its purposes. The most obvious limitation is time. A typical argument lasts no longer than fifteen minutes. Therefore thought must be given to how to use the short time allotted in the most effective way. The second limitation is simply the inability of most people, including judges, to absorb large quantities of detailed information when it is presented to them orally. Law students know from attending their classes how much or how little one can take in at a sitting. Most people understand complicated ideas better in writing. Accordingly, standing before the court and reciting the points in the brief is a waste of precious argument time. Oral argument should be used to supplement the brief and to do what it cannot do rather than to rehash it in a less effective way. If one keeps these ideas firmly in mind, the method of preparing for and presenting a good oral argument becomes clear.

Preparation

1. Know the Record

Many appellate benches today, both real and moot, are "hot." That is, the judges have read the briefs and perhaps part of the record in the case before oral argument. The judges cannot, however, be expected to know the facts in a case as well as the attorneys handling it. One of the principal jobs of the advocate is to answer questions about facts that may have slipped a judge's mind or that a judge simply missed in reading the written material. Even seemingly minor details must be at counsel's fingertips. An otherwise brilliant oral argument can be damaged by any misstatement of fact or by inability to respond to a judge's inquiry about a point in the record. In particular, counsel should be prepared to respond to questions concerning preservation of issues. It is good practice to be able to point to the precise page in the transcript at which an objection was made. There can be no surprise questions about the record. Inability to answer them can only reflect careless preparation.

2. Know the Law

The oral advocate should also be familiar with both the legal principles and the facts contained in the cases on which both sides have relied in their briefs. This is not as obvious as it seems, since weeks and even months may have gone by since the briefs were filed. It is easy to forget the details of cases; while it is unlikely that a court will want a discussion of basic legal principles with which they are familiar, a judge may very well ask whether the case is similar to or distinguishable from a cited case on its facts. Good preparation is simply a matter of rereading the cases and perhaps making a few notes on file cards to serve as a reminder of the holding and important facts in each case. The advocate should also be prepared to answer questions about the appropriate standard of review.

3. Select the Points for Oral Argument

Given the limitations of oral argument mentioned above, it is simply impossible to discuss more than two or, at most, three issues at oral argument. There will not be enough time and the court will not be able to take them in. Counsel must determine which are the key issues on which victory in the case turns and concentrate on them. Other factors to be considered are whether the adversary has made any particularly troublesome arguments that require response or whether a particular issue is so clear and so well covered in the brief that there is little of interest to add at argument. Besides the substantive issues, counsel may also want to deal with any doubts concerning preservation, whether or not a particular error was harmless, and the relief being requested.

4. Anticipate Difficult Questions

Once the points have been selected for argument, the next step is to try to anticipate the questions that may be asked. By the time most lawyers have filed their briefs, they have become entirely convinced of the rightness of their client's cause and the impossibility of losing the appeal. Now is the time to step back from the case and to give it an honest appraisal. The appellant lost below. What was the reason? Respondent may want to think about why appellant has gone to the trouble and expense of the appeal (and in some cases a reason that the court has agreed to hear it). The advocate is well advised to ask the hard questions, the ones that go directly to the weakness of the case.

The place to start looking for the hard questions is the adversary's brief. It should be read carefully to determine the strongest arguments and the best responses. One should remember, however, that courts are not bound by the arguments made in lawyers' briefs. Judges may have concerns of their own that the adversary did not raise. The advocate must be prepared for these questions as well. It is here that the assistance of colleagues and even non-lawyer friends and relations can be a big help. Often an intelligent lay person's skepticism (Well, what *was* he doing on the roof with a hatchet at 1:00 in the morning?) can pinpoint a problem in the case that the attorney has overlooked. Rather than rehearsing a canned speech, it is far better that an oral advocate practice answering difficult questions clearly and confidently.

5. Update the Research

The effective advocate will do some last minute research shortly before oral argument to make sure that in the time between the filing of briefs and argument none of the cases relied upon has been reversed or overruled and that no relevant new cases have been decided. Many lawyers now do a quick computer search for information on the very morning of oral argument. That may be unnecessary, but surely counsel would be embarrassed to learn from the court, at the beginning of the argument, that the precedent on which the case turns was reversed two weeks earlier. Likewise, updating research may afford a great opportunity to buttress an argument with a brand new case having, of course, informed the adversary.

6. Know the Court; Know the Judges

Just as your brief was shaped by knowledge of the different functions of various levels of appellate courts, so should you keep in mind when preparing for oral argument that not all appellate courts are alike. Generally speaking, intermediate courts are more concerned with doing justice on the facts of the particular case, while high courts tend to focus on broader policies and the implications of rulings for other litigants and for the public at large. The higher the court, the more likely it is that you will be faced with questions outside the narrow area of the law you have briefed. After all, if the Justices of the Supreme Court declare a particular criminal penalty imposed on a minor invalid, they have to consider the consequences of that ruling, not just for other similarly situated minors, but also for the law relating to minors in other areas of the law. Therefore, the advocate in a high court would do well to prepare to answer questions related to the legal issue but outside the narrow confines of the case being argued. In an intermediate court, on the other hand, the judges are much more likely to focus on the specific facts of the case at hand, so that here detailed knowledge of the record is more important.

Information about the particular judges sitting on an appellate court may also be useful to counsel. Attorneys arguing before the United States Supreme Court will almost certainly have thought about each Justice's prior opinions on related questions, and may in fact tailor their arguments so as to maximize the chances of securing that one crucial swing vote. Similar research can be done about the judges of other courts. When judges sit in panels, counsel should find out as much as possible about the judges who will be sitting on the day of the argument. The first step is to research other opinions the members of that panel have written. It can be very helpful to know that a judge hearing one's case wrote the majority opinion in another favorable case, or dissented in a case relied on by one's adversary. In these days of computer research, extensive investigation of decisions by individual judges is not difficult.

Checking with an attorney who has argued before the same judges can also provide valuable information about the people who will be deciding the case. For example, one attorney learned to his dismay, after he had dispensed with a microphone at oral argument, that one of the three judges was deaf and could not hear an unamplified word but was sensitive about revealing this fact. Learning some inside information about the personal peculiarities and concerns of the judges, as well as knowing their opinions on various legal questions, can be an important aid in framing an oral argument.

7. Outline the Argument

Most lawyers have a personal preference regarding notes for oral argument, and it makes sense to use what works best for each individual. With the understanding that the advocate will not be giving a speech, but rather simply making a couple of forceful points and answering questions, however, certain methods recommend themselves.

First, it is generally agreed among experienced appellate practitioners that it is not a good idea to write out a whole argument. Not only is it unlikely that one will get a chance to deliver it, but the prepared speech may actually be a hindrance when questions about particular issues are asked in an unexpected order. A lawyer may never get back on track and therefore fail to make important arguments.

A better idea is either to make a short outline on which points can be checked off as they are addressed or to make notes on a few file cards, one issue per card, which can be shuffled as appropriate. This way, if the court asks few questions, counsel can simply make the arguments in the order outlined. If the court interrupts frequently, on the other hand, the advocate will have no trouble reorganizing the points on the spot. The notes should be written in large enough print so that they can be seen just by glancing down. Remember, the point is to know the case so well that only a glance is necessary to jog the memory.

Although the entire argument should not be written out, many lawyers do find it helpful to write out an introduction and a conclusion. A written introduction can be comforting, even if in the end it is not used, if one is afraid of being struck dumb with nervousness upon approaching the bench. A written conclusion can be helpful at the end of an argument, in which questions have been far ranging, to bring the court back to the main point. Both the introduction and conclusion should be short.

The introduction should not begin with a recitation of the facts. It is not a catchy way to start and the first few sentences of an argument can be important in attracting the court's attention. One can assume, moreover, that the judges know the basic facts. If they do not, they will not hesitate to ask. This is not to say that if a particular fact or facts are crucial to the resolution of the case they should not be mentioned. They should, however, be woven into the legal argument and not set out as a separate statement of facts. For example, instead of beginning the argument with a chronology of the identification procedures engaged in by the police, it is preferable to begin by saying that none of the indices of a reliable identification are present in the case and then go on to discuss the facts surrounding the witness's viewing of the defendant.

Appellant has the initial task of capturing the court's attention in the face of what is probably some shuffling of the papers from the previous case and remnants of thoughts, and possibly even discussion, lingering from the issues presented by earlier advocates. If there are such distractions, appellant's counsel may wish to start by reminding the court of the nature of this case and its procedural history. Once the judges are focused on the advocate, however, it is best to seize the opportunity by making a forceful and concise statement of the strongest point that calls for reversal of the judgment or order. Lengthy preambles are to be avoided; today's busy and impatient appellate judges are eager to get right to the heart of the issues in dispute.

Here the difference between real courts and the practice followed in moot court competitions is worth noting. The almost universal practice in law school competitions is to begin with a "road map" listing the issues to be addressed, in the order in which the advocate plans to address them. In part, this introduction allows the first student to signal to the bench which issues he or she will be arguing, and which are reserved to the second member of the team. Only very rarely will argument time be divided in actual courts, so that the judges need not be alerted in this way.

8. Practice the Argument

A moot court with a video camera is obviously the most luxurious way to practice an argument. If, however, there is no one with whom to practice and no camera, one can practice at home with a mirror in the manner of previous generations of appellate lawyers. For the beginning appellate advocate, out-loud practice is the only way to ensure the ability to express the ideas in one's outline. Many advocates find it helpful to express the same idea in a number of different ways, so that the idea becomes second nature, yet the particular way it is expressed does not sound rehearsed. Practicing an argument out loud may also reveal which words you tend to stumble over, awkward transitions, and gaps in logic. Discovered in time, such problems may be solved by finding alternative phrases, reorganizing the order of points to flow more smoothly, and thinking through any logical gaps in your argument. The more you practice, and the more you test your arguments before others, whether they be colleagues in your office, fellow students, or other intelligent willing listeners, the better your argument will be. Indeed, for moot court teams, the conventional wisdom is that the team that practices the most, and before the widest diversity of benches, has a decided advantage in any competition.

When beginning a career in appellate advocacy it is also a good idea to observe other lawyers argue, either in moot or real court. Having a clear idea of what to expect is helpful in overcoming nervousness and becoming acquainted with the rhythm of an oral argument. It is particularly useful to attend a session of arguments in the same court where you will be appearing. Each appellate court has its own way of approaching oral argument: beyond differences in rules (such as permitting or refusing to hear rebuttal), courts also have somewhat different styles, and the more you can adapt to that style, the better your chance of persuading that particular bench of the merits of your case.

Presentation

Moot court societies often stress the formal aspects of oral argument: Don't wiggle but don't stand rigid, use your hands but not too much, look the judges in the eye but make sure your eyes sweep the bench, don't take so many papers to the podium that you look weighed down but don't take so few that you appear cavalier, *ad infinitum*. Often these admonitions become paramount to concern over the content of the legal argument.

When analyzed, however, it becomes apparent that these warnings are simply the common sense rules of civilized discourse. It is not an idea peculiar to appellate advocacy that no one is persuaded by a person who mumbles or shouts, interrupts, harangues, has distracting mannerisms, doesn't answer questions straightforwardly and is either disrespectful or obsequious. Judges are no exception. If one keeps in mind that the purpose of oral argument is to inform and persuade the court, correct behavior before the bench will follow. Whatever behavior serves a lawyer well in formal situations in the rest of life will be equally effective in court. Some people are naturally amusing, others serious, others dramatic and others low key. No particular personality is required to be a good oral advocate. Indeed, the shyness of a lawyer arguing for the first time can serve to make a case stand out. The advocate who is prepared and takes the job of representing a client seriously will do well. That having been said, a few pointers are helpful.

1. Getting Started

Appellants argue first and sit on the left, respondents second and sit on the right. Appellants in some, but not all, courts may reserve time for rebuttal. It is important to find out in advance if your court permits, frowns on, or outright prohibits rebuttal. When the case is called, the appellant should go directly to the podium while the respondent sits down at counsel table. Appellant can wait to begin speaking until the judges appear to be paying attention, but counsel should not wait to be invited to speak. Although there is no particular formula, a standard way to begin is, "May it please the Court, my name is Abe Fortas. I represent the petitioner Clarence Earl Gideon."

While an attorney is arguing, both the opposing attorney and co-counsel should be unobtrusive. Counsel should not make faces or groan while an adversary is arguing. Co-counsel should avoid passing notes to the lawyer who is arguing as it is distracting to both the attorney who is arguing and to the court.

2. Demeanor

A lawyer's demeanor should, of course, be normally polite and respectful to the court. Judges are customarily addressed as "Your Honor." Counsel should not be unduly humble, however. A lawyer at argument is a professional doing an important job requiring intelligence and skill, not a peasant pleading for indulgence from the emperor. One commentator has used the phrase "respectful equality" to describe the appropriate demeanor of a lawyer at the bench.

An argument should not be read and should be made in a sufficiently loud conversational tone of voice to be easily heard. No one can be persuaded by someone who is inaudible. The judge who has to strain to hear may once ask the attorney to speak louder, but then will probably give up. Also to be avoided at argument are quotations and case citations. They break up the flow of an argument.

Finally, counsel should become aware of any distracting mannerisms he or she may have. Most people are unaware of their own bad habits. Videotape is a valuable tool to help one see oneself through the eyes of the court, tapping a pencil or twisting a ring or rocking backwards and forwards. In the absence of a video camera, candid criticism from a colleague should be solicited.

3. Answering Questions

Oral argument provides a unique opportunity to find out what aspects of the case are troubling to the court and to address them. The lawyer should stop talking as soon as the court interrupts, listen carefully to the question and try to answer as clearly and persuasively as possible. An appellate lawyer should never refuse to answer a court's question either by telling a judge, "I'll get to that later," or by answering a different question, or by claiming that the question is not relevant and that something else is. Occasionally a judge's questions may seem off the mark, but even they should be answered without visible impatience. A judge bothered by unanswered questions will remain unpersuaded. To the extent possible, counsel should integrate the court's questions into the argument rather than simply answering and then jumping back to the different argument being made before the judge interrupted.

Because it is so important to answer a court's questions as they arise, it is bad practice for co-counsel to divide their argument time so that each one argues a separate point and has to refer questions to the other. This is often done in moot court simply so that all team members get a chance to argue, but in real life it results in an ineffective argument. Even in moot court competitions, a team member should be able to answer questions on all issues presented by the case.

It sometimes does happen, even to the well-prepared lawyer, that a court asks an unanticipated question. In this case a lawyer must try to answer as best as possible. If it is not possible to answer, it is better not to waffle but to say "I don't know," and offer to find out.

Not all benches behave the same way at oral argument. Occasionally, for example, the advocate is faced by the silent bench. This can be even more unnerving than being bombarded with questions. If the judges ask no questions, the advocate must simply be prepared to make the arguments selected as forcefully as possible and sit down. The hostile bench is another phenomenon encountered at oral argument. Sometimes judges make clear that they simply do not accept an argument. In this situation it is better to move on to the next point than to continue to try to convince a court that has already made up its mind on that particular issue. It may be, however, that only one or two judges are unconvinced; be sure that you have gotten your point across to those silent members of the bench who may be on your side.

4. Concessions

Among the most important skills of the appellate advocate, and one that takes practice and experience to develop, is knowing when to be flexible and when to stick to one's guns. Courts often try to wring concessions from lawyers. It is critical to distinguish ahead of time, as much as possible, between what cannot be conceded without landing on that slippery slope that concedes away the case, and what may safely be given up in the interest of perhaps winning the vote of a judge not willing to go quite as far as the advocate would like. Faced with a posited concession that the advocate has *not* anticipated, the cardinal rule is to think before you speak. The moment you spend thinking may seem endless to you, but it is far preferable to either being saddled with a damaging concession (such as not infrequently make their way into opinions: "Even counsel for respondent agreed. . .") or being forced to backtrack after further questioning demonstrates where the slippery slope has led. In addition, an advocate who spends a moment thinking about a judge's question gives the positive appearance of taking that question seriously – not a bad impression to make.

Advocates should be wary, not only of making dangerous concessions directly, but also of being lulled into agreeing with a judge's characterization of their position that, while not directly contrary to the claim, states it in terms that might amount to a less favorable formulation than is appropriate for the client. When a judge says, "Aren't you really arguing, counselor . . ." it is important to make sure that what follows really is a correct statement of the position being argued. If necessary, a judge may be asked, politely, to restate the question. Again, the embarrassment of appearing not to have paid attention is not as damaging as the possible agreement with a position that turns out not to reflect accurately the claim being presented. Of course, if the judge's formulation *is* correct, counsel should not hesitate to agree.

5. Respondent's Argument

Respondents have a more difficult and, at the same time, an easier job when preparing for oral argument. It is more difficult because the respondent does not know what points appellant will argue. Therefore, respondent's attorney must wait until the argument is actually in progress before making a final determination about the points to which response should be made. On the other hand, respondent has the advantage of listening to appellant's argument and learning ahead of time which issues interest the judges and which they have already made up their minds about.

Respondent's attorney must therefore go into court prepared to argue anything. Once there, the attorney must listen carefully to appellant's argument and quickly organize a response, both to what appellant has said and to questions the court asked during appellant's argument. Respondent is, of course, free to argue any point raised in the briefs, whether or not appellant has chosen to argue it orally, if that will help the client's case. Generally, however, if appellant has nothing to add to the arguments contained in the brief, then respondent, too, may decide to address the issues that appear to be more hotly contested.

One caveat: While the court's questioning of appellant's counsel may give some idea of the court's thinking on the issue, it is dangerous to assume that a judge's questions necessarily reflect that judge's views. Some judges love to play the role of devil's advocate, hammering away at the weaknesses of first one advocate's arguments, and then those of opposing counsel.

6. Finishing Up

When all points have been made, the advocate should sit down even if the argument time has not elapsed. Courts appreciate brevity. If, on the other hand, the time signal goes on before the advocate is finished, the advocate should complete the sentence or answer to a judge's question, and then ask for permission to go on if something crucial has been omitted. Most courts will grant permission if they are interested in what is being said.

7. Rebuttal

Even courts that permit rebuttal generally do not like it. Rebuttal time reserved does not have to be used, and should be waived if a lawyer has nothing to add. Its purpose is only to address new matter raised by respondent at argument that appellant could not have anticipated. For the most part rebuttal is properly used only to correct actual misstatements of fact by respondent. Rebuttal should not be used to repeat an argument already made or to make an argument forgotten the first time around. In moot court, points are taken off for improper rebuttal, and in real life a lawyer risks antagonizing the court.

When Not to Argue

In general, one should not pass up an opportunity to persuade the court of a client's cause. There are infrequent occasions, however, when it may be preferable not to argue.

As a tactical matter, for example, appellant *might* forego oral argument on a clear, well-preserved issue of prosecutorial misconduct in a criminal case with gruesome facts in which the proof overwhelmingly demonstrated the guilt of the defendant. The court in such a situation might be tempted to use oral argument as a forum to berate the prosecution for its error, and then, with a clear conscience, affirm the judgment as unaffected by error declared harmless. Similarly, if opposing counsel has submitted a very weak brief, an advocate may determine that little would be gained and much might be lost during an additional opportunity to communicate with the court.

Index

References are to page numbers.